JUDICIAL DISCRETION IN THE
HOUSE OF LORDS

Judicial Discretion in the House of Lords

DAVID ROBERTSON

CLARENDON PRESS · OXFORD
1998

Oxford University Press, Great Clarendon Street, Oxford OX2 6DP

Oxford New York

Athens Auckland Bangkok Bogota Bombay Buenos Aires
Calcutta Cape Town Dar es Salaam Delhi Florence Hong Kong Istanbul
Karachi Kuala Lumpur Madras Madrid Melbourne Mexico City
Nairobi Paris Singapore Taipei Tokyo Toronto Warsaw
and associated companies in
Berlin Ibadan

Oxford is a registered trade mark of Oxford University Press

Published in the United States
by Oxford University Press Inc., New York

© David Robertson 1998
The moral rights of the author have been asserted

First published 1998

British Library Cataloguing in Publication Data
Data available

Library of Congress Cataloging in Publication Data
Robertson, David, 1946–
Judicial discretion in the House of Lords / D. Robertson.
p. cm.
Includes index.
1. Great Britain. Parliament. House of Lords. 2. Judicial
discretion–Great Britain. 3. Judicial process–Great Britain.
I. Title.
KD7132.R63 1998
328.41'071–dc21 98–24211
ISBN 0-19-827442-4

1 3 5 7 9 10 8 6 4 2

Typeset by Best-set Typesetter Ltd., Hong Kong
Printed in Great Britain
on acid-free paper by
Biddles Ltd., Guildford and King's Lynn

For Ellen

Preface

This book has taken five years to write, and very much longer to think about and sketch. My interest in law as a subject matter for political science began when I first taught in America and was first amazed and then delighted by the seriousness with which American social scientists took law. Part of my argument in what follows is that European political science's refusal to be much concerned with law is not excused or explained by the mere absence of judicial review in the US sense of that phrase. I must, perhaps unconsciously, have become a convert when in America to judicial realism as the only explanatory school of legal theory which makes any sense at all to a political sociologist. Certainly all my reading, writing, and thinking over the last few years have done nothing to dissuade me from the stubborn view that law really is just what the judges say it is, and may very well, at times, depend on what they had for breakfast. But as this book also argues, something can be done to channel and legitimize the inherent and radical discretion of judicial activity if the country has a constitutional code. This country does not, with the consequences I try to spell out for judicial behaviour.

The structure of the book is dictated by the need to establish good grounds for accepting judicial realism as an accurate portrayal of British judicial behaviour before going on to demonstrate in selected areas of law why this matters. Thus the first half, Chapters 1 to 5, examines judicial decision making in the House of Lords, with the primary intent of showing how undeterminative of the result are the arguments made in cases, as well as how extensively important these decisions can be as political acts. Chapter 5 is somewhat of an interlude. It is an attack on what most commentators see as an unusually sensible recent decision, *Pepper* v. *Hart*, in which the Law Lords decided to allow themselves to use the legislative record to interpret statutes. Without anticipating my argument there, I can say that I regard the decision as the wrong route to take if one is worried by the undemocratic nature of judicial discretion absent a guiding constitutional code. The chapters in the second half of the book look in some detail at substantive legal areas. Because I believe that 'politics', when the political consequence of judicial activity is considered, is defined far too narrowly, I start with a seemingly apolitical area, the law of negligence. The remaining chapters do, however, cover the area normally seen as political—various strands of public law. I conclude with a chapter which sketches an answer to the very old problem of what on earth law actually is. This answer, however, is different in nature from the usual answer, because I mean something more radically questioning than is usual in posing the problem at all.

This book is, obviously, not a book inside law as an academic field, and may have little interest to lawyers. In saying this I wish it to be clear that I regard it as completely outside that discipline, including the philosophy of law. It is a work in the discipline of political sociology which takes law, essentially the output of the House of Lords, as material to be explained and characterized, and thus much of what I say may seem to be legally incorrect. I hope this is not unnecessarily true—I have learned a huge amount of law over the years, and where it is relevant I have tried to give legally appropriate answers to questions. But it has seldom been appropriate, because lawyers are required, most of the time, to act as though the courts have to reach the specific decisions they reach, and must therefore treat the alternative answers I may suggest as not alternative, because wrong. In that sense I am perhaps seldom legally correct. This is not, I hope, always because I just do not know the material—one has an obligation as a social scientist, even when treating another profession's work from the outside, to try to see it from the inside. I am unsure this is really possible with law. I call to mind a board game my wife and I used to play with our friends when she was in Law School. The players were given a (real life) legal conundrum and asked to pick, from several options, the answer the judge had given. There were two ways of scoring. One got points either for getting the answer right, or for giving the same answer as a majority of players gave. The non-lawyers amongst us regularly did as well or better on the first scoring system, the lawyers always beat us on the second. One of the Law Lords I interviewed for this book told me frankly that he did not think a non-lawyer could hope to come to understand how judges made their decisions. Assuming this is not just because lawyers are cleverer than non-lawyers, the answer itself is curiously revealing, and some of this book is concerned to tease out what he might have meant.

Which brings me to the acknowledgements. I was surprised and delighted by the way many of the Law Lords were willing to grant me interviews—indeed none refused to do so. They were open, honest, and fascinating, and I am very grateful. I cite no one directly to retain confidentiality. Indeed I have gone out of the way not to use any of the many insights I gained in any way that might be attributable. I was enormously impressed with these judges, and I hope it will be clear that anything negative I say in this book is commentary on the role they are forced to play in our judicial system, not on their personal competence. I must single out for thanks Lord Lowry, who gave me several lengthy interviews and read large parts of this book in draft without, as far as I can tell, disagreeing very strongly with any of it. His comments were invaluable. Otherwise my legal education has been at the hands of many academic and practising lawyers over many years, all of whom I am deeply grateful to. I will mention only the first and last in this long chain. Bill Aughterson, Australian Barrister and English Solicitor I have known and learned from for over twenty years. I first grasped the idea of law as a set of tools for fixing problems from him, and what I understand of the wider, common-wealth development of the common law owes much to the variety of his own experience and practice. In the last couple of years I have leant heavily on two of my lawyer colleagues in College, Joshua Getzler, an-other Australian but now an Oxford academic lawyer, and the Principal of my College, Derek Wood CBE, QC. The latter not only read what I have written, but allowed me to watch him in action in the House of Lords. Seeing may well be believing in a field like this. I have nearly always taken the advice given by all these, and many others. I will disappoint Derek Wood in one respect—for the sake of some degree of variety, I have not always referred to the Law Lords by their full titles, a habit he found quite improper. I am sure their Lordships will forgive me this, if only this. Many social scientists have helped form my views on the law, and I would like to pay tribute to the very useful sessions of the Bristol University 'Law and Politics' colloquium, under the leadership of Richard Hodder Williams, one of the few British political scientists to find the courts as interesting as I do. I have leant heavily on the advice and help of Adrian Moore whose philosophical acumen has strengthened many of the argu-ments. It is traditional to thank one's wife, and for good reason. But I would prefer here to thank her not for wifely support, though it has always been generous, but to thank her instead as Elizabeth Oberle-Robertson MA (Oxon.), JD (Yale), Attorney and Counsellor at Law of the State of New York, and Solicitor of the Supreme Court of Judicature, because her legal talents have been even more important.

St Hugh's College, Oxford D. R.
January 1998

Table of Contents

Analytic Table of Contents

Part One—How the Law Lords Work

Chapter 1
Introduction—Politics and Judicial Discretion

Introduction—brief account of American Legal Realism—discussion of the extent and nature of discretion in the House of Lords—description of the working methods of the Lords and the nature of the case load.

Chapter 2
A Statistical Analysis of Judicial Discretion

A demonstration by the use of various multivariate statistical techniques that results of appeals are strongly correlated with which Law Lords hear the appeal. It is further demonstrated that complex interactions take place between various pairs and even triples of Law Lords, sharply affecting the probability of the 'stronger' or 'weaker' litigant winning the appeal. The data are also used to construct 'dimensions' of judicial style.

Chapter 3
Judicial Methodology in Statutory Interpretation

Detailed analyses of several divided cases show how little constraint there appears to be on how easily judges can justify their decisions. It is also suggested that far from being determined by methodological principles like 'strict interpretation', the principles are adhered to when and as they are useful in justifying the preferred substantive decisions.

Chapter 4
Judicial Methodology and the Common Law

The analytic approach of the previous chapter is extended to common law cases to demonstrate the weakness of precedential argument as a constraint on judicial discretion. Extensive analysis is undertaken of the rival argumentative strategies deployed to justify desired results. The point is developed further from Chapter 3 that a major weakness of appellate argument in the Lords is the ignoring of opposition positions and a failure of rival arguments to meet with each other.

Chapter 5
In *Re Pepper* v. *Hart*: Comments on the Nature of Laws

The recent decision by the Lords in *Pepper* v. *Hart* to allow themselves to consult Hansard to help in statutory interpretation is discussed. The chapter seeks to demonstrate that, far from being a restriction to judicial discretion, the new ruling is likely to obscure further just how much discretionary decision making is indulged in by the Lords. It discusses in some detail the role of value-principles in statutory interpretation, and the constitutional status of such interpretation.

Part Two—What the Law Lords Have Done

Chapter 6
Pure Policy—The Law of Negligence

The law of negligence is one where judges have been forced to engage in law making more openly and frequently than elsewhere. Analysis of negligence cases from the famous *Donoghue* v. *Stevenson* until recent times shows how policy battles between more or less expansionist judicial ideologies have characterized this development, with the victory tending to go to the more restrictivist. The constant theme is one of judicial preference for commerce and for state institutions rather than for plaintiffs.

Chapter 7
Imposing Rationality on the State

The general judicial doctrines on when and why the courts can intervene between the state, in its many forms, and citizens are analysed. Attention is particularly paid to the incoherence of the classic ruling case, *Wednesbury*, especially to the way subsequent treatment of it has raised serious questions of exactly what a precedent is. The general thesis that judges use *Wednesbury* both to allow and to forbid interference with state policy is developed, particularly to show how 'voluntary' judicial intervention really is.

Chapter 8
Public Law and the Liberty of the Person

Public law in its relation to individual freedom, especially in immigration and prisoners' rights cases. It is here at the very core of the liberal conception of courts as protectors of the weak that the seepage of judicial ideology into their decisions shows at its clearest. Implications for future jurisprudence with an incorporated Bill of Rights are considered.

Chapter 9
Judicial Review as Welfare Management

An important part of the Law Lord's work can best be described as 'managing the welfare state' because much of their time is spent interpreting statutes where citizens appear as claimants for scarce goods the state provides. The cases demonstrate a clear preference to support state officials and a generally restrictive orientation towards the generosity with which a statute could be interpreted. This is largely ascribed to the way judges approach the cases as though they were themselves civil servants, rather than seeing claimants as exercising rights.

Chapter 10
Conclusion—Legal Argument and Politics

The arguments of the previous chapters are brought together into one question—is there really such a thing as a 'legal answer' to a problem? This is investigated by looking at legal decision making in crisis, demonstrated through the Anthony Bland case. A sketch of a theory of judicial appellate behaviour based on the Kuhnian approach to the philosophy of science is offered.

List of Tables

List of Figures

PART ONE

How the Law Lords Work

1

Introduction—Politics and Judicial Discretion

> It is not the will of the sovereign that makes lawyers' law, even when
> that is its source, but what the judges by whom it is enforced *say* is his
> will. The judges have other motives for decision, outside their own
> arbitrary will, beside the commands of their sovereign. And whether
> those other motives are, or are not, equally compulsory, is immaterial,
> if they are sufficiently likely to prevail to afford a ground for predic-
> tion. The only question for the lawyer is, how will the judges act?
>
> > Oliver Wendell Holmes

1. The Aim of the Book

This book addresses an old question. Just how much discretion do the
judges have when they makes their decisions? It is primarily about a small
subset of judges, those who comprise the Appellate Committee of the
House of Lords, the Lords of Appeal in Ordinary, usually referred to only
as the Law Lords. They are the highest court in the UK, and if anyone has
extensive discretion, they do. They are chosen for study mainly because as
the ultimate court, they are both the most free, and the rulers of the curial
hierarchy. To a greater or lesser extent all other judges are governed by
their decisions. But it is part of the general approach of this book to treat
all judicial decision making as to some extent discretionary, and the
second reason for studying the Law Lords is that they are the most visible
part of the system. What is true for them will be true, to a degree that
varies for many reasons, for all the judges in the system.

One can indeed broaden that. Judges are only one set of a universe of
public officials all of whom make decisions on people's requests, complaints, and challenges by applying supposedly given and predetermined
rules to sets of facts. There is no absolute distinction between a Law Lord
and a junior Social Security officer establishing a claimant's right to the job
seekers allowance. In the criminal sphere there is no absolute difference
between the Law Lord and the Custody Sergeant determining when CID
must release a prisoner they have not charged. In its broadest scope,
therefore, this book is about rule bound discretionary decision making in
the State. The theme is studied through an investigation of an unusually
powerful body who are forced to carry out their activities in public.

There are several reasons why students of politics should be concerned with the Law Lords, but they all come down to the same problem. The problem is that our democratic theories of political legitimacy have very little to say about judicial behaviour, and have almost no way of justifying judicial discretion. This point is true to a greater or lesser extent in all democracies, but it is especially acute in the United Kingdom, because our largely inchoate constitutional theory is still very largely Hobbesian, in that we recognize officially no source of binding authority other than the Crown in Parliament. Thus political theorists and constitutional lawyers ought to be concerned with the Law Lords. So should those who study political institutions in a more empirical mode. Though in the UK the courts have never been seen as important institutions by political scientists, this is in part because democratic theory has never bothered to account for them. It is also because there is enough truth in the idea that parliament rules to mean that a study of the courts is a study of a marginal institution. Because there is no power of judicial review equivalent to the constitutional override power of the American and Canadian Supreme Courts, or the German Constitutional Court, or even the French Conseil Constitutionel, the Law Lords are not political actors of that degree of importance.

However, in a system like that of the UK, almost all power is marginal if the test is to be an equivalent to the power of a Commons majority. If the civil service departments are worth studying, the courts are worth studying. Indeed it is one theme developed in later chapters of this book that the courts often operate as though they were staffed by civil servants. In any case it is the marginal that affects ordinary people in their daily lives. If a decision of a court means that one claimant does not get an allowance which she might have gained had the courts interpreted a statute differently, and if they could indeed have so interpreted it without triggering the Hobbesian Sovereign to intervene, that person's life is made worse. It is because the courts, led and disciplined and directed by the Law Lords, do indeed make such decisions, and because the Hobbesian Sovereign, in the shape of the House of Commons, only most infrequently bothers to interfere, that the courts are fit for study by political scientists.

The whole idea of what it is to make a discretionary judgment, and the related questions of what constraints there either are, or should be, on judicial decision making, is very complex, and this chapter only sketches very lightly over them. But first it seems sensible to give an example of the sort of judicial decision, important perhaps only at the margin, that the book is concerned with.

AN EXAMPLE

In 1989 one of Britain's more conservative newspaper owners, Associated Newspapers, publishers of the *Daily Mail* and the *Evening Standard*, decided to reduce as much as they could the power of the National Union of Journalists on their papers. They withdrew recognition of the union, and in an attempt to reduce further its influence offered individual work contracts to all the journalists. Those who signed by a certain date were given a pay rise backdated to October 1989. Those who refused were told they would not get any rise before the annual pay review in October 1990. Up to 1991 the National Union of Rail, Maritime and Transport Workers (NURMTW) represented manual workers in Southampton and negotiated their pay and employment conditions. Associated British Ports, who own Southampton dockyards, were also eager to reduce union influence, and offered their workers the choice of signing an individual contract or continuing on whatever terms the union could negotiate. Those who agreed to individual contracts were given significantly better pay rises than those who stayed with the union.

These sorts of employment practice may well have fitted the industrial relations climate at the end of the Thatcher era, but members of both unions had some reason to think they were protected against overt attempts to discriminate against them. The last Labour Government had passed various employment Acts, tidied up in the Employment Protection (Consolidation) Act 1978. Part of this Act, section 23(1)(a) certainly seemed to offer protection:

> Every employee shall have the right not to have action (short of dismissal) taken against him as an individual by his employer for the purpose of—(a) preventing or deterring him from being or seeking to become a member of an independent trade union, or penalising him for doing so.

The employers could not be said to have done anything positive to the workers, but section 153(1) apparently covered their situations nonetheless:

> In this Act except so far as the context otherwise requires—'act' and 'action' each includes omission and references to doing an act or taking action shall be construed accordingly.

There was another reason the workers might have thought they were protected against their employers' anti-union tactics. As early as 1987 the Court of Appeal had already held, in a similar context, that not giving to union members what was given to those prepared to leave the unions was unlawful.[1] Emboldened by this the workers took their cases to Industrial Tribunals, which in both cases upheld their complaints. Inevitably the employers appealed to the Employment Appeal Tribunal. In both cases the EAT panels were divided, the judge, the same in both cases, Wood J, holding for the employers along with one of the lay members, and with isolated dissents from the other lay representative. However, the cases were joined at the next stage and the Court of Appeal held unanimously for both sets of workers. Head counting matters even less in legal argument than it does in moral philosophy, but it is worth noting that by this stage the score, in terms of judicial

---

[1] The earlier case was *National Coal Board* v. *Ridgeway* [1987] ICR 641. The cases discussed here are jointly reported as: *Associated Newspapers Ltd.* v. *Wilson* and *Associated British Ports* v. *Palmer and Others* [1995] 2 WLR 354.

votes, was 11 to 4 for the unions. Now the joined cases went to the Appellate Committee of the House of Lords, which split three to two. Unfortunately for British Trade Unions, the three in majority found for the employers. So even though the final score was 13 to 7, the unappealable final decision was that a Labour Government's apparent efforts to protect unions from discriminatory tactics were not, in fact, the law of the land. Discussing this position, its author, Lord Bridge who gave the only speech for the majority spells out his attitude:

> The line of reasoning I have followed . . . was criticised as unduly literalistic. It was even submitted that the Labour Government which introduced the Act of 1975 could not have intended to provide less effective protection for trade union members than the Act of 1971. A purposive construction to resolve ambiguities of statutory language is often appropriate and necessary. But this is the first time I have heard it suggested that the policy of an enactment to be presumed from the political complexion of the government which introduced it may prevail over the language of the statute. The courts' traditional approach to construction, giving primacy to the ordinary, grammatical meaning of statutory language, is reflected in the parliamentary draftsman's technique of using language with the utmost precision to express the legislative intent of his political masters and it remains the golden rule of construction that a statute means exactly what it says and does not mean what it does not say.[2]

There is much to be said for ostensive definition. This case is what we mean when we talk about judges making politically important discretionary judgments. It is an example of discretion because the result manifestly could have been different—two of five Law Lords wanted a different result and had arguments that satisfied them to justify it. It is politically important because as a result the power of the State is not to be used to protect the weak, in this case an association of journalists, from the strong, in this case the modern equivalent of a press baron. The key idea here, though, is that the result 'could have been different'. That is what judicial discretion is about, and we need to turn directly to a consideration of this thesis, which is the heart of this book.

2. Judicial Decision Making and Judicial Discretion

The basic judicial decision, outside the process of supervising a jury trial, is to decide whether a given set of facts fit an understood rule. This book is written from the perspective of a school of jurisprudence known as legal realism[3] which severely doubts the possibility of this process because it

---

[2] *Associated Newspapers* at 362.

[3] There is a large literature on various aspects of realism, most American. Perhaps the classic statement, vital because it is by a distinguished judge, is Oliver Wendell Holmes early essay 'The Path of Law' in his *Collected Legal Papers*, London, 1920. His view was that law as practised was little more than a matter of predicting what judges will do. This position was developed especially by Kurt Llewellyn in a series of publications, the first and

doubts the 'understood rule' aspect of that description. There is a huge literature on legal realism which makes it otiose to discuss it at any length here. The theory's origins may lie with Oliver Wendell Holmes, a nineteenth-century American legal thinker and vastly experienced judge. Early in his career, as a practising lawyer, he made his name as a legal theorist whose views, especially in his early work on the law of torts, seemed to suggest that law was, indeed, a logical construction of principles, and one could hope to achieve statements of what the law was in some areas which were very close to certainty. He approached his first judicial appointment, to the Supreme Court of Massachusetts, with the expectation that he would be able to work in this manner, to 'invent new problems which should be the test of doctrine, and then to generalise it all and write it in continuous, logical, philosophic exposition, setting forth the whole corpus with its roots in history and its justifications of expedience'.[4] After nearly twenty years on the Massachusetts court he had radically changed his view. By then he saw judging as a much more arbitrary procedure, and contrasted the view that law was 'a system of reason' or 'deduction from principles of ethics or admitted axioms' with the belief that law could only really be described as 'prophecies of what the courts will in fact do'. Holmes saw all judicial activity as the making of policy choices, the decisions as resting on 'general lines of policy blindly felt'. He was aware that 'the language of judicial decision' was 'mainly the language of logic', but insisted that the decisions themselves were 'opinions as to policy' which 'merely embody the preference of a given body in a given place and time'.

Holmes's insights were developed in the inter-war years in the USA into what became a completely dominant view of law by the Legal Realists. They maintained that most, if not all, major judicial opinions could be demonstrated to be every bit as arbitrary as Holmes had thought. Their major tool, often described as 'debunking' has been described as subjecting 'opinions to a logical analysis that exposed their inconsistencies, their unsubstantiated premises, and their tendency to pass off contingent judgments as inexorable'. As one of the leaders of the movement, Kurt Llewellyn, summarized it 'in any case doubtful enough to make litigation respectable the available authoritative premises are at least two and the two are mutually contradictory'.[5] This approach, though we hope we do

most famous being a short book written for beginning law students, *The Bramble Bush*, 1930. A more extensive and developed theory is contained in a collection of his essays, *Jurisprudence: Realism in Theory and Practise*, Chicago, University of Chicago Press, 1962.

[4] The quotations from Holmes are taken from G. Edward White, 'The integrity of Holmes jurisprudence', in *Intervention and Detachment: Essays in Legal History and Jurisprudence*, pp. 75–105, New York, Oxford University Press, 1994. This brief account is the best we know on Holmes.

[5] Cited in G. Edward White op. cit. at p. 276.

it in a spirit too respectful to make it 'debunking', is crucial to our argument here. Lawyers criticize judgments, but usually from the premise that some alternative correct answer was ignored by the judges. Our extensive critique of legal argument in Chapters 3 and 4 is to establish that a legal realist approach to the Law Lords is viable, that Llewellyn's judgement and Holmes's characterization is every bit as true of English judicial argument in the late twentieth century as it was of American judicial opinions earlier. The odd thing about legal realism as a movement is that it was once dominant—the great law schools like Harvard, Columbia, and Yale were completely given over to it, and indeed its doctrines were taught as correct to law students—yet it vanished away. Legal realism was never defeated in intellectual combat—it simply faded out of fashion by the time the Second World War was over. Yet successor movements in American legal thought were deeply influenced by it. Indeed it may be that the basic premise—all judging is policy preference, all judicial argument is artefact, was so completely accepted that it slipped into the entire legal consciousness. Some argue that the highly influential 'Critical Legal Studies' movement in contemporary American law schools is no more than a modernized legal realism presented from a more avowedly politically radical perspective, and that what the 'CLS' movement calls 'deconstruction' is just the old 'debunking'. However that may be, the realist school is the theoretical basis for this book.

There is a more extreme version of the theory, called fact scepticism, which doubts the extent to which judges really are faced with a clear-cut factual situation.[6] Were we writing about judicial behaviour in the lower courts where these factual situations are decided, we might well wish to join that group, but by and large we accept here the given facts aspect. Appellate judging is certainly supposed to accept as given the factual description decided on by lower parts of the court hierarchy, and most of the time the Law Lords do so. Their job is to check that relevant rules have been properly understood and applied conscientiously to those fact situations. Because it is the second level of appeal, after the Court of Appeal (or the equivalent in Scotland and Northern Ireland), and because appeals are restricted by both cost and the need to win permission from the Lords themselves, the few cases which they hear are generally assumed to be 'hard cases'. We discuss the utility of this idea of a 'hard case' later in this chapter. For the time being, let us take it that a hard case is one where it is thought there is real uncertainty about the rules which should be applied. Thus the Lords are not in the business of checking for, as it were, the technical proficiency of the Court of Appeal. That court may well 'make

---

[6] The best statement of fact scepticism is still probably by its pioneer, Jerome N. Frank in *Law and the Modern Mind*, London, Stevens & Sons, 1949.

mistakes', apply a rule wrongly, apply the wrong rule, or in some other way botch the job, but that should not, in itself, mean the case was a 'hard' one in the sense that adjective is normally used in this context. There are several reasons why the rule may be uncertain, and the possibility of such uncertainty is accepted by all schools of jurisprudence, though they differ both in their beliefs about the extent of such uncertainty, and the conclusions they draw from the uncertainty. It is this uncertainty which produces judicial discretion, using discretion here in the neutral sense that means no more than that appellate judges have to make a decision about what rule is relevant, and that there is no institutional way they can be forced to make one rather than another decision.

It is important to grasp this neutral sense, in which the presence of discretion is undeniable. Discretion is often used with other shades of meaning, and can be taken to mean that there is *no* sense at all in which a judge can be criticized for a decision if he had discretion. For example Ronald Dworkin and Herbert Hart, probably the two leading philosophers of law in the post-war Anglo-American tradition, have furiously debated the existence of discretion, in a debate only possible because Dworkin takes this strong sense of discretion.[7] But it is not only legal philosophers like Dworkin who take this meaning, and consequently deny that discretion exists. One Law Lord interviewed for this book insisted that the only discretion the Lords had was 'to get the answer right'. We take no position on this theoretical debate. By judicial discretion here we mean the mere fact that appellate judges must and can make choices and that there is no effective control over their choices.

Let us consider three basic models of the judicial role. Model one corresponds to what is sometimes called 'slot machine jurisprudence', and is quite unreal. In this model there is some equivalent to an 'answer book' which the appellate judge should consult. In a very simple world it would be a published legal code which exhaustively covers all situations which could crop up. Continental code law countries in fact make a pretence that exactly this is provided, often, as with the French, with constitutional doctrines that expressly prohibit the judges from 'making law'. We have a little to say about this model in Chapter 5 where we discuss one attempt to make the UK system a little bit more like a slot machine, at least as far as interpretation of parliamentary statutes. Even if a code cannot be expected to be complete, one might hope to paper over its cracks by a

---

[7] The debate is best seen by comparing their two main works. H. L. A. Hart, *The Concept of Law*, Oxford, 1961 and Ronald M. Dworkin, *Taking Rights Seriously*, London, 1977. A quick entry to the debate is provided by Dworkin's essay 'No Right Answer?' in a Festschrift to Hart, *Law Morality and Society: Essays in Honour of H. L. A. Hart*, P. M. S. Hacker and J. Raz (eds.), Oxford, Clarendon Press, 1977. A good collection of essays covering all the relevant aspects of both sides in the debate is Marshall Cohen (ed.), *Ronald Dworkin and Contemporary Jurisprudence*, London, Duckworth, 1984.

separate set of rules for interpretation of the code. Most jurisdictions do in fact have such auxiliary codes. There have been several interpretation Acts in recent British legal history, and the common law contains several rules of interpretation, some stemming from its formative days. Most such auxiliary codes do little more than provide judges with a ragbag of acceptable ways of expressing their discretionary judgments. Alternatively one could imagine an institutional system of reference to parliament wherever the code seems unclear—something like this was the original idea behind the French system after the revolution, because of the hatred of judicial involvement in politics. Slot machine jurisprudence of this form is quite incompatible with any idea of separation of power between the executive and the judiciary, however. Slot machine jurisprudence is indeed impossible in practice because no one could ever draw up an exhaustive interpretation code. It may indeed by logically impossible, in the same way that a completely consistent account of a formal system like mathematics can be shown to be impossible. Nonetheless it is an important idea, because it is a characteristic assumption about judicial behaviour by the general public, and may be useful as a benchmark against which to test reality.

The second model is roughly what the official English doctrine would be were it to be written out anywhere. One of the difficulties in writing about this field is that judicial pronouncements in England have always tended towards a pretence of a belief in slot machine jurisprudence, a downplaying for the public of the extent of judicial discretion. Roughly the official doctrine would go something like this. Where problems arise because the law is unclear, or a novel situation has occurred, the judges do indeed lay down new law. Where the problem arises in the common law, however, they do this only by drawing out the implications of a pre-existing and very rich body of rules developed over time, aided by general principles embodied in that tradition, and acting only in the most incremental fashion. As well as this, the official position accepts that rarely it will be necessary to make what English judges call a 'public policy' decision. This is where an overt value choice is recognized as necessary because the answer the judges might have to give by incremental extrapolation is undesirable in itself. An example which crops up in cases we analyse later is the public policy rule that one may not sue a police force for negligence. One other area of accepted innovation, very similar to public policy but even rarer, is where an undoubted rule of law is openly changed because it is widely felt in society to be no longer acceptable. The best example in this book is the judicial change in the law of rape where the doctrine that a man cannot rape his wife was abandoned. As will be seen, even when this decision was announced, considerable judicial craftsmanship went into showing that the rule itself was nothing like as well established as had been thought. This model does not deny that choices are made, but minimizes the discretion by limiting the range of choice and suggesting that the technical expertise of lawyers is such as to provide for something very close to a 'correct' answer which is capable of discovery by a process of induction, or sometimes even of deduction.

It would be impossible to deny a certain degree of judicial law making in the common law because of its very history. Common law, that is, the whole body of legal rules and principles which has not been cast into statutory form by Parliament, may today be a learnable body of rules based on specified precedents, but it was originally entirely judge made. In a pre-democratic political system there is no particular problem about entrusting the creation of binding rules to the King's judges, and the very idea that such law actually has precedence over parliamentary law was slow to die. (Some recent comments by judges, not usually from the bench, suggest that idea may be beginning to re-arise. This we touch on in the chapters on public law.) Furthermore this law was consciously made by members of a particular social class, the developing bourgeois, in the interests of that class and to encourage economic development as understood by that class. Most legal history texts on the law of contract, property or real estate show this, none better than the superb treatment of contract by Patrick Atiyah, *The Rise and Fall of Freedom of Contract*.[8] In his book on the Law Lords Robert Stevens gives an extensive account of the way an open acceptance of this massive creative role of judges gave way to a presentation of the judicial function which minimizes, if it does not entirely deny, this creativity.[9] Rightly or wrongly the common law is now presented as a complex body of rules, a 'maze' as described once by Lord Diplock, but a largely fixed body which can generate answers to novel situations by the basic legal methodology of analogy to precedents. This idea is best examined in the context of real cases and real examples of judicial argument, as we present in Chapter 4, rather than in an abstract way in this introductory chapter. Suffice it to say that when they do admit to law making, modern judges think of themselves as acting in an entirely incremental way, and in a way that, because the answers they produce are derived from the older law by professional legal craftsmanship, should not be presented as acts of radically free choice such as to make judicial discretion politically important. A typical example of such a common law hard case coming to the Law Lords involves a claim by a plaintiff for compensation after suffering an injury caused by the defendant. This might involve a form of injury hitherto not seen as entitling a plaintiff to

[8] Patrick S. Atiyah, *The Rise and Fall of Freedom of Contract*, Oxford, Clarendon Press, 1985.
[9] The best historical study of the development of the Law Lords as an institution is Robert Stevens, *Law and Politics: The House of Lords as a Judicial Body 1800–1976*, London, Weidenfeldt and Nicolson, 1979.

recompense, or a claim against a particular type of actor hitherto protected, or a situation where the general type of hurt and the general type
of offender would normally have been covered, but some rule of law had
in the past been of help to deny legal protection to plaintiffs of the instant
type. To decide such a case the Law Lords must extend, or decline to
extend, a complicated web of previous decisions over a new situation. The
official doctrine suggests that there are well understood methods to decide whether or not to do this, and the decision can be made without being
just a judge's own private response, shaped by his values and preferences
in a way which involves outright judicial legislation.

Where problems occur not in common law but in the application of
parliamentary statutes discretion is seen as limited by the simple duty to
discover the intention of the legislators when they passed the Act and to
give effect to it. Again there is choice, but well-intentioned judges using
the various rules of interpretation and having in mind their duty to
discover and apply Parliament's will should be able to come very close
to a correct answer. This is the form of decision that the example at the
beginning of this chapter illustrates. It is clear that in *Associated Newspapers
Ltd.* v. *Wilson* Lord Bridge presents himself as finding a correct answer by
the application of well understood techniques, in such a way as to minimize almost out of existence any troublesome sense of discretion. Any
remaining worries that might occur about judicial creativity are put to rest
by the doctrine of parliamentary sovereignty. Parliament can always
change the law, so if some aspect of the common law has not been affected
by legislation, it can be assumed Parliament approves of it, and therefore
of marginal or incremental developments to it. Judicial interpretation of
statute has attracted a huge literature, and has been openly discussed in
many leading cases. Again, we consider these matters at length both in
Chapter 3 and, in the special context of the recent case of *Pepper* v. *Hart*,
in Chapter 5. (In this case a major modification was made to the official
method of interpretation, with the intention of making parliamentary
intention easier to discover.) The problem for us can be described fairly
succinctly. Modern parliamentary statutes are often complicated documents which do not so much lay down a rule as create a legal institution
to achieve policy ends. Thus if something like the Children's Act needs
interpretation the judicial problem is to fine-tune or tinker with an aspect
of the welfare state. This inevitably involves substantive policy preferences, and referring to the idea of parliamentary intent does nothing but
disguise what judges are really doing. Though it may seem, at first sight,
that statutory interpretation must be a fairly automatic and innocuous
activity, it is here, as much as in the common law, that the creative
discretion of judges comes into play. Much of this book consists of analysis of cases where these techniques of extrapolation and interpretation are

used, and the full richness of this approach will appear in the substantive chapters. There is little point in discussing such matters further in this chapter.

The third model, ours, differs only in one way from the second, the 'official' model, and it follows directly from the American tradition of judicial realism. We simply deny that the law does or even can, produce that form of technical induction. Instead we claim that not only a few, but a very large number of decisions in hard cases are akin to the recognized category of the public policy decisions.[10] We do not believe that law, as an intellectual activity, can generate answers to questions about new situations or to unclarities in statutes. What we suggest happens instead is that judges form a view on what result they want, and then deploy complex and subtle arguments from precedent, or from interpretative rules, to provide *ex post facto* 'justifications' for these preferences. This is not to deny that the preferences may be for the continuation of a previous approach despite the result in the instant case. They may even be preferences for upholding a technique of decision making—a preference perhaps for a very literalistic approach to statutory interpretation, which is what Lord Bridge thought himself accused of in *Associated Newspapers*. But these are all *preferences*, predispositions, and they are fully freely chosen and not entailed or enforced by anything in law. What we are insisting on is that any case that comes to the House of Lords could be decided either way, and that the judges do fully choose the way it will come out, with no important limitations other than those involved in the need to get at least two other Law Lords to agree with them.

Because the difference between our third model and the official model is, in a way, so narrow, there is only one way to support our case. It is, unfortunately, a very arduous way, both to write and to read. There is no alternative but to look very closely at actual examples of judicial argument from a wide range of cases. Most studies of judicial ideology do not do this. They not only normally only consider a very few cases, they tend to look mainly at the result of those cases rather than the arguments. So, for example, the main exponent in the UK of the idea that judges not only make up the law, but do so in a class motivated way is J. A. G. Griffiths.[11] Yet his books, though popular with radicals, have had very little impact on the judiciary, or on main line lawyers, because of this selectivity of cases. What we try to do in Chapters 3 and 4 is to study judicial argument through a wide variety of cases to show, as much as it can ever be shown, that the rival arguments just cannot be seen as determinative of the

---

[10] A very good treatment of public policy in the law, and in general a powerful analysis of judicial legislation, is John Bell, *Policy Arguments in Judicial Decisions*, Oxford, Clarendon Press, 1983.

[11] John Griffith, *Judicial Politics since 1920: A Chronicle*, Oxford, Blackwell, 1993.

results, and can only be seen as the construction of argument from approved material to give a justification, it is not too strong to say a rationalisation, of a preferred outcome. Our attempt is to show that law just does not have sufficiently closed a texture to render judicial discretion unimportant. We tie this up with a final demonstration in the last chapter of judicial decision making in a situation where the judges have to admit there is no pre-existing material, no possibility of incrementalism, and where they nonetheless claim to be producing a technically correct *legal* answer rather than just imposing their value preference. This is the horrific case of Anthony Bland, who had been left in a permanent coma when crushed in a crowd disaster. His case can be taken as an extreme example of judicial discretion, which no one would deny. The difference between our model of judicial behaviour and the second model is that we regard it as extreme only in its clarity (and, of course, in its tragedy) but not logically really different from more routine cases. If the first part of the book, therefore, concentrates on judicial methodology to show the reality of discretion in this strong sense, the second half gives examples of the consequences of this indeterminacy in judicial behaviour. Basically we ask, has it mattered? Can we see law developing in various areas, both common law and statutory, in ways that suited the preferences of the judges who decided the cases when viable alternatives that others would have preferred were ignored or dismissed? Mainly we consider public law cases, as befits a book written from a political science viewpoint. We do, however, dedicate one long chapter, Chapter 6, to an important common law problem, legal protection against negligence, because we believe that a broad definition of politics is relevant. It is a political matter if a house owner cannot be recompensed by a local authority when his shoddily built house falls down, and if this is because judges have chosen that he should not be compensated, and the choice was a free one they did not have to make, we then have a very good reason for holding that judicial discretion exists and matters. There is no real difference between such a situation and one where a local authority is absolved of the duty to house the homeless because of a judicial interpretation of the phrase 'intentionally homeless' in a statute which they were perfectly free to interpret differently. Both are 'political', both are discretionary, both matter.

Before we turn to this difficult effort, it is necessary to consider briefly how exactly we think the Law Lords do come to their decisions. Much depends on the actual method of giving decisions on cases. As we discuss later, the Lords do not sit as a full body except for very rare cases where they want maximum authority for their ruling. The very fact that they do sit *en banc* on these rare cases shows in a way that even they recognize the partiality of normal decisions. It should be noted that decisions of a sub-panel are virtually never used in other supreme courts. Instead the Lords work in panels of five judges, chosen more or less at random from the full Appellate Committee of a dozen Law Lords. Panels of five judges, like any small committees, are subject to all the strains involved in small group dynamics, and the Law Lords follow one rule often found in such situations to minimize one type of undue influence—the reverse seniority rule, which is found, *inter alia*, in the US Supreme Court. This means that the junior Law Lord present gives his opinions first when the case is discussed, followed in turn until the presiding Lord. It is also important that these decisions are given for consideration orally, and immediately after conclusion of argument. As the Law Lords do not have (most say they would not want) the aid of law clerks to brief them on the law and present written draft arguments, it means that first reactions to a possibly quite complex case are thus produced face to face, rapidly, and orally in an atmosphere that very much resembles a committee charged with solving a question rapidly. It cannot be denied that the possibilities here for the influence of personal styles, human interactions, and surface reactions coloured by latent preferences and predispositions are immense. When one adds that several of the members of the panel will not be as expert as others in the area, and that few, conceivably none, of the those deciding a case will have been involved in selecting it for decision one would hardly be surprised if the resulting decisions were apt to reflect strong preferences by only one or two Law Lords. As a way of getting an initial measure of where everyone stood such a procedure might be useful. It is usually the sole method. Very few cases have a subsequent meeting to try to iron out differences, compromise, or convince doubters. It is hard to get a well based figure for the number of cases where there is more than one meeting. Different Law Lords gave different estimates, but one who had thought hard about the process and himself regarded it as a weakness thought he could remember not more than one or two such in around fifty cases he had been involved in. No Law Lord interviewed suggested a much higher rate. After the initial vote the presiding Lord will ask one member to write the opinion, or the opinion of the majority if it is split, or may claim it himself. Any other Lord is free to write an opinion, not only in split, but in the unanimous cases, and these are circulated. But it is very clear that this is a circulation of opinions for information, not for discussion. As far as one can tell it is rare for draft opinions to be changed. What is beyond doubt, and we note this at several places in later chapters, the arguments published by a Law Lord in a case almost never respond to the other arguments. In other words if a minority opinion contains what seems, to an outsider, a severe criticism of the argument of the majority, there will be no slightest defence against these criticisms contained in that majority opinion. The Law Lords do not seem extensively to concern themselves with the cases they are not hearing, however controversial, so that there is no sense in which the opinions of the five, or even the single opinion of an undivided panel, reflect a general consensus of the Law Lords as a group. This is not, of course, to say that particular individuals will not consult colleagues. Obviously they do. Several Law Lords gave examples of specific discussions they had with one or more of their colleagues and even, though only in guarded terms, of discussions with judges not in the Lords. But it appears to be a highly individualistic and entirely *ad hoc* process. To an extent vastly greater than seems to be the case in equivalent courts, the Law Lords make their law as individuals, being satisfied as long as the argument they construct, or consent to, satisfies their own sense of legal correctness.

We know relatively little about the detailed working of any appellate court, but most appear to perform their jobs in a very much more collegial way. To start with, many continental European courts allow only a single unsigned opinion of the court. Such a process inevitably makes for more collegial working, because no decision can be issued at all until a majority can agree. It is a feature of such courts, the French perhaps being typical, that opinions are very short, and lack supporting reasons for their statements of law, it being presumably easier to get a majority to agree to a bare decision if reasons are not annunciated. The US Supreme Court, and both the Canadian Supreme Court and the Australian High Court, however, are well known to work by a process of lengthy negotiation of draft opinions. In these courts not only do the majority try to craft an argument which will maximize their number, but dissenting judges will similarly try to build a broad agreement on reasons for dissent amongst the minority. These courts use law clerks, and go through several, sometimes many, meetings and discussions so that the final result is much less a collection of individual preferences and much more of a collegial product. It is true that the dissent rate in the House of Lords is considerably lower than in the three courts referred to. The Law Lords seldom do disagree with each other—an average over time would be about 10 per cent of all cases resulting in dissents. But this is hardly surprising given that the agreement is essentially only on which side should win. It is in this behavioural context we must place the general position on discretion described above. If law does not in truth contain material that can really determine a decision, if discretion is possible in the quite strong sense we have claimed above, there is only one source of restraint. This is the need for each judge's views to win the approval of other legal professionals. Where a judge is one of nine or ten or, in the international courts often more than a dozen, all of whom are involved and seeking not only to form, but to maximize, a coalition, the need to have arguments that are as proof against other lawyers as possible is very strong. What little we do know about other courts tends to show this process. With the US Supreme

Court, for example, we actually have some information about early drafts of some major decisions which would have shaped the law quite differently had they been able to command as much internal support as the later versions which were officially announced.[12] An English Law Lord cannot feel this pressure very strongly, though they do, of course, care about their public image amongst the elite of the profession. Certainly some 'read their reviews', as it were, particularly the academic journals, though others at least claim to be uninterested in this audience, and to write only for practising lawyers or others—in commerce or other institutions where a knowledge of judicial argument may be expected—who can be seen almost as clients. In general though it seems that there is relatively little institutional pressure on a Law Lord to modify his views, or to give up a preferred outcome because 'the law' will not support it. When we examine specific cases later it will occasionally be possible to demonstrate how the haphazardness of the small semi-random panels plays into this discretion, because it is, though rarely, possible to know how other Law Lords who happened not to sit on a particular case would most likely have decided it.

It is not easy to characterize individual judges in the general terms often used by political scientists in other countries, and it is not useful to look for broad class based ideological affinities. Indeed neither we, nor usually the judges themselves, are likely ever to be able to be very clear about what drives their decisions in easily generalizable ways. In many cases, and the Law Lords admit this easily enough, they work 'bottom up', from a basic instinct that the plaintiff or the defendant ought to win to an argument that makes him the winner. Their own sense of being constrained in this process by the limits of acceptable legal argument is quite strong. Two ideas were common to most interviews. One is that they all claim to be familiar with the sense of having to give up the attempt to decide a case the way they want to, because the arguments cannot be made to work. The other is that they have, in a phrase that cropped up over and again, a sense of 'cheating'—that is, they are aware that some opinions of their colleagues did break this ineffable sense of proper legal argument and constituted 'cheating', not playing the game. Many of the Law Lords interviewed, for example, used this word to describe the man who still horrifies as well as fascinates the English legal establishment, Lord Denning; but they used it also of their current colleagues. Or they used it to describe an inner sense of obligation—'one tries not to cheat'. It is a very inchoate idea, but in itself evidence of just how very free a Law Lord is in exercising his discretion. It is much more useful to demonstrate apparent motives for decisions in the course of analysing the decisions

---

[12] Bernard Schwartz, *The Unpublished Opinions of the Warren Court*, New York, OUP, 1985.

themselves, so we leave any extended discussion of this topic for the substantive chapters. To sum up we would add the following to our model of judicial behaviour. The Law Lords come to their decisions very freely, with little peer group influence or pressure, largely according to individual conceptions they hold about their role, and with an eye either to an immediate sense of justice in the particular case, or to concerns they have about the likely impact in a wider world of the instant decision. This latter point we try to spell out in the substantive chapters and it cannot usefully be summarized ahead of those discussions.

But even a preliminary sketch of a model of judging cannot quite stop there. Granted the Law Lords are free to decide more or less what they want to in any case before them, subject only to the need to persuade two others to agree, however tacitly, what do they use this freedom for? This is where someone committed to class analysis, conspiracy theory, or any neat generalization about the English power structure can wheel in their preferred model of ideology. We very much doubt that any judicial model that fails primarily to treat them as above all else judges and lawyers can be very helpful. Who the Law Lords are, in the way the question is often raised, especially by journalists and political activists is hardly worth asking. That they are all men, most with public school and Oxbridge educations, most from an upper middle class professional home, and most comfortably, some very well off goes without saying and tells us almost nothing. All British institutions are so headed. To the extent that anything in what they do or believe follows from that, it does so only in a very restricted sense. Indeed it is easier to use decided cases to show how they often overcome any blindness that might follow from that background than it is to see them being obviously biased because of it. As an example, the Lords' record on married women's rights is rather better than that of the House of Commons, as we show in some of the cases analysed in Chapter 4. Of course they do share a common ideology, which permeates their thinking and shapes the law. This might be otherwise and probably should be otherwise. A major purpose of the second part of this book is to tease out this ideology. But we insist that if the Law Lords share a common ideology, it is precisely that, the ideology of the *Law* Lords, which is to say that it is a particular version of a judicial ideology. Anyone socialized by a lifetime in a narrow and almost total institution like that of the elite English Bar will, if he comes to the top of it, have a very clear understanding of how to act, and that understanding will be shared by his colleagues and those close to his rank in the profession. To the extent that judges are the product of socialization, the crucial socialization is not into their social class but into the world they have lived in since undergraduate days. The world of the successful English barrister is very small—there are only a few thousand practising barristers altogether, a few hundred successful Queen's Counsel, less than two hundred judges of High Court status and above. These people have lived and worked together intimately, fought each other in court, judged each other in the various rungs of the court system for well over thirty years by the time they get to the Lords. (They even marry each other's sisters, which the great American sociologist C. Wright Mills used as a partial measure of an elite.) They have learned the trade of advocacy with its highly individualistic style—it is useful to remember that no barrister has ever been a member of a law firm, with its emphasis on the 'team player', and they overwhelmingly come from either the Commercial Bar or the Chancery Bar. Hardly any criminal law specialists make it to the higher rungs of the judiciary, and not many more who specialize in family law or, until recently, in public law where financial rewards are dependent on legally aided clients. What this leads to for our purposes is that the Law Lords come to the job with a set of perceptions of their role, with an idea of what the job of a Law Lord is. Any lawyer must have a model of law's social function in mind, and the more intensely he embodies the law, the more powerfully this model will affect his judgments—he will use his discretionary freedom to do what he thinks law is there to do. This is precisely where both the specific expectations of the profession, and more generally the expectations of the whole legal culture, come into play. There are many descriptions one could give of law's function. Sociologists, at least those of a functionalist persuasion, tend to see law as primarily about conflict resolution. English legal practice does recognize this, but interestingly tends to see institutions other than the courts as better at it—hence the growing interest in arbitration, conciliation, and what are generally known as 'alternative conflict resolution' mechanisms. To the extent that the civil law is about conflict resolution, this aim tends to be seen as having failed if a case actually gets to court rather than being settled by negotiation earlier. A more legal conception of law is that it is a system for the protection of rights. It could well be argued that this is a North American conception—or, perhaps, simply one from the USA, because some powerful critiques of the effect of the Canadians introducing a justiciable Charter of Rights and Freedoms has been that it is replacing a consensual legal culture with one all too oriented to rights. The English legal, and in many cases political, culture is not strong on rights. Indeed we argue at length in the later chapters on public law that it is precisely the absence of a strong sense of rights that produces the sort of decisions, especially in welfare cases, that judicial discretion has produced. The very lukewarm reaction given by England's judges to the whole idea of incorporating a Bill of Rights into law is evidence enough of their lack of interest in rights jurisprudence.

If a Law Lord is unlikely to see himself primarily either as a resolver of conflict, or of a protector of rights, what is left? To fill out our third model of judicial behaviour and to help readers follow the extended argument of the rest of this book we suggest, at this stage it can be no more than a suggestion, that overwhelmingly the Law Lords see themselves as problem solvers. A phrase that one hears over and again when the Law Lords discuss their work, either in private, or even in their interjections and questions during oral argument, is 'how can we make this work?' They react to statutory construction in terms of finding definitions that will 'make the statute work'; they deal with claims against public institutions, the police, education authorities, housing authorities, in terms of facilitating the overall functioning of those bodies. They consider prisoners' rights in terms of the problems of the prison governor. They reject arguments in civil common law cases because they might not easily be applicable by lower courts, they restrict negligence claims because it would make the job of those who, for example, write references difficult; they deny the right of access to confidential information because institutions might not function effectively if the ordinary citizen saw internal memoranda; earlier, and sometimes still, they find in favour of employers or manufacturers because the economy might not function as easily if some types of plaintiffs could get damages for negligence. Throughout every area of law there is this emphasis on fine tuning social institutions to facilitate their general working. This image should not be entirely unexpected. The senior judges working in Britain in the mid-nineties are the heir to a tradition of jurisprudence which is deeply utilitarian. The legal philosophy they inherit is a modified Benthamite orientation, turned into a legal theory by the famous nineteenth-century positivist Austin, and modernized by H. L. A. Hart. Hart may have modernized, even humanized, Austin's positivism, but the hostility to ideas of natural rights, and the utilitarian concern with social engineering and institutions, still survived his reworking. Hart's main critic in modern jurisprudence, his successor in the Oxford Chair, was Ronald Dworkin, who argued in direct opposition to Hart for a 'rights based' jurisprudence, and specifically against the idea of a pragmatic utilitarianism. We are in no position to take sides on which of them is normatively correct, but Hart's major work, *The Concept of Law*, is, revealingly, described by its author as 'an essay in descriptive sociology', and though its focus and aim are different from ours, we do think it is sociologically not incompatible with our analysis. At the same time, while we do not think that judges do behave as Dworkin thinks they do, much of our substantive analysis of cases in the second half of the book rests, though sometimes only implicitly, on the belief that a Dworkinian judge, that is, one who does take rights much more seriously than UK judges do, would produce different results.

It is obvious that one cannot go about 'making statutes work', or in our language 'fine tuning the welfare state', or deciding cases according to commercial common sense without, in fact, making value judgements, exercising preferences about who should bear the burdens of systems, discounting individual suffering because of social, economic, or political efficiency. In other words, the very general ideological orientation of judges will come into play via the idea of pragmatically making something work, through the loose texture of the law that not only allows but requires freely discretionary judgment. It is up to others, if they wish, to make assertions about this ideological input. Not only might political radicals have views on this. One modern school of legal analysis which is at least sometimes compatible with our view of the working of English judges would be the Chicago School of Economic Analysis of Law. We do not share its ideas either as normative prescription or, in detail, as descriptions, but the idea that the common law is an economic efficiency mechanism is akin to our observation of judges making choices that fit their conceptions of economic efficiency. Probably the major failing of the Economic Analysis school *vis-à-vis* the British judiciary is that they are nothing like as economically literate as the writers in that school. But it is certainly the case that some of the American legal opinions most favoured by some Law Lords when dealing with issues in negligence are precisely the opinions that the Chicago school themselves hold up for praise. But many other sociological analyses could be made of where the judges get their ideas of what does constitute a pragmatic solution to a problem. It is enough for us to try to show that they are free to give play to whatever ideology, and that they can be shown to do so in as far as 'problem solving' is their mode.

This then is our 'statement of claim', our 'proof of evidence' to slightly misuse legal terminology. Judges are widely free to make creative decisions in both common law and statutory construction cases; they really can choose what to decide, with very little constraint, both because of the nature of law and the institutional setting within which they work; in exercising this freedom they act as problem solvers in a highly pragmatic manner. What remains to do in this chapter is to fill in some technical details about the work and personnel of the Law Lords, and briefly to consider the notion of a 'hard case' as far as this is relevant to what they work on. This section can well be skipped by anyone with any familiarity with the institution.

3. The Structure and Caseload of the Law Lords

There are now twelve Law Lords—Lords of Appeal in Ordinary as they are officially known, though for most of the period covered here there

were ten. In practice the body of men—they are all men—whose arguments and opinions are treated here is a fluctuating group. In strict theory
any member of the House of Lords who has held high judicial office may
hear appeals, though apart from those who are or have been Lords of
Appeal in Ordinary, the only others to do so in our period are Lord Lowry
and the various Lords Chancellor who sit infrequently. Lord Lowry,
though he has recently retired as a Lord of Appeal in Ordinary, had been
given a peerage when Chief Justice of Northern Ireland and occasionally
then had heard appeals to the House of Lords. When there were only ten
Law Lords it was frequently necessary to call on the services of retired
Law Lords to make up the panels of five in which they almost invariably
sit to hear appeals. The practice is likely to continue because at any time
one or more of the Lords is likely to be involved in other business for the
government, like Lord Nolan who chairs the parliamentary Ethics Committee, or like Lord Woolf who spent much of his brief time in the Lords
writing a report on access to justice. We have chosen the bulk of the cases
discussed from the last ten years because it is neither possible nor would
it be useful to write this book as a long-term history. Because of retirements and appointments over the period from which we draw cases
roughly twenty men appear quite frequently in the following pages. The
cases mentioned range over the careers of thirty-six Law Lords from the
post-war courts, and sometimes even earlier judges are quoted. The 'core'
judges, however, are those who have been Law Lords from the early
eighties until the early nineties—some dozen men. A graphical display of
the extent of the problem of lack of overlap is given in Figure 1.1.

Sometimes the work of these men is analysed from a time before they
were Law Lords. Most of the Law Lords come to that post from the Court
of Appeal, and thus it is possible to examine divisions of opinion between
judges all of whom will at some time have been in the Lords, but not
necessarily together. As divided cases naturally provide a better opportunity to examine judicial argument than ones where all the judges vote in
the same way, this addition to the sample of divided cases is useful and
harmless. But we are acutely aware, and readers should bear in mind, that
there is no such thing as 'The Law Lords'. It would be hard to find a period
of more than two or three years when there were no retirements and new
appointments, unlike, say, the US Supreme Court where appointments
are often made younger, and where there is no retirement age, resulting in
lengthy periods of little personnel change. There is another crucially important difference between the Law Lords and most other highest courts,
to which we have already attached much importance. The US Supreme
Court, the Canadian Supreme Court, the Australian High Court, the European Court of Justice, and, effectively, the German Constitutional Court
almost always sit *en banc*, that is, all the judges on the court hear all the

	70	71	72	73	74	75	76	77	78	79	80	81	82	83	84	85	86	87	88	89	90	91	92	93	94	95
Reid	*	*	*	*	*																					
Morris	*	*	*	*	*																					
Hodson	*	*																								
Guest	*	*	*	*																						
Upjohn	*	*																								
Donovan	*	*																								
Wilberforce	*	*	*	*	*	*	*	*	*	*	*	*	*													
Pearson	*	*	*	*	*																					
Diplock	*	*	*	*	*	*	*	*	*	*	*	*	*	*	*	*										
Dilhorne	*	*	*	*	*	*	*	*	*	*	*															
Cross		*	*	*	*	*																				
Simon		*	*	*	*	*	*	*																		
Salmon			*	*	*	*	*	*	*	*	*															
Kilbrandon			*	*	*	*																				
Edmund Davies						*	*	*	*	*	*	*														
Fraser						*	*	*	*	*	*	*	*	*	*	*										
Russell							*	*	*	*	*	*	*													
Keith								*	*	*	*	*	*	*	*	*	*	*	*	*	*	*	*	*	*	*
Scarman								*	*	*	*	*	*	*	*	*										
Roskill											*	*	*	*	*	*	*									
Bridge											*	*	*	*	*	*	*	*	*	*	*	*	*	*	*	
Brandon													*	*	*	*	*	*	*	*	*	*				
Brightman													*	*	*	*	*	*								
Templeman													*	*	*	*	*	*	*	*	*	*	*	*	*	
Griffiths																*	*	*	*	*	*	*	*	*	*	*
Ackner																*	*	*	*	*	*	*	*	*	*	*
Oliver																*	*	*	*	*	*	*				
Goff																*	*	*	*	*	*	*	*	*	*	*
Jauncey																	*	*	*	*	*	*	*	*	*	*
Lowry																			*	*	*	*	*	*		
Browne-Wilkinson																							*	*	*	*
Mustill																							*	*	*	*
Slynn																							*	*	*	*
Woolf																								*	*	*
Nolan																									*	*

Figure 1.1 A Visual Display of Law Lords' Periods of Service 1970–1995

appeals as one group.[13] The Appellate Committee of the House of Lords operates a different system. Appeals are heard by a panel of five Law Lords freshly assembled for that case. (The Lords themselves refer to a 'constitution' of Law Lords not a panel. The usage is so specific, and so easily misunderstood that I have throughout used the Americanism of 'panel'.) On rare occasions a larger group is enpanelled, when the Lords know the result of their decision may be highly contentious. The only case of importance discussed here which had a larger panel is *Pepper* v. *Hart*, to which we devote an entire chapter. Its importance to us, and to the Law Lords, is that it changed a constitutionally important aspect of their procedure.

There is no general pattern of specialization or grouping, except that the two senior Law Lords will not hear cases together and will preside over separate groups of four colleagues—but not the same four except by random accident. Though some effort is made by the civil servants who organize these matters to provide some relevant expertise, this is the only limiting factor. Thus if it is possible there will be a Lord who had Chancery experience on a tax case, someone with an extensive prior history of commercial law on a contract or admiralty case, and there will always be at least one Scots Law Lord for appeals from Scotland. Otherwise availability and supplementation from retired Law Lords produces an *ad hoc* system of who hears which cases, and who hears cases alongside whom or under whose chairmanship. The consequence of this is that it makes very little sense at all to talk about a court having a particular view, tendency, orientation or ideology. Individual judges have all of these, and their private judicial styles interact in an ever varying grouping and regrouping spread over the entire gamut of legal issues. But 'the court' in a real sense does not exist at all, still less does it have, even over a brief year or so, a common character.

This is a vital point about the working of the Law Lords, and worth a brief investigation. A glance at the arithmetic shows how little chance there is for the judges to coalesce into a coherent 'court'. Suppose the Lords hear thirty-two cases per year (an arithmetically convenient figure close to the actual average). The probability that Lord A will hear a particular case is 0.5; the probability that Lord A and Lord B will sit on it together is 0.25. That pairing then will happen probably only eight times in a year. They will probably only overlap for five years—thus they will only hear about forty cases together, spread over time. Were there a third man, Lord C, who might if he worked often together with A and B begin

<hr />

[13] The German Constitutional Court consists of two chambers, which never sit together. However, the chambers are functionally specialized so that all cases are heard by all of the 'relevant' judges, with the effect that any area of constitutional law is developed by a single team.

to develop a coherent group approach, the trio will probably only coincide on some twenty cases over the time they are all on the court. Each of those twenty will be spread over a wide range of legal issues, and will be cases where varying others join in. There simply is not the time for more than an idiosyncratic and accidental coincidence of views to happen. And these figures are maxima. We can calculate examples from the data used in Chapter 2. During the central years covered in the analysis of Chapter 2 three Law Lords, Lords Bridge, Goff, and Griffith, heard more cases than any others except the two senior Law Lords, Keith and Templeman, one of whom chairs the panel for every case. Suppose that these three were of like mind, and might, if they interacted enough, come to form a cohesive majority group in panels, and perhaps have a chance to develop a juris-prudence which would spread to influence other members. (This is entirely heuristic; there is no reason to believe this trio did share to any unusual extent a common legal approach.) During the whole ten years, 1986 to 1995, from which the data are drawn, the trio sat together on only twenty-seven cases, and never on more than eight cases in one year, 1990. Let us further assume, most plausibly, that their agreement is on only one major division of law. We will take public law both because it is the area of more concern to this book, and also because it is the commonest of the broad categorizations we use here. The trio heard only twelve such cases together, by the broadest definition, and never more than three in any one year. In other areas of law the possibility of developing a group approach was still more limited. They heard one criminal case together each year from 1988 to 1992, only four commercial cases together altogether; in one subfield of public law which is highly politically sensitive, immigration law, they heard only three cases together, two in 1987 and one the next year. These figures would be similar or worse for any other trio of judges. Even regular pairings of judges do not produce much chance of develop-ing an active joint approach. Lords Ackner and Bridge sat together as a pair more frequently than any other two Lords in the period under review, hearing ninety-nine cases together over the ten years, sitting together nineteen times in their 'best' year. But even then the pairing never coincided on more than five cases in any one area of law in one year, when in 1990 they heard five public law cases; their next best was four criminal law cases in 1987. Compare these figures with the US Supreme Court, where after only one year a new justice will have heard in excess of one hundred cases together with every one of his or her colleagues, and over a five-year span will have heard five or six hundred cases along with nearly all of them, even allowing for retirements. Furthermore the caseload will have covered a narrower range, because by definition the Supreme Court hears only cases with a substantial Federal Law element.

The consequence is that only in the most rudimentary sense, and then only very rarely, can one talk about 'Lord So and So's Court', in the way that analysts talk of the Warren or Rehnquist Court in America, or perhaps the Mason Court in Australia. The nearest one might find is a tendency to think of the House of Lords for a period in the early and mid-eighties as 'the Diplock Court'. This seems to have been more a recognition of his outstanding legal brilliance combining with a very forceful personality and his own strong sense of his dominance to impress, even perhaps to intimidate, some of his colleagues, and even more the Bar.[14] Even this unusual period was essentially contentless, however—no overarching judicial ideology or value set seems to have been in place. The only externally obvious impact of the Diplock period was a temporary but marked reduction in the number of divided cases, and an even sharper reduction in the number of speeches given in undivided ones. Even less will one find comment on groups or coalitions of judges—they simply cannot form, necessitating the highly individualistic style of judicial impact we survey during this book.

4. What Cases are Heard?

This is really two questions—what sort of legal problems do they decide, and why do some cases get to the Lords when others in the same broad area do not? We take the latter question first. The Law Lords have near complete control over their own caseload, except that litigants have a right of appeal from the Scottish Court of Session. (Though it is not possible to take a criminal case on appeal from Scotland to the Lords.) Such appeals may proceed directly to an Appellate Committee provided that two counsel have certified the reasonableness of the appeal. (This was the old practice for English and Irish appeals, changed by legislation in 1962.) Compared with all other supreme courts, the Lords have a very small caseload, averaging between thirty and forty cases each year.[15] In contrast the US Supreme Court hears over 100 cases each year, and the continental European constitutional courts can have caseloads in the thousands. This difference is not because there are not many potential cases, at least in recent decades. Although there were, on average, only about 40 petitions for leave to appeal per year before the seventies, there were on average 83 each year in 1971–80 and 150 in 1981–90. We know very little about which

---

[14] Robert Stevens' brief account of Diplock as a Law Lord (op. cit., p. 562) supports my contention about him, which is largely based on interviews with judges and barristers.

[15] The data used in Ch. 2 include as far as we can tell all published opinions for the period 1986 to 1995. On this data the annual average of cases before the House of Lords was 31.2. There were also 94 cases before the Privy Council, bringing the total average to 41 cases.

cases seem to the Appeals Committee suitable for a second level of appeal. The doctrine is fairly straightforward—the Lord's Appeals Committee will decide to hear cases where they think a general issue of law of public importance is involved. This matter is something the court below can be asked to certify to even when they refuse, as they usually do, to grant the appeal to the Lords themselves. The formula does not get us very far, because almost any case which does not involve an exceptionally narrow fact basis could so qualify. Furthermore, some cases come up that do have such a narrow empirical reach that it is hard to see how they can qualify as of general public importance, though they may be of fascinating legal complexity. It might be thought that somehow or other the answer would be simple—routine cases would not be allowed on appeal, only those difficult ones where the law is obscure would need the second level of appeal. This is the sort of answer, going under the general name of the 'Hard Cases' approach, one often gets when asking judges or barristers, but it does not get one very far. However, it makes relatively little theoretical sense, because it assumes the problems which Legal Realists find with slot machine jurisprudence somehow or other stop one stage or two stages below the ultimate court. Of course there are thousands of routine cases where the law seems very clear and settled, and the only reason for an initial appeal is the hope that the appellate judges might see the facts differently from the judge at first instance, though technically that should not enter their considerations. But there are two reasons why the idea of a case being 'hard' and suitable for their Lordships' consideration makes less obvious sense. The first point applies equally to the Court of Appeal, where it might be thought useless of a client to appeal unless his was a 'hard' case, that is, one where the law was unclear or, perhaps, missing. The truth is that any competent barrister can always find *some* argument on which to claim both uncertainty and a preferred clarification which suits his client. Working barristers will admit perfectly openly that the question they ask themselves is whether they can persuade a judge to see the arguments their way, not whether they can invent such arguments. It follows from the basic premise of judicial realism, that judges choose which of a set of competing arguments they prefer in order to do what they think should be done in a case, that there is no level of law where a case is objectively hard or easy. There are, however, limits on the argumentative strategies that can be adopted to show that a case is hard and susceptible to one's preferred solution rather than being an obvious case for application of one's opponent's interpretations. The most important restriction applies to the Court of Appeal and not to the House of Lords, thus making it possible to see a wider range of cases as routine at the former level. This is because of the doctrine of precedent in English law. Where a precedent can be seen to apply, both in the common law and in

the previous history of judicial interpretation of a statute, the counsel
whose client will suffer from its application is forced to argue that the
precedent is not, in fact, relevant in the particular case. Technically he
must ask the Lords Justices of Appeal in the Court of Appeal to 'distinguish' the precedent. The Court of Appeal is bound to follow previous
decisions not only of the House of Lords, but of previous panels of the
Court of Appeal itself. Beliefs about how restrictive this is vary enormously from practitioner to practitioner—one Law Lord said that he
never found this restrictive when he sat on the Court of Appeal 'because
you can always find a way around'; some members of the Court of
Appeal, however, clearly think of much of their work as routine because
they do tend to see precedents more clearly restricting their freedom. The
Lords are not so restricted. By their own decision in 1966 they gave
themselves the freedom to reject previous decisions of their own House,
and they have never, of course, been bound by the decisions of the Court
of Appeal. Consequently for a case to be hard rather than routine when
the Law Lords are the potential bench means not only that it may involve
an uncertainty in existing law, but alternatively that it may involve a
manifest injustice in a perfectly clear area of law. If conceptions of
unclarity are largely in the eye of the judicial beholder, conceptions of
injustice are vastly more so. We really cannot hope to learn very much
about when a case will go up on appeal to the Lords because they give no
reasons, and because the idiosyncrasies of the judges are even more important when random committees of four or even three have to make only
a yes/no decision as to whether or not even to grant leave. The truth is
that the truly routine cases are filtered out long before any appeal, and
mostly before they even come to the court of first instance. Furthermore,
the principle filtering mechanism is financial, because of the cost of appeals which is extremely high. Although legal aid is available for criminal,
and for some public law appeals, such aid is itself discretionary, based on
expectations of the likely result. We will later, in the substantive chapters,
come across some examples of cases where the sheer chanciness of
whether it was given right to appeal is demonstrated.

What the cases represent in terms of substance is much easier to say,
and is often amazing to non-lawyers. Because the Law Lords are a general
court of appeal and not the sort of constitutional court more normally
looked at by political scientists, appeals cover the entire range of law. As
such it might be thought that much of their work would not be of interest
to political science, but to take that position would surely be to have an
impoverished view of what constitutes politics. We mean by this not that
political science must consider the whole range of government policy,
though that is true. We mean rather that political science is concerned
with power, its distribution and use. Cases before the Lords, in one way or

another, are nearly all about power imbalances. Indeed the traditional notion that the duty of the courts is to protect the weak from the mighty is a guiding theme of this book.

To give some shape to this account we consider only those cases before the Lords which were reported in either the *Law Reports* or the *All England Law Reports* for 1993. Some cases are certainly hard to see in this power imbalance way in any serious sense, and can best be characterized as sorting out the details of the corporate economy. Of the forty-one cases from 1993, perhaps eight can be dismissed as this, involving as they do matters like powers of the arbitrator in a conflict between a huge construction firm and the Channel Tunnel Group, which national law should apply in a conflict between the Republic of India and the India Steamship Company, the assignment of rights between landlord and tenant when both were major corporations rather than ordinary rent paying individuals, whether a large foreign corporation can sue a foreign bank in an English court for something that happened abroad, and similar issues. (This is not to say that the legal spin-off in terms of precedent might not be relevant at some later date to a more clearly 'political' case, but in themselves such cases seem more akin to, say, the provision of financial services to the world economy than the handing down of fundamental justice. And indeed some of the Law Lords do very much see their court, and the London courts in general, as exactly such providers of international services, and even admit to tuning their decisions in accordance.) There is another category of cases which it is often, but not always, apt to treat as similarly the technical provision of services, though in this case to the State itself, which are tax cases. The Lords hear what may seem a disproportionate number of such cases, but this follows directly from their role as the 'fine tuner' of the governmental system. Six such cases were reported in 1993. A glance at them, however, demonstrates how risky it is to dismiss any general category of cases as routine. One of these cases, *Hart* v. *Pepper*, is the subject of a whole later chapter in this book because it was the vehicle by which the Lords changed their own rules on how to interpret statutes, and this has enormously far-reaching implications. Nor is it necessarily true that tax cases involve huge corporations or incredibly wealthy families, though this is often what a case that gets to the Lords is in fact about, and two of the 1993 cases more obviously demonstrate a protection of the weak, in the guise of rather humble taxpayers, against a revenue authority apparently determined to extract any money it can make a semi-plausible argument for.

It is trivially true that appeals in criminal cases represent a politically sensitive area because the criminal law is, *par excellence*, a conflict between state power and the individual. This is all the more so because criminal appeals have nothing to do with the guilt or innocence of the appellant—

such a matter is firmly for the lower courts. Criminal appeals essentially deal either with the definition of crime—does the State really have the authority to use its power against certain human actions—or about the methods it may use in wielding its power. Thus one case in 1993 dealt with the possibility of jury bias, another with the acceptability of telephone intercepts by the prosecution, a third with the admissibility of evidence derived from computers, these latter two both being typical subject matter for a constitutional court like the US Supreme Court. The other criminal cases directly raised the question of whether the accused had actually committed a crime at all, at least if one believes that criminal law statutes must be interpreted with very strict regard to the clarity. It must be said here that there appears to be almost complete consensus in the legal profession, including the Law Lords themselves, that the Lords have a bad track record in criminal law. It is actually hard to get anyone to specify exactly in what way they fail at criminal law, except in some vague but substantive sense that they do not get the answers right, but probably a majority of members of the Court of Appeal believe that criminal law appeals should no longer go to the Lords, as is the case in Scotland. For this and other reasons we ignore criminal law in the rest of this book, except for some discussion in Chapters 3 and 4 which deal with judicial methodology.

Naturally it is the public law cases which most obviously raise the sort of questions about individuals' rights which are the obvious stock of politically relevant courts. Using the label of 'public law cases' rather more broadly than might a professional public lawyer, there are at least eight cases in 1993 which are very clearly matters of individuals faced with a struggle to assert their rights against the State, in one or another of its manifestations. As fine tuner of the welfare state the court dealt with an important attempt to widen the coverage of local authorities' duties to the homeless (the attempt failed), and, again unsuccessfully, an attempt to challenge the Secretary of State for Social Services over his restrictive interpretation of the rights of the disabled. Another local authority, unusually, lost its appeal when it attempted to deny someone their statutory right buy a council house. Prisoners' rights came up in two cases, one a direct challenge to the Home Secretary's powers over the length of life sentences, a topic which continued to exercise the courts throughout the next few years; the State actually lost in two immigration cases, one of which involved the Lords insisting that they had the power to hold the Home Secretary in contempt. In another case on the fringes of criminal law the Lords refused to allow a prosecution to go ahead against a man who had been illegally extradited to this country. Not only the State in its full persona can be at a great advantage over individuals. One case where the Lords, by a majority, failed to uphold such rights involved a university lecturer made redundant by his university, who the Lords refused to allow to have access to the courts to hear his substantive grievances in a decision which saw universities as, in many respects, outwith the controls of the common law. These boundaries between the State and what might be described as civil society, and between public and private law, are not always as easily drawn for a social scientist as they are for lawyers. How does one characterize the definitely 'rights protecting' decision which held that a local authority could not sue a newspaper for libel? Certainly the judicial argument in the case is full of the rhetoric of fundamental free speech rights, and a local authority is part of the State, though the law in question is, at least technically, neither constitutional nor public law. Similarly the case in which the Lords upheld the right of the Monopolies and Mergers Commission to investigate a potential regional monopoly would qualify for any political scientist as a constitutional law matter, and a case involving the legality of a local council's refusal of planning permission is clearly a matter of individual rights, though the guise it presented itself in was a claim for financial compensation for damage caused by the revocation of such rights. Several of the cases quite clearly within the boundaries of ordinary civil law must equally be seen as rights protecting in a politically interesting way, in one of which where the rights of wives whose husbands mortgaged their matrimonial homes and defaulted on the mortgage were upheld against banks, the Law Lords went a good deal further than any legislation would have been likely to do.

Finally, there are cases which seem tremendously important, manifestly involve pressing human demands for justice, but which defy categorization. In one the Lords refused to lift a time limitation rule in a straightforward civil law case involving personal injury. Or that, at least, is one way of describing it. The injury in question was psychological harm arising, but not understood as such, from sexual abuse during childhood. We discuss the case later, but it exemplifies the way an external description can seem to make a case really no business of a social scientist interested in the role of the court, because too much embedded in technical legal rules of procedure, when in fact substantive policy decisions are involved. The final case we list here is discussed at length in the concluding chapter, has already been mentioned above, and was a major event in the media— the decision of the Lords to allow the withdrawal of feeding to a man in a permanent vegetative state. Which human or civil right this case is involved with is a matter for very deep debate, but that, in allowing a hospital to do something intending to allow a patient to die as a result when he would not otherwise have died, the Lords made a vitally *political* decision is undeniable.

Thus the caseload for 1993, a listing which in itself must justify to anyone the need to investigate very carefully how a handful of unelected men, initially selected for the positions from which they reached this eminence on the basis of excellence as pleaders of causes, come to make such decisions. One further point needs to be spelled out at this stage. Most of the cases discussed in this book, especially in the first part, deal with cases where the Lords were divided, though as noted above only about 10 per cent of cases fail to be decided unanimously. We use such cases simply because the public disagreements make it much easier to analyse legal argument. It is emphatically not part of our thesis that discretion only gets exercised in such cases. The huge majority of cases where there is no overt disagreement are going to be just as subject to judicial discretion. In some, unknowable, percentage of these cases all five judges will genuinely agree with each other, but this is evidence of nothing more than that the specific five men shared a preference for the outcome. Equally a portion of these cases will be ones where one or more of the Law Lords involved had very little interest in the case, or felt it preferable to take the lead from someone who claimed expertise and did have a strong view. That, after all, is how most committees work, and the Law Lords operate very much more like a committee than like some conceptions of a court. It is also certain that there are cases where one or more Law Lords were tempted to dissent but felt that nothing would be achieved. Given the strong sense both of collegiality, and of the value of certainty in law, there is an unwillingness to make pointless dissent public. One Law Lord commented that it was important to reserve the right of dissent to special cases so as not to get the reputation of being awkward. It should be remembered that most of the Lords have had experience on the Court of Appeal (Criminal Division) where dissent is forbidden. Were the culture of legal practitioners one in which arguments are made out of famous dissents, as in the USA, there might be more point in dissent, and more would then be obvious. Some tangential evidence for the role of strong preferences is given in the next chapter. In other cases the possibility of disagreement is shown by disagreement in the courts below. It must be remembered that in the English legal system the Law Lords have no monopoly on legal eminence—even institutionally the holders of offices like that of Lord Chief Justice or Master of the Rolls rank professionally with that of a Law Lord, and it is not at all uncommon to find united Lords' panels overturning decisions in the lower courts lead by such men.[16] (Though disagreement in the courts below is clearly one indicator of when the Lords will decide to hear an appeal—only 6 per cent of Court of Appeal cases are divided, but 15 per cent of all appeals heard from that court are cases involving a dissenting judgment.) Finally, we should note

---

[16] The current Master of the Rolls, Lord Woolf, is by no means the first to step down from the Lords to take the post—Lord Denning was another.

that we almost completely ignore the other role of the Law Lords, who sit also under the guise of the Judicial Committee of the Privy Council. Though that body would richly merit research in its own right, the ways in which it differs from the behaviour of the Law Lords are extraneous to our concerns here.

That then is our model of appellate judging in the UK—small groups of senior lawyers with enormous practical discretion coming to decisions in relatively hurried committee meetings after exhaustive (and exhausting) oral argument. The next chapter presents one form of evidence, statistical in nature, that suggests we can see the impact of particular judicial preferences or predispositions in the results. The following two chapters demonstrate at length, from the nature of judicial argument over a range of cases, that there must indeed be discretion to craft almost any argument that satisfies its author. In the second part of the book the impact of this system is demonstrated in selected substantive areas of law; it is here that we put some flesh on the bones of the model and suggest just exactly what ideological preferences do emerge from this judicial autonomy.

2

A Statistical Analysis of Judicial Discretion

1. Jurimetrics—A Simple British Application

In the first chapter we stressed two things—that we were committed to a legal realist position in which the decisions of courts are policy decisions, or acts arising from the interaction of judges' personal preferences, and that much depends on the way the House of Lords works in ever changing quasi-random panels of only five Law Lords. The methodology of the Legal Realists, called by both themselves and their opponents 'debunking', was to subject cases to detailed argument to demonstrate the essentially arbitrary nature of the decisions, and the extent to which the judicial arguments signally failed to 'determine' the results. There is no alternative to such a method, and Chapters 3 and 4 present our attempt at a similar 'deconstruction' of modern English judicial argument. Such an approach is absolutely necessary, because our thesis requires that there be alternative arguments easily enough assembled to justify almost any decision a judge wishes to come to, and that his colleagues' arguments cannot be logically powerful enough to block his route. This we describe as an analysis of judicial methodology. By itself though such an approach is not quite enough. All that can be established by such conventional methods of socio-legal analysis is that individual judicial preference *could* matter enormously. Given the weight we have put on the arbitrary matter of which five judges hear a case, it would be very helpful if we could present some objective evidence not only that judicial personality could, but actually has, had influence on the outcomes of similar cases. Such evidence we present in this chapter. The techniques of multivariate data analysis we use here are likely to be unfamiliar to most of our readers. We have adopted the following strategy. The results of our analyses are presented, as much as possible, in plain language, and all the techniques are described as simply as possible, with almost no reference to technical matters and methodological problems. (Some details are reported in a brief statistical appendix, which also includes information about how to receive a copy of the data set and a fuller account of the analyses.) We have done everything in our power to ensure that the plain language account in this chapter never misleads or covers up any technical problems, but readers are simply warned where there may be problems, rather than faced with statistical digressions on them. In practice the results we need are sufficiently simple and robust that there is relatively little danger of accidental mystification. The essential result we need to establish is very simple indeed: can we give objective evidence to refute the proposition that it makes no difference to the likely result of an appeal who sits on the panel?

Since the 1950s American political science has deployed ever more powerful statistical techniques, under the general label of 'jurimetrics', in the search for behavioural models of courts. In a country where judicial appointments are overtly political, and often elective, and where the political culture legitimizes the litigation of fundamental political conflict, such an approach is both more apposite and more likely to be fruitful than elsewhere. Except for the High Court of Australia and the Supreme Court of Canada, where the duty of federalist supervision makes an analogy to America relevant, there has been little attempt to apply such techniques to other jurisdictions. As far as Britain goes the technical problems are formidable, and the likely theoretical yield minimal. Most jurimetric techniques involve scaling judges by their votes in divided cases where a clear political value can be given to such a vote. It makes sense, for example, to contrast two Supreme Court justices by how often they grant or deny a criminal appeal under the search and seizure rule of the 4th Amendment, or allow encroachment of the pro-abortion rule in *Roe* v. *Wade*. These are publicly recognized as political issues taken into the courts and judges are known to have conflicting long-term attitudes—indeed recently their appointments will not have been able to pass the Senate without the Judiciary Committee quizzing the nominees in public about their beliefs on such issues. Technically such analysis of the Supreme Court is easier than for the House of Lords for three reasons: nearly all decisions by the US Supreme Court are by majority; all justices hear all appeals; the reported caseload of the Supreme Court is much bigger, over one hundred cases each year, compared with an average of around forty in the UK.

In general there would be little point in replicating US style analyses on UK data—it would be impossible to infer a judge's legal ideology from his voting pattern, so subtle and complex are the attitudes involved, and so difficult would the cases be to categorize. At a very basic level there is one good reason for trying a simple form of jurimetrics. The US exercise is only undertaken at all because no one doubts the importance of particular judicial attitudes to results. In the UK, however, the prevailing belief is still one of neutral technical judging. If the analysis on Chapters 3 and 4 is correct, such technical neutrality is largely mythical. Thus it ought to be possible to show that that which judges sit on an appeal does in fact partially determine the result. Failure to find regular predictive patterning would not disprove the thesis that judicial predispositions are crucial—the argument would be that the predispositions, and the interactions between different judges' predispositions, are too complex to manifest themselves in crude data analysis. But to demonstrate that certain sorts of cases are regularly decided in a specific way partly because of the membership of the committee would go a long way to showing that the possibility of ideological seepage is a reality. In one sense this would not demonstrate anything the legal profession does not know already—lawyers are always happy to guess the outcome on the basis of who is hearing it. But this sort of knowledge, as well as being untestable, is also somewhat esoteric. The same lawyers would refuse to accept that the implication of their predictive competence was unsettling. Most probably the defence would be that such predictabilities iron themselves out, and anyway only apply to rare judges in rare situations. Supposing the patterns were robust, involving most judges and most cases? This is the thesis to be tested in this section.

In fact there is little difficulty in demonstrating crudely but robustly that the mere presence of a particular judge can shift the probability of a particular outcome from what it would be in his absence. Where there is little apparent doubt about the meaning of cases, this might be thought enough. So Table 2.1 demonstrates statistically what any observer of the House of Lords knows already—Lord Templeman was so strongly opposed to tax evasion that his presence on a panel must have pleased the Revenue Authorities. Equally strong, but probably less predictable by court watchers, was the tendency for criminal appeals to go to the defendant when Lord Bridge was on the bench. In tax cases over the period 1986–95 the Revenue won only once when Lord Templeman did not hear the appeal, but won 65 per cent of all cases where he was present. Similarly, though the prosecuting authorities won 70 per cent of all criminal appeals covered here, they won only four of the ten appeals Lord Bridge heard. These numbers are small, but the patterns are easily significant statistically.

I. A Brief Note on Statistical Significance

Significance, for a statistician, has a very precise meaning, and it is one which does not correspond well to an ordinary language usage. All we mean by saying that a result is significant is that a pattern in the data—for example the proportion of cases Lord Bridge heard which went to the defendant—is sufficiently larger than it would have been had the thesis that Lord Bridge had no influence been true. 'Sufficiently' has also a technical definition. A pattern like that of Lord Bridge and criminal appeals could arise by sheer random accident. But we can calculate the probability of such an accident. A result is statistically significant when it is so different from the one that would arise with no 'Bridge effect' that one could only expect random chance to throw up such a difference very rarely. How 'rarely' is for the analyst to choose. In most of what follows we use the most usual such level, known as the 5 per cent level. This means we judge a result to be statistically significant when the chance of getting the pattern in question by random accident is less than 1 in 20.

Thus in Table 2.1A the pattern shown is that the tax authorities won 1 case out of 9 where Lord Templeman was absent, and won 13 out of 20 when he was present. If there was no 'effect' of Lord Templeman's presence, the results would have been that the Revenue won 4 of 9 cases with him absent and 10 of 20 cases with him present. This is the result against which the actual result is tested to answer the significance question, which is essentially the question: 'What is the probability that the observed results would differ so much from the "expected" results if "nothing was going on"?' As the table shows, the result would occur less than once in twenty times, if the entire process is imagined as a repeatable experiment. In fact a precise figure can be given to this probability, though we do not usually bother to do so. In this case the probability of getting so large a departure from the expected values if nothing happened when one added or subtracted the Templeman factor is 0.007—less than seven chances in one thousand trials. What statistical significance does *not* do is measure importance in any substantive way. A result can be statistically

Table 2.1A Tax Cases and Lord Templeman

	Templeman Absent	Templeman Present
Result Pro-Taxpayer	8	7
	89%	35%
Result Pro-Revenue	1	13
	11%	65%

Chi Square = 7.219 with 1 Degree of Freedom, significant at better than 5% Level.

Table 2.1B Criminal Cases and Lord Bridge

	Bridge Absent	Bridge Present
Defendant Wins	4	6
	17%	60%
Prosecution Wins	19	4
	83%	40%

Chi Square = 5.99 with 1 Degree of Freedom, significant at better than 5% Level.

significant, that is, very improbable, but utterly trivial, just as one can find a result in data analysis of enormous theoretical importance, a very strong connection, perhaps, between a particular Law Lord and a pattern of case results, which, alas, could easily arise by accident. The great virtue of statistical analysis is that it forbids one to take the second of those results seriously. The great disadvantage is that analysts are prone to assume that statistical significance *is* substantive importance and to get excited about an highly improbable but trivial result. Fortunately the reader can easily dismiss such overenthusiasm without understanding statistics.

II. Simple Evidence and Inference

Table 2.1 demonstrates that something must be happening along the lines of judicial attitudes determining, or at least constraining, outcomes through discretion. The only counter argument would be that it just so happened that the ten criminal appeals Bridge heard were ones with unusually weak prosecution cases, and any other judge would have re-acted in the same way. One would then have to stretch credulity further by saying that Lord Templeman, by sheer happenstance, almost never sat on cases where the Revenue's argument was weaker. Finally, one would have to explain that while these two judges did experience such random distortions in their caseload, most other judges did not. Because most Law Lords have 'result patterns' on any particular set of cases which do not depart significantly from the overall disposition rate for that category. Thus if we reported a table of criminal cases measuring only the presence or absence of Lord Keith, the expected values in each cell would be very close to the observed values. Remember, an 'expected' value is the number of cases that would fall into the cell if nothing was happening.

The problem, of course, is that such brute facts tell us very little, because we cannot know what, really, was going on by knowing the sheer out-comes. While it could just be the case that Lord Bridge was soft-hearted about criminals, this is deeply improbable. It is less improbable that Lord Templeman had, as an aspect of his judicial ideology, a firm belief that the rich should not get out of taxes because they can afford expensive accountants. The latter constitutes a plausible account of judicial thought, the former does not. But the judgement we have made in the previous sentence is a substantive one based on a largely intuitive sense of what British judges are like, and cannot itself easily be tested. Later these patterns for criminal and tax appeals are revisited and given a substantive interpretation.

Perhaps the greatest difficulty which precludes jurimetrics in an Ameri-can way being applied in the UK is this problem of categorization of cases. It is an objective question whether or not a discrimination case depends on whether a statute treats people differently by using an 'inherently suspect' classification, which would be a typical question in American jurimetric studies of the Supreme Court. It is a fair judgement to say that a justice who does vote to treat gender as such a suspect classification holds to markedly different constitutional and social theories than one who does not. Nowhere will one find equivalent objective grounds for categorizing judicial votes in this country. Even if *James* v. *Eastleigh Borough Council*, an English equal opportunities case analysed in Chapter 3, ultimately did depend on Lord Griffiths' feelings about gender inequality, there is no way one could demonstrate this. Categorizing a case is not only subjective and difficult, but often what the case is actually about. Thus one could not use the case on homosexual sadomasochism discussed in Chapter 4 as part of scale measuring judicial attitudes to sexual liberation in part because the judicial argument was precisely about whether the case concerned sexual behaviour or violent behaviour.

One categorization that is often possible and usually objective is more fundamental. Throughout legal history the courts have, *inter alia*, been seen as protecting, or failing to protect, the weak against the strong. This approach to studying the cases has already been discussed in Chapter 1. The main focus of this book is about such a role—public and constitutional cases concern the conflicts between the State, the strong litigant, and the citizen or claimant, the weaker. Criminal law definitionally is about this. Some, though relatively few, civil law cases can fairly easily be characterized as a weak litigant—Mr Knowles, who hurt his hand, seeking redress from a much stronger litigant, Liverpool City Council, the first case to be discussed in Chapter 3. What one does is to make the categorization depend on the character of the litigants, not the case. *Eastleigh* is perfectly capable of objective categorization—two ordinary citizens sued a local authority in public law. *R* v. *Brown*, whatever else it may be about, is a criminal case in which the coercive power of the State is pitted against defendants; *O'Brien* is about the power of a huge financial institution, Barclays Bank, to take away a woman's home. There are a thousand reasons why one cannot, in most contexts, take just a description of the litigants and the actual result of a case, and deduce anything of consequence. This is not one of the contexts when such is impossible. If some judges do systematically favour the strong over the weak given such categorization, and others do not, that is an adequately objective fact. If the categorizations are too crude, the patterns will not show up in the data. If judges have no such generalized predispositions and really are only influenced by the specific arguments, the patterns will not show up. There is, in other words, an inbuilt fail-safe protection for the court system against the suggestion that predispositions powerfully shape outcomes.

It will be apparent that the focus here is different from that of the American tradition in another way. No extensive attempt is made to predict the behaviour of individual judges. What is to be predicted is the outcome of the case, how the court collectively decides. This avoids the problem otherwise caused by the much greater apparent consensus of British judges: the House of Lords produces majority decisions in only around 10 per cent of cases. Were this to be true in the USA, research would be very much harder, because all the justices on the court hear all appeals. The variance which has to exist before statistical analysis can be applied arises in the UK because of the different administrative structure—only five of the ten or twelve Law Lords hear any one case. If the American system applied in the UK, all we would be able to tell is that the fundamental jurisprudence of the court changes over time as Law Lords retire and new members are promoted—hardly a radical insight. The question we are asking here then is very simple: does it make any difference which five Law Lords are selected to hear those cases which it is possible to categorize as conflicts between stronger and weaker litigants? If the Law Lords do differ consistently in their predisposition to favour the weak, regardless of all other factors, then the absence or presence of particular judges amongst those five should show up by making the outcomes, coded only by that crude Weak Wins/Strong Wins dichotomy, predictable to some degree or other. The resulting patterns will deviate from the values expected on the assumption that it makes no difference who sits on the appeal panel.

2. The Data and the Technique

I. The Data

The question is to be studied by considering nearly all the reported cases before the House of Lords from 1986 to 1995. It is not a random sample because only a few civil law cases, mainly those negligence cases where a crude weak v. strong categorization can be applied, are included. That apart, virtually all other cases enter the analysis at one stage or another subject to one restriction. Because membership of the Law Lords changes continuously and because retired Lords still hear cases from time to time it is impossible to include in the analysis every Law Lord who was part of any decision in that ten year period. Several would have heard only a few. For the same reason it is impossible to include all the cases, because some would have been decided by benches where several of the members heard very few other cases. A 'core' court of fifteen Law Lords present for a major part of the decade's work was selected. Only those cases where the bench had at least four members from this core court are included. These selections are essentially arbitrary. They are driven by that bugbear of all statistical analysis—the need to have at least a minimum number of comparable cases in an analysis to reach acceptable levels of statistical significance. The core court, with the total number of cases each heard, is given in Table 2.2.

Even so simple a categorization as weak wins/strong wins can raise problems of comparability unless some restrictions are placed on comparing like and unlike, so most of the fundamental analysis is carried out separately on five groupings of cases. Tax and criminal law are obvious and separable groupings, with respectively 23 and 33 cases used in the basic analyses. Public law and constitutional law are the next two groupings. There is inevitably some danger of ambiguity in coding, but the fact, to appear later, that the patterning of judicial decisions is slightly different suggests it is worthwhile to make the distinction. Public law cases are those which would normally be so recognized in any textbook on the subject—appeals against immigration and other tribunals, claims against social security and housing decisions, prisoners' appeals against decisions of the Prison Service, and similar. Cases have been coded as 'constitutional' rather than public where the issues have been more serious, or the basis less routinely a matter of *vires* arguments in statutory interpretation.

Table 2.2 Contributions of Law Lords to the Data Set

	Dates of Appointment	Number of Cases
Keith	1977	179
Bridge	1980–92	191
Brandon	1981–92	147
Templeman	1982–93	181
Griffiths	1985–93	156
Ackner	1986–92	162
Oliver	1986–92	130
Goff	1986	166
Jauncey	1988	120
Lowry	1988–94	105
Browne-Wilkinson	1992	61
Mustill	1992	50
Slynn	1992	44
Woolf	1992	28
Lloyd	1993	25

NB Because Lords Woolf and Lloyd heard only a small number of cases from the sample, they are omitted from some of the anlyses.

Sometimes the decision about labelling is made for us because, as with the *Fire Brigades Union* case, or *Derbyshire* v. *Times Newspapers*, the legal fraternity itself has labelled the cases constitutional. (All cases referred to as examples in this chapter are discussed in detail later in the book.) Sometimes it is a matter of subjective judgement. It matters relatively little, because the basic findings would not change substantively were the two categories to be combined. There are 41 public law cases. Sixty-five cases could have been used, but as an extra precaution a tighter selection rule has been used for this relatively large group—only cases where all five Lords hearing the case came from the core court have been included. Constitutional cases are less plentiful because of the selection criterion, and there are 29 such cases selected for analysis. Undoubtedly the last category, civil cases where a weak/strong judgement has to be made, is the most methodologically troublesome. Thirty-seven of the 104 civil cases heard between 1986 and 1995 have been selected. The number could, obviously, have been much larger, but given so subjective a selection criterion it is necessary to use only those which could withstand robust criticism. It must be remembered that the selection is not a judgement on how the Lords who heard the cases would have classified them. For example, one case which seems safely included is *Bradley* v. *Eagle Star Insurance Company*. This case is discussed later, but for the moment let it suffice that Mrs Bradley was prevented from suing Eagle Star Insurance because of an interpretation of the Third Parties (Rights against Insurers) Act 1930. No one could doubt that the elderly lady suffering from byssinosis and suing on legal aid was, quite objectively, 'weaker' than the insurance company. The majority who found for *Eagle Star*, however, cannot have seen themselves as hard-heartedly supporting the company indifferent to her suffering. Nonetheless the result of the case was to uphold the rights of a strong litigant against a weak. These are essentially the sorts of cases that have been selected. One potential criticism is that even civil negligence cases which appear to pit the strong against the weak are frequently, in reality, really just about transfer payments between major insurance companies. This can be true especially for cases like automobile accidents. Indeed it is a common 'off the record' criticism by judges of their colleagues that the object of criticism is over impressed by a mythical poor litigant. Few of the cases included here would seem, on the surface anyway, to be of this type. It is not clear that it matters even where it is true, because the legal arguments and attention still have to focus on the litigants of record, what can be expected of them, and how entitled they are to compensation.

A further restriction was applied—none of these cases were before the Privy Council, though of course the bulk of cases overtly recognized as constitutional come to the Law Lords wearing those hats. Such cases have not been ignored, and are analysed as a separate grouping. The Law Lords often remind themselves that they must defer wherever possible to local experience when hearing Privy Council cases, and they are fully aware of the political consequences of their judgments. It was therefore felt that the likely different methodological attitudes of the judges made it unsafe to combine the two into one grand constitutional grouping. Instead 20 Privy Council cases are analysed as a composite, with 14 being specifically constitutional, three public law, and three civil cases where the weak litigant/strong litigant distinction can be made easily.

II. The Techniques

There is a wide range of statistical data analysis techniques that could have been used. We use two here, though they are often seen by statisticians as alternative versions of the same technique. The first is called *Logistic Regression*, which we use initially to establish the overall plausibility of our approach, and which we describe shortly. The technique we use for the bulk of the analysis is known as *Multiple Discriminant Analysis* (MDA). Its normal application is to provide a predictive technique by which to predict how cases (in the data analytic sense of observations) are classified into two or more discrete categories on a variable, but where no assumptions need to be made about any ordering between the categories. In this case the outcome is victory in the final appeal for the weaker or stronger litigant as described above.

It may help to describe a previous use in a completely different piece of research. We used this method, for example, to see if coding of contents of party manifestos could reliably predict which cell in a typology of European political parties each manifesto belonged to. No possible ordering between Social-Democrat, Christian-Democrat, Liberal, Socialist, Agrarian, Conservative, and so on could have been attempted, yet MDA very accurately cast the manifestos into the right boxes.[1] Here the question is whether the mere presence or absence of a judge amongst the four or five recorded as having heard the case helps predict the outcome. The technique is known to be fairly robust under conditions of sample size and other technical considerations, but it was chosen more for intellectual simplicity than any other. The method takes all the independent variables and forms a predictive equation from the known classifications. First, let us apply logistic regression to a restricted set of judges and cases to establish, more fully than the simple one judge tables above, that the

[1] Ian Budge, Derek Hearl and David Robertson. *Ideology, Strategy and Party Change: Spatial Analyses of post-war election programmes in 19 Democracies*, CUP, 1987.

presence or absence of different Law Lords, in combination with others, does affect the outcome of appeals. We take here ninety-two cases which came from the public law and constitutional law areas, and where at least three of the sitting Law Lords came from a more restricted 'core court' of those who heard most of the 1986–95 cases together. The judges in the analysis are Lords Griffiths, Templeman, Bridge, Jauncey, Goff, Ackner, Lowry, and Keith. Logistic regression is similar to a more familiar technique know as regression analysis, but it works directly with the idea of the probability of getting one rather than another of two exclusive results. For example, a hospital might apply a battery of tests to patients suspected of having cancer to assess the probability that they do, before deciding on the more invasive option of an exploratory operation.[2] The result of applying a logistic regression model to the results of the tests would be a probability estimate that cancer was present. The tests or measurements might themselves be either continuous variables like the person's age or weight, or they might be yes/no dichotomies like, 'Does he smoke?' or 'Is hormone X in his bloodstream?' Here we have logically similar data. For each of the judges in the core court, we ask simply—Was Lord X present (code 1) or absent (code 0)? The result of applying the analysis to each appeal is a single number—the probability that the Lords' panel would uphold the State or the individual, the strong (code 1) or the weak (code 0). In the imaginary example the logistic regression can be checked, after the event, for its predictive accuracy, because we would know whether, in the event, each patient did or did not develop cancer. We can check the predictive accuracy of our model, because we know how the case was in fact disposed of. The model is in the form of a simple equation. It gives a coefficient for each of the predicting variables, which assesses the impact that the presence or absence of each judge, or the result on each diagnostic test, has on the overall probability. Thus we can both say whether knowledge of who was sitting gives us a statistically significant prediction, and also how important the presence or absence of each particular judge was, and what the impact would have been on the result of the case had he been present when actually he was not, and vice versa. It is probably easier to explain the model directly from the results. We will start with an over simple model containing only three Law Lords, Lords Bridge, Jauncey, and Griffiths.

---

[2] This example is modified from the manual for the statistics programme we have used, the *SPSS Advanced Statistics User's Guide*, Marija J. Norusis (ed.), Chicago, SPSS Inc., 1990, ch. 2. Although intended as a user's manual rather than a textbook, we recommend this as an introductory description of the techniques we use here. Chapter 1 covers Multiple Discriminant Analysis. Technical expositions of the techniques can be found in any textbook of multivariate analysis. We suggest D. W. Hosmer and S. Lemeshow, *Applied Logistic Regression*, New York, John Wiley and Sons, 1989, or G. W. Milliken and D. E. Johnson, *Analysis of Messy Data*, Belmont, Lifetime Learning Publications, 1984.

Model 1

(Probability that the State wins)

$$= (0.382) + 1.052(\text{Bridge}) - 1.200(\text{Jauncey}) - 1.133(\text{Griffith}).$$

The first number on the right of the equals sign, 0.382, is a constant term. Effectively it gives the probability if all of the variables in the equation are zero, which would represent a case when none of the three judges dealt with here were on the panel. The actual calculation of the probabilities involves a slightly confusing set of mathematical transformations which need not concern us here. For those interested, an alternative model is set out in complete statistical detail, with the probability calculations shown, in the appendix. In this example the probability of such a case being decided for the State is 0.594. (Over all the 92 cases in this analysis the State did, in fact, win 50, so that the probability of the State winning calculated just from the actual data would be close to this, at 0.544. But the 92 cases of course include those which the three judges did hear, while the probability in this model is for those they did not hear.)

We can work through the full model to show how it works. Each variable can only take the value 1 if the Law Lord in question heard the appeal, or 0 if he did not. So the first term, $+1.05(\text{Bridge})$ is $1.05 * 1$, i.e. 1.05 for the cases where he was present, and $1.05 * 0$, i.e. 0, for the cases when he was not selected for the panel. Take a case where Lord Bridge was on the panel, but the other four places were taken up by judges not in our model. Such a situation is represented by the equation form

$$(\text{Probability that the State wins}) = (0.382\text{—the constant}) + 1.051.$$

The probability derived from this is: 0.81. Thus, everything else being equal, replacing one of the unmeasured judges by Lord Bridge, but still

Table 2.3 A Simple Logistic Regression Model for Public and Constitutional Law

Observed Result	Predicted as Weak Win	Predicted as Strong Win	% Predicted Correctly
Weak Win	16 (10)	26 (32)	38%
Strong Win	7 (13)	43 (37)	86%

This table shows a statistically significant pattern: the figures in parentheses are the number of cases which would fall into each cell if the model had no predictive power. The difference is statistically significant such that so large a departure from the expected values would happen only 8 times in 1,000 trials.

leaving Lords Jauncey and Griffiths off the panel increased the chance of the State winning a public law appeal from 0.594 to 0.81, that is the State wins nearly six out of ten cases in his absence, but eight out of ten cases when he sits. That Lord Bridge would increase the State's chance was given by the positive sign in the coefficient. The full model, for cases where all three judges sat, by the same process gives a probability of 0.289. Because the signs for the coefficients for both Lords Jauncey and Griffiths were negative one could already tell that the weak litigant would be helped by their presence, and one could see also that it would take only one of them to counteract Lord Bridge, because the size of the three coefficients were relatively similar. These coefficients thus give an indication both of the direction of the likely impact on a decision of having a judge present, and the rough comparative magnitude of his effect. Putting two men who appear, statistically anyway, to be sympathetic to the citizen rather than the State on a panel with Lord Bridge radically alters the likelihood of the State winning. A 'perfect' panel from the viewpoint of the citizen litigant, as far as this restricted model can tell, would be three of the unmeasured Law Lords plus Lords Jauncey and Griffiths. This would produce the probability of only 0.125—the State could expect to win only one case in eight presented with such a panel. Analysts usually attach more importance to the overall predictive power of the model than the details of the coefficients, because they can only be interpreted with great care. Above all it must be understood by the reader that any coefficient is relative only to the model in question. We cannot assert that, in any context whatsoever, Lord Bridge is 'worth' a specific probability increase for the State, merely that the measured impact in the context of the comparisons defined by the model is such that his presence, in the absence of the other two named Law Lords, has a particular magnitude and direction. This is quite enough for our purposes—we have shown that the probability of the State winning a public law case is affected, to a significant extent, by who sits on the panel. It is also entirely fair to assert that the direction of the impact shows Bridge, in comparison with some of his colleagues, to have been pro-State in his general orientation. There are actually two separate significance questions one can ask about such a model—one is whether the actual measured impact of any coefficient is significantly different from zero. For all three Law Lords involved in this simple model, the answer is yes. In each case the coefficient is significantly different from zero at better than the 5 per cent level described above. It is more common to be concerned with the overall predictive capacity of the model as a statistical gestalt, and indeed it is relevant to our purposes, because we would have achieved most of what we need theoretically if we could only say that the presence or absence of named judges as a group predicted case outcomes better than guesswork, even were we unable to make the quite refined comparisons of likely outcomes given above. In this case the model does significantly predict—using the model we can (retrospectively, admittedly) predict 64 per cent of cases correctly when chance would give us only around a 50/50 chance of guessing correctly.

Model 2

The three-judge model above was deliberately oversimplified for explanatory purposes, though it achieved all that, in most senses, was necessary. It is worth looking at one more complex model partly to give a fuller account of how the absence or presence of judges works, and partly to introduce an idea which figures more largely later in this chapter, which is the concept of 'interaction' between variables. The equation from the model is:

(Probability that the State wins)

$$= \text{(the constant, } 0.626) + 1.992(\text{Bridge}) - 1.030(\text{Jauncey})$$
$$- 1.070(\text{Griffiths}) + 2.595(\text{Goff\&Ackner}) + 2.492(\text{Lowry\&Keith}).$$

The main difference from the previous model, apart from the fact that Model 2 takes account of more Law Lords, is the presence of two teams (Goff&Ackner) and (Lowry&Keith) which combine into one variable the measured presence or absence of two judges. These terms would take the value 1, and thus contribute to the calculated probability, only when *both* of the Law Lords in question were present on a case. The reason they are coupled in such a way is that individually none of these four Law Lords has a statistically significant effect on the model—the probability of the State winning or losing is not measurably affected. (This shows statistically in two ways—the coefficients for the specific judge effect if one plugs, say, Ackner into the model are close to zero, 0.002 in Ackner's case, and the significance, measured as the probability of getting such a coefficient when it was, in truth, zero showing no effect at all, are very high. Thus a measure of only 0.002 rather than zero could arise by accident in 99 per cent of trials.) However, although the presence or absence of Ackner and of Lord Goff individually has no effect, their joint presence does and strongly so, which is true also of the pairing Lowry and Keith. (We oversimplify again here—Lord Lowry does register an individually significant effect on the probabilities, of roughly the same magnitude as the other single judge effects, but it needlessly complicated exposition to take account of it here, and dropping the single Lowry term does no great damage to the overall predictive efficiency of the model.) It should not be surprising that such pair effects should occur. Technically it is called interaction and analysts are well used to modelling its effect. In the earlier example of cancer diagnosis one could well say that two hormones could be involved in the growth of a cancer in such a way as to matter only if they were both present in the bloodstream above certain levels. In our case we cannot know exactly why the presence of Ackner and Goff together should have a very strong tendency to tip appeals towards the State when the sole appearance of one or the other had no particular effect. There are many stories one could tell here. Perhaps they give each other's arguments support that wins the approval of their colleagues; perhaps they embolden each to press for pro-statist results. If one thinks of a Lords' appeal panel as a small committee, which is all that it is, statistical interaction is nothing odd. We are all used to thinking of committees along the lines of 'I see John is on the committee, but it's OK because he's no harm to our cause as long as Bill isn't on it as well.' But if one looks for and allows interaction effects to be fitted, a much more rounded and complete model can be derived, as with Model 2 here.

Once again the model as a whole is highly significant, with a probability of only 1 chance in 1,000 of getting such results by random accident, and predicting 72 per cent of the cases accurately. Unlike the previous simple model, the predictions, shown in Table 2.4, are symmetric—there is just as high a chance of predicting the weak results as the strong results.

It may be useful to calculate probabilities for some of the possible panels that can be assembled given the richness of this model.

We know already the nature of the effect of having just Bridge, Jauncey, and Griffiths on a panel combined with two judges not in the analysis—now we can add others to make up a full panel. Suppose in addition to those three, both Lowry and Keith heard the appeal. The new model gives a probability of the State winning an appeal before such a panel of 0.853—a situation where the State would win more than eight cases in ten, and a result which follows from having three judges with (+) signed coefficients. That is not, of course, the worst possible scenario for the citizen. Imagine arguing an appeal, on legal aid for a public law claimant, in front of a panel consisting of Jauncey as the one sympathetically predisposed

Table 2.4 A More Complex Model for Public and Constitutional Law

Actual Result	Predicted as Weak Win	Predicted as Strong Win	% Predicted Correctly
Weak Win	31	11	73.8%
Strong Win	15	35	70%

The table shows a significant predictive effect such that the results could only arrive by accident in a vanishingly tiny per cent of trials.

Law Lord and Lords Keith, Lowry, Ackner, and Goff. The resulting prob-ability of success for the *weak litigant* then would be not more than 4 per cent. (It would not be quite this bad, in fact, because of the individual Lowry effect left out in the model, but the directionality and size of the effect is clear.)

Could all this be meaningless? Are the results just too strong to be credible? Well they are not meaningless in one clear-cut sense. These are not estimates, they are precise mathematical descriptions of the patterns in the data. It just *is* the case that the results over the case were such that the results described in the pages above occurred. They can only be meaningless given a tremendously strong and counter-intuitive assump-tion. The assumption, and here we repeat the point made earlier, is that all of these patterns are sheer happenstance—all these combinations of judges just happened to fit together with cases the legal and factual details of which would have driven any combination of judges to the same results. This is not quite the same as the random accident against which statistical significance tests protect us, but it is of the same logical nature. No absolute credence can be given to the details, but the overall picture is clear—Law Lords have had predispositions in the public law domain, and these have resulted in patterned results way beyond the reach of luck. In that sense something very like the realist argument seems proven. The two models we have described here are only some of those that can convincingly be fitted to the data, but they serve to establish the important points. The drawback of this particular type of model is that they are restricted to comparing specific judges in the context of a few others, making any extensive comparison difficult. The advantage is the certainty with which we can demonstrate detailed statistical significance. We turn now to use the similar technique of multiple discriminant analysis on a wider range both of cases and Law Lords.

III. Multiple Discriminant Analysis

In this case fifteen dichotomies coded 1 where a Law Lord did participate in a case and zero where he did not constitute the independent variables. These are the Law Lords listed above as the 'core court'. MDA works much as does logistic regression as far as the reader needs be concerned, and again involves constructing equations in which each Law Lord has a coefficient indicating the direction and strength of his impact, in this case on a classification which could, though here it does not, have more than two cells or possible outcomes. Here though we establish such coefficients for all of the fifteen Law Lords, but we separate the cases more narrowly into different subject domains, though still using only cases capable of the weak/strong coding. What MDA does is to derive mathematical functions which arrange the variables (in this case our judges) along a dimension according to how well their values best classify cases into the predefined categories. Because we are only distributing the cases into the two categories of weak wins and strong wins there need be only one such function, and one set of 'discriminant function coefficients'. We will need to use these coefficients later, and the details for each of the following models is given in the appendix.

IV. The Main Results

The technique predicts well, though this should be no surprise given the earlier results in this chapter. Our first model is for predicting constitutional cases, and gives the results in Table 2.5. Being able to predict over 90 per cent of cases just by knowing who is on the bench would certainly seem substantively significant—in fact only one case was miscalled, one in which the Lords had actually found for the weaker litigant but which was predicted to have been won by the State.

The statistics associated with Table 2.5 back this up. The predictions are statistically as well as substantively significant. In particular the *Chi Square* shows that the chance of getting so clear a pattern by accident is virtually zero. At least where constitutional law was involved just knowing the past record of the four or five judges involved in a case during the last ten years gives a nine out of ten chance of guessing it correctly. Pleasingly the one mistake, a case where a litigant did win against the State was arguably the most constitutionally controversial of the decade—*Factortame*, where the Lords were effectively ordered to find against the Government by the European Court of Justice. Caution is necessary—multiple discriminant analyses almost always perform less well when new, genuinely unknown

Table 2.5 Predictions of Constitutional Cases

Actual Group	Predicted as Weak Win	Predicted as Strong Win	% Correctly Classified
Weak Wins	11	1	92%
Strong Wins	0	17	100%

Overall correct prediction = 97%. The result has a significance level with p = 0.000. (Note: henceforth we show significance, as is usual in the technical statistical literature, by giving the probability of the result arising if the connection assumed was not present.)

data are fed in. If we were seriously interested in predicting future cases we would not expect 9:1 odds. In this case a much lower prediction rate—providing it was statistically significant—would serve the purpose of showing that, completely ignoring case details, the texture of law is permeable by sheer judicial predispositions.

Naturally not all the issue domains predict as well. It makes theoretical sense that the constitutional law area would be most easily predictable from judicial predisposition, because the law is less certain, less bound by established principles, and much less involved in statutory interpretation. In contrast most of the cases covered by the public law category are statutory, reducing somewhat the scope for sheer judicial preference. But as Table 2.6 shows, even this area can be predicted adequately.

A prediction rate of 83 per cent must still be very much higher than counsels' intuitive guesses, and far more repeatable. It should not be thought, despite the convenience of *Factortame* being the one wrong prediction in the constitutional domain, that one can always, or ever should seek to, explain away mistakes. The wrong predictions here are straightforward examples of situations where, despite the predispositions of judges, something, presumably legal doctrine, forced a different result. Case 139, for example, *Janaway* v. *Salford Area Health Authority*, was predicted as a victory for a Ms Janaway. She was a secretary dismissed for refusing to type letters about abortions for her consultant, and who claimed the protection the law gave to people forced to participate in such operations against their conscience. Even without this statistical model one might have guessed that a bench containing Brandon and Lowry would strive to find for her—their discriminant scores (given in the appendix) for this domain put them well towards the 'pro-weak' end of the spectrum. Unfortunately for Ms Janaway they were balanced by Lord Keith, even more firmly on the 'pro-State' end. Thus two far more moderate Law Lords, Goff and Griffiths, whose 'moderate' position in the middle of the spectrum probably comes from having no strong disposition seem to have held the balance. The case was mispredicted because the

Table 2.6 Predictions of Public Law Cases

Actual Group	Predicted as Weak Win	Predicted as Strong Win	% Correctly Predicted
Weak Wins	10	4	71%
Strong Wins	3	24	89%

The analysis correctly predicts 83% of cases, with the highest significance. (P = 0.000.)

discriminant score gave very even probabilities of it falling into either camp, a result of the averaging out of the scores in this bench. Very probably the case really could have gone either way—Lord Lowry records a serious hesitation in his three line concurring speech—but it is, nonetheless, simply a mistake which shows the inherent limitations of this sort of model. What is remarkable is the great general success—only seven of forty-one cases miscalled, and the high statistical significance. So far we have essentially been replicating the work in the first part of the chapter which combined public law and constitutional cases. We can now turn to the other subject domains, with less need for general discussion. Tax cases, or, as coded here, tax and rating cases, represent an obvious choice for a set of lawsuits which would be closely similar, both substantively and in legal approach. Furthermore, it is more likely than in some domains that judges might have deep predispositions, either in favour of the revenue authorities on the grounds that there is a citizen duty to pay taxes, or alternatively a sympathy for the taxed. Indeed we used Lord Templeman's well-known views as our initial example at the beginning of the chapter. Certainly the domain predicts well, with only two errors out of twenty-three cases. One of the errors, where a win for the taxpayer rather than the authorities is wrongly predicted, demonstrates just how dependent this approach is on correct coding. The case, it was actually an appeal against a rating decision not a central tax matter, is arguably not appropriate for this category at all. What was at stake was a public law issue of whether or not the courts could entertain a ratepayer's appeal under certain legislation, and the decision was entirely on this matter and did not touch the original issue of the correctness of the rates demand. Had the case been transferred from the tax to the public law domain the prediction rates are increased in both. However, the coding rule that it is the impact of a decision rather than its rationale that counts is more important than fine tuning. The explanation is adduced here to make the point that mis-codings can only damage the apparent strength of the results, not give them a false authority.

As with revenue cases, criminal law provides an automatic standard-

Table 2.7 Predictions in Tax and Ratings Cases

Actual Group	Predicted as Pro-Taxpayer	Predicted as Pro-Revenue	% Correctly Predicted
Pro-Taxpayer	13	1	93%
Pro-Revenue	1	8	89%

The analysis correctly predicts 91% of cases. (P = 0.000.)

ized coding—a decision simply is one that either favours the power of the State or a coerced individual. Criminal law is, for several reasons, a tricky area to deal with in the Lords, and it would be inappropriate to use the potentially emotive 'weak' versus 'strong' characterization here. For one thing, as shown later, though the domain predicts well enough, the likely internal 'meaning' of a predisposition in this domain is not what might be expected. The first clue to this is that the discriminant function scores are the reverse of the other domains. Normally a high score means that a judge tends to vote for the 'strong', in this case the prosecution side. Here the defendants' victory cases have a higher average score, 2.14, than the prosecution victory cases whose average score is 0.931. Thus judges one might think of as defence minded, Lords Bridge and Keith for example (as can be demonstrated by the logistic regression technique), have much larger discriminant function coefficients, compared with Lord Lowry's coefficient of 0.500. (Details in the appendix.) It turns out, as is shown later, that a systematic tendency to uphold the defence has nothing to do with any 'softness' on crime. Nor would one expect to find such a pattern. Criminal appeals in the Lords—and many of their Lordships acknowledge that it is not an area they have shone in—have next to nothing to do with attitudes to crime, and nothing to do with criminal evidence. The area may indeed be the one where the questions of, 'What is the case all about?', which is shunned in the coding here, and, 'Who benefits?' cannot be as easily separated. This point will become clearer in the last part of this chapter. Table 2.8 gives the details.

Inevitably the idea that civil law cases can be coded systematically to capture the role of the courts in protecting a weaker or more helpless claimant against a large and powerful defendant, and even more that large and powerful claimants may be thwarted by judicial dispositions to protect the helpless, is one of the more controversial aspects of this analysis. Ultimately any such coding is a matter of intuition. Self-discipline has restricted the selection to only thirty-seven cases in the decade studied, which are used as examples, and in no sense should be taken to be an exhaustive list of cases that might come under this heading. It is hardly

Table 2.8 Appeals in Criminal Cases

Actual Group	Predicted as Defence Win	Predicted as Prosecution Win	% Correctly Classified
Defence Wins	9	1	90%
Prosecution Wins	0	23	100%

The analysis correctly classifies 97% of cases. (P = 0.000.)

Table 2.9 Predictions in Civil Cases

Actual Group	Predicted as Weak Win	Predicted as Strong Win	% Correctly Predicted
Weak Win	11	2	85%
Strong Win	3	21	88%

The analysis correctly predicts 87% of cases. (P = 0.002.)

surprising that this more subjective domain should not predict as well as others, but the final results are still remarkable, with only a handful of errors being made.

The final domain covers some cases from the Privy Council. These cannot just be inserted into their logical place in the other technical domains for reasons already discussed. (For convenience PC cases clearly on constitutional issues were attributed to the public law and constitutional cases analysed in the logistic regression section.) But Privy Council cases account for such a large proportion of the Lords' caseload that it would be wrong to omit them completely. At the same time repetition of essentially similar results is pointless. Criminal cases are therefore omitted entirely. If criminal jurisprudence in the Lords itself has to be treated with great care, it would be potentially misleading to include criminal cases arising from very different cultural backgrounds alongside the UK cases. (The caution may be overdone—analyses of the PC criminal cases shows them almost identical in prediction rate, and in the inversion of the discriminant scores, to the British cases.) Consequently the Privy Council cases are those from public and constitutional law which would qualify for separate treatment were they UK cases. Here they are joined, partly because there would be too few to analyse otherwise. The bulk of these are constitutional cases, but because 'constitutional' has a more precise meaning when the cases come from countries which actually have written constitutions, there are in fact only a small handful of cases coming to the Privy Council that could properly be called public law but not constitutional—only four by the conservative judgement used here. As Table 2.10 shows, this grouping can be satisfactorily analysed. The only problem is that the governments of Commonwealth countries do not often seem to win constitutional/ public law cases which make it to London, with a consequent imbalance in the results. Though this does not affect the statistical significance of the results even with the very small sample size, it prompts a certain caution in relying on the analyses substantively.

Were the intention here just to demonstrate the predictability of cases

Table 2.10 Predictions of Constitutional/Public Law Cases from PC

Actual Group	Predicted as Weak Win	Predicted as Strong Win	% Correctly Predicted
Weak Wins	11	1	92%
Strong Wins	0	5	100%

The analysis correctly predicts 16 out of 17 cases or 94%, with probability of the result arising by accident of p = 0.003.

by the presence or absence of various judges the technique used, MDA, would be unnecessarily cumbersome. Simple cross-tabulations like those used in subsection II would have sufficed. At the end we return to such contingency tables, though not simple ones, to explore one area that the MDA technique ignores—that of interaction between the Lords. The reason MDA was used was because the discriminant functions it produces, the weighting of each judge along a dimension that does the discrimination between cases, is vital for the next step. This next step is to put some meaning on the patterns by inference from how judicial predispositions in each domain fit together.

3. Dimensions of Judicial Predispositions

The discriminant functions in each domain can be seen as dimensions contrasting how strongly each Law Lord is predisposed for or against the results represented by the ends. Basically what happens is that in calculating what weight to give to the presence/absence of each judge in order best to predict the case results, the analysis programme ranks the judges themselves on a continuum from the most likely to cause a victory for one side to the most likely to cause a victory for the other, via, inevitably, a mass of 'centrist' Law Lords who seem to have no particular predisposition in the domain under analysis. These scales or continua can be treated as descriptive variables in themselves to allow us to go on to consider the nature of the judicial positions so defined. Most judges lack strong predispositions on most dimensions, and consequently occupy 'middling' positions on most discriminant functions. What do these end and middle positions actually represent? An entirely objective coding is possible for all but the civil law dimension, but, as suggested earlier, we do not really even know what the import is of regularly tending towards the pro-defence versus pro-prosecution end of the criminal appeals dimension, the most obviously objective. For example, when it comes to the tax cases, is a predisposition towards the revenue authorities substantially the same attitude as a predisposition towards the prosecution? Can we see predispositions towards the State authority in public and constitutional cases, and towards the 'strong' side in a civil dispute as representing a pattern of attitudes to the power redistribution aspect of the legal system? For that matter, given that public law and constitutional law domains need to be separated at all, and produce higher predictability when separated, does supporting the weak litigant against the State mean the same thing in the two domains?

All of these are questions about correlation—the only way we can get some sense of the meaning of judicial predispositions through this 'external' analysis, is looking to see how these separate dimensions relate to each other. The correlations have been used to produce a factor analysis. This technique seeks to take sets of original variables and, on the basis of their intercorrelation, to reduce them to a smaller number of derived variables or factors, each of which measures what is common to several of the originals. One way of thinking of factor analysis, familiar from its use to derive IQ measures, is to see each of the original variables as an impure measure of some underlying trait. Thus in research on intelligence a battery of verbal, numerical, and spatial tests are applied, each of which is thought of as being a partial measure of one or more basic intelligence capacities. Each test in the battery may relate partially to different traits, and several tests will each partially measure each underlying trait. Here the idea is that predispositions to vote regularly for the defence, for the revenue, for the State, for the weaker side in civil cases may all be partially and impure reflections of more fundamental, and comprehensible, judicial attitudes.

The intercorrelations between discriminant functions yield the following factor analysis which replaces the original five functions with three dimensions or components. One important feature of such solutions is that the three new dimensions are completely uncorrelated. Consequently the resulting model can helpfully be thought of in spatial terms—each of the components of the solution can represent one of three orthogonal dimensions in a 'space' which characterizes judicial attitudes.

Factor 1 in Table 2.11 measures very strongly a dimension characterized by just two of the original domains, voting in public law and criminal law cases. Some care is needed to keep these patterns clearly in mind. A 'high' score in the public law domain means, as discussed earlier, that a judge has a predisposition to vote for the State or other authority in a public law appeal. But because of the coding of the criminal law domain, a high score there means a predisposition to grant appeals by criminal defendants. Thus it is not, as might casually be expected, a dimension contrasting support for the weak individual in both criminal and public law. Instead

Table 2.11 Factor Analysis of the Five Discriminant Functions

Rotated Factor Matrix:

	Factor 1	Factor 2	Factor 3
TAX	0.01278	*−0.80896*	−0.07956
PUBLIC	*0.90049*	0.17815	0.06913
CON	0.01133	0.01125	*0.99514*
CIVIL	0.02164	*0.79125*	−0.05849
CRIMINAL	*0.90684*	−0.16435	−0.05276

The factor loadings which characterize the factors are italicized.

to get a high score on the first factor requires consistent support for the state in public, but also for the *defendant* in criminal cases.

There is no incompatibility, no great mystery about this. Criminal appeals do not turn on emotive matters of instant justice or criminal desert. They turn rather on matters like the scrupulousness with which the judiciary interpret the precise terms of a criminal statute, the rigour with which they impose a common law restriction on, for example, hearsay evidence, or the exactness of their demands about judicial summing up to the jury. It is precisely the cast of legal mind that restricts public law claimants in their pursuit of aid from the State to the narrower of statutory interpretations which also makes it harder for the State arbitrarily to employ its coercive powers through the criminal law. (We discuss in the next chapter the nature of statutory interpretation required to give an expansive or 'generous' interpretation of public law statutory entitlements.) The dimension that ensues is a highly probable one, and is best thought of as an almost purely methodological component of judicial ideology—restrictivism versus liberality of interpretation.

The second factor again 'loads' very clearly on two and only two of the original domains, tax and civil law. Also similarly, the direction of the domain codings requires careful thought. The tax domain has a negative loading, −0.809. To get a high score on the domain involved regularly voting for the revenue authorities, of course. Thus, given the reversal implied by the sign of the factor loading, a high tax score pushes a judge to the negative end of factor 2, along with scores indicating a preference for the weaker of two parties to a civil suit. Superficially confusing though the arithmetic may be, the interpretation is quite simple—strongly supporting paying taxes goes with a concern for those in a weak economic position—as indeed it does in most ordinary political thinking. The taxpayers whose appeals come to the Lords are not, generally, the poor and

weak. The dimension is one of egalitarianism. The final factor requires no
interpretation, loading very highly only on the constitutional domain. A
low score on factor three means a judge tends to support those pressing a
constitutional claim, trying to have protected some core value of constitutional democracy often, though not invariably, against the State.

There is never a 'correct' or unique solution to a factor analysis, because
the essence of the technique is the partitioning out of the correlation
between two or more variables, all of which are somewhat muddily
measuring or representing more than one underlying dimension. Thus
if one leaves out or adds variables, different solutions emerge, because
different 'commonalities' dominate in the exposition of what the measuring variables represent. In this case a different and notably simplified two-
dimensional model emerges if the criminal law is ignored. It makes sense
to consider a model of judicial attitude space excluding criminal law for
several reasons. The first is that their Lordships are themselves unhappy
about their reputation in criminal law, and much of the criminal law
profession is even more so. Secondly, there is more substantively in common between the other four domains, because the criminal law results do
so strongly reflect methodology not value preference. A natural connection between public law and constitutional law is submerged, and a
methodological dimension given special salience when criminal law is
included. Thus it is worth paying attention also to a second, alternative
spatial model where, by leaving out criminal appeals, the 'restrictivism
versus interpretative liberalism' dimension is suppressed. This is given by
the results in Table 2.12. The first factor in this model is essentially the
'egalitarianism' dimension from the full five-domain analysis, but this
time with the additionally moderately strong loading of the public law
domain at 0.485. To be at the low score end of the dimension is to support
claimants within the public law domain, as well as supporting the Rev-

Table 2.12 Factor Analysis of Tax, Public, Constitutional, and Civil Cases

Factor Matrix:		
	Factor 1	Factor 2
TAX	−0.76180	0.14792
PUBLIC	0.48498	0.34737
CON	0.17548	0.88712
CIVIL	0.72708	−0.29083

*The factor loadings which characterize the factors are
italicized.*

enue against would-be tax avoiders and the weaker side in civil law suits. The full effect of the public law domain is divided in this analysis, because it loads, again moderately at 0.347, on factor two along with the discriminant function from the constitutional law domain. In truth what we call public law is a blend of two sorts of claim against state bodies—welfare style claims pressed in the courts against bodies like Housing Authorities and the Social Service Departments, and liberty claims against, *inter alia*, prison governors and immigration officials. (This distinction is developed considerably in the substantive Chapters 7–9 in Part Two of the book.) It is quite natural that a scale based on judicial voting in such cases would measure two different predispositions that come into a sharper focus when the correlations with other dimensions are considered.

Because factor analysis is a spatial technique, it offers the possibility of looking at the relationships between the Law Lords in a graphical manner. Figure 2.1 presents their Lordships in the two-dimensional space described by the factor analysis in Table 2.12.

No observer of the Law Lords in recent years is likely to be very surprised by this portrayal. Lord Mustill, for example, is indeed an advocate, usually, of the constitutional values of a liberal State, but hardly noted for squeamishness in denying civil remedies, particularly in negligence when his brethren would expand their scope. Lord Templeman in contrast was often in the minority in pushing the rights of bodies like trade unions in civil cases, and defending the 'little old ladies', just as he fiercely supported the Revenue. But otherwise he was not often found

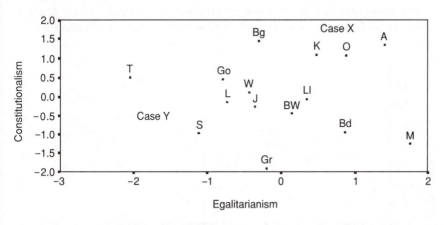

(T: Templeman, Bg: Bridge, K: Keith, A: Ackner, O: Oliver, Go: Goff, W: Woolf, L: Lowry, Ll: Lloyd, J: Jauncey, BW: Browne-Wilkinson, Bd: Brandon, S: Slynn, M: Mustill, Gr: Griffiths.)

Figure 2.1 A 2-Dimensional Judicial Space

supporting restrictions on state activity or being excessively generous with benefit claimants. Most of the other outliers will look similarly familiar to regular readers of the *Weekly Law Reports*.

Because the methodological elements of judicial ideology are crucial, Figure 2.2 reduces the factor analysis reported in Table 2.11 to the first two dimensions, ignoring the constitutional dimension so that it can conveniently be graphed.

The surface plausibility at least of naming the first factor 'restrictive interpretation' is high. No one could regard Lord Keith as particularly 'soft on crime', but there is little doubt that, as with many Scottish judges, he has a considerably greater tendency to insist on narrow and linguistic interpretations in general. But Keith is not a judge over likely to give an expansionary reading to a social service obligation. Lord Lowry is an experienced criminal judge, a one time 'Diplock Court' judge in Ulster, and previous Chief Justice of Northern Ireland, but he is by no stretch of the imagination a hanging judge. Nonetheless his opinions are regularly impatient with technical obstructions to purposive state behaviour, as much in supporting claimants as in upholding convictions even in the face of potential obscurity in the statutory language.

Inevitably both graphs show a few Law lords with clear positions, and a larger centrist group. The question of what happens to cases with a heavy concentration of such centrists is not completely answerable, though some attempt is made in the final section. The dimensionality displayed in these figures will inform much of what we have to say in the chapters of Part Two of the book. There are two further ways these figures can be immediately helpful. First, given this idea of ideological space it is easier to see how, and why, the prediction mechanisms used earlier work.

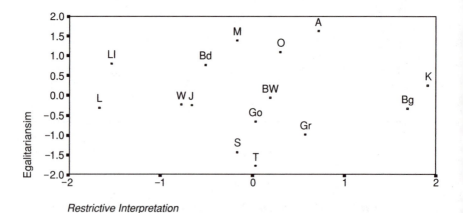

Figure 2.2 An Alternate 2-D Space.

Imagine a case concerning, for example, a challenge to a local authority that it was applying an unfairly restrictive interpretation of its duties to house the homeless, which comes up for appeal before Lords Ackner, Keith, Oliver, and Bridge. One could plot this case itself onto the graph in Figure 2.1 by averaging the dimensional scores of these four Law Lords. Such a hypothetical case is shown in Figure 2.1 as 'Case X'. It would fall clearly in the top right-hand quadrant, almost regardless of the identity of the fifth judge. Who would relish arguing a case expressing the values implicit in that description, in an ideological area characterized as non-egalitarian and pro-Authority? Other paradigm cases can be tested out in this way. Case Y is a hypothetical where a bench of Templeman, Goff, Lowry, Slynn, and Griffiths sits. There is little doubt what sort of a case one would prefer to present. One must remember, however, that these figures are themselves simplifications of much more complex underlying attitude spaces.

Secondly, such judicial 'maps' can give a good idea of natural judicial alliances, of groupings or clusterings which may occur, and explain the outcome of particular cases. Who is like whom? It is not all that easy to make such judgements by unaided visual inspection, but a simple analysis device know as *Hierarchical Clustering* can use the dimensional scores to show how such groups form into broader and broader potential coalitions as one relaxes the criterion of spatial proximity. Such a plot is given in Figure 2.3.

If one requires a very close proximity to recognize a group, Jauncey and Woolf would form one, with Ackner and Oliver forming a pair only slightly less close, with Keith and Bridge uniting at a level of proximity that would turn the original pair into a trio of Jauncey, Woolf, and Goff. Some judges, seen in this perspective, are manifestly loners: Templeman never unites until proximity restrictions are so relaxed that the entire cohort become one group; Mustill is almost as much a loner, and though Griffiths and Slynn become a couple fairly early, they never join a larger group. The most obvious larger groupings show as a group of five centrists—Jauncey, Woolf, Goff, Browne-Wilkinson, and Brandon—which becomes centre-left with the slightly later addition of the Lloyd/Lowry pair, and the restrictivist/Conservative group mentioned above which is really a double pair, Ackner/Oliver and Keith/Bridge. Nothing is implied about the extent to which these have any internal meaning to the members, but it is likely that they reflect something of the group dynamics in the judicial conferences. Again readers of the Law Reports might well find the 'loneliness' of Lords Mustill and Templeman unsurprising—one thing they have in common is a tendency to deliver trenchant dissents in highly individualistic, perhaps idiosyncratic, styles.

Which brings us to the final reason for examining the way the original

This clustering uses distances from 3-D Factor Solution

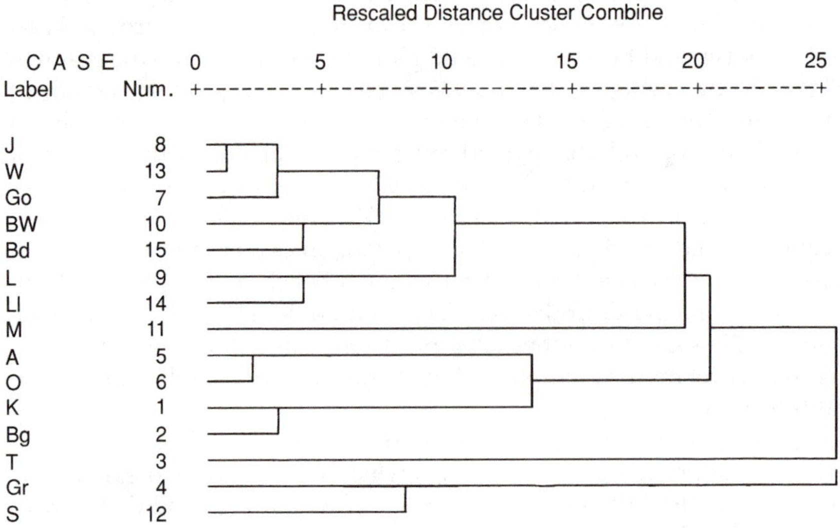

Rescaled Distance Cluster Combine

```
  C A S E       0      5      10     15     20     25
  Label    Num. +---------+---------+---------+---------+---------+

  J          8
  W         13
  Go         7
  BW        10
  Bd        15
  L          9
  Ll        14
  M         11
  A          5
  O          6
  K          1
  Bg         2
  T          3
  Gr         4
  S         12
```

Figure 2.3 Dendrogram Using Average Linkage (Between Groups)

domains interrelate. All the early predictive analysis was carried out inside the separate subject domains. The sample sizes within each are too small to investigate the final question which must be addressed here. Much of what has been discussed in this section, however, seems to justify regrouping cases. Thus we can put together the tax, civil, and public and constitutional cases with some confidence that coding the decisions to represent an 'egalitarian/inegalitarian' dichotomy does justice to their import. This being done a final question can be raised.

4. Judicial Interaction

Multiple Discriminant Analysis, the technique used to demonstrate the predictability of decisions in the Lords, is, like logistic regression, part of a family of techniques called the General Linear Model. In particular they are both *Additive* linear models. Essentially they are based on the equation for a straight line, familiar from elementary calculus. We have seen this in the use of the logistic regression technique. A dependent variable, called y, is defined as the sum of a constant term, a, and a variable, x, which is multiplied by another constant b to give: $y = a + b(x)$. Usually there are several x terms, collectively known as the 'independent' variables, one for each of the factors derived from the substantive theory which is being statistically modelled. Here we have been using the presence or absence of a judge as variables. The first of the linear additive equations we used in the earlier section on logistic regression was, it will be remembered:

(Probability that the State wins)

$$= (0.382) + 1.052(\text{Bridge}) - 1.200(\text{Jauncey}) - 1.133(\text{Griffith}).$$

Just setting the calculations out in this way may make the problem stand out by itself. Where, sociologically or legally, does the 'additivity' assumption come from? It is needed to make the equation work because calculus in its early stages is additive, but does it have any reference to real life? Even if we believe that judges can be treated as independent variables, does their presence or absence on a court just add or subtract from the probability of a case being decided a certain way, independent of context? Effectively the model is asserting that Griffiths acts the same way regardless of who else is on the court, and so does Jauncey, and Bridge is equally indifferent in his behaviour to whom he is discussing the case with. Perhaps that might be true. In fact we already know that it is not always true, because we had to fit special terms to catch the interaction in subsequent logistic models. It might, more particularly in this example, be true of Bridge and Griffiths because they have strong (and opposed) predispositions in this area. But what about Jauncey? A glance at the judicial map in Figure 2.1 shows him as near as can be slap in the middle of both the egalitarianism and the constitutionalism dimensions—in part precisely because his discriminant function score is very close to zero at only 0.322. Is a judge with little predisposition exactly as likely to vote in a certain way when alone with a strong liberal constitutionalist as when with someone from the other end of the constitutionalism dimension? And when all three are present, does not the middle man, according to all tenets of coalition theory, have a disproportionate influence? On those courts most usually studied by political scientists, like the US Supreme Court, the role of the 'swing' voter, the middle judge capable of being won to either extreme on a case by case basis, is well understood. (Indeed US newspaper coverage of the court often focuses on just such an analysis.) There are of course endless other matters which make one doubt that additivity can be anything but a serious oversimplification, even if all the orthodox expectations about the facts of the case mattering are dispensed with. Above all, personality and intellectual dominance are known in all other small groups to be vital. Surely they must be in the Lords?

The fact that the crude simplicity of an additive model works given what it neglects makes that success more impressive, but it does not mean that the models are fully adequate explications of judicial decision making. What we must do now is to follow up the hints of a non-additive relationship suggested earlier, looking for what social scientists call 'interaction', the effects of which are suppressed by all additive data analytic techniques. If it does exist, and we shall show it does, there is no way a fully detailed examination of all the interactions that might more fully explain the data can be undertaken. The possible interactions amongst the fifteen judges in the cohort are vastly too many to study even were the data set huge. But that is not necessary. It will suffice to give one or two examples of interaction at work. Because we are then adding to the possibility that the results of cases are explained by judicial predispositions. They are then even more fully explained by taking note of the highly individualistic interactions between the bearers of these predispositions, still without reference to the details of the cases. This, however predictable by sociologists or barristers, takes us yet further from any model of merely limited judicial discretion.

The technique chosen here to examine interaction effects is LogLinear modelling.[3] It is too complicated to be explained here, but is commonly used, is specifically designed for use on data of our type, and is very robust, making very few measurement assumptions, none of which are violated by our data. LogLinear modelling was originally designed to allow highly sophisticated model building on data presented in the simplest way known to social science, basic cross-tabulation tables of straightforward contingency counts. This is the data presentation used at the beginning of this chapter to make a prima facie case for the effect of judicial predisposition on case outcome. Then we presented two by two contingency tables relating a judge's presence or absence to outcome, one for Templeman on tax, one for Bridge on crime. At this stage we use a table which is clumsier but intellectually of the same level, cross-tabulating the presence/absence of three judges with the results of cases taken from all the four related domains: tax, public, criminal, and civil. The Law Lords covered by this table are Lords Ackner, Lowry, and Keith, chosen more because they heard a large number of cases together or in various permutations than because they are particularly likely to have demonstrated interaction in their judicial work.

Table 2.13 is cumbersome but not difficult to read. The first column specifies what combination of judges the row refers to. The first double column shows how the cases heard by that combination did, in fact, divide between victories for the 'weak' and 'strong' litigant. The six cases heard by all three split 5:1 in favour of the strong side. The next three double columns show how this result would have been predicted under

---

[3] An extremely approachable guide to LogLinear modelling, requiring nothing more than simple arithmetic, is G. Nigel Gilbert *Modelling Society*, London, George Allen and Unwin, 1981.

Table 2.13 Predicted and Actual Results of 167 Cases from Tax, Constitutional, Public, and Civil Law Domains

Membership	Actual Counts		Prediction—no effects		Prediction—single effects		Prediction—interaction effects	
	1	2	3	4	5	6	7	8
	Weak	Strong	Weak	Strong	Weak	Strong	Weak	Strong
A,L,K, +2	1	5	3	3	2	4	1	5
A,L, +3	7	12	8	11	7	12	7	12
A,K, +3	4	9	6	7	3	10	4	9
L,K, +3	4	5	4	5	6	3	4	5
A, +4	6	25	13	18	6	25	6	25
L, +4	20	5	11	14	17	8	20	5
K, +4	25	21	20	26	23	23	25	21
+5	11	20	13	18	14	17	11	20
% Misclassified	n/a		16%		8%		1%	

All entries in the table are rounded to the nearest integer.
A,L,K, +2 means the case was heard by Ackner, Lowry, and Keith, and two other unidentified judges who may, but need not, come from the cohort studied; A, +4 etc. means that only Ackner of the three sat on the case; +5 that none of the three heard it.

three assumptions. First, assuming that there were no effects attributable to the presence of any of the three judges, it would be expected that the split between weak and strong would be exactly even. Clearly there must be some relationship, therefore, between the presence of judges and the results, because the real split was as nearly uneven as it could be—more strong victories happened than weak ones. The third double column tests the assumption that has been used through most of this chapter—there is an effect of judicial presence but it is a straightforward additive one—each judge has the same effect depending on his presence or absence, in a way that is independent of who else sits on the case. The prediction here is still wrong, at 4:2, but it is getting nearer. The final assumption testifies that some form of interaction between the judges does exist, and in this case the split is correct—that is, the model predicts the same figures that actually happened—a 5:1 split in favour of the strong side. The same logic applies to all the rows. So, for example, row six refers to those cases where Lowry, but neither Keith nor Ackner, was amongst the Law Lords hearing appeals. The results are striking. In reality twenty out of twenty-five Lowry cases go to the weak side. This is a major demonstration of the impact one judge can have in itself: in the entire data set the weak side only won in 43 per cent of cases, but where Lowry sits, *in the absence of Keith and Ackner*, the weak side wins 80 per cent of cases. Not surprisingly such a result would not be predicted on the assumption that these three judges have no personal impact on the results. Under that assumption, only about half as many cases would have gone to the weaker side. But the results are only slightly more accurate allowing single judge correlations but not interaction effects—then the model predicts seventeen of the twenty-five cases for the weak side. Lowry is important, but the full impact of his presence is obviously mediated by the absence or presence of the other two, because allowing interaction produces a perfect fit. (The interaction model only misclassifies 1 per cent of all cases.)

We can see what the main effects of the judges are from inspecting this table. Just as Lowry inclines the court heavily towards the weak, Ackner does the reverse: where he sits without the other two, only 20 per cent of cases go to the weak. Furthermore, Ackner does not seem to be involved in interactions. Columns 5 and 6 which report the results of the 'direct effect without interactions' model get the results exactly right for this row of the table. Actually the 'no interactions' model fits pretty well when Ackner is sitting with Lowry but without Keith, and vice versa. Keith has little impact by himself—there are more weak victories than the expected value for no effects at all, 54 per cent to 44 per cent , but the contrast is not at the level of the 'Lowry alone' or 'Ackner alone' effects. This is as one might expect from glancing again at the graph in Figure 2.1—the trio was chosen for analysis in part because Keith lies neatly in between the 'egalitarian' Lowry and the 'conservative' Ackner. By itself mere inspection of the table cannot really establish that interaction is going on at a significant level, or, if it is, which interactions really count. This is where LogLinear modelling comes into play.

LogLinear modelling allows one to fit any set of terms to the data, in increasing complexity, until some sort of 'best fit' is arrived at. Most analysts regard the best fit as the model which explains the largest amount of variation with the smallest number of terms, following the orthodox preference for scientific parsimony. Satisfaction is measured in several ways. Primarily one considers a term, G^2, which measures the total deviation between the cell entries predicted by the terms in a particular model and the actual terms—one strives to reduce G^2 to zero. Associated with each model and G^2 is a probability, the probability that such a fit would not happen by accident. The probability tests are those discussed earlier—we settle for any model which passes at the 5 per cent level—that is, one which could happen by accident in only one trial in twenty. Finally, it is possible to calculate what is known as a Proportional Reduction in Error measure, or PRE. This takes the amount of error in a baseline prediction—in this case the assumption of no effects at all, and calculates how much one has reduced this error with any particular model. The PRE here takes values only between zero—no reduction in error—and one—no remain-

Table 2.14 LogLinear Models to Explain Case Results by Presence or Absence of Lords Ackner, Keith, and Lowry

Model	G^2	PRE	Probability	Degrees of Freedom
Base model—no effects	28.3	0	0.000	7
A	14.3	0.49	0.026	6
L	24.0	0.15	0.001	6
K	27.9	0.01	0.000	6
A,L,K	8.5	0.70	0.074*	4
A,L	8.6	0.69	0.12*	5
A,K	14.2	0.50	0.014	5
L,K	22.8	0.19	0.000	5
L+K,A	1.7	0.94	0.65*	3
L+A,K	7.9	0.72	0.049	3
A+K,L	8.5	0.70	0.036	3
L+K,L+A	0.2	0.99	0.92*	2
L+K,L+A,A+K	0.2	0.99	0.92*	2

Models significant at better than the 5% level are marked*.

ing error. It is not a directional measure, like its more familiar equivalent the correlation coefficient, and cannot have negative values. Table 2.14 gives a summary of results from fitting various LogLinear models to this data, in the search for the precise interactions that are needed.

The nomenclature used in the table is straightforward: A is the model taking account only of Ackner's presence or absence, ignoring the other two Law Lords. A,L involves fitting the separate effects of Ackner and Lowry, ignoring Keith; A,L,K uses all the direct effects, but still ignores interactions; L+K,A = fitting the direct effect of Ackner and the interaction between Lowry and Keith, which necessarily incorporates the direct effects of each of them; L+K,L+A = fitting the interactions between Lowry and Keith, and the interactions between Lowry and Ackner. (Three way interactions, A+K+L are possible but unnecessary in this data.)

Clearly Ackner has the biggest effect on results by himself. The Proportional Reduction in Error from the baseline using only Ackner in the model is 0.49—nearly a 50 per cent error reduction, compared to only 15 per cent reduction with just Lowry, and no appreciable reduction with Keith alone. However, none of the models using a single judge reach significance. Indeed Keith's presence or absence is irrelevant at the level of direct effects, because the three term model A,L,K, which represents a major improvement on the baseline with a PRE of 0.70, is hardly damaged with the removal of Keith to produce the model A,L. Where Keith becomes enormously important is in interaction with Lowry—the model L+K,A; fitting the direct effects of all three and the interaction of Keith and Lowry reduces the original error in prediction by 94 per cent, with a minimal G^2 of 1.7, and a healthy significance level of 0.65. (The way the measures are calculated leads us to need to maximize the significance value here, while in the logistic regression models we were seeking to minimize it. It is merely a consequence of which way round one calculates, and the logic remains the same.) No other model at this level improves seriously on the simple additive model of A,K,L. The model can be improved, but only by adding another interaction term between Lowry and Ackner, to make the model L+K,L+A. There is no Ackner/Keith interaction of any significance.

So, if by an apparently over-technological route, we can establish a terribly simple thing—complex, unguessable, but specifiable and testable interpersonal interactions between judges with established predispositions are what constrain, if they do not determine, the outcomes of cases. Without such technology, however, much would be missed. It appears, after all, that Lord Keith has no personal effect on the cases he hears. Naturally we do not mean this in a full-blooded jurisprudential sense. Doubtless his views were always taken most seriously by his colleagues. And we know, and document in Chapter 6, that in one particular area of the law of negligence he fought and won a long campaign to change the law. But it must be the case that in the cases we consider here no special tendency of Keith's to prefer one sort of outcome existed, or, if it existed, it did not successfully influence his colleagues. His presence is crucial, but it only appears when he is joined with another judge, Lowry, who must somehow or other bring out from Keith a similar 'egalitarian' tendency. Or the pair of them are impressive in conference in a way that is greater than either can achieve by himself. It comes to the same thing. Just to show that the results in the previous table are not a carefully

Table 2.15 LogLinear Models on Lords Ackner, Bridge, and Templeman

Model	G^2	PRE	Probability	Degrees of Freedom
Base model—no effects	22.4	0	0.002	7
A,B,T	6.1	0.73	0.19	4
A+B,T	4.4	0.80	0.22	3
A+T,B	6.0	0.73	0.11	3
B+T,A	2.0	0.91	0.58	3
B+T,B+A	0.6	0.97	0.90	2

selected fluke we will much more briefly report a similar analysis with a mainly different cast. The same set of cases yields equivalent results for the trio of Lords Ackner, Bridge, and Templeman. We report only the LogLinear model, and only in truncated forms.

First we fit the direct effects model for all three Lords, which demonstrates an immediate good fit, with the original error from the base model of no effects reduced by 73 per cent, by cutting the G^2 term from 22.4 to only 6.1, with an entirely adequate probability level of 0.19. (Again, to remind, anything over 0.05 indicates acceptable significance.) All three judges are needed in the model, but unsurprisingly, given the results immediately above, the single effect of Lord Ackner is greater than that of either of his brethren. Is there any interaction? Two obvious interaction models, each with Ackner, need to be tested because he does seem to be so dominant. Ackner and Bridge do seem to interact as a pair, reducing G^2 by another third, but there is no evidence of interaction between Ackner and Templeman. Returning to Figure 2.1, one can see this is fairly obvious—Templeman and Ackner were chosen to be opposites, with Bridge in between. There can, of course, be interaction between those who are radically opposed, but the more natural interactions are between centrists and one or other extreme. This is very much what one gets here, because the still relatively parsimonious model B+T,A is highly successful, with PRE up to 0.91, a very small G^2 of only two, and a probability up to 0.58. One might stop there, but the fuller model, accepting that Bridge interacts in an important way with both the extremes, though they do not interact together, is even more successful, reducing G^2 to only 0.6, with a 97 per cent reduction in the base error, and a very high probability of 0.90. It is the way we can swap back and forth between the visual depiction of judicial similarities in the spatial account given by the factor analysis, and the quite independent testing of effects with LogLinear modelling, that makes this whole statistical approach useful and persuasive. Further examples could be given, but are surely unnecessary, especially given that the data are too sparse for the examination of every possible combination, or for exploring even higher level interactions. All the theoretical work we need has been done, and we can proceed to examine the real impact of these interactions of judges within their ideological attitude space in the remaining chapters of the book.

5. Recap

In sociological terms this chapter has taken a highly positivist approach to the institutional behaviour of judges. The individual judicial vote has not been the focus. Indeed the search for judicial ideological profiles has intentionally been made harder by this decision. Though dissents are rare—over time less than 10 per cent of cases are decided by public majority voting—they do occur, so on occasion the Law Lords have been coded as in support of cases where they were actually in dissent. A more individualistic approach—and much of this book does concentrate on individual argument, seeking to understand judicial role though the judges' own words—would have taken these individual votes rather than the group decision as what had to be explained. The aim has instead been to infer what goes on inside a black box, the secret—if rather 'leaky'—judicial conferences in which cases are decided. Three major points emerge. First, a good prediction can be made of case resolution by knowing who is on the panel which hears the appeal. Initially these predictive models were derived on separate domains of cases to make the coding of results more transparent and objective. It was further shown that the results of these separate domain analyses can be used to examine the coherence of the domains, and generate a meaningful ideological space into which the Law Lords can be mapped. Finally, this possibility of interpreting the decisions allowed for the recombination of the domains along a consistent coding of egalitarianism. When all domains are combined a larger sample of cases could then be used to tease out the complexities of interaction between the judges to show how highly personalized the conference decision making must be. It seems fair to conclude from all of this that a major factor in determining case outcome is the relative positions of the Law Lords on a basic dimension, for convenience labelled 'egalitarianism', which mirrors a traditional view of the courts doing justice by acting as a counter to social power imbalances.

This chapter then has added strength to the theoretical sketch of Chapter 1. We believe that legal realism, taking judicial decisions to be largely unconstrained individualistic policy preferences, is a valid interpretation of the higher English courts, and we have now shown that the actual outcome of cases is entirely compatible with such a theory. Certainly the predictability of outcome based only on knowing who heard the appeal is inconsistent with anything like the idea of slot machine jurisprudence. There is a major question left to be dealt with in this first part of the book. If Chapter 1 is broadly right, and if the analysis in this chapter is valid, how can this come about? Judges, after all, do not just vote. They give complex opinions, deriving their preferred decisions by long chains of difficult logic from precedents. Do these arguments not constrain and shape their decisions? Surely the Law Lords must be terribly unfree, massively restricted by the need always to justify their preferences? Or is the legal realist idea that argument is, as it were, *post hoc*, constructed out of pliable material to justify rather than to discover the result valid? The next two chapters complete this theoretical and methodological part of the book by looking in great detail at just how binding judicial argument actually is.

3

Judicial Methodology in Statutory Interpretation

> There is no better way of exercising the imagination than the study of law. No poet ever interpreted nature as freely as a lawyer interprets the truth.
>
> Jean Giraudoux
>
> It is a hallucination: this search for intent. The room is always dark.
>
> Charles Curtiss

1. Introduction

There are two logically separable types of judicial decision in a British appellate court, the application of common law rules and the application of statute rules. Both involve the fitting of rules to fact situations taken as given, whether arising from the decision by a jury in a criminal trial or a first instance judge in a civil trial. In practice this sharp distinction between fact and law does not always work easily—their Lordships at times find ways of overturning factual analyses which would lead to legal conclusions they dislike, but in theory at least appellate decisions refer to prior mistakes of law only. Both types of decision involve interpretation, but the techniques of statutory interpretation and of interpreting the true nature of the common law rule to be found in precedents differ somewhat. Consequently we have divided our analysis of the nature of legal argument in the courts into two sections. Here we discuss what should be the more limited area of judicial discretion, the interpretation of statutes. Very few cases, however, are pure types. There are few problems coming before the court where no statute at all can be said to be relevant (though the Lords may interpret it away to give themselves a clear common law run). More typical of a mixed situation is the usual job of statutory interpretation where there is no doubt which piece of parliamentary legislation applies. Once an important statute has been on the books for any length of time the more difficult clauses will have been subject to prior interpretation, and the meaning given by the Law Lords in the instant case will have to be shown to be compatible with the meanings given before, as well as with the all-important 'intention of Parliament'. It has to be remembered throughout this discussion that the Lords differ from the Court of Appeal because the Court of Appeal is bound to follow not only precedents of the House, but also its own prior decisions. The Lords are entitled to overrule Court of Appeal decisions and frequently do so. Since 1966 they have also given themselves the power to overturn their own precedents, a power they use very sparingly, so strong is the commitment to precedent. One can find cases, Lord Reid in *Knuller* v. *DPP* for example, where a Law Lord believes that the precedent was wrongly decided, dissented in that case, thinks that following it requires him to give the wrong answer in the instant case, but still follows the precedent for the sake of 'certainty' in the law.[1] More typically a ruling case may be thought inadequate, and to cause problems in developing some area of law, but the Law Lords will prefer to try to 'distinguish' it, or partially redefine it rather than overrule. This happens because it is easier to see that the precedent did not fully capture the way the law should be going than to come up with a perfectly satisfactory alternative, and 'certainty' then argues for holding back from an outright overruling. A current example is the ruling case on when a tax avoidance scheme is too fanciful to allow, the 1984 case of *Dawson* v. *Furniss*.[2] For at least some of the Law Lords *Furniss* has become somewhat of a straitjacket, even though it was a major breakthrough at the time, ending the traditional view that a taxpayer could do anything which was not illegal to minimize his obligation to the Revenue. But tax planning is so complex a business, and so important to the economic life of the country, that even the opponents of the ruling in *Furniss* shrink from overruling it. The fact that nearly all tax cases are ultimately about statutory interpretation, makes overruling no easier. Indeed Lord Reid is also on record as refusing to use the 1966 Practice Direction at all in statutory interpretation, on the grounds that there is no possibility of an objectively correct decision about the meaning of an unclear statute.[3] The thought in itself is suggestive for the study of statutory construction.

The Lords sometimes extend this respect for precedent to the rulings of the Court of Appeal, and will often go to great lengths to chart a path through a thicket of their precedents to arrive at the conclusion they want, rather than just rule a previous Court of Appeal decision to be wrong. However, in practice, respect for a line of cases in the Court of Appeal seems only to be mentioned as a supporting reason for coming to a conclusion the judge wants to come to. It is rare to find such a line of cases respectfully dissented from—in such cases they are just ignored. (This, as Chapter 4 will show, cannot be done as easily where a fully common law issue is involved.)

This brings us to the nature of judicial argument. As we have said, the

---

[1] *Knuller* v. *DPP* [1973] AC 435.
[2] *Dawson* v. *Furniss* [1984] 1 AC 474.
[3] *Jones* v. *Secretary of State for Social Services* [1972] AC 944.

aim of this book is primarily to understand how the discretionary nature of law allows the seepage of private attitudes and ideologies into decisions. Following the legal realist perspective, we wish to take apart the reasoning in a series of cases to show how optional their Lordships' decisions are. But we want also to show how some types of arguments are easier and others harder to manipulate to a desired end. Much of this chapter relates to the 'interpretative' dimension of judicial voting analysed in the last chapter, but it is important to note that we also argue here that such a methodological preference is itself optional—judges will adopt it when convenient, but not necessarily bow to it when they wish to select a result which requires a freer interpretation of the law. It would be foolhardy to argue that there are absolutely no constraints on what a judge may argue, and thus what decision he can support. There should be two sorts of constraint which fetter judicial decision, whether it be the decision of a single judge who must look over his shoulder at the appellate court, or the member of an appellate panel who must seek to carry his peers. These constraints are (1) the range of acceptable arguments, which is a methodological constraint, and (2) a commonly shared set of principles which can be referred to when ultimate value judgements have to be made. This sort of constraint on discretion is much in the minds of the Law Lords. Lord Keith, for example, in a recent and very controversial case, begins his short dissent thus:

I am unable to reconcile the allowance of the plaintiffs' claim with principle, or to accept that to do so would represent an appropriate advance on the incremental basis from decided cases

and ends it by linking principled and methodological objections:

I have found the conceptual difficulties involved in the plaintiffs' claim, which are fully recognised by all your Lordships to be too formidable to be resolved by any process of reasoning compatible with existing principles of law.[4]

By 'conceptual difficulties' he means effectively that no one doubted what instant justice required, and he cannot see how to get there. But note that Keith has included a methodological rule as beyond doubt—that cases must develop the law 'on an incremental basis', and alludes to another, which is that if a decision cannot be justified 'with existing principles of law', it must not be chosen. More informally, when discussing their work, the Law Lords are prone to use the language of games, and to talk of 'trying not to cheat'. The phrase crops up with many of them—'The trouble with Denning was that he cheated', 'Perhaps I was cheating a little in X v. Y', 'I dissented because the majority were cheating'. (All of these are genuine, though disguised, quotations from private discussions.)

---

[4] Lord Keith in *White and another* v. *Jones and others* [1995] 1 All ER 691, at 695.

The problem is that there is precious little evidence that the methodology of judicial argument does have much of this constraining element. On close inspection it is rare to find arguments determining conclusions and forcing agreement. Rather, judicial argument seems to consist much more in deploying standard forms of argument picked because they lead to conclusions, rather than adopting a methodologically appropriate argument and deriving the conclusion. At some level this is not a controversial point. Most of the Law Lords will agree that they come to their conclusions 'bottom up', from an intuitive sense of what justice requires in the case, and seek to find an acceptable way to the conclusion. Conveniently Lord Mustill, Lord Keith's companion in dissent in the case mentioned above, almost throws this in the majority's face:

> I will proceed at once to explain why I have felt it difficult to join company with those who, judges and commentators alike, have almost unanimously found it too plain to need elaboration that the plaintiffs' claims ought to succeed, if only an intellectually sustainable means can be found, . . . The soundness of these assumptions must, I believe, be confronted at the start, because they dominate the landscape within which the whole inquiry takes place.[5]

But their Lordships also believe strongly that they only rarely cheat, and will give up their pursuit if that 'intellectually sustainable' route cannot be found. It is a question perhaps for another field of enquiry whether argument can ever determine conclusion completely. It is a question with an especial importance here, however. This is because much of the traditional discussion of statutory construction presents the judge as essentially passive, as being forced into choosing an interpretative technique because of a difficulty in the language of the statute which exists inherently in the statute, only to be perceived, neutrally, by the judge's mind. This is not at all often what happens. Rather, the judge makes an initial decision to find something in need of interpretation. Only then, after this decision, does he use, and too often present himself as being forced to use, one or other of the interpretative techniques. This is what happened in *Associated Newspapers*, the case used as an example at the beginning of Chapter 1. The plaintiff needed to show that *deliberate omissions to act* were covered by the clause guaranteeing employees 'the right not to have action . . . taken against him as an individual by his employer for the purpose of . . . penalising him for doing so' (being a member of a union). This would appear to be relatively simple because section 153(1) of the Act states:

> In this Act . . . *except so far as the context otherwise requires*—'act' and 'action' each includes omission and references to doing an act or taking action shall be construed accordingly [our emphasis].

---

[5] Mustill in *White* at 719.

If there is no ambiguity about the language of section 153(1), then the judge must interpret the language of the 1978 Act by itself, and, at least according to the minority here, and the Court of Appeal in a previous case, this can be done perfectly easily, to the plaintiff's benefit.[6] If, however, there is an ambiguity, a whole alternative interpretive tactic is available—to go back to the original Acts of which the 1978 Act is a consolidation, and seek there for an answer. If one does search the earlier Acts a case can be made, though not one that Lloyd and Slynn, in the minority here, think strong, for denying the union members the apparent protection against their employers. It is necessary, in other words, to *deem* the original language to be ambiguous. Bridge does this, though only by importing an otherwise unjustified assumption about drafting techniques:

The crucial phrase to be construed in section 23(1) is 'the right not to have action . . . taken against him'. If this phrase is to be construed as embodying the extended meaning, one must first expand the language so as to include the verb 'omit' or the noun 'omission' to see how it reads. The attempt to do this grammatically without substantially recasting the phrase and introducing additional words at once exposes the difficulty. If the concept of taking action against some person is to embrace the concept of omitting to act, the omission must be an omission to act in that person's favour. I cannot believe that any competent parliamentary draftsman, intending that an omission by an employer to take action in favour of an employee should have the same consequences as positive action taken against him, would fail to spell out the circumstances in which the obligation to take action in favour of the employee was to arise.

Thus Bridge essentially finds for himself the loophole—the ambiguity he perceives 'gives rise to a real and substantial difficulty' in the interpretation 'which classical methods of construction cannot resolve'.[7] But is there here an ambiguity existing independently of Bridge's assumption? Lloyd certainly did not see one:

It is said that to read 'action' in section 23(1)(a) as if it included 'omission' presents a grammatical difficulty, and that therefore the context . . . excludes the application of the definition in section 153(1). I accept at once that the inclusion of omissions within the scope . . . means that the phrase has to be recast. It is not possible to substitute one word for the other. For you cannot 'take' an omission. But this is no bar to the application of section 153. It was foreseen by the draftsman. That is why it is provided by section 153 that 'taking action' is to be 'construed accordingly'. I cannot easily visualise a context in which 'taking action'

---

[6] *National Coal Board* v. *Ridgway* [1987] ICR 641, CA.

[7] Bridge in *Associated Newspapers* at 359. He is here quoting from Lord Wilberforce in a case, *Farrell* v. *Alexander* [1977] AC 59, 73, which is held to lay down the rules for when the previous legislative history of an Act may be examined. Note that this is not the same sense of legislative history as in *Pepper* v. *Hart*, which authorizes looking at the debate on an Act. The two techniques could, presumably, be combined.

has to be construed so as to include an omission which would not involve substantial recasting.[8]

He goes on to point out that in such extensive definitions there will always be 'some difficulty in finding the neatest form of words' and to stress that the problem is 'inherent in the drafting technique'. Most tellingly he notes that in the previous case 'it never occurred to the employers to argue . . . that the definition did not apply. It was common ground that it did.' It is examples like this that force one to see interpretation as the result of a judicial *decision* to interpret, which then allows the choice of construction tools, not as something forced upon the judge. Here, after all, we have the same words used to show either a careful piece of parliamentary drafstmanship, or a drafting failure that can be remedied only by looking at the original Acts that were meant to be consolidated. What we seek to show in this and the next chapter is that inspection of judicial argument makes their preferred model of their behaviour seem hardly accurate. It is through the weaknesses in the structure of judicial argument, we suggest, that the inevitability of some discretion becomes the much more troublesome seepage of private ideology.

In a real sense the Lords seldom argue, because they do not address each other's points. Only relatively rarely will a dissenting opinion actually take on the logic of the majority and try to rebuff it. Still more rarely do the opinions destined to form the ruling seek to defend against the minority's criticisms. There is not a word in Bridge's speech in *Associated Newspapers* which even recognizes that Lord Lloyd has, quite bluntly, denied that Bridge's interpretive technique is even legitimate. It is absurd that this clash of view, this precisely defined and complete contradiction as to the correct technique even for starting to find the true meaning of the Act, is not in any way resolved or reconciled. This tendency to bland assertion rather than the often quite brutal attacks on other judges' reasoning found in American or Australian opinions has probably become worse since a development in the early eighties. Until Lord Diplock's period as senior Law Lord the Appellate Committee was providing so many speeches even in consensual cases that it was sometimes hard to find which of a set of arguments only compatible in that they ultimately all found for the same litigant actually contained the *ratio decidendi*. Whose view of the case was to become the precedent? Under his guidance the Lords have moved to the expectation that there will only usually be one major speech unless there is an actual dissent. Whatever value this may have for legal certainty and an appearance of curial consensus, it has reduced the extent of genuine argument and discussion of issues in a way that not only academic lawyers but many leading counsel find distinctly

---

[8] *Associated Newspapers* at 373–4.

unhelpful. (In fact by the latter part of the period covered in this book the old tendency to multiple opinions was beginning to reassert itself.) As the first of the ensuing case studies shows, it can also cause problems for their Lordships themselves, who sometimes find that they are deemed to support interpretative positions they later have to withdraw. The rest of this chapter, then, describes the typical methods of argument and analysis used in cases which are predominantly about statutory interpretation. Chapter 4 attempts to do the same for the rather different situation where a case is primarily one of precedent and common law.

It should be said that the technique used here, which involves rather detailed explication of their Lordships' arguments from several cases chosen to demonstrate several types of problem, is not the norm in such discussions. Books on statutory interpretation written by and for lawyers are legion and doubtless perfectly well serve their intended function. They tend, however, to be very light on examples. More problematic for our purposes, they largely ignore the fact that interpretations are rivals, either in comparison with others offered in a dissenting case, or as chosen between contentions by counsel. Thus a sense of consensus in how to interpret comes across. One recent and generally admirable comparative study of statutory interpretation contains not one example of a disputed interpretation in a dissenting case in the whole chapter on the UK.[9]

2. A Note on Parliamentary Intent

Before we proceed we must signal here that some of what we say needs to be considered in connection with the argument in Chapter 5. Chapter 5 discusses just one recent case, alluded to earlier—*Pepper* v. *Hart*. A major tactic in statutory interpretation is to claim that one must interpret legislation according to the intention Parliament had when it passed the statute. There are very many reasons this is a much more complicated, and some would think philosophically dubious, proposition than it might seem. One specific problem that has always plagued the English courts is a self-denying ordinance that they will not consult the record of parliamentary debate to discover this 'intent' from the mouths of the legislators. In 1993 the Law Lords granted themselves the right to do this. So important is this decision that we have taken all discussion of it, and much of the general discussion of the problems inherent in seeking to know parliamentary intent, and placed it all in a special chapter. Consequently there

---

[9] D. Neil MacCormick and R. S. Summers (eds.), *Interpreting Statutes: A Comparative Study*, Aldershot, Dartmouth, 1991.

is less in the rest of this chapter on 'intent' arguments than a reader might expect, and no discussion at this stage of *Pepper* v. *Hart*.

Some Examples of Statutory Construction

I. An 'Objective' and 'Expansionary' Ruling

The law on sexual discrimination in England and Wales is largely determined by the Sex Discrimination Act 1975, which was applied, with no serious problems, for some years before its meaning was tested in two cases at the end of the eighties. Two definitions of discrimination are given by section 1, quoted in full below:

A person discriminates against a woman in any circumstances relevant for the purposes of any provision of this Act if—(a) on the ground of her sex he treats her less favourably than he treats or would treat a man or (b) he applies to her a requirement or condition which he applies or would apply equally to a man but—(i) which is such that the proportion of women who can comply with it is considerably smaller than the proportion of men who can comply with it, and (ii) which he cannot show to be justifiable irrespective of the sex of the person to whom it is applied and (iii) which is to her detriment because she cannot comply with it.
    [By clause 2(1), the Act applies equally where men are the subjects of discrimination.]

There are, in general two rather different models that anti-discrimination law can take. In America, which has longer experience of such legislation than elsewhere, one is known as the 'strict scrutiny' model. Under this model the mere fact that unfavourably differential treatment is given to groups defined by the relevant characteristic—sex, religion, race or whatever—makes it illegal, regardless of any aims or reasons the discriminator has. In the jurisprudence of the US Supreme Court only race has become such 'an inherently suspect category'. Other differentiations are subject to a weaker test where differential treatment may be allowed if there is a strong 'rational connection' to an otherwise legitimate policy goal.[10] Thus different welfare provisions might be allowed on a gender basis if they pursued a positive welfare goal. To which model does the 1975 Act seem nearer? On the face of it, section 1(a) would seem to be a 'strict scrutiny' test. If people are treated differently because they are women, unlawful discrimination takes place. By section 1(b), two people being treated differently because they fall into different social categories where membership of these categories is itself partially or completely

---

[10] This is a much oversimplified account of the US jurisprudence. A brief discussion can be found in David Robertson, *A Dictionary of Human Rights*, London, Europa Publications, 1997.

gender determined, may also be an example of unlawful sexual discrimination. Because of the escape clauses in 1(b), the second limb of the test is nearer to the American 'rational connection' idea. So far so good. But 1(a) provides that someone discriminates against a woman when *'on the ground of her sex'* he treats her less favourably than he treats or would treat a man. (Our italics.)

The interpretation of these five words in two cases in 1989 and 1990 demonstrates vividly the entire problem of statutory construction. Nearly all the classic techniques are brought to play by one judge or another, the problem of the Lords sitting in panels rather than *en banc* is evident, personal interests and private attitudes to the functioning of the legal system show themselves, and the end result is a blunter and tougher law than might have been. All in all one cannot read these two cases together and not conclude the actual impact of law has as much to do with the appointed as the elected circles of the British political elite. But also that much depends on the happenstance of which Law Lords actually hear an appeal. One caution is necessary before continuing. The 1975 Act was passed in the middle of a period when the House of Lords was gaining a decidedly unenviable reputation for its interpretations of three Acts aimed at restricting racial discrimination, the Race Relations Acts 1965, 1968, and 1976, all, like the 1975 Sex Discrimination Act, passed by Labour Governments. In a series of cases in the mid-seventies the Court of Appeal and the House of Lords gave decisions which many felt emasculated the Acts and severely limited the powers of the supervisory bodies, the Race Relations Board and the Council for Race Relations, which they created.[11] It seems extremely probable that the Law Lords at the end of the eighties were determined not to seem to continue the restrictive behaviour of their earlier brethren. It should also be remembered that by the end of the eighties the Lords had become used to operating with an eye to sex discrimination legislation and legal decisions emanating from the European Communities. Against this background one can readily imagine a felt need to give an expansionist rather than a restrictivist reading to discrimination legislation.

These two closely related cases were heard by eight Lords of Appeal, with only two overlapping both cases. Lord Goff gave the only speech in the first case, *Birmingham City Council* v. *Equal Opportunities Commission*,[12] with Lords Keith, Roskill, Brandon, and Griffiths saying nothing at all. (Roskill and Brandon had both been on the panel which effectively put a stop to the restrictive interpretations of the race relations cases, and had reproved the Court of Appeal under Lord Denning for

---

[11] A good account of the cases and the legislation is given in J. A. G. Griffiths, *The Politics of the Judiciary*, London, Fontana (3rd edn.) 1985, pp 95–103.

[12] *Birmingham City Council* v. *Equal Opportunities Commission* [1989] 1 AC 1155.

their criticisms of the Council for Racial Equality, in 1982.[13]) Less than a year after *Birmingham* came *James* v. *Eastleigh Borough Council*[14] where Lord Griffiths now dissented, along with Lord Lowry, against a decision which turned on Lord Goff spelling out what he had actually meant in the earlier case. Eastleigh Council lost by a majority of three to two therefore, two of whom in the majority had not heard the earlier case. To make matters worse Lord Browne-Wilkinson heard the *Eastleigh* case in the Court of Appeal when he was still Vice-Chancellor, and his judgment makes it plain that had he been on either case in the Lords he could not have supported what turns out retrospectively to be the ratio (that is, the rule of law the case is said to stand for) in *Birmingham*. By 1991 Browne-Wilkinson was a Lord of Appeal in Ordinary. We shall quite often in later chapters use this method of demonstrating a lack of consensus in the Lords by pointing out clearly contradictory views held by men who were on the Court of Appeal when a case came up but were subsequently promoted to the Lords. The point is, *inter alia*, that the happenstance of who sits on an appeal panel is worsened by taking account of *when* a case comes up.

The stories of the two cases are thus. Birmingham City Council maintained a selective secondary school system with some single sex schools such that, as there were fewer places in selective schools for girls than for boys, girls had to gain a higher mark on the 11+ exam to gain a grammar school place than boys. Eastleigh Borough Council operated a concessionary scheme for its swimming baths which allowed those of 'pensionable age' free swimming sessions when the rest of the public had to pay. As men legally reach pensionable age at 65, and women at 60, men are disadvantaged by this concession. In both cases sexual discrimination was claimed though in neither case was it alleged that the council in question intentionally sought to advantage one sex over the other. In both cases the issue fought over was the applicability of section 1(a), although an easier case could probably be made out for 1(b). (This was suggested, certainly, by Browne-Wilkinson in *Eastleigh*.) The avoidance of 1(b) was probably because differential treatment there *may* be justified under 1(b)(ii), whereas *all* differential treatment to someone's detriment is discrimination if it can be brought under 1(a). The problem for the plaintiff in both cases was to establish that the lack of any intent to discriminate *per se* did not mean the defendent had not treated people differently as implied by the 'on the ground of her sex' phrase. Simply put, what does 'on the ground of' mean in legislation?

The way the argument was framed in the *Birmingham* case allowed Goff to dispose of the question very quickly. His depiction of the

---

[13] *Mandla* v. *Dowell Lee* [1983] 2 WLR 620.
[14] *James* v. *Eastleigh Borough Council* [1990] 2 AC 751.

defendant's argument was that 'less favourable treatment on the grounds of sex . . . involved establishing an intention or motive on the part of the council to discriminate against girls'.[15] In answering this Goff simply states abruptly that 'on the ground of sex' means 'if the relevant girl or girls would have received the same treatment as the boys *but for* their sex'. (Emphasis ours.) This phrase 'but for' came to be the test as part of a very robust sweeping away of any questions about the intentions of the discriminating actor, as shown by Goff's continuation here:

> The intention or motive of the defendant to discriminate . . . is not a necessary condition of liability; it is perfectly possible to envisage cases where the defendant had no such motive, and yet did in fact discriminate on the grounds of sex . . . if the council's submission were correct it would be a good defence for an employer to show that he discriminated against women not because he intended to do so but (for example) because of customer preference, or to save money, or even to avoid controversy. In the present case, whatever may have been the intention or motive of the council, nevertheless it is because of their sex that the girls in question receive less favourable treatment than the boys and so are the subject of discrimination.[16]

The argument, in the context of Birmingham City's manifest discrimination in educational provision, may have been all well and good, but because there were no further opinions, and because Goff's opinion is so notably not discursive, the implications of treating 'on the ground of', which clearly refers to the reasons for a discrimination as identical with 'but for', which is an external description of the effect of a classification, were never explored. As it happens the Court of Appeal's decision in the ensuing *Eastleigh* case was given before the reasoning in *Birmingham* was published, so they were not directly acting despite of the 'but for' test when they found that the Borough Council's concessionary fees policy in their leisure centres was lawful. Even had they read Goff's opinion, however, there would have been no reason to assume that the precedent really swept away all consideration of the reasons for differential treatment when it held that intention was not relevant. As Browne-Wilkinson argued, there would appear to be no need for the separate rule in 1(b) were 'but for' to be taken so sweepingly. The whole scheme of the Act does appear to have been to ban discrimination in two ways. The Act totally bans what has been called 'direct discrimination' where a gender classification is used under section 1(a). It further bans some forms of 'indirect discrimination' where non-gender classifications are very highly correlated with gender. Browne-Wilkinson's argument seems strong. To make every case where there is a causative link between sex

---

[15] *Birmingham* at 1193.
[16] *Birmingham* at 1194.

and different treatment an example of the 'but for' test is not what the Act is about:

This plainly was not the intention of Parliament which was drawing a clear distinction between, on the one hand, those cases where the defendant expressly or covertly acts by reference to the sex of the plaintiff and, on the other, those cases where the defendant acted on grounds not expressly or covertly related to sex but his actions have caused a disparate impact as between the sexes.[17]

The attack on this line was led by Lord Bridge in the Lords, who objects to construing 'on the grounds of' as referring subjectively to the alleged discriminator's 'reason' for doing the act complained of. This, he says, is directly contrary to the ruling in *Birmingham*:

Lord Goff's test, it will be observed, is not subjective but objective. Adopting it here the question becomes: 'Would the plaintiff, a man of 61, have received the same treatment as his wife but for his sex?' An affirmative answer is inescapable.

There is very little argument here as to why Goff's test, so bluntly stated in *Birmingham*, actually has this effect of removing reasons from consideration, because, according to Bridge, the two cases cannot be distinguished. Yet in fact they are very different. In the *Eastleigh* case pensionable age is being used as a measure of likely disposable wealth which happens to correlate (as indeed does disposable wealth) with sex, where the policy aim genuinely has nothing to do with sex. In *Birmingham* the whole policy is centered round a sexual difference in educational provision. Lord Goff, accepting that 'I expressed myself . . . I fear too tersely' in *Birmingham* expanded what he meant in correcting Browne-Wilkinson. But his new argument amounts to no more than asserting that 'on the grounds of sex' does not only refer to cases where there is an intention to discriminate, but all cases where 'a gender based criterion is the basis on which the complainant has been selected for the relevant treatment'.[18] Similarly he disposes of Browne-Wilkinson's structural argument that such an interpretation makes 1(b) otiose by assertion that 1(b) applies only to gender neutral classifications like height, and not to gender based classifications like pensionable age. The latter is an entirely plausible legislative policy, but not one that it can remotely be said is obvious, whereas 'on the grounds of' would, normally, seem to imply reasons, and not facts. Yet Goff does go on to expound on what one might call 'intention language' in a way which gives somewhat of a clue as to why he has been so adamant on this 'objective' mode of interpretation. The problem for Goff is that he dislikes all of what he calls 'subjective' language, a trait shown in other opinions of his like *R* v. *Maginnis*.[19] He insists that in a legal

[17] Quoted by Bridge, *Eastleigh* at 763.
[18] *Birmingham* at 772.
[19] *R* v. *Maginnis* [1987] 1 AC 303.

context if words such as intention or motive are to be used as a basis for decision, they require the most careful handling'. He goes on to explain the motivation for his interpretation:

For these reasons I am reluctant to have to conclude that those who are concerned with the day to day administration of legislation such as the Sex Discrimination Act 1975, who are mainly those who sit on industrial tribunals, should have to grapple with such elusive concepts as these.

Advocating his 'but for' test he stresses 'it avoids, in most cases at least, complicated questions relating to concepts such as intention, motive, reason or purpose and the danger of confusion arising from the misuse of those elusive terms'. This same sense of the terrible complexity of this legislation is given in Lord Ackner's curious short concurring opinion which starts 'in case it might be thought that your Lordship's decision involves such complex reasoning as not to be readily comprehensible to the senior citizens of Eastleigh, two of whom have generated this litigation, I add this short contribution'. More importantly, Ackner too insists that the men of Eastleigh were discriminated against 'on the ground of, i.e., because of, their sex'. It is of no avail for the council to insist that they were to be treated thus because, being still employed, they could expect to be better off. As long as 'on the grounds of' is equated to 'because of', section 1(a) must apply.

Despite the simplicity of Goff's approach, the fact is that 'on the grounds of' is not necessarily an apt phrase to express an objective test. Against this majority position others, including Browne-Wilkinson in the court below, deploy variously almost the entire armoury of interpretive weapons, as well, of course, as continually playing the judicial 'full stop' counter of 'I cannot believe that Parliament intended . . .'. Browne-Wilkinson's use of that move is quoted above. Griffiths shows what explicitly it is that Parliament cannot have intended:

The result of your Lordships' decision will be that either free facilities must be withdrawn from those who can ill afford to pay for them or, alternatively, given free to those who can well afford to pay for them. I consider both alternatives regrettable. I cannot believe that Parliament intended such a result and I do not believe that the words 'on the grounds of sex' compel such a result.[20]

Browne-Wilkinson, as was shown, used mainly a form of structural interpretation whereby a meaning is given to 1(a) partly on the grounds that otherwise another section, 1(b), is empty. Griffiths deploys another form of structural or analogical argument by pointing to the long established and common use of 'pensionable age' to carry out concessionary policies in other statutes. Lowry uses yet another form, the analysis of almost

---

[20] *Eastleigh* at 768.

identical words in a directly analogous anti-discrimination statute. Before that, though, he shows himself master of the classic, though increasingly little used, Grammatical and Linguistic method. The argument is too subtle to demonstrate without over extensive quotation, but the style can be represented by a couple of excerpts. Lowry begins by accepting counsel for the defendant's contention that a subjective interpretation involving the reasons for action is crucial:

[On] reading section 1(1)(a), it can be seen that the discriminator does something to the victim, that is he treats him in a certain fashion, to wit, less favourably than he treats or would treat a woman. And he treats him in that fashion on a certain *ground*, namely, *on the ground of his sex*. These words, it is scarcely necessary for me to point out, constitute an adverbial phrase modifying the transitive verb 'treats' in a clause of which the discriminator is the subject and the victim is the object. While anxious not to weary your Lordships with a grammatical excursus, the point I wish to make is that the *ground* on which the alleged discriminator treats the victim less favourably is inescapably linked to the subject and the verb; it is the reason which has caused him to act. [Stress in the original.][21]

Lowry goes on to approve counsel's citation from the *Oxford English Dictionary* making 'ground' a reason or motive, and points out that opposing counsel 'conceded that in ordinary speech to ask on what grounds a particular decision is taken invites consideration of the mental processes of the decision maker'. The words, for Lowry, then, introduce a subjective element and 'pose the question "was the sex of the appellant a consideration in the council's decision?"' Putting it this way around is to ask the question in such a way that the council can seem innocent, because it invites the answer: 'No, the person's income was the consideration.' In the *Birmingham* case, which Lowry has no desire to invalidate, the answer would have had to be: 'Yes, the girls' sex was the consideration, because the council was allocating places to single sex schools.' Lowry hammers the point home:

Putting it another way, a 'ground' is a reason, in ordinary speech, for which a person takes a certain course. He knows what he is doing and why he has decided to do it. In the context of section 1(1)(a) the discriminator knows that he is treating the victim less favourably and he also knows the ground on which he is doing so. In no case are the discriminator's thought processes immaterial.

After a detailed consideration of his own interpretation of a similar phrase in the Fair Employment (Northern Ireland) Act 1976 which allows for reasons to be counted in, thus buttressing his argument analogically, Lowry sums up the ordinary language attack on the majority's interpretation. It does indeed have the virtue of simplicity and avoids consideration

---

[21] *Eastleigh* at 775

of 'such protean and slippery concepts as intention, purpose, motive, desire, animus, prejudice, malice and reason':

The basic difficulty of this approach, I consider, is that one has to disregard or distort the phrase . . . in order to make it work. Counsel argued that the subjective meaning construction 'artificially confines the meaning of "ground" '. I must disagree: the subjective construction uses 'ground' in its natural meaning. The phrase 'on the ground of' does not mean 'by reason of'; moreover, 'ground' must certainly not be confused with 'intention'. [Counsel] rightly submits that the policy of the Act is to discourage discrimination . . . but the Act pursues that policy by means of the words which Parliament has used. . . . the phrase . . . does not, as alleged, constitute an exception to the policy and therefore does not fall to be narrowly construed. The words in question constitute an *ingredient* of unlawful discrimination. [Emphasis mine.][22]

Lowry is here invoking part of the plain meaning rule which allows strained construction in order to achieve the purpose of the Act by the reminder that purposes can only be achieved by statutory words, and claiming to show the purpose is compatible with the unstrained meaning:

It can thus be seen that the causative construction not only gets rid of unessential and often irrelevant mental ingredients . . . but also dispenses with an essential ingredient, namely the ground on which the discriminator acts. The appellant's construction . . . reduces to insignificance the words 'on the grounds of'. Thus the causative test is too wide and is grammatically unsound.[23]

The arguments go on with increasing complexity. Yet what is striking about the case is that no argument convinces the opposition, and, above all, that the arguments do not really meet. In a seminar it would be easy to show what was happening. First, the majority insist that a distinction— pensionable age—which is itself based on another distinction—gender— is banned. To do this they have to remove the argument that the reasons, whatever they may be, for making women retire earlier than men have nothing to do with the reasons for the discrimination, which have to do instead with a consequence of retirement. They do this by (intentionally?) equating motive with reason, because it is accepted that a good motive does not legitimize discrimination. But a seminar involves actually face to face discussion, and is not satisfactorily ended without some conclusion. The conclusion may be a meeting of minds, or an overt recognition of irreconcilable value differences. Because there is no need to reach an agreement the former does not happen in a law case, and because the judges are not supposed to bring their values with them, the latter cannot be stated. The main point in discussing at length this example, apart from displaying the battery of techniques, is to demonstrate just this—judicial

---

[22] *Eastleigh* at 778.
[23] *Eastleigh* at 780.

argument does not in fact resolve problems. Suppose Lowry had joined Goff and Griffiths in the *Birmingham* case. All three believed that Birmingham was discriminating. That case could not then have been resolved as it was. No one would have dissented, because they all agreed on the result. Thus at most there might have been two statements of why Birmingham lost, one of which, authored by Goff and, conceivably joined by Brandon and Roskill might have continued to use the 'but for' test. Another, by Lowry and Griffiths, would have admitted the relevance of reasons. The case would not then have been a precedent when *Eastleigh* came up, and the united Court of Appeal which wanted 'on the grounds of' to have some part to play in the Act would probably have been upheld. Indeed Mr James would probably not have been granted leave to appeal, because, absent the precedent in *Birmingham*, there would not obviously have been a major issue. It is in this way that judicial preferences or ideologies seep into the law, even when their activity is apparently only that of interpreting another's words.

II. Simple Phrases and Single Words

Interpretation is not, despite many assumptions to the contrary, always necessitated by any unclarity in language at all. In 1993 there was one case, *Knowles* v. *Liverpool City Council*, which comes as close to the paradigm of simple interpretation as any case could which made it as far as the Lords. Mr Knowles, a labourer for Liverpool City Council, injured his finger when a flagstone he was manhandling broke. The flagstone broke because of a defect in its manufacture. The *Employers' Liability (Defective Equipment) Act 1969*, section 1(1), provides that the employer shall be liable for injury caused by defective 'equipment', even when the defect is actually the fault of a third party, in this case the makers of the flagstone. The council appealed against the verdict in the County Court, first to the Court of Appeal, and then to the House of Lords. They claimed that the flagstone was not equipment, because 'equipment' meant such things as tools and machinery, and not 'stock in trade'. Who is right? The case does matter, not because the effect on any individual is great, but because of the huge number of similar claims thrown up each year. As lawyers say, the world is full of 'trippers'—the accident prone. In this situation the Lords have a chance to fine-tune the industrial injuries climate—to make the UK a more or a less caring society, to tilt the balance one way or another in the endless apportionment of economic costs. In another context it is the sort of matter dealt with, to the political fury of those with a strong sense of populist democracy, by Directives from the European Union. If it is politically pertinent whether or not unelected officials in Brussels decide such matters, it is politically pertinent whether or not unelected judges do so.

Counsel cited precedents, inevitably. They tended only to show that 'equipment' could apply to large-scale plant, a direction away from its being taken to mean material. One, for example, showed that the Lords had treated 'equipment' to include an entire large ship!

There are two broad techniques that can be applied here, according to the tradition of statutory interpretation. Some would favour what has come to be known as the 'plain meaning' rule. Others would prefer a 'purposive' interpretation. This roughly equates to the 'strict' versus 'liberal' construction debate in America. There are quite clear parallels inasmuch as their Lordships do vary amongst themselves according to their general predilection, as do Justices of the US Supreme Court. Though, as argued in the last section of this chapter, Law Lords tend to prefer ideological consistency, over time, to technical consistency. A strict construction, the use of the plain meaning rule, assumes that Parliament can be expected to use language much as any ordinary citizen, and the words of a statute should be given their normal meaning, unless this would produce an obvious absurdity. Further help may be gained from the text of other parts of the statute, or indeed of other statutes. A purposive interpretation takes the actual text as a general guide, to be fleshed out by the actual purpose of the statute, so a meaning is given that will best further the policy aims of the Act. In general British courts have shifted firmly towards the purposive definition school over the last two decades though there are still plenty of occasions when a judge will find the meaning quite plain, in order to give a restrictive reading to an Act.

In *Knowles* there is an open acknowledgement that a purposive strategy is being used, when in the leading opinion Lord Jauncey points out:

[T]here can be no logical reason why Parliament, having recognised the difficulties facing workmen, as demonstrated by *Davie and New Merton Board Mills Ltd.*,[24] should have removed those difficulties in part rather than in whole. [*Knowles*, at page 327.]

But what makes a restrictive, plain meaning interpretation almost impossible in *Knowles* is that the Lords knew, they had it pointed out by counsel, why the 1969 Act was passed. The 1969 Parliament (a Labour controlled Parliament let it be remembered) passed the Act specially to change the law as it had been determined by the Lords in the 1959 case cited above, *Davie* v. *New Merton Board Mills*. In that case the Lords had made a common law ruling specifically that an employer was not liable if a tool he had provided for a workman was defective, provided he had, in good faith, purchased it from a reputable supplier. Faced with an Act which was itself a reaction to a restrictive legal interpretation, and with no constraining precedents, the result was one a court perhaps predisposed

---

[24] *Davie* v. *New Merton Board Mills Ltd.* [1959] 1 All ER 346.

towards a particular vision of industrial justice could easily arrive at. But that result was not preordained. A different court could, for example, have made the following argument:

Davie laid out the usual common law duty of employers. This can sometimes leave employees in an unfortunate situation. Recognising this, Parliament has imposed additional duties, making the employer responsible for defects which are the suppliers fault, and which the employer can do nothing about. We should not take it upon ourselves to widen this imposition further than Parliament intended. The normal meaning of the word 'equipment' does not cover raw material, nothing else in the Act suggests such a wide meaning, and no other court has ever felt it necessary to give such a meaning to the word.

Many a set of Law Lords in the past would have given this ruling, which is not logically different in form from the one that Jauncey does give. (One Law Lord who did not sit on *Knowles,* and thought the decision wrong, indicated in an interview that he would have approved of precisely our constructed argument had it been presented to him.) It is very similar to an argument that counsel for Liverpool did address to the Lords—which was that the case that caused the Act to be passed had most definitely involved a tool, and therefore the Act could best be seen as dealing specifically and only with faulty tools. Certainly there are analogous cases with quite different outcomes to the interpretation decided by earlier courts. A generation before, in the 1964 case of *Sparrow* v. *Fairey Aviation,*[25] the 1937 Factories Act was treated to a particularly narrow and literal interpretation in a rather similar situation. Section 14(1) of the Factories Act requires 'any dangerous part of any machinery shall be securely fenced'. Sparrow was working on a lathe. He had to use a metal scraper to clean off a metal burr from the disk he was smoothing. The scraper slipped against the unfenced jaws of the lathe, smashing his hand onto another part of the machine, damaging his little finger so badly it had to be amputated. However, the actual part of the machine his hand struck was not, itself, dangerous. The Lords held, with one dissent, that the Act only required that machinery be fenced to prevent a worker's body hitting a dangerous part, not a tool he was holding. There was a line of precedents holding in this way from at least 1946. In fairness to the Lords it must be said that they had not yet, in 1964, given themselves permission to over-rule previous cases. But had they wished to the precedents could easily have been distinguished. If a restriction on the direct duty of an employer such as this was an adequate interpretation of the Factories Act, why should an indirect duty of an employer be interpreted so widely thirty year later? The lead opinion then was given by Lord Reid, a legal giant of his generation, and the rest of the majority were perfectly distinguished

---

[25] *Sparrow* v. *Fairey Aviation Co. Ltd.* [1964] AC 1019.

judges. In fact, Lord Reid had also given the leading opinion in *Sparrow*. There is no obvious way of choosing between the two rulings, except a substantive one. Nowadays the two rulings by Reid would be ideologically improper. But the legal methodology has not changed.

It is useful to compare *Knowles* with a formally very similar case which also turns on the interpretation of just one word, the 1994 tax case of *National Westminster Bank plc* v. *Inland Revenue Commissioners*.[26] This case depends entirely on the definition of the word 'issue'. NatWest was involved in a tax reduction scheme which involved lending money, at an advantageous rate, to people who used it to buy shares in a special tax exempt investment scheme. The law was changed on 16 March 1993, disallowing the tax exemption for anyone who had taken a loan to finance such investment. (The point was to ensure that only genuine individual investors benefited from what was meant to be a special incentive for business expansion, while under the NatWest scheme the bulk of the benefit went to the bank.) In this case investors had applied for, and been allotted the shares, and so notified before 16 March, but they were not actually registered until 2 April. All the help the Act gives is the plain words:

An individual shall not be entitled to relief in respect of any shares in a company issued on or after 16th March 1993 . . .[27]

But nowhere does the Act define what it is for a share to be issued, though the concept is crucial at several stages. It was agreed by all concerned that English law distinguishes between the allotment of shares by the directors of a company, and their being fully issued. It was further agreed that 'issue' in this sense is not a technical legal term, not a 'term of art', and must be given a 'mercantile meaning'. How were their Lordships to decide the question? It might be more honest here to ask rather, how were they to justify their answer? The temptation to see the division of opinion (Lords Templeman, Slynn, and Lloyd for the Revenue, Lords Jauncey and Woolf for the bank) as really motivated by attitudes to tax avoidance in general is very strong. The nine judges who heard the case at various stages split 5:4 in favour of the Revenue. Two completely different approaches were taken. The majority followed Templeman's technique, which was purely precedential. A number of cases, going back to an 1867 Chancery Division case interpreting the 1867 Companies Act,[28] and including a 1949 precedent from the High Court of Australia[29] were shown to have one thing in common. They all demonstrate that 'issuing' is

[26] *National Westminster Bank plc* v. *Inland Revenue Commissioners* [1994] 3 All ER 1.
[27] S. 111, Finance Act 1993, amending s. 299A Income and Corporation Taxes Act 1988.
[28] *Re Ambrose Lake Tin and Copper Co. (Clarke's Case)* (1878) 8 Ch. D 635.
[29] *Central Piggery Co. Ltd.* v. *McNicoll* (1949) 78 CLR 594.

a complex process of allotment, notification, paying, acceptance, all finalized by registration. Therefore the only single date that can be affixed to the idea of an issue is the registration. Furthermore, as Lloyd says as well as Templeman, if Parliament had wanted any other date, such as allotment, they could have said so. So the bank loses. The opposition dispensed with all initial reliance on precedent:

Whatever else may be said about the previous authorities, they are certainly not conclusive. They could not be so because they deal with different statutory contexts and it is not in dispute that context can effect the meaning. [Woolf, at page 22.]

Though it must be noted that, for safety's sake, both Jauncey and Woolf go through each of the cases cited by Templeman showing how they can be differently interpreted. Which interpretations of the cases is correct is beside the point, because Woolf and Jauncey have no intention of accepting their relevance.

The minority cannot replace precedent with an 'intent of Parliament' argument because the only clear thing is Parliament's lack of forethought in never providing a definition. Instead they rely on an essentially purposive interpretation. What is the whole thing about? Providing funds for new companies which would not attract investment without the tax deal. When is this aim achieved? When the shares have been paid for and allocated. The rest of the process is a mere formality that no one has any real interest in. Given that a precedential approach is being abandoned, some stress on 'ordinary language' is needed as well:

It seems to me that as a matter of language it is not only legalistic but artificial to import into the issue of shares a requirement of registration. You would expect a person to whom shares have been issued to be a holder of those shares but not necessarily a member of a company.

Furthermore:

All that can be said is that if the legislator had intended that the registration of the holder of shares was essential for their issue, it is surprising that this was not made clear.

Quite the opposite expectation was shared, of course, by Templeman and Lloyd. Finally Woolf makes an appeal to principle, thus incorporating two of the three sources of decision—precedent, statutory meaning, and general legal principle. It is a double principle, appealing both to basic fairness and to the need for self-restraint by courts, both of which we shall meet over and again:

I conclude with what I regard as being a general point which is not without importance. The dispute here is as to steps which have to be taken by the deadline if the taxpayer is to avoid losing an existing tax relief. If Parliament has not made it clear that any particular step has to be taken before that deadline the courts should be slow to require that step to be taken, in order to avoid unfairness.[30]

III. Interpretation and Statutory Rights

In the cases above one can see how different methodologies produce different interpretations, even if one might be tempted to think the causation is the other way around. The next example of the methodology of statutory interpretation comes from the area we have described as involving the Lords as fine tuners of the welfare state. *Mallinson v. Secretary of State for Social Security*[31] is very much a situation where the 'restrictive' versus 'liberal' conception of interpretation applies—a liberal reading of the statute may significantly extend the coverage of a social security benefit, a restrictive one will not. The Social Security Act 1976 provides in section 35(1)(a):

A person shall be entitled to an attendance allowance if he satisfies prescribed conditions as to residence or presence in Great Britain and either—(a) he is so severely disabled physically or mentally that, by day, he requires from another person either—(i) frequent attention throughout the day in connection with his bodily functions, or (ii) continual supervision throughout the day in order to avoid substantial danger to himself or others . . .

Mr Mallinson is blind, and he requires help with certain activities—cutting up food, getting in and out of the bath, making drinks and dealing with hot liquids, and walking in unfamiliar situations. He hoped to qualify for an attendance allowance primarily because of his need for assistance walking out of doors. In order to qualify he needed to establish two things. First, that the assistance counted as 'attention', not 'supervision', and secondly, that the help was 'in connection with a bodily function'.

The process for making a claim under this section, and having it adjudicated when denied is complex. The appeal got to the courts, after several medical examinations, on a point of law only. The legal point is the claim that the Social Security Commissioner erred in law in holding that the assistance required by the appellant while walking out of doors in unfamiliar surroundings was not 'attention . . . in connection with his bodily functions' for the purpose of section 35(1)(a)(i). This claim was dismissed by the Court of Appeal. The majority argued either (1) that though walking is a bodily function, Mr Mallinson could walk without assistance, and walking in unfamiliar circumstances is not a separate bodily function, however much he might like getting out of his flat, or (2) attendance in

---

[30] Woolf, *NatWest* at 25.
[31] *Mallinson v. Secretary of State for Social Security* [1994] 2 All ER 295.

order to enjoy the practical enjoyment of an unimpaired bodily function is not a required attendance in connection with that bodily function. Nolan LJ dissented (he had become a Law Lord by the time the case came to the House, but naturally was not on the committee that heard the appeal), disagreeing with the whole conceptualization. For Nolan, Mr Mallinson suffered from 'a physical disorder of mobility' because he could not see to walk. Yet another way of conceptualizing the problem, in order to bring Mallinson's situation under the Act, was to argue that the attention was required in connection with his bodily function of seeing. The majority of the Court of Appeal dealt with that claim by the saying that as he could not see, he could not require or receive attention with seeing.

The House of Lords overturned the Court of Appeal by a majority of three to two. Precedents did not much matter in either of the approaches taken because they serve only to define the sort of things covered by bodily functions, and are cited with approval by both sides. There is, however, a stress in the only House of Lords opinion cited,[32] on reaching an answer which will be practicable in running the welfare services, to which Lloyd's minority opinion attaches much importance. Even a purposive approach can do little, because no one is proposing not to grant help to the disabled in carrying out a bodily function. Nor is the Act, in itself, intended to deal with the variety of problems the blind face, so one cannot argue for a purposive interpretation on the grounds of a general conception of blindness as a special human condition. The problem really does arise because of conceptual difficulties. The only way this case could be handled was by fine linguistic analysis, so that both majority and minority are, more or less, applying the same methodology.

Lloyd's more restrictive view is easier to argue, as is so often the case. In fact he both narrows and widens the definition of the problem, first by refusing to discuss blindness, and then by attaching much importance to the administrative convenience of his suggested decision. Lloyd accepts the Appeal Court's insistence that the case is all about walking, noting of Mallinson's counsel:

> Mr Drabble a most experienced advocate in this field, was accepting that the relevant bodily function is walking. Nowhere in the printed case is it suggested that the relevant bodily function is seeing, or a combination of the two bodily functions of seeing and walking.

It is a common tactical move to refuse to discuss a line of argument on the ground that it was not fully argued, or not relied on by counsel—it all goes to the way counsel's arguments and ability can be used, though not necessarily as they would wish, to bolster judicial argument. It is very much a matter of choice, however, whether to do this or not. A path

---

[32] Lord Bridge in *Woodling* v. *Secretary of State for Social Services* [1984] 1 All ER 593.

breaking majority decision in 1994 relied in part on Lord Goff's somewhat unwillingly joining the majority. *Spring* v. *Guardian Assurance plc*[33] established, for the first time, what was thought not to be the case, that the writer of a reference could be liable for negligence if he carelessly wrote an inaccurate reference that cost the subject a job. He felt unable to accede to the main majority argument presented by Lord Woolf, which was straight on the merits of the arguments relied on by counsel. Instead he developed an entire argument of his own, relying on quite different precedents, so much so that he actually begins by saying that he would normally have sent the case back for further argument on his points, had he not known that a majority would decide it, for different reasons, the way he felt it should go. This case is discussed further in Chapter 4.

In Mallinson's case Lloyd did take this route out of dealing with an argument, though he bolstered it by a typical piece of linguistic analysis. Admitting that Mr Mallinson is blind, Lloyd stresses that the Act requires 'attention in connection with some bodily function', and asks 'Is seeing then a bodily function?' Referring to a test approved in an earlier decision, he points out the Act is thought to refer to 'functions which a fit man normally performs for himself', and goes on:

... but whereas eating drinking walking and washing, to take a few examples, are all bodily functions which a fit man *performs* for himself, it would not be a normal use of language to say that seeing is a function which a fit man *performs* ... If you were to ask a blind man's guide what his purpose was he would reply 'I am helping him to walk because he cannot see'; he would not say 'I am helping him see to walk'. [Emphases by Lord Lloyd.]

The final blow against Mr Mallinson, for Lloyd, is the impracticability of any test that would let a medical examiner decide that his need for help walking counted. Several times he points out obiter in previous decisions by Lord Bridge in one case and Lord Denning and Lord Justice Dunn in another 'all stressed the need for a test which can be easily and uniformly applied'. And again, 'As Dunn LJ and O'Connor LJ both said in Packer's case, the line has got to be drawn somewhere.' So in Mallinson's case:

The same applies to 'walking in unfamiliar surroundings'. It is much too vague and imprecise to count as a separate bodily function. It would mean that the examining medical officer would have to inquire how often the disabled person needed to walk in unfamiliar surroundings, and for what purpose. Fine distinctions would spring up between one case and another, and the delegated medical practitioner's task would never be done.

Clearly these are persuasive arguments—what sort of technique, other than a one on one rebuttal of the points made, could the majority use to

---

[33] *Spring* v. *Guardian Assurance plc* [1994] 3 All ER 129.

give a liberal interpretation of the Act? Lord Woolf had the job to do, because the other opinion in the majority was by Lord Templeman, who frequently offers short supporting arguments going entirely to the substantive merits. His contribution is interesting as an example of a methodology based on ignoring legal argument. The actual task for the medical examiner is to aggregate the various ways in which a claimant needs help, to see if it amounts to 'frequent attention throughout the day in connection with his bodily functions', a fact largely ignored by others. What Templeman does is to use this to make the analysis of his walking problems seem rather trivial. Mallinson needs help in eating, by cutting up his food, in bathing by help in getting in and out, with walking in the form of guide and help when outdoors. Thus:

true it is that Mr Mallinson can walk within the confines of his flat without attention but this facility is only a factor which the adjudication officer will bear in mind in deciding whether the aggregate attention required . . . amount to 'frequent attention throughout the day'.

It is as though for everyone else the picture is that 'Mr Mallinson can walk perfectly well but . . .' whereas for Templeman the picture is 'Mr Mallinson can only manage to walk when . . .'.

However, law is not, predominantly, made by Templeman's methodology, and Lord Woolf must mount a convincing counter-attack. What methodological tools are available for a construction which will expand social welfare? Lord Woolf's first move is to show how important the decision is going to be by pointing out that it will affect people entitled to allowances for providing the sort of attention Mr Mallinson needs, as well as to the disabled themselves. Clearly the only successful interpretation will be one which refers to Mr Mallinson's 'bodily function of seeing', and Woolf immediately says that he thinks the approach which rejects this line 'out of hand' is wrong. Instead of arguing that he cannot be helped in seeing because he is blind, Woolf asserts 'the only help that can be given to a person 'in connection with' a sight handicap is to provide the assistance to enable that person to do what he could physically do for himself if he had sight'.

The technique Woolf goes on to argue is a common one in legal argument—to appear to reduce the opposition view to a *reductio ad absurdum*. There is no substitute for quoting extensively to show the method of argument. The steps go like this:

If, for example, a person with a sight handicap receives correspondence, someone has to read their contents to him if he cannot read them for himself. That I would regard as being the active personal assistance which constitutes the attention which a normal person does not require which the subsection demands. It would be inconceivable that Parliament intended that in those circumstances, a partially sighted person should qualify for an allowance but in the same circumstances a totally blind person should not qualify.... while a one-legged man who was supported when walking or standing if he received assistance from someone else would be receiving attention, the person who had lost the use of both his legs and was therefore pushed in a wheelchair rather than supported would not be receiving attention in respect of his bodily function of walking because he was incapable of performing the function of walking. Such a result is obvious nonsense and does not cease to be nonsense because there is a different allowance which can be payable for lack of mobility.

This apparently provides the conclusion Woolf needs:

The fact that your disability is so severe that you are incapable of exercising a bodily function does not mean that the attention you receive is not in connection with the bodily function if it provides a substitute method of providing what the bodily function would provide if it were not totally or partially impaired.

In fact the conclusion is exactly what the majority of judicial opinion, two in the Court of Appeal and two in the Lords (plus the Social Security Commissioner) deny. The rhetorical work is done by the development of the apparent absurdities—help for the partially sighted but not the blind, and for the one legged not the man with no legs. There is no substance here. The Act does not provide help of this sort for the partially blind, and the situation of the man with no legs is provided for by mobility allowance and would not be covered by the section of the Act in question. But the technique of drawing a line out to conclusions of obvious absurdity, which allows the judge to insist that Parliament never intends absurdities is a vital weapon in statutory construction. The absurdity here is strengthened, according to Woolf, by yet another reference to whom else may suffer:

Thus reading to or guiding of a man with a sight defect remains attention in connection with bodily functions even if it replaces a total rather than a partial incapacity. If the position were otherwise, this would disqualify not only the person receiving the attention from receiving the care allowance ... but also the person providing the attention from receiving invalid care allowance.

The statement may seem pointless, as it is obviously true that if someone does not qualify for attention, no one can qualify for payment for giving that attention. But it has the effect of demonstrating how narrow the minority interpretation is. The final step is to deal with the administrative convenience argument that Lloyd deployed. This is just denied by a factual assertion:

For a doctor having to answer such questions should not be an over-demanding task. While there are always going to be a minority of cases where it is difficult for him to decide on which side of the line a case falls, in the majority of cases the answer will be straightforward and a result should be achieved without creating any sense of justified grievance between one claimant and another.

In fact both Lloyd and Woolf operate by assuming factual situations they cannot know—but Lloyd is on safer ground because he only needs to point out that a complex test inevitably provides greater chances for inequity, whereas Woolf has to quantify the risks. In apparently being highly critical of Woolf's arguments we have not intended to take sides, or suggest that the minority's position is in some sense 'correct'. We have intended rather to show the way in which liberal, they might better be called 'extensive', interpretations are likely to have to fall back on very different, and often logically less tidy, techniques. Reliance on precedent is almost never going to be easy, because law develops in a ratchet-like way—once rights have been granted, they are hard to take away, so the case would not even come up if there were liberal precedents. Close textual analysis, on the other hand, is likely to produce restrictive inter- pretations because the parliamentary draughtsman will be careful not accidentally to give more welfare rights or whatever than the civil serv- ants wished. It simply is true that law, in its statute form, is inherently conservative—the mere stipulation of a right is a limiting exercise by logical form. If Parliament, having debated the issue, decides that the infirm can have X and Y, it has clearly decided that they cannot have A, B, and C. Consequently either one goes very much by the substantive merits, as with Templeman, or one has to find some way of making the narrow interpretation seem just too grudging. Actually destroying it will never be easy.

Just how resistant statutes can be to generous interpretation where there is no desire to make them generous is well demonstrated by *Bradley v. Eagle Star Insurance Company*[34] in which Lord Templeman battled unsuc- cessfully against his brethren to give a more generous reading to a statute. The reason for picking this case is that there is good reason to think his brethren were being over restrictive.

Mrs Bradley had worked in a cotton mill on and off from 1933 to 1970 in which year she was certified by the Pneumoconiosis Medical Panel to be suffering from byssinosis. Byssinosis is a respiratory disease caused by the inhalation of cotton dust, and it was generally accepted that this gave her a prima facie case for some form of compensation from the firm she had worked for, Dart Mill Ltd. Unfortunately for Mrs Bradley Dart Mill had been wound up in 1976, and Mrs Bradley did not seek to start proceedings until 1984, long after the period during which a liquidated company can be revived, under the Companies Act, to face legal proceed- ings. However, during the whole time Mrs Bradley worked for Dart Mill

[34] *Bradley v. Eagle Star Insurance Co. Ltd.* [1989] 1 AC 957.

the company had an insurance policy with Eagle Star Insurance to cover liability for personal injuries to its employees. Eagle Star was very much still in business, and had profited from Dart Mill's premiums. Had Dart Mill still existed Mrs Bradley would either have won damages from the company in a court action, or come to an out-of-court settlement. Dart Mill would have passed on the cost of her compensation to Eagle Star. Why then did it matter that Dart Mill no longer existed? Parliament would appear to have taken notice of just this problem. Not recently, either, because the relevant statute is the Third Parties (Rights against Insurers) Act 1930, an Act passed during the second Labour Government of British history. Section 1(1) of that Act states:

Where under any contract of insurance a person . . . is insured against liabilities to third parties which he may incur then—(b) in the case of the insured being a company, in the case of a winding-up order being made, or a resolution for a voluntary winding-up being passed, with respect to the company . . . if, either before or after that event, any such liability as aforesaid is incurred by the insured, his rights against the insurer under the contract in respect of the liability shall, *notwithstanding anything in any Act or rule of law to the contrary*, be transferred to and vest in the third party to whom the liability was incurred. [Our emphasis.]

We have no way of knowing how many similar cases have been settled by agreement between insurers and third parties, or dealt with by unreported trials at first instance. Unfortunately for Mrs Bradley one roughly similar problem did lead to litigation, and was ultimately resolved in the Court of Appeal in 1967. The ruling in this case, *Post Office* v. *Norwich Union*[35] was binding on the Court of Appeal in Bradley's case, though not, of course, on the House of Lords which could have overruled it. In this earlier case two members out of the Court of Appeal (Lord Denning MR and Salmon LJ) gave an interpretation to the 1930 Act that wiped out its protection for people in Mrs Bradley's position. They accepted that all rights that the insured company would have had against the insurers passed to the third party, but essentially claimed that there were no rights in this situation. The insured company had no right to reimbursement until it had legally become obliged to pay one of its workers, either after losing a case in court or settling out of court. Because Dart Mill died irretrievably before becoming thus legally obliged, it could have no rights against Eagle Star, and there was therefore no claim to be passed on to Mrs Bradley. Salmon LJ in the *Post Office* case was very clear on this point:

It is quite unheard of in practice for any assured to sue his insurers in a money claim when the actual loss against which he wishes to be indemnified has not been ascertained. I have never heard of such an action and there is nothing in law that makes such an action possible.[36]

---

[35] *Post Office* v. *Norwich Union Fire Insurance Society Ltd.* [1967] 1 All ER 577, CA.
[36] *Post Office* at 377-8.

The House could easily have distinguished *Post Office* v. *Norwich Union*, the facts being rather different, or have overruled it. It chose instead to uphold it, thus finalizing the disembowelment of the Act. Because the Act now can only protect people in a very restricted way. If, and only if, an insured company goes bankrupt after accepting liability but before actually paying out will the injured worker be able to claim against the insurers. This is an extraordinarily restrictive interpretation of the Act, and one which clearly rests on a preference for procedural tidiness over substantive justice. Lord Brandon, writing for the majority in *Bradley*, openly admits that the result is a victory for procedure over justice:

> The complaint may be made, and has been forcefully made on behalf of the appellant in this appeal, that the decision reached by the Court of Appeal, with which it is apparent that I fully agree, depends really on procedural technicalities and produces a result which is unfair to the appellant and gives an unmerited bonus to the respondents.[37]

But, at least as the concept is used here, a preference for procedure is in itself no less ideological than, say, a predisposition to find for insurance companies. If there are judicial ideologies, they will indeed be *judicial* ideologies. Templeman's argument is simple. Had Dart Mill still existed, and had it been sued by Mrs Bradley, Eagle Star would in fact have fought the case in Dart Mill's name. There was no practical difficulty at all, therefore, in allowing her at this stage directly to sue Eagle Star, simply removing what would have been the quite artificial presence of Dart Mill's name on the court reports. After all, had Dart Mill been less than two years dead, it could have been forcibly legally resurrected to fight the case, but, as Templeman point out:

> To restore the Dart Mill company in these circumstances would do no more than authorise Mrs Bradley to make use of a name carved on a tombstone. The use of the name could not restore life to the skeleton.[38]

The four Law Lords in the majority clearly preferred procedural tidiness, but, of course, this in itself is not an argument against what might seem to be the whole point of the Act. Again, in Templeman's words:

> The Act of 1930 was intended to protect a person who suffers an insured loss at the hands of a company that goes into liquidation. That protection was afforded by transferring the benefits of the insurance policy from the company to the injured person. In my opinion, Parliament cannot have intended that the protection afforded against a company in liquidation should cease as soon as the company in liquidation reaches its predestined and inevitable determination in the dissolution of the company.

[37] *Bradley* v. *Eagle Star* at 967.
[38] *Bradley* v. *Eagle Star* at 970.

Brandon has to show that it is most probable that Parliament intended just that. Two characteristic tools are used. First, the history of the Act, by way of Brandon's own explanation of what it was that was concerning Parliament at the time. It happens that Parliament had been concerned by two recent cases in which similar obligations had arisen against companies undergoing bankruptcy. The receivers had grabbed the moneys paid to the companies and put them to the general purpose of paying off the companies' debts rather than passing them on to the claimants. To remedy this Parliament had passed section 1(2) of the Act. Brandon cites section 1(2) of the Act, but argues that as Parliament did provide for debts in bankruptcy but said nothing about Mrs Bradley's type of case, they obviously did not mean to cover it. The idea is a basic one in interpretation— that there is an assumption that Parliament does not mean to do legally unorthodox things unless it makes it very plain indeed that it does. It is legally unorthodox to allow Mrs Bradley to press her claim. Parliament made it clear in section 1(2) that it was intending to do something unorthodox. Therefore if it had meant to allow Mrs Bradley her unorthodoxy, it would also have said so. The consequence is to suggest section 1(1), the relevant section, actually had no purpose whatsoever. Templeman is obviously right, but he has no ammunition. Brandon, in contrast has two weapons—a 'principled' assumption of expectations about how parliaments behave, and the further fact that in one part of the Act they made clear that they were not behaving as expected.

The actual language of section 1(1) *'notwithstanding anything in any Act or rule of law to the contrary'* (our emphasis), though emotionally powerful, and the fact that it was a Labour Government that passed the Act at a time of considerable industrial tension, count for nothing against this technical weaponry. We have chosen this case to demonstrate the use of a restrictive form of parliamentary intent argument as judicial strategy for a special reason. Very unusually, the decision in the case was reversed by legislation. A committee of the Commons was persuaded to put an amendment in a piece of legislation going through the House at the time, and furthermore to make it retrospective. Lord Templeman gave one of the main speeches in the Lords defending the Bill against the concerns some Peers had about its retrospectivity. If a Conservative dominated Parliament in 1993 favoured a more liberal reading of the old Act than had been intended by a Labour controlled Parliament in 1930 it would be very strange indeed. Of course it can be objected that since the decision in *Pepper* v. *Hart*, parliamentary intent will no longer be such a powerful interpretative technique. The full effect of the decision in *Pepper* remains to be experienced, and the entire issue is discussed in Chapter 5. But *Pepper* will not entirely, and may actually very little, replace this form of argument where an intent is deduced by combining details of one part of an Act with general 'principles', like the preference for procedure. Certainly the ability to look at debates and 'travaux préparatoires' in continental jurisdictions has not removed the problem.[39]

IV. *Methodological versus Substantive Consistency*

It should not be thought that there is, in the UK, any natural coincidence between a preference for restrictive interpretation and an unwillingness to restrict traditional property rights or otherwise to exhibit a conservative ideology, just because we have all become used to such an equation in American jurisprudence. English legal technique requires far more sub-tlety. The same judges can often only maintain ideological consistency over different cases precisely by switching backwards and forwards between restrictive and expansive interpretation.[40] At the same time the very question of what constitutes a restrictive or a literal interpretation can be extremely unclear. It is useful to consider a few cases where it is fairly obvious that a sheer political preference exists. Such an assumption is usually dangerous because Law Lords naturally deny overt political preferences. There are only a few exceptions to this in recent legal history, involving Lords who cannot plausibly deny a political stance. Lord Dilhorne who sat as a Law Lord from 1969 to 1979 is one such exception. As a former Conservative MP, and both Attorney-General and Lord Chancellor in Conservative administrations, it is fair to assume that he came to public law cases with an ideological predisposition. Two divided cases of his from the mid-seventies, one where he dissented, one where he was in the majority demonstrate well both the difficulty of actually char-acterizing opinions as 'literal' or not, and the practice of switching between approaches to maintain a coherent set of values.

The first of these cases, *Suthendran* v. *Immigration Appeal Tribunal*[41] is one of the purest examples of very strict, very literal interpretation, relying on a grammatical argument to the point of pedantry, that one can hope to find. The case involves immigration rights, one of the more controversial areas of social policy, especially at the time. It is simple enough, though the dates need to be followed carefully. Suthendran was given leave to enter the UK for twelve months ending 23 July 1974. On 2 June 1974 he started work in a hospital, which applied for a work permit for him. This was refused by the Home Secretary and a complicated set of appeals ensued. After he lost these appeals the hospital, on 20 May 1975, made a

---

[39] See D. N. MacCormick and R. S. Summers, *Interpreting Statutes*, op. cit., and especially the chapter by Robert Alexy and Ralph Dreier on Germany.
[40] See David Robertson, 'The Courts in the Political System' in Ian Budge and D. McKay (eds.), *The Developing British Political System*, Longman (3rd edn.), 1993.
[41] *Suthendran* v. *Immigration Appeal Tribunal* [1977] AC 359.

further request that he be allowed to stay in the UK to finish his training as a pupil nurse. This was refused, again by the Home Office, on 17 June, and he was ordered to leave the country by 17 July. He appealed to the adjudicator set up by the Act, and won this appeal, on 16 January 1976. Now the Home Secretary appealed, to the Immigration Appeal Tribunal, who upheld the Home Office on the grounds that as his original limited leave to remain in the UK had expired back in July 1974, 'he had no right to appeal from the Secretary of State's refusal to the adjudicator'.[42] The case falls under section 14(1) of the Immigration Act 1971. The terms need to be set out:

> . . . a person who has a limited leave . . . to enter or remain in the United Kingdom may appeal to an adjudicator against any variation of leave . . . *or against any refusal to vary it*; and a variation shall not take effect so long as an appeal is pending . . . nor shall an appellant be required to leave the United Kingdom by reason of the expiration of his leave so long as his appeal is pending under this subsection *against a refusal to enlarge or remove the limit on the duration of the leave.* [Our emphases.]

Until a decision in the Court of Appeal on a similar case only the year before,[43] it had been the Home Office's invariable practice to interpret this section to mean that someone who had had a limited leave could apply for a variation extending his stay even though his original leave to remain in the country had expired when he made the application. It was generally agreed that to interpret the section otherwise would mean, *inter alia*, that someone who applied for an extension during the period of his permission to be in the UK and had it turned down, through administrative slowness, after that initial period had ended could never appeal against the decision, despite the fact that the Act clearly intended there to be an appeal procedure. The problem is very simple, if taken as a matter of literal interpretation. 'Has had' does not mean the same as 'Has'. Dilhorne approvingly quotes Bridge LJ in the earlier case: 'Once a limited leave to enter has expired, there is nothing left to which an application to vary can sensibly relate.'[44] As Dilhorne himself says:

> If Parliament had intended to give a right of appeal to someone who had had a limited leave but whose leave had expired, it would have been easy so to provide by the insertion of the words 'or had' after 'has' in section 14(1). Parliament did not do so . . . I see nothing in section 14 to support any inference that Parliament had any such intention.[45]

Later, adding some substantive reasons for making this assumption about the intention he expresses the view:

[42] *Suthendran* at 365.
[43] R v. *Immigration Appeal Tribunal, ex parte Subramaniam* [1977] QB 190.
[44] R v. *Immigration Appeal Tribunal, ex parte Subramaniam* at 204.
[45] *Suthendran* at 366.

It would indeed be surprising to me if a person not a patrial who was liable to deportation and to prosecution for remaining in this country beyond the period for which he had leave to do so was, though illegally here, given a right to appeal after his leave had expired against a refusal to extend it. If section 14(1) applied to such a person, proceedings for deportation would by virtue of that subsection be held up so long as the appeal was pending.

The conclusion in the last sentence is correct but irrelevant, the assumption in the first simply tells us how Dilhorne would have legislated, and he need really say none of this at all—because his argument rests entirely on the tenses of the verb 'to have', and is correct. Or at least, it is correct unless such a reading makes some element of the Act unworkable. This is the argument of the minority, on whose behalf Kilbrandon accepts readily enough: 'The literal argument in favour of [the interpretation the majority want] is certainly persuasive: how can a person whose limited leave has expired be described as "a person who has a limited leave".[46] The real argument of the minority is straightforwardly that it is not absolutely necessary to give a literal interpretation, especially given that the Home Office itself had not done so for some years, and that to do so produces a real danger of injustice. Kilbrandon nonetheless feels obliged to try a rather shaky piece of semantics, because the majority has chosen to play it that way. As he clearly does not even convince himself, we can leave it, and settle for his summation:

My Lords, faced with two interpretations of this somewhat perplexing statute, both of which are possible though perhaps neither of them altogether convincing, I prefer that which, whatever maybe the administrative inconveniences . . . at least avoids giving statutory sanction to a possible injustice which I do not believe Parliament would knowingly have countenanced.[47]

Just as Kilbrandon cannot deny that Dilhorne is literally correct, the latter does not attempt to deny the argument from injustice. He admits it could happen, but that such an eventuality is simply irrelevant:

I accept that could happen . . . If it did happen the person concerned would have a legitimate grievance. Failure to provide for this possibility is a flaw in the Act but the existence of this flaw does not in my opinion justify reading section 14(1) so as to give all those who had leave to be in this country but whose leave has expired . . . a right of appeal . . . to read that word in that subsection as meaning 'has or had' . . . would in my view not be interpreting the language of a statute but, to remedy a flaw in the Act, encroaching on the province of the legislature.[48]

But if such a straightforward linguistic approach, coupled, of course, with the parliamentary sovereignty argument, will do when one does not want

---

[46] *Suthendran* at 370.
[47] *Suthendran* at 371.
[48] *Suthendran* at 367–8.

to extend rights that might otherwise seem 'natural', how does one extend rights that are apparently not given? In *Daymond* v. *South West Water Authority*,[49] the year before, Dilhorne had faced this other sort of problem. The SW Water Authority sought to use its powers under the Water Act 1973 to charge Mr Daymond a total of £4.89 for provision of sewerage services, even though Mr Daymond's house was not connected to the public sewers. It was estimated that there were so many people in Mr Daymond's position that if he won this test case about £30 million would have to be levied instead in addition to their own charges on people across the country who were so connected. Once again the relevant statutory language is perfectly simple and clear, and we cannot be said, without straining language, to be dealing with any form of legislative ambiguity. Section 30(1) of the Act provides:

Subject to the provisions of this Act, a water authority shall have power to fix, and demand, take and recover such charges for the services performed, facilities provided or rights made available by them (including separate charges for separate services, facilities or rights or combined charges for a number of services, facilities or rights) *as they think fit*. [Emphasis ours.]

That is essentially all it says about charging, though there are other sections giving the Secretary of State power to impose certain charge levels, and there is a general duty to move towards a charging system that does not discriminate against any class of persons. Nowhere does the Act say who should be charged for what service. This is hardly surprising. The money was to be collected by local authorities as agents for the Water Authority via a general rate, the usual method for covering the cost of all such public services. It had been settled law since as early as *Soady* v. *Wilson* in 1835 that 'public benefit' is a legitimate reason for charging in such matters. As Wilberforce, for the majority, points out, this battle was fought long ago, during the great public health debates in the nineteenth century, and for well over 100 years it had been normal practice to share the cost of sewerage in an area over all ratepayers. This fact, plus the complete silence of the Act, produces, one might think, not ambiguity but clarity. The Water Authority can charge what they think correct and, nothing being said to the contrary, can charge whoever they think right. Surely this must be the type of argument that must recommend itself to Dilhorne.

But, as a Conservative, Dilhorne clearly thinks that property rights, or at least the right not to be taxed without the most explicit statutory reference, trump. Here parliamentary silence produces an Act that cannot be made to work at all without the courts adding words. Parliament did not say

---

[49] *Daymond* v. *South West Water Authority* [1976] 1 AC 609.

who should pay. Obviously a non-elected body like a Water Authority cannot make such taxing decisions itself. Thus the courts must find a way of making up for Parliament's inattention. (In fact Dilhorne tries to suggest that the silence of the Act was intentional, to avoid political controversy during the passage of the Act. As the Act was passed by a Conservative controlled Parliament it is a little improbable that the Cabinet feared much trouble, at least from the opposition, in continuing a policy of charging for public services on the general rate.) So for Dilhorne this omission is one that must be remedied by the courts, and it must be done by inference from what is in the Act, not from past practice:

In my opinion this is a wrong approach for it is not to be assumed that in the absence of a contrary indication a new statutory body inherits the powers of its predecessors. Its powers are governed by and contained in the provisions of the Act under which it is established and it is to that Act that one must look to see what its powers are.[50]

It is then a matter of inference from within the Act. His argument goes like this. Can we infer the SW Water Authority could charge anyone in the whole UK? Obviously not—undemocratic. So must we infer that they can only charge people living in their own area? Obviously yes. Therefore can we infer that, within the area, they can charge anyone they like? No, because the natural inference drawn from a provision that talks about providing services 'is in my opinion that it can charge only those who avail themselves of its services . . .'. In many ways the argument is a good one, if, but only if, we do in fact ignore both the whole history of public health politics in the UK, and the fact that provision of sewerage is the provision of a collective good—no one can fail to avail himself of the benefits from sewerage whether or not his benefits include the disposal of his own household waste. Whether this form of interpretation is restrictive or literal, or whatever the opposite of those concepts may be, is rather hard to say. There is a glaring conflict with the style of thought between *Daymond* and *Suthendran*, but they have in common two things. First, in both cases recourse is made only to words in the Act, and any external knowledge or public value is excluded. The history of public health administration, and the history of Home Office application of the Immigration Act, are irrelevant. Secondly, there is no sense of the value often found in public law cases, that somehow or other the Lords 'have got to make the Act work'. £30 million will go uncollected and possibly hundreds of would be immigrants will be denied a statutory right of appeal if Dilhorne's views prevail. Both cases do rest on narrow readings, in the sense that Parliament is limited to a specific verbal tense in one case, and

[50] *Daymond* at 641.

a very specific meaning to the phrase 'providing services' is used in the other. But in truth the only way to make the two approaches consistent is to claim that there is a vital difference between Parliament saying something and Parliament saying nothing. It is not an unacceptable invasion of parliamentary sovereignty to fill in a gap Parliament has left, but it is such an invasion to alter what it did say to correct a flaw. It is somewhat doubtful that this could be generalized to make a working rule of interpretation. What the story of the two cases is really about is manifestly clear—property rights are vital, and immigration rights are not. Ambiguity in an Act arises when one has a strong sense of what Parliament would have said had it thought of it, and if one can find a general principle of English legal practice to generate this expectation. There is a general principle that taxation requires representation (water authorities are not directly elected). As Parliament said nothing, it can be deemed to have overlooked something it would have said had it thought. But with immigrant rights, if Parliament did not think about the problem of an appeal arriving after a leave had expired, there is no way we can deduce what they would have said had they thought, because there is no general principle available. Hence there is no infringement of parliamentary sovereignty in the first case, but there would be in the second case. And the principle of parliamentary sovereignty is, always, supreme.

Kilbrandon, agreeing with Dilhorne in *Daymond* though he had opposed him in *Suthendran*, makes an agonized complaint that might seem to summon up the whole mess of statutory interpretation:

this, of all cases is one in which there could have been some source or sources upon which the courts could draw, in the exercise of their constitutional duties to interpret legislation, over and above those to which custom, or vis inertiae, has arbitrarily limited them . . . It is certain that there are other and more satisfying ways of arriving at the meaning of an Act of Parliament . . . than by prolonged linguistic and semantic analysis.[51]

But no one forced Kilbrandon to use such techniques—he could have joined Wilberforce and given a historically based backing to the argument that if Parliament just said the authorities could set what charges they thought fit, that was all Parliament needed to say. Wilberforce gives a liberal reading in *Suthendran* to protect a liberal value—rights to appeal against the executive—and a literal reading in *Daymond* to protect the liberal value of public welfare provision. Dilhorne, in reverse, switches from literal interpretation because he does not care very much about immigrant appeal rights, to a more flexible method of interpretation to protect the conservative value of property rights. Kilbrandon, obviously with a great sense of strain in both cases, tries complex semantic analysis

---

[51] *Daymond* at 652.

and backs essentially contrasting political values. But Kilbrandon is also wrong in thinking there was some way out. The great revolution of *Pepper v. Hart,* reading *Hansard* to find out what Parliament did intend, would avail him nothing. In both cases Parliament said nothing at all.

4

Judicial Methodology and the Common Law

A Judge is a law student who marks his own examination papers.

H. L. Mencken

In contrast to the highly linguistic methods of statutory interpretation, purely common law argument from decided cases and their enshrined principles has a greater fluidity. Contrary to much lay opinion, common law still accounts for perhaps as much as half of the cases before the higher courts. In this book the common law is mainly studied in terms of criminal law, public law, and the general law of obligations, although large parts of contract and land law are predominantly uncodified. From the overall perspective of this book our task in this chapter is harder than in Chapter 3. There is very little in democratic thought, or in the working assumptions of the British constitution, that can legitimize judicial discretion in statutory interpretation if that discretion is widely used to make legislation mean what an individual judge can persuade his colleagues to agree it means in pursuit of his own beliefs. If slot machine jurisprudence can be expected anywhere, it is in statutory interpretation. Consequently we did not have to show very much to demonstrate that there is too much discretion too freely exercised when the Law Lords interpret statutes. But the common law is *supposed* to be judge made. What is it, then, that we must demonstrate? Well, to say that the judges are supposed to make the common law is not to say that they are free to come to whatever decision they believe in, and to 'rationalize' the decision with essentially *ad hoc* legal arguments. The common law is supposed to be a drawing out of general principles in a principled manner. And, of course, after several centuries of common law development, and after a century of extensive and massive legislation, there ought not to be many or frequent cases where new law needs to be made. Our task here is therefore not to show that judges make law sometimes, but that the law in almost any case that comes before the Lords turns out to be whatever their Lordships feel it ought to be at that moment. The task is more difficult, but not impossibly so—indeed the freedom with which the Law Lords create doctrine, and the resoluteness with which they ignore each other's contending arguments is often more obvious.

1. Examples from Criminal Law

I. Violent Sexuality

It is perhaps a little unfair to start with criminal law. By common consent, including some at least of the Law Lords themselves and many of their juniors on the Court of Appeal, the Lords have not shone in their task of controlling and developing the criminal law. To some extent it is not their fault. Criminal law in England is an unhappy combination of statute and common law, in comparison with jurisdictions in Continental Europe or North America where it is almost entirely codified. Some of the statutes, especially the laws on murder, are deeply unpopular with the judges, because they refuse discretion in sentencing. Others are manifestly out of date and regularly produce absurdities. The first example concerns one of these statutes. As suggested before, there are relatively few cases where *no* statute bears at all, so it is helpful to start this chapter with a case involving a statute, but one so old, and so manifestly inadequate for modern conditions, that much of the judicial debate is about precedent, though ultimately none of the precedents help.

The case, *R* v. *Brown*,[1] revolves round the interpretation of the 1861 Offences against the Person Act.[2] The police had come across video tapes of a group of men engaging in multiple homosexual behaviour, some of it sadomasochistic. It was accepted by all parties that any pain or wounding that had been caused was with the eager consent of the victims, and that the whole enterprise had been carefully controlled, and precautions had been taken to protect against infection, or against violence going further than the volunteer victims were prepared for. The participants were clearly guilty of the offence of gross indecency under the Sexual Offences Act 1967, which had legalized homosexual activities only where not more than two men took part, and where the activities were conducted in private. Unfortunately for the police, prosecutions under this Act were time barred, because the Act requires them to be brought within twelve months of the offence. Determined to get convictions for what even the Law Lords saw as quite horrendous and shocking behaviour, the prosecution tried to treat the case as purely one of assault. All of the participants were charged under section 47 of the 1861 Act, which penalizes an assault causing 'actual bodily harm'. Three were also charged under the more serious section 20, which provides that: 'Whosoever shall unlawfully and maliciously wound or inflict any grievous bodily harm upon any other

---

[1] *R* v. *Brown* [1994] AC 212.
[2] This Act, which forms the basis for nearly all criminal law dealing with violence, short of murder itself, is the subject of continual complaint by the judiciary. Its inadequacy is said to be at the heart of much of the inefficiency, as well as injustice, of the criminal justice system in England and Wales.

person . . . shall be guilty of an offence.' Both sections carry a maximum punishment of five years in prison.[3] Originally Brown and his co-accused pleaded not guilty, but when the trial judge ruled that the prosecution would not have to prove the absence of consent, they all changed their pleas to guilty and were sent to prison.

As presented to the Lords, therefore, the legal question was whether or not the consent of the victim is a defence to a charge of assault occasioning either grievous or actual bodily harm, or resulting in a wound. It was common ground that common assault, where there is no imposition of physical harm, does provide that consent is a defence.[4] As one of the Law Lords who, to his enormous relief, did not sit on the case pointed out, everything depended on which end you came from. Did you see it as a case about sexual freedom, where violence happened to be involved, or did you see it as a case about violence, which happened to occur in a sexual context? From the first position, which seems to have been that taken by the minority, Lords Slynn and Mustill, consent is of the essence. From the majority position, Templeman's, Jauncey's, and Lowry's, consent is largely irrelevant. The case is really pure common law, because the statute itself was seen when passed as no more than an attempt to codify the existing common law. There are precedents about the role of consent in assault, though they are few and have no very clear import. Above all they do not involve a question of sexual freedom in a context of fully fledged, informed, and unconstrained consent.

R v. *Brown* indeed is illustrative of how sparse material can be in precedent-based cases. Only three cases were important, the earliest being *R* v. *Coney*, a case from 1882.[5] This involved the legality of prize fighting, where it was argued that the consent of the two pugilists negated the offence of assault. Unfortunately, although there were eleven judges involved, and five separate opinions, most of them seem to have believed prize fighting should be outlawed because it was a breach of the peace, and/or that prize fighting in general raised the danger of really serious injury of the level that no one believed could be consented to. For some curious reason the fighters and their supporters had only been charged with common assault. The emphasis therefore had to be on the presence of special reasons why the normally acceptable defence of consent could not

---

[3] Actual bodily harm means any physical assault of a more than trivial sort, grievous bodily harm means a 'serious bodily harm', and courts are reluctant to define it further. Wounding involves actually breaking the skin.

[4] At common law an assault is an act by which a person intentionally or recklessly causes another to apprehend immediate and unlawful personal violence and a battery is an act by which a person intentionally or recklessly inflicts personal violence on another. Hence a non-physical assault, a common assault. Though what would be implied by my consenting to be frightened of violence but not consenting to receive it is unclear. The definition is quoted in Templeman's speech in this case, at 230.

[5] *R* v. *Coney* (1882) 8 QBD 534.

here apply. What intellectual effort can be discerned in these nineteenth-century opinions was directed to making sure that 'many activities' such as ordinary boxing, single stick fighting, and so on were not caught in the net. Nor are these arguments very persuasive. One of the Lords who heard the appeal, in private admitted that his study of the law in this case had led him to the conclusion that modern boxing matches probably were illegal.

The second, and apparently more apposite case, as it concerned the beating of a prostitute, was *R* v. *Donovan*, from 1934.[6] Donovan paid a prostitute to allow him to cane her, and the result was sufficiently severe to leave bruises several days later. She complained and he was charged with indecent assault and common assault. Unfortunately for any clear statement of the law, indecent assault is also, like common assault, a charge to which consent is a defence, and on the actual facts of Donovan's case, everything depended on technical questions of whether or not the jury was properly instructed on the question of consent. There was a clear statement of law in this case, to the effect that assault causing actual bodily harm is an act *'malum in se'*, and as such something which cannot be made legal by the consent of the victim. This is the form of argument relied on, for example, to justify murder convictions on doctors who practice euthanasia.

The final case, and this shows us something about the non-determinative effect of precedents, was relied on by both appellants and respondents in argument before the House. Somewhat unusually the case was one in which the accused was acquitted and the Attorney-General used his power of reference to the Court of Appeal to get the statement of law involved corrected, even though the accused could not be retried and convicted. Known as *Attorney General's Reference (No. 6 of 1980)*, it concerned two youths who, engaged in a bitter argument, agreed to settle their disagreement then and there by a fight in the street, during which one of them suffered a bloody nose and facial bruising. The 'winner' was charged with assault causing actual bodily harm.[7] He was acquitted when the judge instructed the jury that the fighters' mutual consent and their restriction to 'reasonable force' might mean there had been no assault. Such a ruling could have been said to follow from either or both of the previous cases. Or not. The restatement of law in the Attorney-General's Reference was described by Lord Lane CJ as 'a partially new approach'. The trouble is that it ruled neither that consent was irrelevant because assault was a *malum in se*, nor that lack of consent was a necessary element of the offence and therefore consent would prevent conviction. Instead Lane argued 'ordinarily, then, if the victim consents, the assailant

---

[6] *R* v. *Donovan* [1934] 2 KB 498.
[7] *Attorney-General's Reference (No. 6 of 1980)* [1981] QB 715.

is not guilty', and, showing that he thought this was the existing law, amplifies:

Bearing in mind the various cases and the views of the textbook writers cited to us, and starting with the proposition that ordinarily an act consented to will not constitute an assault, the question is: at what point does the public interest require the court to hold otherwise?[8]

Lane's answer is that it is 'not in the public interest that people should . . . cause each other actual bodily harm for no good reason' and, he stresses, 'This means that most fights will be unlawful regardless of consent.' The trouble with this formulation is that it starts out by apparently saying 'consent vitiates unless . . .' and ends up meaning, and being taken to mean, 'even with consent assault is illegal unless . . .'. This is because the public interest exception is defined so widely, as 'for no good reason', that it actually becomes the background condition or, as it were, the 'rest state'. Mustill, who attempted to use the case for the appellants in his minority argument, valiantly admits that others see the case as inconsistent, though not he. It may not be inconsistent, but it is a beautiful example of how a particular way of stating a rule can allow judicial creativity much play, as we shall see. The problem is to see in what respect it is a 'partially new approach'. Was there previously a rule that made consent a defence, so that the instant decision was extending the law against assault and 'legislating judicial paternalism'? This was the view of Glanville Williams, perhaps Britain's foremost academic expert on criminal law.[9] Or was it breaking new ground and disregarding all the old cases, and establishing a rule that consent was a defence except in special cases, as Mustill characterizes it?[10] It is because of this uncertainty that the case law can, essentially, be used by both sides. Hence the problem for the Law Lords in making a common law determination of the case. However it may be, these were the precedents when the case appeared before the Lords. They were not, of course, binding on their Lordships—none even came from the House of Lords, so the 1966 doctrine did not even have to be invoked. Nonetheless there is a strong preference for appearing to follow cases—they lend an authority that is missing if a decision is too obviously a new venture.

The muddiness of the precedents in this case presents both the majority and minority even more difficulty than might otherwise happen because of the substantive subject matter. This is, essentially, a brand new question. To a layman it is quite obvious that neither common law nor statute have an answer to the question stated by the Court of Appeal:

[8] *Attorney-General's Reference (No. 6 of 1980)* [1981] QB 715, at 718.
[9] Glanville Williams, *Textbook of Criminal Law*, 2nd edn., 1983, pp. 582–9, cited by Lord Lowry in this case.
[10] *Brown*, op. cit. at 270.

Where A wounds or assaults B occasioning him actual bodily harm in the course of a sado-masochistic encounter, does the prosecution have to prove lack of consent on the part of B before they can establish A's guilt under section 20 or section 47 of the Offences against the Person Act 1861?

One counsel specifically asked the Lords to give a new ruling on the matter. Even the DPP, in her submission, makes it clear that the waters are uncharted:

In the end it is a matter of policy. Is/are the state/courts right to adopt a paternalistic attitude as to what is bad or good for subjects, in particular as to deliberate injury.[11]

Unfortunately for their Lordships, and for English criminal law, there were very powerful reasons why neither side could be seen to do this. The majority have an essentially constitutional need to insist that they are simply applying existing law, quite apart from any inherent dislike of admitting to judicial legislation. It has been accepted since the mid-sixties that the Lords have a particular duty not to innovate in criminal law, whatever they may do in other areas. There are examples to the contrary, discussed below in connection with *R* v. *R* which removed the rule that a man could not rape his own wife, but this at least involved abolishing an exception to a rule, not creating a new offence. In European jurisdictions this special horror of judicial creation of criminal laws, an inheritance from the French revolution, shows in the very tight rules on interpreting criminal statutes. Indeed in *Brown* there was also argument from European law that it was particularly inappropriate to innovate in criminal law. Templeman, Jauncey, and Lowry, all of whom dismiss the various attempts to use European human rights law, were therefore even more eager to insist that no new law was being created.

Even though the minority, supporting the appeal, did not run this particular risk, there were very good reasons why they also should not seem to be innovating, and they too stress the conformity to existing law of their legal opinions. The public's attitudes are unlikely to be very permissive in an area like this, so to seem to create a licence for sexual deviance of this kind—and the majority were careful to mention just how extreme was the behaviour—would not incline future courts towards the minority's arguments. Above all though, the innovators, whichever side they were, would be guilty of a sin the Law Lords find it persuasive to accuse their opponents of—infringing legislative prerogatives. According to the majority, to justify making an exception in the law of assault to allow sadomasochism would require massive psychological and sociological investigation that only Parliament can manage. To the minority

---

[11] *Brown* at 274.

only Parliament has the legitimacy to extend the criminal law to penalize something already legal. Lord Slynn, in his minority opinion, is emphatic. Noting that counsel for Mr Brown actually asked for a new ruling in law, he insists:

My conclusion is on the basis of what I consider existing law to be. I do not consider that it is necessary for the House in its judicial capacity to give what is called 'a new ruling' based on freedom of expression, public opinion and the consequences of a negative ruling on those whom it is said can only get satisfaction through these acts . . . Nor do I think that it is for your Lordships to make new law on the basis of the position in other states so that English law can 'keep in line'. All these are essentially matters, in my view to be balanced by the legislature *if it is thought necessary to consider the making criminal of sado-masochistic acts per se* . . . I agree [with the DPP's submission] that in the end it is a matter of policy. It is a matter of policy in an area where social and moral factors are extremely important and where attitudes can change. In my opinion it is a matter of policy for the legislature to decide. If society takes the view that this kind of behaviour . . . *should be brought now for the first time within the criminal law* then it is for the legislature to decide. [Emphases mine.][12]

Mustill similarly insists that ruling that sadomasochism should be made criminal would be:

an altogether more difficult question and one which I would not be prepared to answer in favour of the appellants, not because I do not have my own opinions upon it but because I regard the task as one which the courts are not suited to perform, and which should be carried out, if at all, by Parliament after a thorough review of all the medical, social, moral and political issues, such as was performed by the Wolfenden Committee.[13]

The starting point then is a consensus amongst the Lords that consent cannot be given to absolutely any degree of violence whatsoever. The precedents, however little use they may be in detail, certainly establish this. They also establish that the general context of the violence, including the reason for it, limit the extent to which consent can render violence not an assault. Alternately the context may limit the situations in which consent can be a *defence against* a charge of assault—the whole case is bedevilled by these alternate ways of seeing the issue.

It is also a matter of agreement that common assault, involving nothing much more than mere touching, does not occur where there is consent. Neither side can therefore avoid drawing a line, somewhere above com-

---

[12] *Brown* at 279–80.

[13] *Brown* at 273–4. The Wolfenden Committee reported on the desirability of legal sanctions against prostitution and homosexuality, as a result of which homosexual activity between two consenting adults in private was decriminalized in 1968. Its report was the occasion for a famous jurisprudential debate between Patrick Devlin, a Law Lord, and H. L. A. Hart, a Professor of Jurisprudence: P. Devlin, *The Enforcement of Morals*, Oxford, 1965 and H. L. A. Hart, *Law, Liberty and Morality*, Oxford, 1963.

mon assault, and somewhere below grievous bodily harm, above which a person cannot vitiate a crime by consenting to it. For those who wish to uphold the convictions the rest is fairly simple. The precedents all involved charges below the level of grievous bodily harm. It is judicial child's play to show how allowing violence at the level of actual bodily harm is too dangerous in practice, and too likely to lead to unfair randomness in charging. Consequently those in favour can plausibly argue that the existing common law already makes it an assault to cause actual bodily harm, and that consent cannot vitiate this, following Lane's rule in *Attorney-General's Reference* that it is 'not in the public interest that people should . . . cause each other actual bodily harm for no good reason'. Sado-masochism is not going to seem 'a good reason' to a very wide audience. Templeman can only command respect from a general audience if he can get away with characterizing the decision as he does:

I am not prepared to invent a defence of consent for sado-masochistic encounters which breed and glorify cruelty and result in offences under sections 47 and 20 of the Act of 1861.[14]

Thus, even against the criticism that the Lords are repressively invading private morality, Lowry can defend the majority's technical position thus:

[The] approach which has characterized every submission put forward on behalf of the appellants, is derived from the fallacy that what is involved here is restraint of a lawful activity as opposed to the refusal to relax existing prohibitions in the Act of 1861.[15]

But if the majority's position can be portrayed as a relatively orthodox application of precedent-based rule by a court unwilling to usurp the legislature's role, the minority has a much harder task. They have no choice but to dismiss the precedents as neither apposite nor, in any case, binding. But nor, as noted, do they dare launch into overt judicial creativity. In fact they have two problems. One is to find authority for any position that will give consent enough power to negative an assault charge, given they do have to dismiss the precedents. The second problem is to justify their line drawing at the point they need. The majority argument ensures that the second task is actually very difficult. Though it is not a question at a high theoretical level. For the minority, violence which causes either actual bodily harm or wounding must be capable of legitimation by consent, despite the obvious potential dangers of infection, AIDS, and of violence accidentally escalating above the 'actual' into the 'grievous' level. Mustill's only answer to this aspect is unsatisfactory intellectually because it requires him to drop below the level of producing

---

[14] *Brown* at 236.
[15] *Brown* at 256.

a principled definition of the law to dealing with it in an *ad hoc*, case by case manner, which he has to disguise as, yet again, a deference to parliamentary supremacy:

> Of course things might go wrong and really serious injury or death might ensue. If this happened, those responsible would be punished according to the ordinary law, in the same way as those who kill or injure in the course of more ordinary sexual activities are regularly punished. But to penalise the appellants' conduct even if the extreme consequences do not ensue, just because they might have done so, would require an assessment of the degree of risk, and the balancing of this risk against the interests of individual freedom. Such a balancing is in my opinion for Parliament, not the courts; and even if your Lordships' House were to embark upon it the attempt must in my opinion fail at the outset for there is no evidence at all of the seriousness of the hazards to which sado-masochistic conduct of this kind give rise.[16]

Exactly what the 'more ordinary' sexual activities during which people regularly kill and meet punishment are is somewhat unclear.

Mustill makes exactly the same point about AIDS, while dismissing the risk of genito-urinary infection and septicaemia on the grounds that 'the risk of serious harm must surely have been greatly reduced in modern times'. (This dip into empirical knowledge, know as 'taking judicial notice' of common facts, he resolutely regards in the earlier quote, of course, as something only for Parliament.) Two quite separate but symbolically related judicial techniques are at play here, based on a specific role description of 'The Judge'. First is the broad strategy of brushing any awkward question under the rug of judicial restraint and deference to Parliament, the second of insisting on the purity of the judicial role in deciding only the extant case on evidence actually before the court. Were these roles really adhered to as strictly as Mustill is forced to encourage here, common law would be enormously weakened, because precedents would be rules with very narrow coverage indeed.

Lord Slynn, in the other minority opinion takes an even more curt approach to the line-drawing exercise. Denying that one can treat common assault as the only category to which consent can be a defence he points out:

> In the first place the range of injuries which can fall within 'actual bodily harm' is wide—the description of the two beatings in the present case show that one is much more substantial than the other . . . I can see no significant reason for refusing consent as a defence for the lesser of these cases of actual bodily harm . . . If a line has to be drawn, as I think it must, to be workable it cannot be allowed to fluctuate within particular charges and in the interest of legal certainty it has to be accepted that consent can be given to acts which are said to constitute actual

---

[16] *Brown* at 279.

bodily harm and wounding . . . None of the convictions in the present case have been on the basis that grievous bodily harm was caused. Whether some of the acts done in these cases might have fallen within that category does not seem to me to be relevant for present purposes.[17]

Again there is the stress on the judicial function as dealing only with the extant case and the evidence and arguments that counsel have chosen to bring to the court's attention, without generalizing from possibilities. There is also an appeal to one of the basic general principles judges are supposed to be motivated by—the high value of legal certainty. Though it must be said that his own account of the fluctuation in level of violence suggests that his opinion would reduce certainty compared with the simpler formula of the majority. These are relatively straightforward techniques for making an argument, and essentially defensive—a restrictive portrayal of the judicial role can usefully avoid arguments that are not otherwise easily dealt with.

However, the line-drawing exercise will not solve the problem by itself. Some principle has to be found, to counter the majority's ability to insist they are simply applying the existing legal principles. The first principle Slynn quotes is: 'it is inherent in the conception of assault and battery that the victim does not consent'. But the main source for this is an academic article by Glanville Williams.[18] His other sources include an Australian case on boxing, a nineteenth-century case on indecent assault, the Criminal Code of Canada, and a passage from one of the dissenting judges in *R* v. *Coney*, a case he regards as, in any case, not determining the issue. It is not particularly surprising that he earlier dismisses the relevance of *Coney*, given the rather uncertain benefit he gets from his quote, by Stephen J:

In cases where life and limb are exposed to no serious danger in the common course of things, I think that consent is a defence to a charge of assault, even when considerable force is used that, as for instance in cases of wrestling, single-stick . . . but in all cases the question whether consent does or does not take from the application of force its illegal character, is a question of degree depending on circumstances.[19]

Only Lord Mustill makes an effort to derive a principle in a more structured way, and it is an interesting comment on his high standards of judicial craftsmanship that he is clearly dissatisfied with the methodology he has to use. In a rare comment on judicial methodology by a practising judge, Mustill says, at the beginning of his lengthy judgment, that all forms of theoretical analysis he tried would not work, largely because:

[17] *Brown* at 283.
[18] Glanville Williams, 'Consent and Public Policy' [1962] *Criminal Law Review*, 74.
[19] *R* v. *Coney* (1882) 8 QBD 534 at 549.

for all the intellectual neatness of this method I must recognize that it will not do, for it imposes on the reported cases on the diversities of human life an order which they do not possess . . . In these circumstances I must accept that the existing case law does not sustain a step-by-step analysis . . . I thus see no alternative but to adopt a much narrower and more empirical approach, by looking at the situations in which the recipient consents or is deemed to consent to the infliction of violence upon him, to see whether the decided cases teach us how to react to this new challenge.[20]

What Mustill is doing is using previous cases not as precedents which stand for rules that can then be either applied or held irrelevant, but as instances of problem solving from which one can generalize to a suitable principle. It is, essentially, a game of induction. He is, in effect, creating a theory of the meaning of the cases, by looking, as he does in great detail, at the specifics of each case, rather than asking the simple question 'is the analogy close enough to apply the rule?' In the usual sense of applying precedent Mustill is quite clear that there is no close analogy:

The purpose of this long discussion is to suggest that the decks are clear for the House to tackle completely anew the question whether the public interest requires s. 47 of the 1861 Act to be interpreted as penalising an infliction of harm which is at the level of actual bodily harm but not grievous bodily harm; which is inflicted in private . . . which takes place not only with the consent of the recipient but with his willing and glad co-operation; which is inflicted for the gratification of sexual desire, and not in a spirit of animosity or rage; and which is not engaged in for profit.[21]

By stating the question with this degree of precision Mustill, of course, makes it impossible that there should be a precedent as such. In fact he approaches the case as what it technically is, a piece of statutory interpretation of the 1861 Act. But his approach of seeking to shift attention from the simple version—do the cases show that assault can be vitiated by consent for purposes like sadomasochism—to the need to answer such a specific question based on *why* the cases were handled as they were, rather than on what answer was given in each case, pays off far more successfully than simpler techniques. Because all the cases contain much discussion of the consent defence, even if obiter, and because Mustill can show how complex and situation specific the refusals to grant the defence were, there is little left of any general rule for either side. His arguments, considered above, for why public policy does not require a ban on consent for sadomasochism is weak, but by forcing the argument around in this way he is able to negative the idea that he, any more than the majority, is creating 'new' law. He is quite open about the reason the technique works:

[20] *Brown* at 104–5.
[21] *Brown* at 115.

... if the question were differently stated it might well yield a different answer. In particular, if it were held that as a matter of law all infliction of bodily harm above the level of common assault is incapable of being legitimated by consent, except in special circumstances, then we would have to consider whether the public interest required the recognition of private sexual activities as being in a special exempt category. This would be an altogether more difficult question ... Thus, if I had begun from the same point of departure as my noble and learned friend Lord Jauncey of Tullichettle I would have arrived at a similar conclusion.[22]

And though no precedent does say that sadomasochistic consent vitiated assault, the previous cases, taken *collectively*, fail to set up the general rule that Mustill attributes to Jauncey's analysis. This general method of constructing 'a theory' of the cases is further demonstrated in other cases considered in this chapter and especially in Browne-Wilkinson's methodology in the case of *O'Brien* v. *Barclay's Bank*. One might, in the alternative, see what Mustill is doing as creating a straw man out of the majority's opinion, the easier to oppose it, a familiar if dubious technique in philosophical argument.

II. Duress, Rape, and Children's Moral Capacity

The general problem remains—where precedents are of no use, how to establish common law principles? Sometimes overt judicial legislation is seen as acceptable, and a new principle will be created avowedly on the back of commonly understood contemporary morality. A House of Lords comprised of men most of whom would be seen as rather more traditionalist and even conservative than the five involved in *Brown* recently took such a bold step in *R* v. *R*.[23] In this case a single opinion by Lord Keith, with Lords Brandon, Griffiths, Ackner, and Lowry agreeing, abolished outright the rule dating at least from 1736, that a man cannot be guilty of raping his wife. No suggestion was made that the courts should wait for Parliament—Keith cited approvingly the Chief Justice's argument in the Court of Appeal:

The remaining and no less difficult question is whether ... this is an area where the court should step aside to leave the matter to the Parliamentary process. This is not the creation of a new offence, it is the removal of a common law fiction which has become anachronistic and offensive and we consider that it is our duty having reached that conclusion to act upon it.[24]

In fact there is almost no argument at all in this case—there is a bald statement that the traditional rule:

[22] *Brown* at 116.
[23] *R* v. *R* [1992] AC 599.
[24] Lord Lane CJ in *R* v. *R* [1991] AC 603 at 611.

. . . involves that by marriage a wife gives her irrevocable consent to sexual intercourse with her husband under all circumstances and irrespective of the state of
her health or how she happens to be feeling at the time. In modern times any
reasonable person must regard that conception as quite unacceptable.[25]

Actually the possible legal problems of abolishing the rule, given the
untidiness of rape charges at their clearest, and the fact that Parliament
has always avoided taking action even though there has been a series of
Sexual Offences Acts in the last twenty years, could have been used quite
respectably had the judges chosen the role model that characterized
debate in *Brown*. The difference, of course, is the assumption, though it is
an untested one, that there is wide consensus in the general public on the
question of marital rape. A better example of equally bold judicial legislation on woman's rights is found in a case discussed shortly. It is instruc-
tive to compare *R* v. *R* with a recent case where their Lordships were
equally unanimous that another ancient rule of common law, similarly
limiting criminal responsibility, was absurd, but felt they could not
remove it. *C* v. *DPP*[26] in 1995 involved a common law rule on the age at
which a child can be convicted of a crime. The rule, which goes back to the
time of Edward III, is that between the ages of ten and fourteen a child is
doli incapax, incapable of knowing good from bad sufficiently clearly to
have the *mens rea* to be held criminally responsible. This is, in fact, a
rebuttable presumption—the prosecution is allowed to lead evidence
showing that the child does in fact have this capacity to know what he was
doing was bad or immoral rather than merely naughty or mischievous,
but the evidence must be over and above the mere facts on which the
charge itself was based. Thus when a boy of twelve was seen helping
another try to steal a motorbike, this, combined with the fact that he ran
away from the police, was not in itself enough to rebut the presumption
and render him *doli capax*. Where the prosecution does not, or cannot, lead
such evidence then the defence can stand up after the prosecution case,
however damning the evidence, and successfully submit that there is no
case to answer. The Divisional Court judge who heard C's appeal from his
conviction by magistrates had held outright according to the headnote:

the presumption that a child was doli incapax did a serious disservice to the law
and its abolition would cause no injustice to the defendant, and that since there
was no impediment to the court's authority to abolish it, the presumption was no
longer part of the law of England.

Of the five Law Lords who held unanimously that the rule was too
entrenched in common law to be abolished, Lords Jauncey, Bridge,
Ackner, Lowry, and Browne-Wilkinson, four said outright that they

---

[25] Lord Keith in *R* v. *R* at 616.
[26] *C (A Minor)* v. *Director of Public Prosecutions* [1995] 2 WLR 383.

agreed substantively with the Divisional Court. The latter refused to say what he thought the law should be. No judicial or academic argument was cited in favour of retaining the rule. It was common ground that the original purpose, to protect young children from draconian punishment, including the death penalty, was no longer apt. Indeed it was pointed out that the effect, by preventing conviction, was to prevent children getting treatment and help. Not surprisingly their Lordships were invited by counsel for the prosecution side to take courage from *R* v. *R*, and Lowry accepted the challenge of showing that abolishing the rule that a man cannot rape his wife was 'very different from what the respondent asks your Lordships to do in the present case'. Some of his argument is fair, especially that recent White Papers and draft legislation showed that the Government had at least been thinking about children's criminal responsibility, though little has actually been legislated, while in contrast there had been an almost systematic refusal by the Home Office to think about marital rape. But Lowry's main point is that the abolition of the rule in *R* v. *R* 'was based on a very widely accepted modern view of marital rape, and it derived support from a group of up-to-date decisions.'[27] If this is meant to contrast with the context of *C*, it can only be described as specious. The abolition of the rule on rape, though occasioned by a rape where the man and wife were separated, would in fact apply inside an ongoing marriage. It is sociologically extremely unlikely that this view would command anything like as much support amongst the mass public as would a rule that allowed the conviction of thirteen-year-old auto-thieves. The fact that there had been several cases where judges had attempted to convict husbands for rape is on par with the attempt by the Divisional Court to change the *doli incapax* rule, where there was extensive quotation from judges who had wanted to but were dutiful to precedent. What is true is that liberal elite opinion was uniform in the rape context, and largely missing in the criminal capacity case. Asked how to square the two results, one Law Lord who had been a member of the bench in *C* but not in *R* v. *R* threw his hands in the air and admitted he could not imagine how *they* squared it. Another though, who had heard *C*, indicated that his decision was prompted by a desire to force the Government's hand and make it legislate.

These two cases notwithstanding, the Lords are more likely to act as in *Brown* and maintain the appearance of simply applying existing common law principles, however absent the supporting precedents. One effective method is an extension of the general legal strategy of argument by analogy which underlies the routine application of precedent. Even if there are no precedents, there may be logically, or morally, equivalent

---

[27] Lowry in *C (A Minor)* at 401.

situations where a satisfactory rule exists and can be borrowed. This technique is demonstrated in another recent divided case, decided by a group overlapping with the bench in *Brown*. In *R* v. *Gotts*,[28] for the first time in English legal history the question arose as to whether or not the defence of duress could be used when someone was charged with attempted murder. Gotts's father had threatened to kill him unless he murdered his mother, which he attempted to do. Two things were clear. Duress is not a defence against murder, and this had been re-established, after some uncertainty, as recently as 1987 when duress was denied as a defence not only to the one who actually killed the victim, but to those involved in the murder as principals in the second degree.[29] Secondly, there has long been a general principle of English law that duress is a defence to nearly all other crimes except, possibly, treason. The majority dealt with this very simply as stated in the headnote to the case:

> in the absence of any common law rule, statutory provision or judicial authority compelling a decision either way, the question whether the defence of duress extended to the offence of attempted murder was at large, and accordingly it was a matter of policy how it should be answered: that the defence was not available to a charge of murder because the law regarded the sanctity of human life and its protection as of paramount importance: and that there was no justification in logic, morality or law in affording the defence to a charge of attempted murder when it was not available to a murder.

In this case the majority, Templeman, Jauncey, and Browne-Wilkinson, were prepared to base their announcement of principle of common law on sheer logic. Rather than engage in a battle of policy-logic, the opposition, Keith and Lowry, had to find a rule without recourse to precedent. Like the minority in *Brown*, they seem to have felt they could not risk an a priori argument for their more liberal answer. It may, in fact, be a general rule of thumb that minority opinions have a greater need to cover themselves with the aura of legal orthodoxy—if so it would partly explain why dissents are relatively rare in the Lords. This, perhaps, is the key puzzle in much of modern legal philosophy. How can one 'find' a rule, for the first time, avoiding the charge of using pure, unfettered, discretion? In the language many of the Law Lords use themselves, how does one get the result one wants without cheating? If straightforward application of precedent is not an option, and there is no available analogy from case law or statute, what are the sources of legal principles?

The answer appears to be that almost any source that can be treated as authoritative will do, in a pinch. Keith and Lowry relied heavily on

---

[28] *R* v. *Gotts* [1992] 2 AC 412.
[29] *R* v. *Howe* [1987] AC 417, which overruled a 1975 decision that duress was a defence for complicity in the second degree.

statements from legal scholars, especially where age had well cured them. Thus the bulk of Lowry's argument come from Hale's *Pleas of the Crown* and Blackstone's *Commentaries on the Laws of England*. The former dates from 1736, the latter from 1766. Both works stand for the proposition that duress is, in general, a defence against any crime short of murder or treason, though neither deal with attempted murder, which was not recognized as a felony at the time the works were written. This process is highly selective, of course. Jauncey, in the majority in *Gotts*, quoted instead from an equally eminent though later writer, Sir James Fitzjames Stephen, whose *History of the Criminal Laws of England* published in 1883 is equally often called upon, who thoroughly disparaged the idea that duress should be a defence. Despite the nature of his sources, Lowry has no doubt of his position—first that there can be binding principles not based on precedent—he quotes approvingly from Lord Lane in the Court of Appeal in *Gotts*:

if the common law recognised that murder and treason were the only excepted crimes, then we are bound to accept that as the law, whether it seems a desirable conclusion or not; the fact that there is no binding decision on the point does not weaken a rule of common law which has stood the test of time. [Stress in the original.][30]

But, then:

My Lords, having considered all the arguments on either side, I am of the opinion that your Lordships *are* constrained by a common law rule (though not by judicial authority) from holding that the defence of duress does not apply to attempted murder. [Stress in the original.][31]

This view that such a common law rule *already exists* rests on eighteenth-century reasoning. Attempted murder, before 1861, was only a misdemeanour punishable by at most one year in prison. There would never have been occasion for anyone to consider, therefore, whether or not it *should* be excused by duress *were* it to be a serious felony! The question must be asked—had Hale's *Pleas of the Crown* or Blackstone's *Commentaries on the Laws of England* shown that eighteenth-century public opinion felt attempted murder was as heinous as murder, would this have deterred Lowry for one moment from mounting a policy argument in favour of allowing the defence of duress? In fact Hale and Blackstone might well have felt thus about attempted murder, because, as the majority point out, a conviction for attempted murder involves showing an actual intent to kill, while a murder conviction can come about when all that was intended was grievous bodily harm.

[30] *R v. Gotts* [1991] 1 QB 660 at 664.
[31] *Gotts* at 441.

2. Protecting the Vulnerable Against the Law

I. Banks and Mortgagees

Here, in a case called *Barclays Bank* v. *O'Brien*, we find, if we find it anywhere, a clearly thought out and open application of the judicial power to legislate. Mrs O'Brien's case was the latest in a stream of cases, at least eleven in the Court of Appeal in the previous eight years, on the same point. At issue was a typical problem of contemporary society. Mr O'Brien had mortgaged the family home to secure an overdraft to help his ailing company. The house was held jointly in his name and Mrs O'Brien's. She had signed the relevant legal documents with no serious consideration, and under the impression that, worse come to worse, they would be liable for at most only £60,000 rather than the actual final debt of £154,000. The bank attempted to foreclose and Mrs O'Brien claimed that as her consent had been gained by misrepresentation by her husband, it could not take her home away.

The previous cases had resulted in conflicting outcomes, and on unsure and uncertain bases. In fact Mrs O'Brien had won in the Court of Appeal, as had many of her predecessors, but the law was shaky. Lord Browne-Wilkinson presented to his colleagues in the House of Lords a clear challenge which sums up exactly what one would hope was the justification for the discretion and power of a final appeal court:

... the present law is built on the unsure foundations of the Duval case. Like most law founded on obscure and possibly mistaken foundations it has developed in an artificial way, giving rise to artificial distinctions and conflicting decisions. In my judgment your Lordships should seek to restate the law in a form which is principled, reflects the current requirements of society and provides as much certainty as possible.[32]

The effort to produce a 'principled' restatement is what primarily concerns us here, because that is exactly what judicial methodology should be about. But it is interesting to see what he has in mind when talking about 'the current requirements of society' because this is precisely the area where judges are prone to hide behind a self-denigrating submissiveness to the supposedly greater capacity of Parliament. One might expect, given that general self-denial, to find Browne-Wilkinson referring to some very simple and very obviously consensual element in public morality. In fact the 'Policy Considerations', as he heads the section of his opinion which sets out the goals, are far more complex. He identifies

---

[32] *Barclays Bank plc* v. *O'Brien* [1994] 1 AC at 195. The Duval case was a Privy Council case, originating from Jamaica, in 1902, which turns out to be the basis, though a very shaky one, for the law on wives' rights against husbands who use matrimonial property in dubious ways to shore up their business ventures. (*Turnbull & Co.* v. *Duval* [1902] AC 429.)

several intersecting factors of modern society which occasion cases like Mrs O'Brien's:

Wealth is now more widely spread. Moreover a high proportion of privately owned wealth is invested in the matrimonial home. Because of the recognition by society of the equality of the sexes, the majority of matrimonial homes are now in the joint names of both spouses. Therefore in order to raise finance for the business enterprise of one or the other of the spouses, the jointly owned home has become a main source of security. The provision of such security requires the consent of both spouses. In parallel with these financial developments, society's recognition of the equality of the sexes has led to a rejection of the concept that the wife is subservient to the husband in the management of the family's finances.[33]

Left like that we would have an adequate description of the relationship between spousal rights and the economics of investment. There would be no obvious policy problem for the courts. The problem comes because Browne-Wilkinson and others are not prepared to take the formal position as an entirely correct description of the reality of family life: 'many wives are still subjected to, and yield to, undue influence by their husbands'. This, again, is a fairly uncontroversial empirical statement. The social-psychology on which Lord Browne-Wilkinson supports this assumption about wives' vulnerability is similarly intuitively appealing:

The sexual and emotional ties between the parties provide a ready weapon for undue influence: a wife's true wishes can easily be overborne because of her fear of destroying or damaging the wider relationship between her and her husband if she opposes his wishes.[34]

However, even if that assessment is not seen as patronizing it is certainly an empirical judgement that might well be seen as the province of some profession other than that of the lawyer, and more properly expert opinion of the sort we are so often told is available only to Parliament, and not to the courts. (On this point it should be noted that the sort of professional amicus brief extensively allowed in the US is very rare in the UK, though recent suggestions from Law Lords indicate the practice might change. From our point of view such a change would be interesting, because the American use of such briefs goes hand in hand with the idea of a 'Brandeis Brief', that is, an opinion openly legislating on the basis of sociological rather than legal reasoning. It would improve the quality of judicial policy making, but at the cost of making much of our claim here rather less controversial. But would it be constitutionally less controversial to make policy openly rather than in a largely unacknowledged way?) What is certain is that enshrining that judgement in a protective law is a blatant

---

[33] *O'Brien* at 188–9.
[34] *O'Brien* at 190–1.

policy act, and one that feminists might well object to. The next several points are even more clearly normative, however:

Such wives can reasonably look to the law for some protection when their husbands have abused the trust and confidence reposed in them . . . It is easy to allow sympathy for the wife . . . to obscure an important public interest viz., the need to ensure that the wealth currently tied up in the matrimonial home does not become economically sterile . . . it is therefore essential that a law designed to protect the vulnerable does not render the matrimonial home unacceptable as security to financial institutions.[35]

It is very clearly a matter of substantive political judgement how to balance the interests of a category thought to be vulnerable to financial risk, always assuming their vulnerability is thought apt to be protected, against any risk there may be of making investment funds sterile. Indeed that latter judgement again seems to be one requiring a technical expertise not, *de jure*, in the realm of lawyers. It should be clear these comments are not addressed to the impropriety of the assumptions and arguments made by Browne-Wilkinson. The decision seems eminently just, and remarkable for putting a lie to the current notion that social justice cannot emanate from a court comprised of 'old white upper class men'. The problem is to explain why all of these moves are acceptable in this case when logically similar, and empirically less difficult ones, would be interference with parliamentary privilege in, for example, the *Brown* case.

In order to achieve his aims, especially the aim to ensure a 'principled' restatement of the law, Browne-Wilkinson has to remove the existing case law and replace it with a rule drawn from an equally persuasive and authoritative base. Removing the case law turned out to be relatively easy, despite the large number of Court of Appeal cases and their complexity. These cases all stem from the 1902 case *Turnbull & Co.* v. *Duval*.[36] In this case a Mrs Duval pledged her interests under a will as guarantee of payment for her husband's trading debts with Turnbull & Co., at his instigation, though she was under the impression that she was only guaranteeing a relatively small part of the debt. The Privy Council refused to allow Turnbull & Co. to enforce this on the grounds that she was unduly influenced by her husband to sign a document which was, in any case, not what she thought it was. Turnbull could not proceed because 'it is impossible to hold that [they] are unaffected by such pressure and ignorance. They left everything to Duval and must abide by the consequences.'[37] From there developed, according to the Court of Appeal judgment in *O'Brien*, two different lines of cases, justifying the protection of wives

[35] *O'Brien* at 188.
[36] *Turnbull & Co.* v. *Duval* [1902] AC 429.
[37] *Duval* at 434–5.

under different theories. One was the agency theory—it saw Duval, and would have seen Mr O'Brien, as effectively acting as agents of the creditors, so that if they misbehaved in pressuring or misinforming their wives, the original creditor's rights were infected, it being good law that the principal cannot be in a better position than his agent. This is one of the things that might be meant by the Privy Council when it said that Turnbull had 'left everything to Duval and must abide by the consequences'. The alternative line of cases has been to recognize wives as deserving 'special equity' because of the risk of undue influence arising in the way that Browne-Wilkinson noted. There is again good law that someone disadvantaged by undue influence can set aside a claim against the influencer. The problem here, as throughout these cases, is to see how a third party, the lender, can be affected. If the husband is not acting as an agent, how can the bank's title to the property be invalidated? Over the years the courts, when unable to rely on the agency theory, have treated Duval's case as necessarily implying a special duty towards wives, a duty to ensure they are fully aware of the implication of any agreement they make to a proposal of their husbands which affects their property rights, even though a lender would owe no such duty in any other context or to anyone else. The law, it has been said, treats married women 'more tenderly than others', and recognizes, in transactions between husbands and wives, 'an invalidating tendency'. Browne-Wilkinson's objections are well put—such an uncertain base makes the outcome both more uncertain, and less principled, because sheer recognition of a peculiar special case, in order to make sense of a dated ruling, hardly has the logical power of a principle from which the law could develop. For example, Browne-Wilkinson is at pains to show that his own solution does not protect wives, in some sense of nineteenth-century gallantry, but all cohabitees, of either sex and married or otherwise, because of a common vulnerability to sexual and emotional blackmail. But such an extension cannot be productive if wives are simply seen as a special case in equity without some principled reason to impose such duties on banks to them as a special category.

Clearly *Duval* has to go, because with it goes the chain of cases relying on it, and the slate is clean. Duval is disposed of simply enough, but in a way that raises a potentially serious question about the logical status of a precedent. Browne-Wilkinson deals with *Duval* by asking two questions: (1) 'Was the husband in breach of duty to his wife?' (2) 'Was the creditor under a direct duty to the wife?' He then goes, very unusually, to the actual case lodged on appeal to the Privy Council, that is, the arguments and facts the councillors were presented with. On this basis he argues that the Privy Council had no right to think, as they clearly did think, that Mr Duval had behaved improperly. Lord Lindley for the Council wrote:

In the face of such evidence their Lordships are of the opinion that it is quite
impossible to uphold the security given by Mrs Duval . . . having been obtained by
a husband from his wife by pressure and concealment of material facts . . . It is, in
their Lordships' opinion, quite clear that Mrs Duval was pressed by her husband
to sign, and did sign, the document, which was very different from what she
supposed it to be, and a document the true nature of which she had no conception.[38]

In contrast Browne-Wilkinson says that there is no evidence from which
Lord Lindley could have arrived at this decision: 'Therefore the . . .
ground of decision sprung wholly from the Board and Lord Lindley's
speech gives little insight into their reasoning.' Consequently if the Board
could not properly find as it did, 'it is impossible to find a sound basis for
holding that Mrs Duval was entitled to set aside the transaction against
her husband. How then could she set it aside against Turnbulls?'[39]

He goes on to suggest that it is the very inchoateness of the original
opinion—an inchoateness dependent entirely on rejecting the Board's
own firm conviction that they did have reason to believe Mr Duval had
misbehaved—that has lead to the tortuous line of subsequent cases. To
overturn a precedent on the grounds that the earlier generation of judges
simply had no good reason for making their decision is very much like
second guessing a trial judge, and leaves one very unclear about exactly
what a precedent is, and when one could ever be safe. It would be disingenuous not to admit that this is precisely one of the reasons we have
selected this case. At no stage in this book will the reader find us offering
an answer to the questions, 'What is a precedent?' or, 'When does a
precedent bind and when does it not?', because the most sense we are able
to make of the idea of precedent is that precedents are argumentative
tokens to be deployed or not as suits the construction of a rationalization.

However, if *Turnbull & Co.* v. *Duval* is, and has always been, simply
wrong, there is no good reason why a third party to a transaction should
not foreclose on a mortgage because a joint owner did not bother reading,
or could not understand, the terms of his or her surety for a cohabitee.
Theoretically it is not obvious that this strategy is permissible. At best it
would involve treating the law in *Turnbull* as based on a counter factual,
because the logic of the rule would apply still. Except, of course, that
Browne-Wilkinson does have a reason, a 'principled' reason which
will produce certainty and not impose an undue burden on lending
organizations.

What Browne-Wilkinson does is to incorporate a long-standing doctrine, the doctrine of notice, which he remarks 'lies at the heart of equity',
and which he notes was alluded to in several of the recent cases on this

[38] *Duval* at 435.
[39] *Barclays Bank* at 192–3.

point. Under this doctrine the bank only takes rights over the property subject to any pre-existing rights a third party—the wife—may have. The bank ought to have realized when making a deal with a husband that the matrimonial context raised a risk that the wife would be over pressured or misinformed . Therefore the bank in this case had not taken the normal precautions to investigate potential prior rights that the law of equity requires.

Consequently Browne-Wilkinson can present the desired result—the protection of vulnerable cohabitees—as flowing directly from the logical basis of a whole branch of law, rather than depending on any precedent at all. Furthermore, the doctrine of notice allows him to generate specific rules that banks must follow in order to show that they are not 'fixed with constructive notice' of a prior right over the property. (Which he conveniently finds to be very similar to the rules set out in the 1992 Code of Banking Practice.) Thus the certainty requirement and the 'principled' requirement are met. What Browne-Wilkinson is doing is essentially to provide an explanation of the established cases, to provide, as described earlier, a 'theory of the precedents'. He notes 'facts' about the law—the 'tender treatment of married women', the 'invalidating tendency':

This tenderness of the law is reflected by the fact that voluntary dispositions by the wife in favour of her husband are more likely to be set aside than other dispositions by her: a wife is more likely to establish presumed undue influence . . . by her husband than by others, because in practice, many wives do repose in their husbands trust and confidence in relation to their financial affairs. Moreover the informality of business dealings between spouses raises a substantial risk that her husband has not accurately stated to the wife the nature of the liability she is undertaking, i.e., he has misrepresented the position albeit negligently.[40]

'Therefore', he goes on to say, 'a creditor is put on inquiry when a wife offers to stand surety'—that is, the situation already prevails, and his opinion is a theoretical explanation of the world, rather than a policy choice inside it. The model is essentially that of the scientist deriving a generalization which accounts for observations, as suggested of Mustill in *Brown*: it is an induction game. Yet another way of putting it is that Browne-Wilkinson is giving us a language in which to describe what judges are already doing with 'matrimonial property as surety' situations, because the language provided by the opinion in Duval, which would lead to the same result, is insufficiently rich. In fact he refers earlier to the way in which preceding cases have nearly all simply applied *Duval* rather than giving 'any analysis of its jurisprudential basis'.[41] The two cases which did provide an analysis he regards as wrong. Thus it is quite easy

---

[40] *O'Brien* at 196.
[41] *O'Brien* at 194.

to overlook the fact that a very specific group is still singled out for preferential treatment on the basis of what is, in the end, a private value judgement based on amateur social-psychology. Legally one might want to ask about the possible extensions of this doctrine—what further requirements might lenders find themselves under when one applies the age-old doctrine of equity to modern social conditions? But such a question is inappropriate inasmuch as law must necessarily be open ended. As was said long ago in another context, 'the categories of tort are never closed'. What is relevant here is to note that the methodology of judging seems to lie in this process of redescribing lines of cases so that actual changes in law, or developments, are presented as the automatic interaction of unchanging principles and given 'facts'. Nothing 'new' ever happens. All that changes is our understanding of what the law always has been. And the trouble with the 'induction game' is that there is always a large, conceivably an infinite, range of possible generalizations that equally well fit the facts.[42] Absent something like the scientist's *Occam's Razor* test, one is left unsure how to select amongst the alternative candidates. It is interesting to speculate about what the opinion in *O'Brien* would have looked like had, as is perfectly possible, a different bench of five judges contained someone who disagreed substantively with Browne-Wilkinson. If that Law Lord bothered to provide a minority opinion, one would have found then, as happened in *Brown*, two quite different theories of the precedents, both purporting to show what the law always had been and continued to be. This is precisely what one gets in the next case which has a substantive, but no legal, proximity to *O'Brien*.

II. Domestic Partners and Shared Houses

In many ways the area of law that has most been involved with politically relevant questions of social justice has not been the common law, properly so called, but equity. Originally equity involved the application of broad principles of justice by a separate set of courts to solve problems that the rule-bound common law courts could not handle. Equity sought to give instant justice in a fundamental way according to the precise details of the conflict brought to the Lord Chancellor (who was exercising the sovereign's right to give *ad hominem* justice). Thus, for example, equity used a rule, to be discussed below, that one had to come to court 'with clean hands'—even if some rule implied you should win in a conflict, evidence that you were personally in no better moral a position than your opponent

---

[42] This is one of the arguments against Dworkin's account of how a judge decides in 'Hard Cases'. See D. Robertson in M. Freeman, and D. Robertson, *The Frontiers of Political Theory*, Harvester, 1980.

might lead you to lose your case. Because equity was, by its very nature, *ad hoc* it ended up being turned into a system of rules almost as inflexible as common law precedential rules at their worst, because otherwise it could not be applied in a consistent manner once it was the business of large numbers of professional judges rather than literally the King's mercy. Shortly before equity ceased to function as a separate branch of law it was pilloried in one of the few major literary works on the courts, Dickens' *Bleak House*, precisely as having become a mass of over-complicated rules. The essence of equity style thought still depends, however, on the original notion of doing specific justice in all the circumstances of the case, rather than the common law ideal of applying a known rule to selected aspects of the case.[43] Though equity and law have long been fused, and the separate equity courts abolished, many of the doctrines of equity remain. Even more important for us, the mode of thought of equity lawyers, those who practise in the Chancery Division of the High Court, is very much alive. To the extent that judicial ideology is a professional ideology, equity is a partially distinct ideology from that which infuses the minds of common law or commercial court judges. Lord Browne-Wilkinson, Mrs O'Brien's protector, is perhaps the arch-practitioner of equity law, as befits his previous office as Vice-Chancellor, the head of the Chancery Division of the High Court. In *Tinsley v. Milligan*[44] he repeated much the same role by protecting Ms Milligan's interest in her domestic home. Ms Milligan and her lover Ms Tinsley lived together in a house they jointly paid for and ran as a boarding house. The house was legally only in Ms Tinsley's name. When the relationship ended she attempted to gain complete possession of the house, ignoring Ms Milligan's contribution to buying and running it. Were there no more to be said Ms Milligan would have a clear right to a half share in the proceeds of selling the house, by long established equity doctrines, and indeed the courts, both at first instance and the Court of Appeal (by a majority), accepted this. But Ms Tinsley appealed to the House of Lords, insisting that her former lover could not rely on this equitable right because the original reason they had put the house only in one name was so that Ms Milligan could fraudulently claim various social security benefits that she would not have been entitled to as a joint owner of the house. There is a long established principle of equity known by a suitable Latin tag—*ex dolo malo non oritur actio*—and by an English epithet we mentioned above—one must come to

[43] Although there is a huge professional legal literature on equity, little of it is useful for a non-legal reader. The best way to approach equity is through a basic legal history like J. H. Baker, *An Introduction to English Legal History*, London, Stevens & Co., 3rd edn., 1990; alternatively the introductory chapters of a textbook on modern equity law will help see where someone like Lord Browne-Wilkinson developed his professional views. Try H. G. Hanbury, *Modern Equity*, London, Stevens & Co., 1989.

[44] *Tinsley v. Milligan* [1993] 3 All ER 65.

equity with clean hands—which effectively means that equity courts (nowadays all courts are equally courts of equity and common law) will not lend themselves to aiding wrongdoing by enforcing an equitable right which comes about by fraud. The question in the case was whether this long established rule, which dates at least to the eighteenth century, should now be abolished or relaxed. The minority in the Lords, lead by Lord Goff, and Ralph Gibson LJ in the Court of Appeal, thought it completely inappropriate to throw away the principle, though Goff is on record as regretting having to apply it in the instant case, feeling instead that it was needed for deterrent purposes in more serious frauds. One aspect that makes the case interesting here is that the Lords were unanimous in very firmly rejecting the grounds on which the Court of Appeal itself upheld Ms Milligan's equitable right. Indeed the Law Lords' majority has been severely criticized in academic legal circles, even though they did drop the old principle, for not doing so in a more emphatic and radical way.[45] The Court of Appeal wanted to accept as a general principle that illegal behaviour involved in accruing some property right might give the Courts the *discretion* to refuse to enforce that right, rather than compel them to do so. This would be discretion in the very full sense of Chapter 1, often better described by the American concept of a 'judgment call'. The idea, in the words of the majority judgment by Nichols LJ was to recognize an underlying principle:

the so-called public conscience test. The court must weight, or balance, the adverse consequences of granting relief against the adverse consequences of refusing relief. The ultimate decision calls for a value judgment.[46]

And, as he went on to say, 'far from it being an affront to public conscience to grant relief in this case, it would be an affront to the public conscience not to do so'. An approach like this would be in keeping with the original point behind equity which was that the fixed rules of common law inevitably threw up anomalies from time to time which only a fully discretionary judgment, originally by the Lord Chancellor as 'the keeper of the King's conscience', could resolve. The Lords would not entertain so overt a role for 'value judgments' in the law, and, most certainly, were not going to allow the Court of Appeal a freedom they would not grant themselves. One cannot know why they took this approach. In some countries it would be fairly the result of bargaining during a process of coalition building, but we are unused to seeing the Law Lords in this guise. It would be more usual in this country, were there such a split amongst those who wanted to find for Ms Milligan, to have two partially contradic-

---

[45] See Hugh Stowe, 'The "Unruly Horse" has bolted: *Tinsley* v. *Milligan*' [1994] *Modern Law Review* 57 at 441–8.

[46] Nichols LJ, *Tinsley* v. *Milligan* [1992] 2 All ER at 398.

tory speeches on her side. Whatever the reason for the shape of their judgment, the shape of the problem as the Lords felt they had to see it was stark—either a policy rule of great antiquity developed by such heroes of English law as Lord Mansfield in 1775 and Lord Eldon in 1802 is still good law, or it must go. The arguments are technically very complex, as arguments involving both common law and equity approaches to property inevitably are, and they required a huge number of citations to old cases. Unusually all members of the majority, Lowry, Jauncey, and Browne-Wilkinson give speeches, and while they each pay the usual courtesy of saying they agree with each other's conclusions, the approaches are rather different. There is no need here to go into them at any length; what is notable is the way they vary precisely as to how openly they admit they are rejecting an established rule. For this reason alone it does seem as though some form of bargaining must have been involved. Jauncey accepts that Eldon's rule:

would have been decisive of the present appeal. The question in 1993 is whether the law remains the same or whether in the intervening 180 or more years the very broad principles . . . have been to any extent modified.

He carefully characterizes the decision to support Ms Milligan as requiring only a rather minor adaptation to Lord Eldon's 1808 rule—'I find this a very narrow question'—and one that has already been taken in a series of cases, the first itself rather old as dating from 1873.[47] Thus the minimum possible damage is done to the sense of an unchanging though developing legal system. (This idea of a body of thought developing but not changing is otherwise not seen so starkly outside theology, as witnessed perhaps best by Newman's *An Essay on the Development of Christian Doctrine*. But then, much legal argument is reminiscent of the casuistry of theology.[48]) Lowry takes in many ways a more forceful tack, though one many judges would shy away from, because it is open about how law works. 'I am unable to accept and act upon Lord Eldon LC's wide principle despite its eminent authorship and its impressive antiquity':

. . . under the wide principle, someone in the position of Miss Milligan, who has only to show a trust, resulting from the fact . . . that the property was acquired . . . by the use of his money, is said to be defeated by the maxim that he who comes into equity must come with clean hands, on the ground that the original transaction was undertaken for a fraudulent purpose. But in the latter case the claimant . . . is merely said to be defeated by a *rule of policy*, despite the fact that he already has an equitable interest [Emphasis in original.][49]

---

[47] Lord Jauncey, *Tinsley* v. *Milligan* [1993] 3 All ER at 82.
[48] On legal casuistry see Richard Posner, *Overcoming Law*, Cambridge, Mass., Harvard UP, 1995, ch. 24.
[49] Lowry in *Tinsley* v. *Milligan* at 83–4.

Even more boldly he dismisses Goff's lengthy citations thus: 'but even a plurality of examples does not in my opinion endow the wide principle with validity'. Finally he rejects the prudential argument from deterrence rather neatly:

I am not impressed by the argument that the wide principle acts as a deterrent to persons in A's position. In the first place they may not be aware of the principle and are unlikely to consult a reputable solicitor. Secondly if they commit a fraud, they will not have been deterred.

The whole of Lowry's strategy depends on this translation of Eldon's principle from a rule of law or of equity into a 'mere' rule of policy. If it is only policy, then perhaps numerous cases applying it do not fix it into the structure of law as such, and, of course, empirical doubts as to its deterrent effect are relevant. Lowry is in general much more sceptical of the validity of 'policy' arguments, as witness his comments in the last case discussed here, *Spring* v. *Guardian Assurance*. Given how often policy arguments are used to support legal decisions it is unclear that many of Lowry's brethren would accept the implication of his argument, but it serves him as a way to avoid tackling head-on the sheer weight of Goff's scholarship in support of the equity rule. Indeed Goff, who accepts that it is a policy rule, makes the opposite inference. To Goff *because* it is a policy rule it is more natural that it will, from time to time, cause injustice, and the resultant injustice would not necessarily make it suspect, as it would were it a rule of law.

Ultimately *Tinsley* comes down to a clash between Goff and Browne-Wilkinson on just what the law is, or has become, since Eldon's time. The clash revolves round technique in citing cases, because Goff clearly has a huge armoury of applications of the 'clean hands' principle. He cites at least fifteen cases from the early late eighteenth century onwards, starting, to get the historical edge, not with Eldon's formulation of the exclusion principle in 1801 but with Lord Mansfield in *Holman* v. *Johnson* in 1775:

I do not feel able to say that it would be appropriate for your Lordships' House, in the face of a long line of unbroken authority stretching back over two hundred years, now by a judicial decision to replace the principles established in those authorities.

He simply does not accept Browne-Wilkinson's historical judgment. 'Lord Browne-Wilkinson has discerned a development in the law since the late nineteenth century which supports [his] approach . . . I have been unable to discover any such development in the law.' And later, minimizing Browne-Wilkinson's claim, 'I have already expressed my respectful disagreement with the view . . . that the law has already developed *at least in the direction of* the conclusion which he favours'[50] (my emphasis).

[50] *Tinsley* v. *Milligan* at 78.

It should be noted here that such an overt disagreement is rare. As we have pointed out earlier, it is much more common for conflicting opinions simply to ignore rival arguments than to admit to conflict. This makes the case all the more useful for us. We must look to see how such a flat disagreement on the case law can come about, because its explanation shows us further how the methodology of precedential argument can have weak enough a force to allow the clear imposition of personal values. Clearly Browne-Wilkinson cannot defeat the 'two hundred years of unbroken principle' argument by denying them—no one of Goff's eminence is going to be quite so massively wrong in legal scholarship. Nor does Browne-Wilkinson, unlike Lowry, bring himself to accept them as a policy and therefore not binding. The trick, and there has to be a trick, is a professionally highly technical one. Ms Tinsley's argument that her ex-partner cannot enforce her right to a share is accepted, by everyone, to depend on the fact that the partner's right is a right *at equity*, and not *at common law*. This has to be the case because the 'clean hands' rule is an equity rule. First, Browne-Wilkinson points out that *common law* property rights cannot be prevented by the idea that the initial ownership is tainted by illegality. Then he shows that the law versus equity distinction would have produced different results in some of the cases cited by Goff had the claims been in law not equity. None of this is disputable, and none of it strictly relevant given the fact that there are two different ways that one can have what a layman would think of simply as a property right. But then comes the statement:

In my judgment to draw such distinctions between property rights enforceable at law and those which require the intervention of equity would be surprising. More than 100 years has passed since the fusion of the administration of law and equity. The reality of the matter is that, in 1993, English law has one single law of property made up of legal and equitable interest . . . in my judgment the same rule ought to apply to any property right . . . whether such a rule is legal or equitable.[51]

If Browne-Wilkinson's 'judgment', expressed at this stage as a preference, is right, then all he has to do is to show that in practice a common law rule with rather different import is really what the courts have been using all along (without, of course, ever realizing that that was what they were doing), and, of course, there turns out to be such a rule, known as the *Bowmaker* rule, from a 1945 case. To get to this point he takes a different approach to the fact that a case has been cited as authority. Goff offers a set of cases in which Lord Eldon's rule is cited as the authority. Browne-Wilkinson says of them all, that 'none of the English cases are decided *simply* by applying the rule' (my emphasis). What he means is that, as it happens, each case depended only on a narrower version than Eldon's formulation, which narrower version happens to accord with the common

---

[51] Browne-Wilkinson, *Tinsley* v. *Milligan* at 86.

law rule in *Bowmaker*. Ergo, apparently, the common law rule has become the only rule through the fusion of law and equity. Thus Goff's scholarship ends up being shown to be accurate scholarship about, as it were, a counter factual.

It is hard to know exactly how one would characterize an argument like this in any other arena of discourse. (Though, to borrow one of their Lordships' favourite notions, the word 'cheating' comes to mind.) For our purposes it is enough to say the methodological difference rests on a question about the specificity of citation. Just how much congruence of argument does one need before a case is a precedent? Can a precedential model in fact ever determine a result? If not there seems to be no obvious limit to the imposition of judicial preference. Yet it is hard to see how much more watertight an argument from authority could be found than Goff's case here.

3. The Courts and Protection of Common Law Rights

The cases so far surveyed have all, in one way or another, shown the lengths the Lords will go to reinterpret a line of cases, or to construct a 'theory of the cases' when they want to make new law. It is not always like this though. Sometimes, at least, the House of Lords will openly acknowledge that they are extending or even creating rights, overtly ignoring the case law. It may not be surprising that this will most typically happen when it is the very power of the courts themselves that is in question. (This idea, that courts are more forceful in defending their own power in society than when only supporting an individual against the State in an area fully granted to them, is developed more fully in Chapters 8 and 9.) *R* v. *Horseferry Road Magistrates' Court, ex parte Bennett* in 1993 is such a case. Bennett was wanted on fraud charges in the UK, and had been traced to South Africa. The police and Crown Prosecution Service had decided not to try to extradite him—there being no routine extradition treaty with South Africa the process would have been complicated and lengthy. Instead, or so it was alleged, the Metropolitan Police, possibly in agreement with the CPS, arranged for him to be arrested by the South African police on warrants relating to charges in New Zealand (Bennett was a New Zealand citizen). Under pretext of repatriating him to New Zealand he was forcibly flown to London, where he was arrested and brought before a magistrate for committal on the fraud charges. He appealed to the Divisional Court of the Queen's Bench Division of the High Court, claiming they should refuse to allow a trial to go forward because of the illegality by which he was brought before them. Feeling themselves bound by a 1986 case on the point, the Divisional Court held that they had no power to inquire into the way in which someone appearing before a court had been brought into the jurisdiction.

The case law seems to have been fairly clear cut, being based primarily on a trio of cases in 1829, 1890, and 1949 which had been followed on all but one occasion since, the one occasion being a case in 1981 later judged to have been decided on an inadequate consideration of the previous cases.[52] In all the cases the line was taken that, though courts undoubtedly had the right to stop or prevent prosecution if there was danger that the trial process itself would be unfair, their jurisdiction did not, and ought not, to concern itself with how it came to be that a person was in a position to face a fair trial. The most the cases would allow was that if bringing the charge at all was unfair, the trial would be banned. This could happen, for example, when the accused had been promised immunity from prosecution for helping the police. So clear is the case law that the majority of the court neither seek to 'distinguish' it nor ignore it—Griffiths, giving the lead opinion, describes it exhaustively. The existing position is well described by Woolf's opinion in the Divisional Court—at that time he was still a Lord Justice of Appeal:

However quite apart from authority, I am bound to say it seems to me [the previous approaches] must be correct. The power which the court is exercising, and the power which the court was purporting to exercise in *Ex parte Mackeson* is one which is based upon the inherent power of the court to protect itself against the abuse of its own process. If the matters which are being relied upon have nothing to do with that process but only explain how a person comes to be in the jurisdiction so that the process can commence, it seems to me difficult to see how the process of the *court* (and I emphasise the word 'court') can be abused by the fact that a person may or may not have been brought into this country improperly.[53]

The extent to which the majority in the Lords, in rejecting this traditional approach, were acting quite unpredictably is highlighted by the very fact that Woolf's own track record as a public law judge, both on the Court of Appeal and subsequently as a Law Lord, is impeccably 'liberal'. (This reputation is now being developed even more fully in his office of Master of the Rolls.) Were anyone to want to overthrow the traditional rule it would be him. His first major act as a Law Lord was to write the sole

---

[52] The Divisional Court here felt itself bound by *R* v. *Plymouth Justices, ex parte Driver* [1986] QB 95. This had reversed a 1981 case which would have allowed them to refuse a prosecution of someone in Bennett's situation. But the earlier case, *R* v. *Bow Street Magistrates, ex parte Mackeson* (1981) 75 Cr. App. R. 24, DC was held to have been decided *per incuriam* on the grounds that the full previous case law was not adduced for the Court's consideration. The classic cases to which *ex parte Driver* reverted were: *Ex parte Susannah Scott* (1829) 9 B & C 446; *Sinclair* v. *HM Advocate* (1870) 17 R (J) 38; *R* v. *Officer Commanding Depot Battalion, RASC Colchester, ex parte Elliot* [1949] 1 All ER 373.

[53] Woolf LJ in *R* v. *Horseferry Road Magistrates' Court, ex parte Bennett* [1993] 2 All ER 474.

opinion in a hallmark case establishing the courts' powers to control and discipline the executive in which they held that even Secretaries of State were subject to contempt proceedings.[54] But the quotation from Woolf above is not that of a man forced to follow a line of cases he disagrees with.

Furthering the case against his own position Griffiths even notes the US Supreme Court decisions on the point. These are unusually important because the American/English contrast in this field runs quite counter to normal expectations. Generally courts in the UK are much tougher and more prosecution minded when it comes to using court powers to discipline police and prosecuting authorities. US Courts will frequently exclude evidence or otherwise prevent conviction where there is a suggestion of abuse of police powers, but have ruled repeatedly that no relevant constitutional right is abridged when an accused is wrongly arrested *abroad* and forced into the United States—only events after entering the jurisdiction can lead to a court's interference. In contrast in the UK it is difficult to have illegally obtained evidence rejected on the picturesquely named ground of being 'the fruits of the poisoned tree'. Lowry, supporting Griffiths, actually himself makes the point that the decision to free Bennett seems illogical for these reasons. The only real case law, and that necessarily only of a 'persuasive' nature, that Bennett's counsel could find is a curious hodgepodge: the minority dissent in the leading US case; a South African case which appears only to have been available in the form of its headnote, rather than the judicial reasoning, and a New Zealand case. Even the New Zealand case is slightly tainted by the fact that the President of the court which heard it went out of his way in a subsequent case to mention his reservations about earlier holding that an analogous prosecution had been an abuse of process. (All of these hesitations about the case law come from members of the majority—Lord Oliver's dissent is hardly concerned to do more than note the almost unbroken line of English and Scottish authority on his side.) The case can be seen as an unusually clear-cut example of Dworkin's theory that judging consists of balancing principles,[55] and Lord Bridge at least is prepared, uncharacteristically for an English judge, to admit this outright:

I fully recognise the cogency of the arguments [in denial of the right of the court to forbid prosecution in this context] sustained as they are by the public interest in the prosecution and punishment of crime . . . if there is another important principle of law which ought to influence the answer to the question posed, then your Lordships are at liberty, indeed under a duty, to examine it and, if it transpires that this is an area where two valid principles of law come into conflict, it must, in my

---

[54] *M v. Home Office.*
[55] R. M. Dworkin, 'Is Law a system of rules?' in R. M. Dworkin (ed.), *The Philosophy of Law: Oxford Readings in Philosophy*, Oxford, OUP, 1977.

opinion, be for your Lordships to decide as a matter of principle which of the two conflicting principles of law ought to prevail.[56]

What, though, are the two principles to be 'balanced' in this case? For Bridge the principle which will free Bennett is the protection of the very rule of law itself. He quotes approvingly from the minority in the most recent US Supreme Court case on the matter:

I suspect most courts throughout the civilised world will be deeply disturbed by the 'monstrous' decision the court announces today. For every nation that has an interest in preserving the rule of law is affected directly or indirectly, by a decision of this character.[57]

Similarly he cites Woodhouse J in the New Zealand case that most closely fits *Bennett* holding that the issue is 'basic to the whole concept of freedom in society'.[58] For Bridge, this upholding of the rule of law is tied also to a respect for international law and comity, and for the very integrity of the legal system as a whole, as shown by his acceptance of the language of a South African case which uses the old equity language in asserting that the state 'had to come to court with clean hands, as it were, when it was itself a party to proceedings'. This is the key to the majority principle, because the anger of the majority is directed at the involvement of the British state in illegal behaviour outside its frontiers. Lowry's attack is very specific. After repeating the clean hands argument by describing the proceedings as ones that 'have only been made possible by acts which offend the court's conscience as being contrary to the rule of law' he focuses on the point:

If British officialdom at any level has participated in or encouraged the kidnapping, it seems to represent a grave contravention of international law, the comity of nations and the rule of law generally if our courts allow themselves to be used by the executive to try an offence which the courts would not be dealing with if the rule of law had prevailed.[59]

This—their Lordships' outrage at the executive—is the key. The real point the majority is pressing home is the fundamental need, in their eyes, for the courts and not the executive to control the criminal law system in general. Lord Devlin's words in an earlier case had already been cited in the New Zealand court and Griffiths echoes them: 'the courts cannot

[56] *Ex parte Bennett* at 65.
[57] Stevens J in *United States* v. *Alvarez-Machain* 119 L Ed. 2d 441 at 466. The Supreme Court held by a majority that the kidnapping of Alvarez-Machain and his smuggling into the US to face a murder charge for killing a US Drug Enforcement Officer in Mexico was not constitutionally barred.
[58] *R* v. *Hartley* [1978] 2 NZLR 199. The Lords in the majority in Bennett all make use also of a follow-up New Zealand case, *Mauve* v. *Department of Labour* [1980] 1 NZLR 464 where Woodhouse expands on this theme.
[59] *Ex parte Bennett* at 76.

contemplate for a moment the transference to the Executive of the responsibility for seeing that the process of law is not abused'.[60] His own statement clearly locates the principle their Lordships are creating in *Bennett*
within a much wider statement of constitutional jurisprudence:

> If the court is to have the power to interfere with the prosecution . . . it must be
> because the judiciary accept a responsibility to oversee executive action and to
> refuse to countenance behaviour that threatens either basic human rights or the
> rule of law. My Lords I have no doubt that the judiciary should accept this
> responsibility in the field of criminal law. The great growth of administrative law
> during the latter half of this century has occurred because of the recognition by the
> judiciary and Parliament alike that it is the function of the High Court to ensure
> that executive action is exercised responsibly and as Parliament intended. So also
> should it be in the field of criminal law, and if it comes to the attention of the court
> that there has been a serious abuse of power it should, in my view, express its
> disapproval by refusing to act upon it.[61]

Thus the clash is between an absolutely basic constitutional principle, a
structural principle indeed of the distribution of power, and the public
interest in the efficacy of the criminal justice system. But is it? If this is
what it was all about we should have nice balancing and a thorough
working out of just how these two principles do weigh against each other.
Unfortunately it takes two, as it were, to balance. The trouble is that Lord
Oliver, in the minority, is blithely unaware of any such constitutional
clash at all. To the extent that Oliver is prepared to see a constitutional
clash it would be, at most, the suggestion that Bennett's civil rights had
been infringed by unlawful or illegal behaviour. Thus it would be a clash
between individual liberty and public interest, not a structural constitutional clash on the separation of powers. Discussing the terms of the
Extradition Act 1989, Oliver has no difficulty dismissing the idea of such
a right:

> A person who is returned only as a result of extradition proceedings enjoys, as a
> result of this statutory inhibition, an advantage over one who elects to return
> voluntarily or who is otherwise induced to return within the jurisdiction. But these
> are provisions inserted into the Act for the purpose of giving effect to reciprocal
> treaty arrangements for extradition. I cannot, for my part, regard them as confer-
> ring upon a person who is fortunate enough successfully to flee the jurisdiction
> some 'right' in English law which is invaded if he is brought or induced to come
> back within the jurisdiction.[62]

By avoiding this debate, sticking to an analysis of the situation in terms of
improper police behaviour, and taking a very tight definition of abuse of

---

[60] Lord Devlin in *Connelly* v. *Director of Public Prosecutions* [1964] AC 1254 at 1354.
[61] *Ex parte Bennett* at 62.
[62] Oliver in *Ex parte Bennett* at 72–3.

court process, Oliver systematically wins the 'normal' legal game. His hypothetical example gives the flavour of the argument. Suppose two terrorists flee to Dover after planting a bomb in London. A gets into an argument with a ticket inspector, is wrongly detained by the railway police and, while still in wrongful custody, is arrested by the bomb squad and charged. B gets all the way to France but, disembarking, is recognized by English police officers returning from holiday, forced back onto the ferry, and formally arrested when he gets back to Dover. Should A have his prosecution quashed? If not, why on earth should B get away with it? Pushing on with this line Oliver shows that the inevitable variance in how courts would exercise such a discretion, depending on their sense of how outrageous various illegalities by the police had been, would produce great uncertainty into the criminal law. Oliver's argument is full of such typical tactical moves, similar to the ones we have seen both elsewhere in this chapter and in Chapter 3, including a floodgates argument based on his surprising acceptance that: 'Experience shows that allegations of abusive use of executive power in the apprehension of those accused of criminal offences are far from rare.' But, given his way of conceiving of the problem, such illegalities 'having no bearing upon the fairness of the trial process' do not entitle an accused 'to demand that he be not tried for an offence with which he has been properly charged'.

Of course, if the argument is set like this, the clarity of the case law allows Oliver to depict the majority as rather arbitrarily carrying out judicial legislation where there is 'neither any inexorable logic calling for such an extension nor any social need for it', an extension which 'will be productive of a good deal of inconvenience and uncertainty'. As he says, the results of assuming such a jurisdiction to stop proceedings are 'surprising': (1) a possibly guilty man will escape 'a just punishment'; (2) the civil remedies he would have had against wrongful behaviour will be unenforceable; and (3) 'the public interest in the prosecution and punishment of crime will have been defeated not by a necessary process of penalising those responsible for executive abuse, *but simply for the purpose of manifesting judicial disapproval*' (our emphasis).

Obviously any reader of the case can see that what is going on is, in fact, a very serious clash of constitutional positions. The case is a stark example of the sort of material that makes up judicial ideology—but as an exercise in public debate that might clarify a fundamental constitutional issue it is useless. The intellectual battle is never joined, because of an inner logic of judicial rhetoric which operates always to re-characterize opponents' positions rather than confront them. Surely this is one of the key reasons legal argument does not strongly constrain judicial discretion. If issues are fought out, one argument must prevail, and to that extent the opponents of the stronger argument are then deprived of their discretion. But if the opposing arguments do not yield a victor, no one has to change their preferred vote.

After that resounding support for the powers of the courts, we turn to a curious withdrawal of curial support for individual rights in the same year. *Page* v. *Hull University Visitor*[63] is a case within a very important and terribly difficult area of public law dealing with the power of courts to control administrative bodies. Later chapters discuss this area in detail, so *Page* will be dealt with very briefly at this point. Mr Page was made redundant from his post of university lecturer in philosophy not for cause but just because he was the oldest member of his department. Rather optimistically he tried to challenge this decision (with the backing, for what it was worth, of the Association of University Teachers) on the grounds that his contract only allowed dismissal for good cause, the old layman's conception of academic tenure. Initially, and as required by the statutes of the university, Mr Page petitioned the University's Visitor. The Visitor's decision was that the university was entitled to make him redundant. (The Queen being the Visitor, the Privy Council dealt with the matter, taking the advice of a Law Lord, Lord Jauncey.) Page appealed against this decision to the Divisional Court, in much the same way that an employee in much of industry could appeal to the Employment Appeal Tribunal after losing before a first instance Industrial Tribunal. (Technically, a matter explained in Chapter 7, he 'applied for judicial review' of the decision.) He won, the Divisional Court refusing to accept that a Visitor's decision could not be challenged in the courts, and also thinking the Visitor wrong in his actual decision. The university appealed to the Court of Appeal which upheld the powers of the courts to supervise the decisions of Visitors, though they also held that in this case the Visitor had got the law right and the university could make Mr Page redundant. From there it went to the Lords, Page appealing against the substantive decision that he could be sacked, the university cross-appealing against the idea that the courts could supervise a Visitor.

Legally the issue is very simple, and by now no reader will be surprised to discover that its simplicity did not prevent a three to two split in the Lords. Ever since a case in 1694 Visitors of a special class of institutions, eleemosynary charitable foundations (mainly universities and colleges, but also Anglican Dioceses and some schools), have been recognized as internally governed not by the common law, but by private law handed down by their founders and interpreted solely, where the founder has so wished, by a Visitor. They are by Lord Browne-Wilkinson's testimony, unique in this respect as islands where the ordinary law does not run. This fact was enough for the majority, Lords Browne-Wilkinson, Griffiths, and

---

[63] *Page* v. *Hull University Visitor* [1993] 1 All ER 97.

Keith. In his lead opinion, Browne-Wilkinson admits that there has been an explosion of public law over the last forty years, much of it involved in giving the courts the power to ensure that tribunals and other public bodies apply the law properly. As recently as *Thomas* v. *University of Bradford* in 1987 the Lords had agreed that at least in some respects the courts would have to intervene to control a Visitor—where he exceeds his rightful jurisdiction by doing something he was not empowered to do.[64] The Law Lords often speak with pride of the extension of the protection of judicial review and their increased powers to control the executive. Lord Griffiths, for example, is witness to that in his speech in *Bennett*. How then could the majority deny that, not withstanding a long history of special treatment for universities, their teachers were entitled to the same sort of protection as other workers? The argument is technical but for present purposes the legal basis can be put in the following form. (All the steps in this argument are capable of being backed by citation, but as the whole field is to be discussed later, only a skeletal version is needed in this chapter.)

1. No tribunal (including a Visitor) may act outside its jurisdiction, i.e. do something unauthorised.
2. An error in applying law means that a tribunal has, in fact, done something it should not have done.
3. Therefore courts can grant judicial review to correct errors of law, as well as for more obvious or wider extra-jurisdictional acts.
4. However, Parliament can, by statute, reserve to inferior *courts* a right to make non-reviewable legal interpretations.

Lord Browne-Wilkinson uses the following strategy to release university Visitors from this net. First, university law has always been recognized as private law:

a member of a college puts himself voluntarily under a peculiar system of law, and assents to being bound by it, and cannot thereafter complain that such a system is not in accordance with that adopted by the common law [Lord Kenyon CJ in 1794].

Consequently, it would make sense to place a Visitor in logically the same position in interpreting his 'domestic law' as an inferior court can be placed by Parliament in interpreting ordinary law. The proper analogy is between court and Visitor, not tribunal and Visitor. Then, to get round the fact that Parliament has not, as it happens, passed such an empowering statute:

For myself, I can see no relevant distinction between a case where a statute has conferred such final and conclusive jurisdiction and the case where the common

---

[64] *Thomas* v. *University of Bradford* [1987] 1 All ER 834.

law has for 300 years recognised that the visitor's decision on questions of fact and law are final and conclusive and are not to be reviewed by the courts. Accordingly unless this House is prepared to sweep away long-established law, there is no jurisdiction in the court to review a visitor's decision for error of law committed within his jurisdiction.[65]

Two pragmatic points are also pleaded—that it is invaluable for universities to have an informal mechanism that produces a 'speedy, cheap and final answer', and Lord Griffiths' reminder that:

Many decisions may turn upon the interpretation of the statutes and other decisions of a more factual nature can all too easily be dressed up as issues of law ... The learning and ingenuity of those members of the foundation who are likely to be in dispute with the foundation should not be lightly underestimated.[66]

In Chapter 3 it was shown that judges cannot be seen as systematically 'strict' or 'liberal' constructionists, but rather accept methodological inconsistency to retain some kind of substantive consistency. Browne-Wilkinson's approach here shows the same pattern. In general a man prepared to ride very roughly over long lines of precedent which fail to fit modern conditions, becomes so attached to precedent in this case that he is prepared to equate a common law precedential rule with statutory enactment. It is actually extremely unlikely that he would in general wish to take this stance, but here it serves a particular purpose. Similarly in *Bennett*, Griffiths happily dumped two centuries of precedent to expand the powers of the court, but will not now tamper with them to expand the court's role against a university.

Against this, what can Mustill and Slynn do? Slynn does point out that, far from being a recondite matter special to university culture, the legal question Page was raising was perfectly orthodox employment law. He adds that there would be little point Visitors being, or being advised by, Law Lords were they in practice unable to understand the complexities of university law. Above all he insists that 'the old cases I have cited must be read subject to the development [of administrative law] ... not least what was said in *Thomas's* case'. The development is that of the scope of judicial review, which he depicts as so well known and thoroughly accepted that 'it is obviously not necessary to cite cases ... it is more than enough to refer to the analysis of Sir William Wade's *Administrative Law*'. Slynn must have known, it was widely accepted at the time, that had the listing clerk by happenstance put on that bench one particular Law Lord with extensive experience of public law in place of Browne-Wilkinson who is a Chancery Lawyer, as well might have happened, the law of judicial review would have taken yet another incremental step. Would Lord

---

[65] *Page* at 109.
[66] *Page* at 101.

Griffiths, who was responsible in *Thomas* for accepting jurisdiction over the jurisdiction of the Visitor, have insisted then that he meant jurisdictional error only in the narrow sense of the word used by Browne-Wilkinson? Why *did* a superior court which was prepared to take on the Metropolitan Police and the Crown Prosecution Service leave university authorities in such a privileged position? That question cannot be answered. What can be said is that it is beyond credulity that the Lords were forced to that position by any principle or any methodology. If there is an explanation that squares both *Bennett* and *Page*, it lies in some ideological depth. But, another alternative, there may simply not be an explanation.

4. Justice, Rights, and Public Policy

It would be wrong to leave this survey of common law methodology and discretion without an example of the Lords at their most creative. The intentional development of basic common law rights of action is where the Law Lords best represent their heritage as avowed judicial legislators. We can only treat briefly here an example which, like the previous one, is deeply embedded in a modern legal development to which a whole subsequent discussion, Chapter 7, is dedicated. The case, *Spring* v. *Guardian Assurance*,[67] is one of the more recent ones in an area known as liability for negligence for economic loss. We need not consider the technical complexities of the whole field here, but it is useful to know that it has perhaps been the most controversial area of common law development in the last two decades. The case is especially useful for our purposes because it displays a structure of judicial opinion much more like the multi-opinion cases of the pre-Diplock era. Not only is it divided, with Lord Keith in dissent, but Lord Goff's reasons for finding for the plaintiff are, subtly but vitally, different not only in argumentative strategy but in legal implication from the reasons shared by Lords Lowry, Woolf, and Slynn, each of whom gives a separate speech. The case also serves as an introductory discussion of one of the main ways in which judicial discretion opens up possibilities of private ideology influencing the making of law, the use of 'public policy' arguments, so far only touched on in *Tinsley* v. *Milligan*.

The question is this: does a previous employer who, negligently but not maliciously, gives a damning reference containing false allegations commit a tortious act for which he should pay damages because his ex-employee's chances of further work in his profession was effectively foreclosed? The natural expectation that this would be a matter of libel law is untrue because of a particular doctrine of English law. Anyone who

---

[67] *Spring* v. *Guardian Assurance plc and others* [1994] 3 All ER 129.

wrote a letter like the one describing Mr Spring, a former insurance salesman, would normally be committing a libel because of the falsehood of the allegations. However, there exists a 'rule of policy' in the law of defamation which removes liability for defamation where the writer has a special immunity known as 'qualified privilege'. Privilege occurs, *inter alia*, in the context of references because it has long been felt that society needed to encourage frank and honest reference writing. Consequently employers in such a situation are protected from the risk of libel so they will not be tempted to write blandly and uninformatively. This privilege immunity can only be disposed of if the defamed person can show intentional malice on the part of the writer. Malice is hard to prove, as this case showed. One of those supplying the information on which the reference was based had actually lied about meeting him, and the general context involved clashes of personality and Mr Spring's being sacked by a new boss. Nonetheless the plaintiff was held not to have demonstrated malice.

Germane here is the fact that the rules of LAUTRO, which govern the insurance industry, require a potential employer to get a reference from a past employer in the industry, and require that past employer to give one. The judge at first instance accepted both that the letter was negligent, and that it completely doomed Mr Spring from any hope of future employment in the insurance industry. The question for the Lords was whether to develop a relatively new area of the law of negligence to give Mr Spring an alternative to the unavailable defamation route as a way of recouping his losses from the way his previous employers, Guardian Assurance, had treated him.

Since the late seventies a general possibility has arisen to sue for what tort lawyers call 'economic loss'—in the past actual physical harm to person or property had been the basis of negligence cases. As a result of *Anns* v. *Merton*[68] in 1977, when plaintiff and defendant are in a certain sort of relationship to each other and particular other characteristics apply to the situation, plaintiffs can sometimes get damages because the defendant has caused, for example, loss of an expectable income stream, without suffering actual physical hurt. Mr Spring hoped to get this line of development extended to cover his situation because a negligent communication had cut off his expected income as an insurance salesman.

An alternative attack exists which was not argued by Spring's counsel. Since the early sixties, and particularly since a seminal decision in *Hedley Byrne*[69] in 1963, English law has specifically recognized that negligence in preparing a reference in certain very tightly defined situations may be

---

[68] *Anns* v. *Merton London Borough* [1977] AC 728.
[69] *Hedley Byrne & Co* v. *Heller & Partners* [1963] 2 All ER 575.

actionable. *Hedley Byrne*, however, had only asserted the right of the *recipient* of an incorrectly favourable reference about a third party to sue when, as a consequence of relying on the reference, he lost money by trusting the subject of the reference. Thus Spring's situation was not directly covered by the rule in *Hedley Byrne*, which had been controversial in itself. Although the possibilities opened up by *Hedley Byrne* and *Anns* both deal with economic loss, the rationales for the two lines of argument are rather different, and the *Hedley Byrne* rule is considerably more restrictive. On the other hand the Lords have shown themselves definitely cautious, but not consistently so, in developing the coverage of the *Anns* v. *Merton* liabilities.

Lord Keith, who wrote the lone dissent, is one of the leaders of the cautious approach to extending negligence liability into new areas, and his approach in *Spring* was typical of his arguments in the area in previous cases. He focused on the public policy grounds for denying a duty of care in writing a reference, the argument that the public interest requires referees to feel free to write whatever they think is correct, without unduly worrying as to whether they had checked everything properly. He was able to make this argument particularly strongly because the originating case, *Anns* v. *Merton*, had specifically noted the likelihood of public policy restrictions on recognizing a duty, a note of caution Keith himself had relied on in several ensuing cases. Indeed he cites his own previous findings of public policy restrictions at the beginning of his argument here. So intent is Keith on developing the public policy attack that he makes no attempt to argue that *Spring* is not, otherwise, a case of unlawful negligence:

My Lords, if no reasons of policy intervened there might be much to be said for the view that Mr Spring is entitled to succeed in his claim based on negligence, on the basis that it was reasonably foreseeable that damage to him would result if the reference were prepared without reasonable care and it thus incorrectly disparaged him, that there was proximity between him and those who prepared the reference, and that it would be fair, just and reasonable to impose a duty of care on the latter.[70]

What makes the policy argument more powerful than it might have been is the very fact that it has so long been recognized in another area of law, the law of defamation, which might be thought to be all the law that was needed in this area. After all, but for the qualified privilege enjoyed by referees, a letter 'incorrectly disparaging' Spring would entitle him to damages for libel. There being no real cases on the point in English law, Keith relies heavily on cases from New Zealand, all the more useful to him because he feels free to characterize New Zealand courts as somewhat

[70] Keith in *Spring* at 135.

more liberal than English courts in many areas. (It will be remembered that New Zealand jurisprudence was also relied on by *Bennett*.)

The views expressed in these three cases decided in a jurisdiction which is well known to be tender in its approach to claims in negligence involving pure economic loss are of great importance.[71]

The essence of the New Zealand approach, which Keith accepts as good law, can be given in a couple of short quotations:

The common law rules, and their statutory modifications regarding defamation and injurious falsehood represent compromises gradually made and worked out by the Courts over the years with some legislative adjustments, between competing values. . . . The important point for present purposes is that the law as to injury to reputation and freedom of speech is a field of its own. To impose the law of negligence upon [it] . . . would be to introduce a distorting element.[72]

The same New Zealand judge in a later case simplified the argument further:

The suggested cause of action in negligence would therefore impose a greater restriction on freedom of speech than exists under the law worked out over many years to cover freedom of speech and its limitations. By a side-wind the law of defamation would be overthrown.[73]

Finally, quite clearly stating the need to keep the distinct areas of defamation and negligence distinct, Hardie Boys J in the third case:

Any attempt to merge defamation and negligence is to be resisted. Both of these branches of the law represent the result of much endeavour to reconcile competing interests in ways appropriate to the quite distinct areas with which they are concerned, but not necessarily appropriate to each other. An inability in a particular case to bring it within the criteria of a defamation suit is not to be made good by the formulation of a duty of care not to defame.[74]

These seem to add up to a rather powerful reason for not granting Mr Spring the relief that Keith has already admitted he probably deserves. In fact the impression is misleading if one considers even briefly what has actually been shown. First, only one of these cases actually concerns a reference at all, and in another, *Bell-Booth*, the issue was actually about whether or not NZ Television should have broadcast something everybody agreed was actually true. Secondly, all one has here (these shortened

---

[71] *Spring* at 141. The cases, discussed by all the Lords of Appeal in this case, are: *Balfour v. A.–G.* [1991] 1 NZLR 519; *Bell-Booth Group Ltd. v. A.–G.* [1989] 3 NZLR 148; *South Pacific Manufacturing Co. Ltd. v. New Zealand Security Consultants and Investigations Ltd.* [1992] 2 NZLR 282.

[72] Cooke in *Bell-Booth* at 155–6.

[73] Cooke P in *South Pacific Manufacturing Co.* at 301.

[74] *Balfour v. A.–G.* at 529.

versions of Keith's quotations are not unfairly selective) are merely the conclusions the courts in question came to, not their reasons. Thirdly, the New Zealand cases cannot be technically anything more than 'persuasive'. Thus we are in fact given merely examples of the conclusions a court in a different country came to in a set of cases that have factually no bearing at all on Spring's problem. And the conclusions themselves actually amount to saying no more than 'The Law of Defamation doesn't allow this sort of action and it has been developed over a long time.' Even this might not call into doubt Keith's argumentative method were it not for one fact—there *is* an English case to point, in which it was found by the trial judge that a former employer did owe a duty of care in giving a reference. But Keith dismisses this simply by saying that the arguments about the law of defamation were not discussed at length and producing the neat counter factual: 'If Tudor Evans J had received fuller argument on the point he might well have reached a different decision. As it is I am of the opinion that his decision was wrong.' Thus a set of dubiously relevant cases from another jurisdiction are preferred as the basis for opposing this extension of negligence to a bluntly dismissed case directly on the point by an English court. What Keith's position actually amounts to is a personal empirical assumption about the behaviour of employers in writing references, coupled to a rather stark indifference to personal rights in the interest of protecting the public. Having pointed out that LAUTRO's rules are necessary to protect against dishonest or incompetent insurance salesmen, and taken judicial notice of 'the many instances of misselling that have recently been uncovered' the real core of his argument follows in one paragraph:

If there exists some suspicion that a person in respect of whom a reference has been asked for has not acted with complete integrity, the public interest requires that such suspicion should be communicated. If liability for negligence towards the subject of the reference were to be held to exist, there would be a temptation not to communicate the suspicion. In the present case it required a protracted trial . . . to establish that in relation to the Fennell transaction Mr Spring had on balance of probabilities acted incompetently but not dishonestly. An inquiry of comparable scope would not be within the powers of the ordinary employer. Faced with the possibility of an action of damages for negligence . . . there are grounds for expecting that the employer would be inhibited from expressing frankly any reservations which he might have about the honesty of the employee.[75]

Just to really rub home the point, Lord Keith goes on to talk about the importance of honest references for jobs involving contact with children and the difficulty of proving that someone has interfered with young children.

---

[75] *Spring* at 141.

It is not appropriate here to express any judgement on Keith's preference for public interest solutions at the risk to individuals. All that is relevant is the way in which the whole of his argument amounts to an exercise in amateur industrial sociology and to markedly pusillanimous conception of employers' human nature. It also involves completely ignoring the fact that, as a member of LAUTRO, there is already a countervailing legal duty to divulge what one legitimately believes. Given that law is, in essence, a set of deterrent mechanisms aimed at interacting with human nature to produce desirable results, it is vitally important to see how easily particular conceptions of human nature act as the main argumentative force in developing law.

There were two tacks, as mentioned earlier, that the other Law Lords could take in the face of Keith's argument. One, the one used by Spring's counsel and favoured by the majority, was to tackle directly the public policy thesis coupled to the interference with the law of defamation. For this the arguments have to be strong, because there is, *pace* Tudor Evans, no existing case law, and *Anns* v. *Merton*, the precedent such as it was for even beginning such a development, very clearly invited policy restrictions. The alternative tack was favoured by Lord Goff who did find the public policy arguments compelling against such an innovation in negligence. This was to carry out the much more automatic act of bringing the facts of Spring's case directly under an existing principle, that in *Hedley Byrne*:

> I have come to the conclusion that if the Hedley Byrne principle cannot be relied upon by the plaintiff, the appeal ought to be dismissed; because in those circumstances it would be a simple case of the defendants having negligently made a statement damaging to the plaintiff's reputation. In such a case, in agreement with the reasoning of the Court of Appeal, I do not see how there can be a liability upon the defendants in negligence consistently with the policy of the law established in the law of defamation in relation to the principle of qualified privilege which, in the absence of malice, protects from liability the maker of a statement made on the privileged occasion.[76]

It is an interesting side point that Goff, aware that his argument is one that was never addressed to the Lords or the Court of Appeal, is made hesitant by this fact. He would have preferred to send the case back for further argument had he not known that a majority were going to decide on the broader grounds that he cannot himself accept. He goes so far as to stress that, made in the absence of argument from counsel, his opinion 'must be regarded as being of limited authority'.

The reasoning behind *Hedley Byrne* must be left to a later chapter. The differences between the two approaches can be seen, by laymen, to be

---

[76] Goff in *Spring* at 144.

vanishingly small. The crucial aspect of *Hedley Byrne* is that it operates only when the relationship between the one who writes an incorrect reference and anyone who relies on it is very close to contractual. In the overall logic of English law it is thought acceptable to impose far more onerous duties where there is a contract, even if the actual contract is silent on some matter, than when one is requiring an involuntary obligation. Goff thinks that the conditions of modern employment and the need for references to get any job comes logically close to importing such a contractual relationship. What is really important for present purposes are two points. The first is Goff's belief, aptly to be described as a methodological belief, about the difference between what he is doing and what the majority are doing:

In a series of well-known cases, your Lordships' House has commended a gradual case by case approach to the development of the law of negligence, particularly in cases concerned with claims in respect of pure economic loss. Even so, one broad category of cases has been recognised in which there may be liability in negligence for loss of this kind. These are the cases which spring from, or have been gathered under the umbrella of, the landmark decision of your Lordships' House in *Hedley Byrne*.

'Even so . . .' indicates for Goff a quite clear-cut difference from a 'gradual case by case approach' of developing the law, that is, making new law, and the firmly recognized 'broad category of cases'. Secondly, Goff thinks, for reasons quite unexplicated by his speech, that bringing the facts of *Spring* under *Hedley Byrne* means that the otherwise, to him absolute, need to protect the public policy restrictions in defamation no longer applies. Presumably this is partly because public policy is recognized in the general methodology of overt negligence extension, hence the 'case by case approach', and partly simply and directly because it was not recognized in the reasoning in *Hedley Byrne*. The empirical fact remains that if accepting the broader position the majority calls for means that 'By a side-wind the law of defamation would be overthrown', this overthrow will be still accomplished whenever his new version of *Hedley Byrne* fits. And given Goff's reasons for that version, it will fit very often. In practice Goff does not, anyway, believe in the reality of the chilling effect on references of allowing liability for negligence. After effectively disposing of the New Zealand cases on the grounds that they are about quite different problems, he briefly disposes of the impact problem:

It is true that recognition of a duty of care to an employee in cases such as the present, based on the *Hedley Byrne* principle, may have some inhibiting effect on the manner in which references are expressed, in the sense that it may discourage employers from expressing views such as those which are encouraged by r. 3.5(2) of the LAUTRO rules. For my part, however, I suspect that such an inhibition exists in any event. Employers may well, like many people, be unwilling to indulge in unnecessary criticism of their employees: hence the perceived necessity for r. 3.5(2). In all the circumstances, I do not think that we may fear too many ill effects from the recognition of the duty.[77]

The rather odd consequence is that Goff has refused to join the majority on the grounds that their principle runs against a policy argument that his own principle is subject to, and which he does not think is empirically valid in any case. There are only two explanations for his taking this position. The first is that he ascribes, as an aspect of his personal judicial methodology, to a principle of great formalism which would go something like this:

1. Though empirically invalid, the law of defamation contains the qualified privilege rule.
2. To introduce a new ground of liability in an area where public policy arguments have been recognized as relevant would-be to breach this other recognition of privilege and therefore constitute making new law in a radical way.
3. But making a minor extension to a clear precedent where the public policy exception has never been recognized does not constitute radical law making.

If Goff does hold to such a view, it would of course be an acceptable judicial methodology, but it can hardly be said to be one so determining in its impact that it removes the problem of discretion. It is a methodology that, at most, controls the decisions of those who choose to be bound by it, when they feel like been bound by it.

An alternative interpretation of Goff's position is that it is a technical device to produce a limitation on the sorts of reference writers who would be at risk if they were negligent, essentially employers, and leave free others, for example academics writing about would-be graduate students. This supposes Goff is making a deliberate choice of who should be covered by the new rule. For some reason or other, in this scenario, he finds it more likely to command acceptance to make his restriction implicit by technique than explicit by his own set of policy arguments. Quite probably, both interpretations are partially correct.

Although we have referred, for convenience, to 'the majority' it is not entirely clear that there is one, as all three of the other Law Lords offer their own arguments. However, Lord Woolf seems to be accepted as the main spokesman for the rule that *Spring* has now probably established. Woolf has little difficulty, Keith after all had conceded as much, in establishing that the preconditions now understood to be necessary for an

---

[77] Goff in *Spring* at 151.

extension of liability negligence in economic loss cases apply here. He puts it at its most convincing by likening preventing someone from getting a job by a negligent reference to more traditional ways an employer has been held liable for harm to his employees:

This is the position if an employer injures his employee physically by failing to exercise reasonable care for his safety and I find it impossible to justify taking a different view where an employer, by giving an inaccurate reference about his employee, deprives an employee, possibly for a considerable period, of the means of earning his livelihood. The consequences of the employer's carelessness can be as great in the long term as causing the employee a serious injury.[78]

Woolf goes on to identify two separate possible objections rather than one—the impact on the law of defamation directly, and the defamation-like policy problem—where previously both in the Court of Appeal and in the New Zealand cases they had been interlinked. The point of doing this appears to be to remove the objection made in the New Zealand cases and repeated in the words of the Court of Appeal as:

His [the giver of a reference] duty to the subject is governed by and lies in the tort of defamation. If it were otherwise, the defence of qualified privilege in an action for defamation where a reference was given, or the necessity for the plaintiff to prove malice in an action for malicious falsehood, would be bypassed. In effect, a substantial section of the law regarding these two associated torts would be emasculated.[79]

For Woolf the two torts are very separate sets of rules, 'not directed at the same mischief, although they admittedly overlap'. A decision in favour of Spring 'will leave the law of defamation in exactly the same state as it was previously'. Which is, of course, correct in as far as it goes. No one will win a defamation case they would not have won before. As Woolf points out, somewhat redundantly, Spring could not win in defamation. Instead they will bring actions under the new negligence rule. But he is entirely ignoring the reason the New Zealand cases were quoted so extensively. It was not some curious legal purism, a matter as he suggests of 'erecting a fence around the whole of the field to which defamation can apply and treating any other tort . . . as a trespasser'. It was because of the claim that the defamation exceptions were the result of a lengthy and deliberate experience of attempts to balance rights and duties in the public interest. However, having separated the two objections he can treat the question of public policy protecting writers of references fairly quickly, and quite appropriately, by setting the question not as to whether there is one public policy consideration, but rather as a need to balance two conflicting public policy principles:

---

[78] Woolf, *Spring* at 169.
[79] Glidewell LJ in *Spring* v. *Guardian Assurance plc* [1993] 2 All ER 273 at 294.

It is obviously in accord with public policy that references should be full and frank. But it is also in accord with public policy that they should not be based upon careless investigations.

And, slightly later:

However the real issue is not whether there would be any adverse effect on the giving of references. Rather the issue is whether the adverse effects when balanced against the benefits which would flow from giving the subject a right of action sufficiently outweigh the benefits to justify depriving the subject of a remedy unless he can establish malice.[80]

Woolf never really attempts to show why the balance should be drawn in favour of the new protection against unfair references. The most he does is to note that modern employment practices as demonstrated, amongst other things, by Civil Service annual reports suggest that: 'There is now an openness in employment relationships which did not exist even a few years ago.' Perhaps there is no way a judge can convincingly do this, but if so, it would be better to dismiss the entire area of consideration. As it is, Keith's public policy objection is outmanoeuvred rather than disposed of, and an onlooker is still left to wonder where the public interest does lie in this case.

There remains the alternative of outright dismissing the relevance of public policy, which would, if it did not actually remove many situations where private ideology creeps in via discretion, at least make it much more obvious when and where that happens. As we discuss in Chapter 6, the idea that policy matters are not justiciable has been mooted, only to be scorned by other Law Lords. Here also, though not in terms, Lowry, in a characteristically honest, if somewhat impatient and judicially probably rather dangerous way, more or less does this. Referring to 'the possibility that some referees will be deterred from giving frank references', he admits:

I am inclined to view this possibility as a spectre conjured up by the defendants to frighten your Lordships into submission. I also believe that the courts in general and Lordships' House in particular ought to think very carefully before resorting to public policy considerations which will defeat a claim that ex hypothesi is a perfectly good cause of action. It has been said that public policy should be invoked only in clear cases in which the potential harm to the public is incontestable, that whether the anticipated harm to the public will be likely to occur must be determined on tangible grounds instead of on mere generalities and that the burden of proof lies on those who assert that the court should not enforce a liability that prima facie exists.[81]

[80] *Spring* at 177.
[81] Lowry in *Spring* at 153.

The only odd aspect of Lowry's speech, which may say something about the nature of the entire debate, is his opening when he claims to agree not only with Woolf and Slynn, but also with Lord Goff's interpretation of *Hedley Byrne*, suggesting that it actually does not matter how their Lordships reach their conclusion.

5. Conclusions

From our point of view *Spring* seems yet again an example of Mustill's pithy observation quoted in Chapter 3. It was a case where four men simply felt the plaintiffs' claims ought to succeed, 'if only an intellectually sustainable means can be found'. But, as in all these examples, the means seem only to need to be sustainable *to the writer*. The happenstance of method shown over and again in these two chapters led one to think of appellate judging as a rather solipsistic activity. Generally the point of examining these cases has been to demonstrate that the range of argumentative techniques, and their manner of deployment, makes it extremely improbable that they are anything but *'post hoc'* arguments, intellectual edifices erected around a value position selected otherwise. The use of precedents shows this particularly clearly. Sometimes the precedents are simply piled up, the argument being that the mere fact of these repeated findings in a certain direction solves the problem. At other times they were used as the building blocks of a 'theory of the precedents', usually leading to a conclusion that they were not previously seen as supporting. Absent precedents, principles are derived on the flimsiest of evidence, or just asserted. Principles are 'balanced', though in fact all that happens is that it is stated that the balance comes down one way or another—we are never shown the scale. Most important, these arguments are seldom tested. In most forms of argument interlocutors are forced to meet the points of the other side, and only *in extremis* will the argument end with one side resorting to 'I don't agree'. This is why the description of 'solipsistic argument' seems appropriate—the only audience for the argument appears to be its exponent. Naturally this is an exaggeration. *Spring* is an unusually important case because it shows that the actual argument does matter, sometimes at least. Goff could have just gone along with Woolf's argument; it cannot have been completely unsustainable, because it satisfied Woolf and two of his fellow judges. Yet there we had relatively rare evidence of how the availability of argument does constrain results. Such evidence used to be more common in the days of multi-opinion cases. Then, though, there was the problem of exactly what rule a case was precedent for, with the resulting distinction, rarely made nowadays, between that part of an opinion necessary to the decision, and that part that was, strictly speaking, *obiter dicta*. It might be argued that the switch to single opinions in cases reflects a much greater unanimity amongst the Law Lords. This is highly improbable, because the actual dissent rate has, if anything, increased. And where cases are divided it is evident from the examples in these last two chapters that there is very little agreement at all on the proper method of approaching any particular fact set. It is much more likely that the minimum standard that Mustill refers to—the 'intellectually sustainable means' suffices. Such a standard can suffice precisely, and perhaps only, because it has nothing to do with how the judges actually reach their own conclusions. Consequently there is no great need for argument unless there is no consensus on the precise decision in the instant case. Where there is no such agreement, there is also no need particularly to do more than find two, instead of just one, minimum satisficing arguments. This has all been said before in the famous advice to young judges: 'Never give your reasons; your decision will probably be right, but your reasons will certainly be wrong.' Normally. At least one leading judge in a common law jurisdiction, Richard Posner, Chief Judge of the US Court of Appeals for the Seventh Circuit, makes this point vividly in an essay titled 'What Judges Maximise'—the answer he gives is voting results, and never arguments.[82]

Normally the counter argument to this would be that the judge must care about the reasons given, because the reasoning provides the rule the case will establish. But there is so little reason to believe this is how precedents are, in fact, used. When reasons matter, they matter because some of the reasons that can be given touch upon aspects of the ideologies that drive the decisions. Because judges' ideologies are, specifically, *judges'* ideologies, deeply infused by legal patterns of thought and professional values, the results they want are sometimes the instantiation of classic arguments. The best example is perhaps 'certainty': the predictability of the law is both a value in itself to some judges some of the time, and an argument that can always be deployed. But the argument from certainty will have no effect on a judge who either values it relatively little, or sees it as outweighed by some demand of justice in any particular case. Arguments matter, as it were, when they matter, but substance more usually matters more. When we turn in the second part of the book to see how the law has been developed by judicial decision in several politically and socially important areas, these judicial ideologies, individual and group, will become clearer. These last two chapters have been necessary, as similar analyses were to the American legal realists, to establish that the legally determinative argument is a rarity.

[82] Richard A. Posner, *Overcoming Law*, Harvard, 1995, pp. 109–44.

5

In Re Pepper *v.* Hart:
Comments on the Nature of Laws

In October 1992 a minor change was made to the British Constitution, largely unnoticed outside the legal profession. The Appellate Committee of the House of Lords changed a procedural rule that has governed their decision making since the beginning of modern appellate jurisdiction. In order to interpret the true meaning of a statute, they consulted *Hansard* to find out what the minister responsible had told the Commons he intended the effect of the proposed legislation to be. They then drew the inference that a parliament so informed must also have intended the statute to have that meaning, and interpreted it so as to give effect to that intention. In most other common law jurisdictions this would be unremarkable. The US courts, for example, regularly consult what they call 'the legislative record', just, indeed, as they sometimes refer to the recordings of debate in the constitutional convention to interpret the constitution. The Law Lords defended their own decision by copious though unspecific references to Australian and New Zealand practice. It has, however, always been a firm taboo in the UK. From time to time judges have tried to get round the ban—Lord Denning in particular admitted in one famous case to having examined *Hansard* in private.[1] The Law Lords have always slapped down such manoeuvres. This time they prayed Denning in aid of their argument. It must be obvious that the use of *Pepper* v. *Hart* as the vehicle for changing the rule was no accident. It had long been the private ambition of at least one Law Lord to effect this change, and he chose this case because, having in fact read *Hansard* as was his regular custom, he believed, rightly, that he had found the perfect case. Even then, as the record of the case shows, the appeals panel that heard the case were originally minded to find for the tax authorities. It was one Law Lord's stated intention, had that occurred, to enter a dissent in which *Hansard* was quoted to demonstrate that his colleagues were wrong in their interpretation that led to a new and larger group of Law Lords being empanelled specifically to face up to the constitutional question. Part of our argument here has to do with the very special sense in which *Pepper* could be seen to be a good illustration of the problem.

[1] *Hadmor Productions Ltd.* v. *Hamilton* [1981] 2 All ER 724.

Although it is a tax case, *Pepper (Inspector of Taxes)* v. *Hart*[2] is surprisingly interesting because it involves an attempt to impose income tax on a category of payer capable of arousing rather conflicting political reactions. To demonstrate the exact way in which recourse to *Hansard* operated it is worth discussing the case first as it seems to have appeared to the House of Lords before the enlarged committee opened Pandora's box.

1. The Old-Style Interpretation

Mr Hart and several others were masters at Malvern College, an English public school. As commonly happens in such schools, they were entitled to have their children educated at the school for only 20 per cent of the normal fees. Until 1976 fringe benefits provided to those who worked for educational or charitable institutions were exempted from any tax. The 1976 Finance Act sought a complete overhaul of this area of taxation. Section 63(1) of the Act provides:

Subject to section 63A where in any year a person is employed in director's or higher-paid employment and—(a) by reason of his employment there is provided for him or for others being members of his family or household, any benefit to which this section applies; and (b) the cost of providing the benefit is not (apart from this section) chargeable to tax as his income, there is to be treated as emoluments of the employment, and accordingly chargeable to income tax under Schedule E, an amount equal to whatever is the cash equivalent of the benefit.

The definition of the 'cash equivalent' of the benefit is given in section 63:

(1) The cash equivalent of any benefit chargeable to tax under section 61 above is an amount equal to the cost of the benefit, less so much (if any) of it as is made good by the employee to those providing the benefit.

(2) Subject to the following subsections, the cost of the benefit is the amount of any expense incurred in or in connection with its provision, and . . . includes a proper proportion of any expense relating partly to the benefit and partly to other matters.

The argument is about how to calculate the expense incurred by the school in providing the places for these schoolmasters' children. The teachers claimed that the legislation meant marginal cost, the cost specifically attributable to the benefiting child. As such it would refer only to costs for extra food, laundry, stationery, and so on, and would be more than covered by the 20 per cent fee. Consequently there would be no net cost to the school, and no imputed emolument to tax. The Revenue claim

---

[2] *Pepper (Inspector of Taxes)* v. *Hart* [1993] 1 All ER 42.

the relevant cost is the same as the cost of educating all the other children at the school, the proportionate or average cost which, given that Malvern is a non-profit charity, means more or less the official fee. Although the taxpayers won the argument before the Special Commissioners for Taxation, the Revenue's interpretation was agreed to by the High Court, by the Court of Appeal, and by four of the five Law Lords who heard the case the first time round.[3]

The first question is whether or not the relevant clauses are ambiguous. Browne-Wilkinson set this up as the first part of the test—parliamentary materials may be consulted where 'legislation is ambiguous or obscure or leads to an absurdity'.[4] It is ambiguous in the general sense that there are various meanings that can be given to the word 'costs', but it is certainly not an unusually difficult problem in statutory construction. This is important, because if *Pepper* passes the test of ambiguity which now entitles the Lords to consult legislative history, the breach in previous practice is actually very wide. Lord Oliver, a reluctant convert to using *Hansard*, insists that, but for the parliamentary record in this case, he would still find for the Revenue. He points out that:

although I recognize that, in popular parlance the provision to one individual of a service which is, in any event, being provided for reward to many others may be said to cost the provider little or nothing, 'cost' in accountancy terms is merely a computation of outgoing expenditure without reference to receipts.[5]

Lord Browne-Wilkinson says that his argument would also have been in favour of the Revenue, on the following grounds, which he says are those given by the Court of Appeal:

I accept Mr Lester's submission [counsel for the taxpayers] that there must be a causal link between the benefit provided for the tax payers and the cost of the benefit referred to in s. 63(1). But in my judgment s. 63(2) provides a statutory formula for quantifying such a cost: it requires one to find 'the amount of any expense incurred in or in connection with' the provision of the benefit, such expense to include 'a proper proportion of any expense relating partly to the benefit and partly to other matters'.

After describing what the taxpayer is getting Browne-Wilkinson goes on to argue that:

On the literal meaning of the words the expense to the school of providing those facilities is exactly the same for each boy in the school, i.e. a proportion of the total costs of running the school. Even if it could be said that, because the school would have incurred the basic expense of running the school in any event such expense was not incurred 'in' providing the facilities for the tax payer's child, on the literal

---

[3] Lord Griffiths testifies to this: *Pepper* at 51.
[4] *Pepper* at 69.
[5] *Pepper* at 52.

meaning of the words such expense was in any event incurred 'in connection with' the provision of such facilities. The words 'in connection with' have the widest connotation and I cannot see how they are to be restricted in the absence of some context permitting such restriction.[6]

Browne-Wilkinson reviews quickly the arguments for the taxpayers' interpretation which rest on supposed anomalies likely to be produced by the Revenue's construction, but finds as many and as good arising from their preferred version. He describes very well the main problem about interpreting this statute, which is that there is an odd absence of something one would expect to be there:

What is taxable is the benefit to the employee and *one would have expected the quantum of that benefit to be assessed by reference to the value of the benefit to the employee.* But the statutory formula does not seek to value the benefit to the employee as such, but requires the quantum of the benefit to be fixed by reference to the cost to the employer of providing it. [Our emphasis.]

Because there is therefore no guidance to parliamentary intention, he argues, it is necessary to interpret the statute literally, and the Revenue must win. One might well ask why the statute has such an odd form. Now we can look at *Hansard*, this becomes clear. But what becomes clear is that, in a fundamental way, the literal interpretation is actually the correct guess at the core meaning of the statute, but that Parliament cannot, indeed, be said to have intended to give effect to its core meaning. It is useful quickly to note that the main arguments given, by Griffiths, for interpreting in favour of the taxpayers without looking at the legislative history are classical parliamentary intent arguments of the form which involve deducing an unpleasant consequence of the Revenue's interpretation and then asserting that Parliament could not possibly have wanted to do any such thing. Much of the force of Griffiths' argument comes from an analogy with the way in which the Government slowly phased in taxation of company cars, the most common 'perk', rather than hitting the beneficiaries immediately, the suggestion being that this shows what Parliament can be expected to intend such policies. Griffiths, it must be remembered, is the only one of the original committee who does claim to have derived a pro-taxpayer answer before looking at *Hansard*. It is fairly well known that Lord Griffiths, after working out this answer and his justification, then privately read the debates and brought them to the attention of his brethren as a clear example of where the Lords would give the wrong answer if they did not relax the exclusionary rule. Lord Griffiths, along with Lord Templeman, had long sought to have the rule changed. Indeed he admits in the course of his opinion:

[6] *Pepper* at 72.

I have to confess that on many occasions I have had recourse to Hansard, of course only to check if my interpretation had conflicted with an express parliamentary intention . . .[7]

Griffiths does not, alas, tell us how often his interpretations have turned out to conflict, and even more interestingly, he does not tell us what he did when there was conflict.

2. The Parliamentary Record

The parliamentary record is fascinating—but more as an example of lobbying at work than anything else. For those whose only knowledge of the case is that *Hansard* was consulted, and what was found therein forced several Law Lords to change their mind about the meaning of the Act, exactly what they found and relied on may come as somewhat of a surprise. Because they did not find a speech by a minister which said, 'Oh, by the way, the word "cost" in section 63 means marginal not average cost.'

In the draft legislation the original plan was to distinguish between two sorts of benefit in kind. One was a benefit which the employer would himself have to purchase or subsidize, which would be taxed on the basis of the cost to the employer. The second were in-house benefits, the provision to an employee of the services the institution was in business to provide for fees to the general public. These, covered by clause 54(4) of the Bill, were to be taxed on the price to the public. The overall aim was fairly clear—where someone gained from his employment a service or benefit he would have to buy for himself otherwise, this was to be treated, as indeed it is, as a direct increase in his consumption capacity. As such he would be taxed for a benefit worth £x as though his salary was increased by £x. However, the Financial Secretary to the Treasury was obviously lobbied intensely—his phrases were 'Representation has been made . . .' and 'I have had many interviews, discussions and meetings on this matter . . .'.[8] These representations and so forth seem to have been mainly concerned with concessionary travel for workers in the rail and airline industry. They were effective, because the Treasury withdrew clause 54(4), and the rest of clause 54 became the section 63 of the Act which caused the problems.

The reasons the Financial Secretary gave for withdrawing clause 54(4) were interesting, because they did not begin to relate to what must have been the original thinking—instead the clause was to be removed because

[7] *Pepper* at 50.
[8] Taken from Browne-Wilkinson's account, *Pepper* at 58.

(1) the cost to the employer was trivial compared with the taxable value of the benefit, (2) the high cost of the benefit would depress use of the benefit and therefore no one, including the Revenue, would gain, and (3) there would be administrative and enforcement difficulties. No replacement clause was written, however. Various rather muddy statements were made in response to questions from MPs, which implied that taxation of such benefits would continue on the past basis. The past basis in fact was largely the result of non-legislative agreements between the Revenue and various bodies, and was certainly not the result of any clear judicial pronouncement. Furthermore, there was no past basis for schoolteachers, as they had previously been exempted, as employees of charitable bodies, from any taxation on benefits. What happened, therefore, was that the machinery for taxing the out-of-house benefits was left in place and allowed to become the machinery for taxing all benefits. All of the examples raised by MPs related to aspects of travel services, including free use of empty rooms for hotel workers and free steamship trips for merchant seamen's families. It was taxation of such benefits that had been the original concern in the Select Committee; this was the area in which there was a past experience of Revenue and beneficiaries colliding; and this was the area about which the 'representations' had been made. In other words, the problems were seen as arising in connection with minor, attractive, but 'extra' perks of working in rather specialized industries. Furthermore, because of particular problems in subsidized travel industries, there were (and continued to be even on the basis of the rest of clause 54) seriously logical problems of costing. Nothing in the committee discussions or the Government's justifications dealt with the very different situation covered by the appeal. Except that one MP did ask the crucial question in committee:

the . . . matter applies particularly to private sector, fee-paying schools where, as the Financial Secretary knows, there is often an arrangement for the children of staff in these schools to be taught at less than the commercial fee in other schools. I take it that because of the deletion of clause 54(4) that is now not caught . . .

The Financial Secretary responded:

He mentioned the children of teachers. The removal of clause 54(4) will affect the position of a child of one of the teachers at the child's school, because now the benefit will be assessed on the cost to the employer, which would be very small indeed in this case.

Are these parliamentary quotations a clear guide to the meaning of the Act? In one sense they certainly are—the Financial Secretary to the Treasury specifically promised that a specific category of worker whose case was brought up would pay very little, if any, tax on their special benefit.

Once their Lordships took judicial notice of such a highly particularistic promise, the resolution of this case was ordained. Lord Bridge puts it clearly—'I should find it very difficult, in conscience, to reach a conclusion adverse to the taxpayers on the basis of a technical rule of construction . . .'.[9] But there is, after all, a good reason why we have the general conception of judicial notice, and the position their Lordships put themselves in by reading *Hansard* may be one that should be avoided. Because there is something very unsatisfactory about the equation of Parliament's intention with such *ad hocery*. Bridge's sentence goes on to read '. . . requiring me to ignore the very material which in this case indicates unequivocally which of the two possible interpretations . . . was intended by Parliament'. There is a huge leap of reasoning, or perhaps of faith, to conjure up anything that could valuably be called an intent of Parliament from this material.

Suppose that particular question had not been asked but some other, non-travel industry group had a champion in the House? Let us imagine that nurses in private sector hospitals are entitled to hospital care at no charge except the surgeon's fee and the cost of drugs, on the grounds that all the beds, theatres, and machinery have to be provided anyway. Had the question been asked about them, rather than teachers, and received the equivalent answer, would recourse to *Hansard* have solved *Pepper*? If the answer is yes, it is so by a process of induction, not because the minister made any general interpretative statement.

What we know from the legislative history is:

1. All benefits are to be taxed under the same regime.
2. The regime, section 63(1) and (2), was designed to cover cases where the basis, the cost to the provider, was more or less the market price, because it was to cover bought-in benefits.
3. In several cases the minister estimated that the tax would be low because the costs would be low.

It is point (3) which is doing the work, in that it is being treated as a general answer to the original question of whether costs, in the legislation, are to be average or marginal costs. They have to be taken as marginal costs in order to make the minister's *ad hoc* promises come true. But is this the sort of general 'intent' of Parliament that in principle should underlie the making of general rules in a political system hallowing the democratic value of 'rule by laws and not by men'? The Revenue, cast throughout this case as villains, were pressing for an interpretation of the Act which was in keeping with the original plan, which had been to tax benefits at something like the value to the recipient, a policy which still applies to any

---

[9] *Pepper* at 49.

benefit which is not 'in-house'. That is why, after all, there is no statement of intent. The Act as envisioned did not need such a statement because equality between recipients of different sorts of benefits on the basis of taxation at rough market value followed automatically. The irony is that if the exclusionary rule, first established in 1769, had not been abandoned, the judges would have reimposed the original plan of the Act. Indeed clause 54(4) was never needed to carry out this plan because the effect of treating costs as equal to average costs is to set in-house benefits at the same costs as bought-in benefits. The reason there was never a general statement after clause 54(4) was withdrawn could well be that it would have forced the Financial Secretary to justify a glaring inequality in treatment where there appears to have been no thought out rationale at all. It was no less a judicial personage than the first Presiding Judge of the European Court of Justice who insisted that parliamentary debate had, as a major role, not the explicating but the hiding of legislative intentions. It may be apposite that the Act in question is a Finance Act. Such legislation by its very nature is unlike most of what Parliament does—it is not really an example of Parliament carrying out the political rule-making function of the classic division of powers. Passing the Finance Acts is, instead, an exercise of the 'power of the purse', an equally vital but constitutionally rather different function. It could be argued with some force either that recourse to *Hansard* is especially inappropriate in cases like *Pepper*, or, in the alternative, that it is only when considering Parliament's exercise of this power that legislative history should be noted. And it may be relevant here that when Browne-Wilkinson tries to deal with arguments against the new relaxation he leaps on a rare comment by Lord Wilberforce, a major supporter of the exclusionary rule, in favour of using *Hansard*. The comment, made in his extrajudicial capacity in a seminar, specifically refers to another occasion where a minister, during passage of a Finance Bill, expressly stated that it was not intended to tax a particular class of beneficiaries.[10] But depending on which of these two arguments were made, a very different theory of the constitution would be implied.

With this as a background, we can turn to consider some general issues about curial interpretation of legislation that raise questions about the real and the ideal nature of legislated rules.

3. When, Why, and How Should Parliament's Intent be Applied?

In *Pepper* the Law Lords write as though the only serious arguments for the exclusionary rule were tiresome practical matters, largely to do either

---

[10] Browne-Wilkinson in *Pepper* at 65.

with the difficulty of finding the parliamentary matter, or the likely explosion in its use resulting in longer and more expensive cases. But this is to equate what some at least think is a constitutional principle to a mere rule of convenience. Scott Styles, for example, refers to the Lords having 'unwittingly set in motion a fundamental change in the nature of the British constitution'.[11] 'Unwittingly' may be unfair—in private some at least of their Lordships express basic democratic and egalitarian justifications, whilst others, less sure of the desirability, worry about likely changes in ministerial behaviour, a 'chilling effect' from knowing what use may be made of their words. Although mention is made of the constitutionality of the exclusionary rule, the arguments against which are actually met in Browne-Wilkinson's opinion are essentially practical. Two references to the constitutionality of the rule which Browne-Wilkinson himself quotes seem very powerful. The first is by Lord Diplock, the giant of the court in the eighties and never a man to let ill-based tradition stand in his way:

The constitutional function performed by courts of justice as interpreters of the written law laid down in Acts of Parliament is often described as ascertaining 'the intention of Parliament'; but what this metaphor, though convenient, omits to take into account is that the court, when acting in its interpretative role, as well as when it is engaged in reviewing the legality of administrative action, is doing so as mediator between the state in the exercise of its legislative power and the private citizen for whom the law made by Parliament constitutes a rule binding upon him and enforceable by the executive power of the state.[12]

Evenly more bluntly, Lord Wilberforce took a line which echoes American debates about the rival claims of courts and legislatures to interpret rules. In a 1975 case where it was sought to use parliamentary material he makes the constitutional claim very strongly:

[there is an argument] . . . of constitutional principle. Legislation in England is passed by Parliament, and put in the form of written words. This legislation is given legal effect on subjects by virtue of judicial decision, and it is the function of the courts to say what the application of the words used to particular cases or individuals is to be. This power which has been devolved on the judges since the earliest times is an essential part of the constitutional process by which subjects are brought under the rule of law—as distinct from the rule of the King or the rule of Parliament; *and it would be a degradation of that process if the courts were to be merely a reflecting mirror of what some other interpretation agency might say.* [My emphasis.][13]

In the same case he gives his own version of Diplock's interpretation of the 'metaphor' of 'intention of Parliament':

[11] Scott C. Styles, 'The Rule of Parliament: Statutory Interpretation after *Pepper v Hart*', *Oxford Journal of Legal Studies*, vol. 14, 1994, pp. 151–8.
[12] *Fothergill* v. *Monarch Airlines Ltd.* [1980] 2 All ER 696 at 705.
[13] *Black-Clawson International Ltd.* v. *Papierwerke Waldhof-Aschaffenburg AG* [1975] 1 All ER 810 at 828.

We often say that we are looking for the intention of Parliament, but that is not quite accurate. We are seeking the meaning of words which Parliament used. We are seeking not what Parliament meant, but the true meaning of what they said.[14]

Both the constitutional doctrine and the gloss on the phrase 'intention of Parliament' could be replicated from many leading judges in the recent past including, interestingly, Lord Scarman, famous for his support of an entrenched Bill of Rights. It is not necessary or useful to pile on such quotations. Both points are neatly summarized by Diplock later in the speech quoted above: 'Parliament, under our constitution, is sovereign only in respect of what it expresses by the words used in the legislation it has passed.'

Clearly what is at stake is an entire theory of the nature of legislation, an account of what the British Constitution really means in enshrining the 'rule of law'. To justify the exclusionary rule we need a concept of a law under which it is quite acceptable to ignore what was said in Parliament, while at the same time believe that Parliament is sovereign. There seem to be three broad avenues one can explore towards this end. The first and most obvious involves asking whether the relevance of statements in Parliament is affected by the age of the statute. The second avenue considers what happens to other existing canons of construction if legislative history is taken into account. Finally, we can ask whether or not there are good reasons to take the meaning of a statute as actually independent of what any, or indeed all, parliamentarians of the time thought the words meant.

All of these are interwoven with a general acceptance that what a statute means is connected to Parliament's intention in the specific sense of the purpose for which Parliament passed it. Purpose certainly is vital, but it is a mistake to believe, as the Lords seem to have believed in *Pepper*, that (1) there is a simple contrast between (anachronistic) 'literal' interpretation and (modern) 'purposive' interpretation, and (2) that because a variety of documentation is already allowed to help conceive of the purpose of a statute (White Papers, Law Commission Reports, Statutory Instruments), reading *Hansard* is just a logical extension of existing practice. To start with, there is really nothing all that new in the idea of purposive interpretation which is not contained in one of the oldest of the canons of interpretation, the 'Mischief Rule'. Secondly, although the Lords refer only to common law jurisdictions, the legislative record in all its manifestations has always been part of the interpretative armoury of judges in Code Law countries. In such jurisdictions, however, there is no equation of statutory intent with parliamentarians' intent—what any member of the legislature says is only one amongst a range of many. Here

---

[14] *Black-Clawson* at 815.

it is necessary to stipulate one assumption that all the rest of this chapter depends on, which is particularly important for the second and third avenues of comment outlined above. Though they do not discuss the point, from the way the opinions in *Pepper* read one can only presume that, where recourse to *Hansard* is allowed, a suitable parliamentary statement trumps. Certainly in subsequent cases where the exclusionary rule has been set aside, those who have relied on legislative history have not thought it necessary to justify defining the intent in this way. In contrast those who have not liked such a result have simply insisted that the initial obscurity that justifies recourse to history was not present. Two of these cases will be discussed shortly. Let us first turn to the relationship between the meaning or purpose of a statute, the age of the statute, and the age of the legislative history.

4. The Problem of Elderly Statutes

The speeches in *Stubbings* v. *Webb* were delivered on 16 December 1992, three weeks after those in *Pepper*. Thus it was one of the first cases where the Law Lords had a chance to take advantage of the new ruling, a chance eagerly leapt on by Lord Griffiths, the most ardent enthusiast for abolishing the exclusionary rule. *Stubbings* was very much 'a case for the nineties'. It was an attempt by Ms Stubbings to sue her adoptive father and brother for personal injuries amounting to mental illness arising from rape and sexual assault taking place at various times between the ages of two and fourteen. The writ was issued in 1987. She was claiming not for the original injuries, but for long-term consequent psychiatric problems, which she had not realized were caused by these assaults until she went to a psychiatrist in 1984, by which time she was thirty. Clearly the long gap between the offending acts and realization of their consequence, inevitable in a case such as this, was going to cause problems about time limitations. Originally her claim was struck out on the grounds that it was a claim in respect of personal injuries coming under section 11(1) of the Limitations Act 1980, which allows only a three-year gap between a plaintiff knowing of the injuries and suing. On appeal from the master the judge ruled that the relevant date was her realization in September 1984, and the claim was not statute-barred. This was upheld by the Court of Appeal.

The case is a procedural nightmare because of the legislative history of the various Limitations Acts, and the impact of the ruling case, a Court of Appeal case from 1965, *Letang* v. *Cooper*.[15] In a nutshell there are two ways

---

[15] *Letang* v. *Cooper* [1965] 1 QB 232.

it can be seen. Either it is a personal injury case, with a time limit of three years, which may be extended under section 11 of the Act, or it is excluded from that section. In the latter case there is a fixed six-year term which ran out before Ms Stubbings issued her writ. It is the section 11 route that the plaintiff was taking. It is clear from the past history of cases that there is uncertainty about the coverage of section 11, in this case as to whether an injury arising from the tort of trespass to the person as in the alleged rape and indecent assaults can qualify for the time extension. The ruling case would allow injuries from trespass against the person to qualify. It is worth citing Bingham LJ in the Court of Appeal's decision on Stubbings' writ to make as clear as possible why they decided this:

In *Letang* v. *Cooper* the Court of Appeal construed the language here in question as embracing a claim based on unintentional and intentional trespass to the person. Cooke J so understood the judgments in *Long* v. *Hepworth* and I consider the Court of Appeal's ruling to be binding upon us as he held it to be binding upon him. The Limitation Acts 1975 and 1980 were enacted in the same terms against the background of this authority, which they must be taken to have endorsed. *Even in the absence of authority I would, like Cooke J, reach that conclusion on construction of the statutory language alone, unless I could see some reason why Parliament should have intended to draw the suggested distinction, and I can see none.* I am satisfied this is an action falling within section 11(1) of the Act. [Our emphasis.][16]

Griffiths denies, in a rather curt way, Bingham's entirely orthodox argument that the recurrent passage of parliamentary language which ought to be known to have been interpreted in a particular way by the Court of Appeal gives that interpretation authority:

The Limitation Act 1963 was enacted to meet the problem of . . . industrial disease and the Act of 1975 was passed to cure the imperfections of the Act of 1963. The 1980 Act merely re-enacts the Act of 1975. In my view no light is thrown on the true construction of the section 11(1) by this sequence of Acts which were passed to deal with a very different problem to that with which your Lordships are now faced.[17]

The Acts may not throw any light on this issue, but it is nonetheless a fact that Parliament had considered limitations on three separate occasions after 1954, and never once said anything Griffiths could use. Griffiths could not find an episode in legislative history which allowed him to avoid this very difficult problem until 1954. But there is a history. Opening *Hansard* Griffiths shows that the original language of section 11(1) was section 2(1) of the Law Reform (Limitation of Actions) Act 1954. This was a private member's Bill, with government support, intended by its sponsor to implement the Tucker Committee Report of 1949. This fact was

---

[16] Bingham LJ in *Stubbings* v. *Webb* [1992] QB 197 at 204.
[17] *Stubbings* v. *Webb* [1993] AC 498 at 507.

attested to by *Hansard* quotations from the Bill's sponsor, and by the Committee's chairman, who had by now become Lord Tucker. It is, in fact, less than clear that the Tucker Report, even if legislated by an Act which had said no more than 'The Tucker Report is now law', would have the consequence Griffiths wants it to have. This is in part because the only way in which the 1954 Act does not follow the Report exactly is that the Report had actually recommended a two-year limit on personal injury extendable to six, and the sponsor's Act substituted a flat three. The later Acts then introduced the methods of timing which allowed Ms Stubbings to start counting from 1984 when her psychiatrist pointed out the causality between her childhood experience and her adult mental problems. There is nothing in the Tucker Report itself which would have solved the problem. And the reason the later Acts were passed was precisely to take account of illnesses, albeit industrially caused, which, like Ms Stubbings' psychological problems, by their very nature did not show up until long after the events that lay at their root. In other words the substantive history, if not the textual history, of the series of Acts presses directly towards opening up the chance for people to recover damages for ills done to them long before. The point for us is that until *Hansard* could be opened, it was possible for the courts to develop a jurisprudence, a 'purposive' reading of the Acts, to keep them in tune with the world. What Griffiths' discovery in the Tucker Report does is actually the opposite of purposive interpretation—it is brutally literal. He discovers a parliamentary intent which categorizes Ms Stubbings' cause of action in such a way—by stressing that it counts not as personal injury but as a different tort—that she cannot avail herself of parts of a much later Act. Griffiths says, somewhat triumphantly, of Denning in *Letang*:

. . . Denning was not prepared to assume that Parliament did intend to give effect to the Tucker Committee's recommendations, but we can now look at Hansard and can see that it was the express intention of Parliament to do so.[18]

Denning presumably had very good reason for not wanting to make that assumption, and could not, then, be forced to. But do we have any evidence that it was Parliament's intention in 1975 and 1980 to give effect to the Tucker Committee? The original sponsor was no longer in Parliament, and only a very strong theory of 'continued implied intent' could actually fix the MPs of 1980 with such an intention. In what conceivable way can it be said that Parliament's intention *vis-à-vis* recovery for injuries such as Ms Stubbings', when passing the ruling 1980 Act, is disclosed by a non Parliamentary Committee's intention when dealing with a completely different issue twenty-six years before, and very long before the medical profession was aware of the tremendous adult life horrors caused by (very

[18] *Stubbings* at 507.

common) childhood sexual exploitation? Would it, in fact, have been possible for Parliament to have had any intent in relation to recovery for such injuries before it was known that such a problem existed?

One way one might use the Tucker Report would produce the opposite result. This is to argue that what the Committee was doing, in 1954, was intentionally giving a longer time-to-sue for victims of intentional harm, the tort of trespass, than victims of negligence—the Act of 1954 allows, after all, six years for the former, and only three for the latter. As time passed subsequent legislation recognized the problem of knowledge in negligence cases, with the result that the initial more generous treatment of those who suffered intentional harm has, accidentally, been inverted. If the courts were allowed to continue blurring that distinction, as the ruling in *Letang* v. *Cooper* did, the consequent injustice was avoided.

It is a problem recognized in Code Law countries where the legislative history version of intent is simply disregarded where legislation is too old for it to be apposite, but a particularly complex problem in the USA, where the whole question of anachronism in legislation has been discussed at length, and has seen considerable effort, both judicial and legislative, to overcome it. It may help to look briefly at one American example, well analysed in a book by the then Dean of the Yale Law School, and now a judge on the US Court of Appeals for the Second Circuit.[19] The book, *A Common Law for the Age of Statutes*, indicates by its very title that courts may have a special job to do, or special problems in doing their job, when a legal system becomes very highly statute in structure. Calabresi is particularly concerned with the sort of case where the legislative intent is crystal clear, in the American sense of 'original intent', that is, what the legislators really did intend the words in the statute to mean at a particular time, but where subsequent social changes have led to a situation where giving the statute its unavoidable meaning not only produces what judges and others may see as injustice but, specifically, produces a result one can clearly see the legislature would not have wanted, given their motivation for the original intent. Such a situation, where no plausible purposive interpretation can get round clear meaning, where one really can be quite, indeed unavoidably, certain about the historic intent, such unwelcome clarity is in fact very hard indeed to achieve unless recourse is allowed to the legislative record. He gives many examples, of which his first will suffice.[20] During the depression years in America the Democrat controlled Congress under President Roosevelt had passed a series of laws to compensate injured workmen in particular industries where, for whatever reason, the common law tort rules were not giving adequate

---

[19] Guido Calabresi, *A Common Law for the Age of Statutes*, Harvard, 1982.

[20] Calabresi, ch. 4, which is also a generally useful study of interpretation, especially if read with the lengthy note on pp. 230–1.

protection. These laws, collectively known as the *Federal Employer Liability Act* (or FELA), and a similar piece of legislation known as the *Jones Act* gave, *inter alia*, very considerably better protection for employees of the railroads and maritime workers than the common law generally provided, and this preferential treatment was clearly intended. However, as time passed tort law was massively reformed in the US so that anyone able to bring an ordinary common law suit for injury came to be himself advantaged over those who could only sue their employers under FELA/Jones rules. These rules, particularly because they had originally been generously interpreted by the Supreme Court of the day, and because Congress's original intent was so clear, were set in stone. The only possible way of preventing rail and maritime employees being kept to 1940s levels of compensation was by a particular interpretative trick that is not available in the UK. The Supreme Court, against, the dissent of one of its most distinguished members, Felix Frankfurter, regularly (mis)interpreted FELA/Jones to allow the settlement of the level of damages to go to a jury, knowing that the jury would ignore the legal technicalities and produce a *de facto* modernization of the rules, thus restoring a situation that the New Deal Congress would clearly have wanted, one in the spirit of, but absolutely against, the 'formal intent', of FELA/Jones. Frankfurter's motivation for his restrictive ruling was in fact to try to force Congress's hand, because a combination of legislative inertia and special interest politics had produced a parliamentary logjam. The whole of Calabresi's book is a study of a phenomenon we are hardly aware of in this country, the need to find interpretative mechanisms to produce what he calls 'Sunset Laws', that is, laws that will die if they cannot be modified to keep up with changing circumstances. The reason the problem arises in America and not, or not visibly, in the UK is that so many of their jurists are wedded to the 'original intent' doctrine, a doctrine which is only applicable with any force where the legislative record can be consulted. Political scientists, of course, are particularly aware of the problem in the USA, because sticking to the original intent of the framers of the constitution, as evidenced by the history of the constitutional convention, has become a prime methodological tool for ideologically conservative judges.

It is a problem that Britain did not have until *Pepper*. Griffiths' speech in *Stubbings* so very clearly shows his lack of concern with litigation like hers that there is little doubt that he would have interpreted *Letang* out of order in any way he could. But the case is a very good example of how powerful a conservative tool the abolition of the exclusionary rule may now provide. The problem is, essentially, that reference to *Hansard* necessarily sets an interpretation within the immediate contemporary understanding of the government of the day. It does, as suggested above, risk imposing a

literalism in interpretation rather than an interpretation in keeping with
the spirit of the law.

5. Other Canons of Interpretation

We have already remarked that *Pepper* gives no explicit guidance on
priorities. The use of *Hansard*, in Bates's apt words, 'entered a judicial
melange of canons of construction to which unregulated weight may be
given'.[21] In fact the implication is clear that a judge who ignores a clear
ministerial statement of meaning will be in defiance of a democratically
elected government, with attendant risks, a point well argued by Styles.[22]
Bates refers to a point which requires considerable amplification. He notes
that references to *Hansard* raise a question about the previous practice of
having a stock of rebuttable presumptions on the intention of Parliament.
These are rules to the effect, for example, that Parliament can never be
assumed to have created a criminal offence, or imposed a tax, unless they
state this with complete clarity. Equivalent interpretative canons, especially with relation to criminal offences, exist in Code Law countries,
where the presumption would trump anything in the legislative history
in a case of linguistic unclarity. The role of these canons in the British
Constitution may generally be underestimated. In some ways they act as
a surrogate for a more formal written constitution or Bill of Rights, functioning much as did the Canadian Bill of Rights before repatriation of the
constitution and the enshrining of the *Charter of Rights and Freedoms*. By
saying that the courts will never read a statute as breaching one of the
canons except where the language is at its clearest they have the same
effect as a Bill of Rights which says that Parliament may not legislate in
breach of an enumerated right unless the legislation openly states that the
Bill should not apply to it. The difference, of course, is that there is no
complete and agreed list as to what these rebuttable presumptions are.
Probably the only two that would be agreed completely are the bans on
interpreting into existence a tax or a criminal offence. Bates, interestingly,
suggests a presumption against Parliament legislating in breach of
European Union Law or international law. These may be the only ones
with quite that force, and in the former case the existence of the Treaty of
Accession makes the role of the presumption uncertain. Such a list could
be extended, certainly. Recently an attempt has been made to do this by
using the idea of an interpretative canon functioning as constitutional

---

[21] T. St J. N. Bates, 'The Contemporary Use of Legislative History in the United Kingdom',
Cambridge Law Journal, vol. 54(1), 1995, pp. 127–52.

[22] Scott C. Styles, 'The Rule of Parliament: Statutory Interpretation after *Pepper v Hart*',
p. 156.

restraint in a private members Bill which sought to give legal force to the European Convention on Human Rights. The Bill stipulated that an English court should interpret any obscure legislation such that 'So far as the context permits, enactments (whenever passed or made) shall be construed consistently with' the Convention.[23] This Bill was supported in the Lords by many of the Law Lords, including Browne-Wilkinson. At the time of writing the Government has announced its intention to legislate to give the Convention some sort of force in English law, and the implications for this are briefly considered in chapters in the second half of this book. At this stage it is entirely unclear what the consequence for the ruling in *Pepper* will be, because no one can tell how ministers may change their style of presentation in the House. Would a reply to a question in the Commons which bluntly said that the Government did not intend some clause of the Convention to interfere with the policy enshrined in a Bill be enough, via *Pepper* v. *Hart*, to oust the new protections? Or will they be especially strong wherever a minister fails to make a reference to the Convention? Considering the fears already expressed about the possible 'chilling effect' of *Pepper*, it is hard to see how ministers will be able to risk not thinking in this sort of way. We have no choice at this stage but to ignore the Government's intention—it is unlikely to change any point of substance made here.

Even if rebuttable presumptions with the very strongest impact are few, there is no doubt that there is a stock of potentially powerful assumptions of this form which can act, depending on the judge's strength of mind, as serious constitutional restrictions on all but a determined Parliament. Indeed part of the inspiration behind Lord Lester's Human Rights Bill, which was avowedly modelled on the New Zealand Bill of Rights, was to overcome a Lords decision in which they failed to use such a presumption. In *Brind*, 1991, the Lords had disappointed liberals by refusing to use the European Convention on Human Rights to restrict the powers of the Home Secretary when he issued directives banning the broadcasting of IRA terrorists.[24] (We discuss *Brind* at some length in later chapters, so no extensive treatment is given here.) Yet this case in fact does disclose just such a presumption as far as statutory interpretation goes, one acknowledged by all the Law Lords who gave speeches, and well represented by Bridge:

. . . it is already well settled that, in construing any provision in domestic legislation which is ambiguous in the sense that it is capable of a meaning which either conforms to or conflicts with the Convention, the courts will presume that

---

[23] Lord Lester, 'The Mouse that Roared: The Human Rights Bill 1995', *Public Law*, Summer 1995, pp. 198–203.

[24] *R* v. *Secretary of State for the Home Department, ex parte Brind* [1991] 1 AC 696.

Parliament intended to legislate in conformity with the Convention, not in conflict with it.[25]

Lord Lester's problem with *Brind* is that the grant of power to the Home Secretary in the Broadcasting Act 1981 is entirely unambiguous and contains no possibility of interpretation—his real argument in *Brind* was that the Convention should replace the accepted doctrine of *Wednesbury* unreasonableness as a test in judicial review of administrative action, not that section 29(3) of the Broadcasting Act would turn out to mean something new if looked at through the Convention. It is not certain that his Human Rights Bill, were it to become an Act, would change this situation.

The Convention has its interpretive force via the general notion that, once a treaty is signed, the words of statutes must be interpreted 'if they are reasonably capable of bearing such a meaning, as intended to carry out the obligation, and not to be inconsistent with it'.[26] There are several similar presumptions with less clear general justification, because the justification is common law based. But if a common law origin is less concrete, it is no less powerful. After all, we are told all the time by judges that we do not need the European Convention, or a legislated Bill of Rights, precisely because the English common law is such a powerful protector of freedom. If this dogma means anything at all, it means that statutes will always be interpreted so as to preserve such traditional freedoms and rights unless Parliament is very determined in its language. The trouble is that such protective presumptions are only as good as the judge is brave. So many of the cases one finds, in searching for examples of this form of constitutional protection via interpretation, turn out to be in minority opinions. They are nonetheless good examples of this aspect of the British Constitution, one which is very seriously at risk after *Pepper*. If one considers the example below it is obvious that powerful and ringing arguments against executive power probably could not have been given at all had the State been able to quote parliamentarians. We have selected a classic Denning-style liberties case, *IRC* v. *Rossminster* from 1980.[27] The revenue authorities, proceeding under powers granted by section 20C of the Taxes Management Act 1970 staged a raid on the offices of Rossminster Ltd. and the private homes of some directors, seizing huge numbers of papers, and refusing to tell any of those raided what they were looking for or what they were suspected of, over and above fraud in general. Denning characteristically starts: 'It was a military style

[25] *Brind* at 747.
[26] Lord Diplock in *Garland* v. *British Rail Engineering Ltd.* [1983] 2 AC 751 at 771.
[27] *Inland Revenue Commissioners* v. *Rossminster Ltd.* [1980] AC 954.

operation . . . Everything was highly secret . . . The other side must not be forewarned.' He goes on to describe it:

As far as my knowledge of history goes, there has been no search like it—and no seizure like it—in England since that Saturday, April 30th 1763, when the Secretary of State issued a general warrant by which he authorised the King's messengers to arrest John Wilkes and seize all his books and papers.[28]

The case shocked the judiciary fairly generally. Browne LJ, agreeing with Denning, makes, for a senior judge, an extremely rare comment on his own reactions:

I have found it difficult to approach this case without emotion, but I hope that I have not allowed my emotions to influence my decision. . . . the events of this case are deeply distasteful to my own old-fashioned, and perhaps now unfashionable, instincts.[29]

The only way that the courts could see to support Rossminster and its directors against the IRC in this case was by querying the warrants they had used, because in every other way the raid, if unusual, was statute covered. But the statute is hardly unclear at all. Section 20C(1) authorizes searches where:

If the appropriate judicial authority is satisfied on information on oath given by an officer of the board that—(a) there is reasonable ground for suspecting that an offence involving any form of fraud in connection with . . . tax has been committed and that evidence of it is to be found on premises specified in the information . . .

All members of the Court of Appeal were agreed that such statutory language cried out for a strict interpretation because of the whole thrust of common law defence against searches and seizures, and used every way they could think of to interpret the section in such a way that the warrants that were issued would turn out to be invalid. Denning:

Once great power is granted there is a danger of it being abused. Rather than risk such abuse, it is, as I see it, the duty of the courts so to construe the statute as to see that it encroaches as little as possible on the liberties of the people of England.

Browne:

The powers given by section 20C . . . are very wide and may involve very serious interference with what would normally be the liberties of individuals. In my judgment the section should be construed literally.

For these judges anyway, there is an interpretative presumption latent in the very tradition of the common law for a particular way of reading a statute in a context like this. Their particular answer is that the warrants

---

[28] *Rossminster* at 970.
[29] *Rossminster* at 977.

are void for lack of specificity, though it is hard to see how they get that out of the words of section 20(C). In any event it would have taken one brief ministerial statement in the House, as a result, perhaps, of a civil liberty motivated question from the opposition along the lines 'Section 20C does indeed allow for less specificity than is usual because of the need for great secrecy in fraud cases', to utterly defeat the unanimous Court of Appeal. Yet, and this is what is so crucial, no MP would have actually had to vote for a piece of legislation which said, on its face, that it was suspending normal common law liberties. It would be pleasant to report that the Law Lords agreed with the Court of Appeal in this case, but, of course, four of the five did not. Lords Diplock and Wilberforce, and Viscount Dilhorne, went so far as to mock Denning's reliance on eighteenth-century doctrines about general warrants as having nothing to do with the modern world, and gave a pro-government reading to 20C. Lord Salmon, however, overtly supporting the duty to construe narrowly, discovered a technically more sophisticated way of reading the section, and one which his fellow Lords rather carefully avoid discussing in their speeches. For Salmon the words of 20C(1) 'if the appropriate judicial authority is satisfied on information on oath given by an officer . . .' clearly mean that the judicial authority must be satisfied *by the information itself*, and not just be satisfied that the officer of the board is satisfied. But the wording of the warrants as issued, and the affidavit evidence of the Board Officer as to what he had said to the judge both make it at least possible, and actually very likely, that the weaker of these two protections was all that had occurred. Here we do have a good example of a genuinely restrictive reading, justified by Salmon's commitment to a constitutional presumption . . . 'the courts should construe a statute which encroaches upon liberty so that it encroaches no more than the statute allows, expressly or by necessary implication'.[30] Salmon's argument could have won the day because it is so easy a reading of the section that judges minded to the same result as the Court of Appeal could easily have adopted it—but it would equally be fatally easy for a ministerial statement to have undermined it. It is very improbable that any US court would have allowed the antics of the Internal Revenue that day to get past the search and seizure liberties in the 4th Amendment, and countries governed by the Napoleonic Code have long had quite strong protection against such raids. Yet it is one of the, perhaps self satisfying, beliefs of English lawyers that the common law does all and more than such systems. It is time now to address some rather more general and theoretical problems about the nature and validity of statutes, and the intentions and motives of those who pass them.

---

[30] *Rossminster* at 1017.

6. What Exactly Is a Rule, and How Does Intent Matter?

In the end we are talking about that deeply important, yet more deeply obscure notion, 'the rule of law'. Part of the reason there are any doubts about the legitimacy of using the parliamentary record is that purposive interpretation is fairly recent in the UK. Indeed it was once quite hotly opposed, in contrast to an ideal of literal interpretation, once aptly described as 'the statute, the whole statute, and nothing but the statute'. The European label is perhaps more suitable. Teleological interpretation avoids prejudging the role of human authors when interpreting a statute partly in terms of its object. A related reason for confusion is that we are prone to treat all statutes as identical logical animals because constitutionally they all have the same form. We treat this form as being that of a rule, or a 'law' in the classical, almost Aristotelian sense in which 'rule of law' is contrasted to 'rule of men', involving the a-personal imposition of a general form conduct in generalized conditions. In reality statutes can be seen as arrayed along a dimension of what one might call 'ruleness'. At one end, the least like the classical form of rule, is a statute containing a series of *ad hoc* executive decisions with no internal cohesion, no basic 'purpose' or 'end' to the statute as a whole which one could use in interpretation. Were our constitution to allow rule by edict in some circumstances, the business of such statutes would be carried out by ministerial fiat: their legitimacy would rest on the fact that the government could be punished electorally, not because of the myth that they represent, themselves, the result of a democratic process through which the general will of the people is put into rule form. French constitutional practice, with its distinction between 'décret' and 'loi' has something of this about it.

To put some flesh on this theoretical skeleton we can return to a point we made earlier discussing *Pepper*. We suggested that as it arose from a Finance Act it could be argued that it was either a particularly suitable, or a terribly unsuitable, vehicle for launching the new interpretation rule. A Finance Act has no coherent purpose except the administrative one of satisfying the needs of the Treasury and sometimes, and not often in a manner compatible with that, of macroeconomic fine tuning. The contents of the Act, the individual taxing powers and exceptions, are nothing but the result of political, and deeply pluralistic, bargaining. In that sense we do need to know whether ministers intended to tax public school masters on their sons' cheap education. And that is precisely what we need to know, rather than to understand some illusory general rule of equitable burden sharing the Act might purport to enshrine. Tax policy in a pluralist democracy just bluntly is a matter of taking money where it is politically least dangerous to do so and giving tax breaks to those, in the current and very revealing jargon, who are part of a political party's 'natural constituency'. Any judicial interpretation of a Finance Act which purports to develop its purpose in extending or refining its categories into rule-like generalizations is slightly unrealistic because the categories are there as cover for a rewards and punishments list. In this sense *Pepper* is a perfect case to justify abandoning the exclusionary rule, but the very reasons that make the rule sensible in *Pepper* argue against the new interpretative technique in other statutes which actually approximate to the formal conception of a law forming part of the doctrine of the rule of law.[31]

Though there are no pure examples, the sort of statute which comes closer to a general rule is a statute that alters or modifies some aspect of the common law. The common law necessarily developed incrementally with general categories of actors or behaviour meant to be widely applicable. To this day it is a frequent criticism of common law decisions in, say, the law of negligence that clear generalizing rules or 'bright lines' are disappearing in favour of over-specific 'pockets of common law'. Such a statute is the Third Parties (Rights against Insurers) Act 1930, which was discussed in Chapter 3. It is a typical alteration in the common law statute, in that it removes the effect of the doctrine of privity of contract in special cases. In Templeman's words:

The Act of 1930 was intended to protect a person who suffers an insured loss at the hands of a company that goes into liquidation. That protection was afforded by transferring the benefits of the insurance policy from the company to the injured person. In my opinion, Parliament cannot have intended that the protection afforded against a company in liquidation should cease as soon as the company in liquidation reaches its predestined and inevitable determination in the dissolution of the company.

The Act, however, has been interpreted so as not to cover someone where the injuring company has gone into liquidation long before the plaintiff could discover the injury, as in *Bradley* v. *Eagle Star Insurance Company*, where Mrs Bradley, discovered belatedly that she was suffering from byssinosis, a respiratory disease caused by the inhalation of cotton dust. One reason for choosing the case, which happened long before the relaxation of the exclusionary rule in *Pepper*, is because it is, nonetheless, an example of the use of legislative history, and it is useful to remember that in some ways *Pepper* does no more than legitimize a mode of argument than was already common. Section 1(1) of that Act states:

Where under any contract of insurance a person . . . is insured against liabilities to third parties which he may incur then— . . . (b) in the case of the insured being a

---

[31] In fact we do not believe that Finance Acts and the like should be a special exception. The argument here is intended to show why other forms of Act should not be brought under a *Pepper* rule which can, at best, be justified for Acts like a Finance Act.

company, in the case of a winding-up order being made, or a resolution for a voluntary winding-up being passed, with respect to the company . . . if, either before or after that event, any such liability as aforesaid is incurred by the insured, his rights against the insurer under the contract in respect of the liability shall, *notwithstanding anything in any Act or rule of law to the contrary*, be transferred to and vest in the third party to whom the liability was incurred. [My emphasis.]

What Brandon for the majority did in this case was to make an argument of the following form:

1. There are procedural problems about letting Mrs Bradley sue.
2. The irregularity arises because as Mrs Bradley can not sue her defunct employer, it cannot lose the case, and therefore cannot accrue any rights against Eagle Star Insurance, so there are no rights that can be transferred.
3. We know why Parliament passed this Act—it was because difficulties had recently arisen in bankruptcy cases. This is made clear in section 1(2).
4. So the Act has nothing to do with cases like hers, and there is no need to interpret 'rights' in a way that involves a procedural irregularity.

This really is a legislative history argument. There is no difference between Brandon's use of his own historical knowledge about 1930 and Griffiths' use of *Hansard* to show that a 1954 Act was intended to implement the Tucker Report. In either case we would suggest that the judges are making a rather crucial mistake, if a rather philosophical one. They are taking the 'intention of Parliament' or the 'purpose of the Act' as synonymous with the reason an Act was passed. In individualistic terms, they are equating intention with motive. The vital point is that a statute of this form creates a rule, and rules have their own domain, their 'extension', their logical power, and these are not exhausted by the particular reasons Parliament or anyone else had in passing them. We are all too frequently aware of statutes being used for ends their authors never shared. A whole branch of the legal industry, tax lawyers, exists to find ways of using particular tax structures to enrich clients where that was never the motive behind the enactment.

Rule by law is not rule by a mass of one-off specific legislative fiats to fix very precise problems. It does not matter why the 1930 Act was passed— what matters is the meaning of the rule it enshrines. And when a statute uses language like 'notwithstanding anything in any Act or rule of law to the contrary', there is good reason to see such a generalized rule as being brought into force. A similar description would suit another statutory liability case discussed in Chapter 3, the relatively simple interpretative problem thrown up in *Knowles* v. *Liverpool City Council*. It will be remembered that Mr Knowles, a labourer for Liverpool City Council, injured his finger when a flagstone he was manhandling broke. The flagstone broke because of a defect in its manufacture. The Employers' Liability (Defective Equipment) Act 1969, section 1(1) provides that the employer shall be liable for injury caused by defective 'equipment', even when the defect is actually the fault of a third party, in this case the makers of the flagstone. Liverpool argued, of course, that a flagstone was not equipment. The Lords said it was. The only way of dealing with a case like this is to decide what general standard of employer liability the rule itself imposes. Here the Lords did interpret in the 'generous' way—but even here they applied legislative history, in the sense of looking for the motive of the legislators. They were clearly swayed by the fact that the 1969 Act was passed to overcome their own earlier lack of generosity in interpreting similar statutes, as admitted by Jauncey:

> there can be no logical reason why Parliament, having recognised the difficulties facing workmen, as demonstrated by *Davie and New Merton Board Mills Ltd.*,[32] should have removed those difficulties in part rather than in whole.

A simpler way of putting it would be that the Act itself would be an internally incoherent rule, by making a pointless distinction, if flagstones were not to be equipment.

These two polar ends of the 'ruleness' dimension leave many types of statute in between, but in most cases the best characterization is to see a statute as a rule, whose terms constitute it and give it its meaning. This meaning is distinct from, and should be superior to, the understandings of those who passed it, for whatever private reasons, which reasons may anyway not be truly disclosed in Parliament. If some people benefit in a way not anticipated by the authors of a statute there may be a political judgement to be made that will issue forth later a new and more restrictive statute. If some fail to benefit who the authors want to protect, because the language is 'under inclusive', the same applies. But the fact that a rule has consequences that its authors did not expect and do not like is not an argument about the meaning of the terms in the rule. Rather, it is a vital aspect of rules that, if we truly believe in them, we are obliged to accept, indeed can in some contexts be taken to have 'willed' or 'meant', those very consequences. It is crucial for the democratic legitimacy of the rules we call statutes that Parliament be in this position, but this can only be the case if the statute as enacted, the verbal formula put to the vote on the floors of the two Houses, rather than as glossed by a minister, is taken to constitute the rule.

Of course interpretation is sometimes required, though the reason it is needed is seldom simplistically that language is ambiguous. The interpretation is best done by the application of canons of construction by a body

---

[32] *Davie v. New Merton Board Mills Ltd.* [1959] 1 All ER 346.

which was not responsible for the initial formulation. There are two related reasons for this preference. First, it is inaccurate to describe the process of defining a troublesome phrase in a statute by reference to a gloss put on it in Parliament as 'interpretation'. It is, rather, the transmission of a policy choice, because when a minister answers a question about an as yet unratified Bill he is exercising such a choice, and the choice, if it is to be thought of as ratified by the democratic process, requires to be fully in the formula that is the subject of the ratification. Secondly, rules are cultural artefacts, and what they mean is a function of the overall culture of the society at the time of application, not of the restricted culture shared by a handful of legislators on the government payroll at the time they were debated. This is effectively what the old 'plain meaning' or 'golden' rule of interpretation strove to ensure. It is intriguing, for example, that American jurisprudence has tended to solve problems about negligence law by allowing more and more types of cases to go to juries as the statutes became more and more out of date. The Law Lords at any particular time are hardly representative of society in a statistical sense, but if they are doing their job well they will nonetheless interpret through a core understanding of the culture, even if it is a filtered and elite understanding.

Interpretation by the application of canons of construction to handle difficult choices, to make them less capable of criticism as merely a reflection of judicial ideology, has another virtue. It is a desirable quality of any set of laws that they should, as much as possible, be consistent with one another, if not in precise terms of consequences, at least in terms of basic values. Parliamentary legislation is hardly consistent in this way even within the lifetime of one Parliament, and with Britain's notoriously adversarial party system, consistency of core values between statutes passed over any length of time is negligible. If ambiguities in statutes are always dealt with by presuming Parliament does not lightly create criminal offences, levy taxes, breach civil liberties, clash with international law, give wide discretionary power to administrators, and so on, some underlying consistency can be maintained. In fact one traditional interpretative technique seldom used now but previously well thought of by the more literal of judicial interpreters, construing a word by what it clearly meant in a different but related statute, took this value very seriously.

The polar contrast between common law style rule-statutes and legislative Gladstone Bags like Finance Acts leaves an uncomfortable middle ground. This is not the place to develop, though it is sorely needed, a full theory of statute types, but it is necessary to note that the suitability of recourse to *Hansard* does depend on the type of statute. One form of statute that is seldom recognized as *sui generis* is what one might call a 'structure creating' statute. Thus legislation like the Housing Acts or

Social Services Acts do not only hand out benefits, they create complex administrative, decision-making, and adjudicatory mechanisms. Much of the work of the Lords, as discussed in the second part of this book, consists in acting as a longstop referee of these structures. The sort of statutory construction puzzle that arises from this type of legislation varies, and with it the potential suitability of legislative history varies. When it comes to rights claims there is a clear choice between seeing the selection of interpretations as similar to a taxing statute, an irredeemably political matter where ministerial statements might be thought to have a special force, or requiring instead that the Exchequer live with the implications of parliamentarily ratified general rules. Many of the decisions that have to be made, however, refer to the shape of the structure itself. Here one might say that the decisions are deeply political, though in the 'nobler' rather than 'baser' sense of politics, in that they are architectonic institution building decisions. Typically these involve grants of power to various bodies, especially, nominally at least, the Secretaries of State. One of the post *Pepper* 'Hansard' cases, *Chief Adjudications Officer* v. *Foster*[33] is of this nature, and reading it one sees that it might have been a situation where, because it was a question about power distribution inside a purpose built institution, the creating ministry should have the last word. (Although in fact Lord Bridge, who wrote for the court, shows he would have got to the same end without opening the parliamentary record.) Unfortunately there seems to be no acceptable way in which *Pepper* could be held to authorize recourse to the legislative history for some, but not for all, statutes. Once again courts could develop such a selective approach, as arguably they have in Code Law countries, were it the case that *Pepper* had ruled that *Hansard* could be used as one of a set of equally valid interpretative tools. But unfortunately the crude identification of purposive interpretation of parliamentary intent with ministerial preferences makes it impossible to develop a justification that would allow such delicacy of use.

7. Concluding Example

Of the handful of cases that came before the Lords in the immediate aftermath of *Pepper* which were clearly decided on *Pepper* principles, only one, *R* v. *Warwickshire County Council, ex parte Johnson*,[34] was really an example of fundamental textual ambiguity. The drafting of a section left it

---

[33] *Chief Adjudication Officer* v. *Foster* [1993] AC 754.

[34] *R* v. *Warwickshire County Council, ex parte Johnson* [1993] 1 All ER 299. One example of a court applying the new ruling with no doubts as to its utility or validity is *Shorts Trustee* v. *Keepers of the Registers of Scotland*, 1994 SLT 65. This could have been important because it would have been open to Scottish courts to see themselves as not bound by an English procedural rule.

entirely unclear whether Johnson, who was the manager of a retail chain store, was guilty of a trading standards offence, or whether only the owners of the chain could be. There was a clear parliamentary statement, because the exact language had been challenged, by Lord Denning, in a committee. In defending the language used the government minister made clear that the form of words was intentional, and that it was intended to prevent managers being guilty of the offence, and even gave a reasoned justification for this policy choice. No harm was done by reference to *Hansard*. But the same result would have come about anyway, because the presumption against the creation of a criminal offence would have won the day. It is alarming, however, that it was thought appropriate to use the *Pepper* relaxation, because this implies that state coercion can be used even through the criminal punishment system, on the basis not of a formal set of words for which all parliamentarians can be held responsible, but on the basis of an interchange, possibly in a nearly empty chamber late at night, indicative only of what the Home Office would like the law to mean. It is in this way that the decision in *Pepper* threatens to alter some fundamentals of British constitutional law, largely, it would seem, because of a laxness in thinking about what a statute, constitutionally, actually is. It may seem curious that, in a book largely dedicated to demonstrating, and to some extent decrying, the extensive presence of and use of discretion in English appellate procedures, we should so object to *Pepper* v. *Hart*. Some of the Law Lords responsible defend their decision, both in public and private, as stemming from a respect for democratic principles. But the rule in *Pepper* is not going to reduce interpretative discretion—it is going to be another way of wielding that discretion, and a method of doing so which hides what is actually going on. No legal realist can be expected to favour a procedural change which provides yet further mystification in the judicial process. This chapter concludes the preparatory half of the book. The five chapters of Part Two demonstrate some of the effects that judicial use by the Law Lords of their discretionary law making powers have had.

PART TWO

What the Law Lords Have Done

6

Pure Policy—The Law of Negligence

I do not think so ill of our jurisprudence as to suppose that its principles are so remote from the ordinary needs of civilised society and the ordinary claims it makes upon its members as to deny a legal remedy where there is so obviously a social wrong.

Lord Atkin in *Donoghue* v. *Stevenson*

The Good Samaritan was a Bad Economist.

Charles Dickens, *Hard Times*

Lord Atkin's view of the role of the law of negligence was not popular in his time, and to this day represents rather the far reaches of judicial thinking than the norm. But it demonstrates why this branch of private law, every bit as much as public law, is redolent of political importance. Quite simply, it is in the development of the civil law of negligence, the law governing when someone is liable to recompense another for a hurt he has unintentionally caused, that the State gives legal effect to its conception of general moral obligation. One way of thinking about the law of torts, of 'civil wrongs', of which negligence is the major part, is that tort law attempts to legislate via the judges to impose the more far-reaching moral obligations which governments prefer not to try to encapsulate in statute. Of course all areas of law are substantively political. The history of English law is the history first of the arrangement of titles in real property—land—to enable the landed to make more money out of their holdings, and then of the development of legal machinery, the laws of contract, to let rich individuals deal freely to multiply this wealth. One does not have to be a quasi-Marxist from the so called 'Critical Legal Studies' school to see legal history like this (although the Critical Legal Studies movement, being the heirs to American legal realism, come nearer to our approach than most of modern jurisprudence.). The great classical statements like Atiyah's *The Rise and Fall of the Freedom of Contract*[1] are full of acute political analysis. Similarly the 'Economics of Law' school associated with writers like Posner[2] and the University of Chicago takes it as

[1] Patrick S. Atiyah, *The Rise and Fall of Freedom of Contract*, Oxford, Clarendon Press, 3rd edn., 1979.
[2] See, in particular, Richard A. Posner, *Overcoming Law*, Cambridge, Mass., Harvard University Press, 1955. Ch. 3, 'What do Judges Maximise?', is an economics of law approach to the same problems this book addresses.

definitional that the common law is, in the language of economics, an efficiency maximizing institution. But to a large extent a combination of statutory codification and common law development has brought most areas to a state where development is largely technical, and where the enshrined values are largely unstated because too commonly accepted to arise in argument. There is no equivalent in the law of the negligence, and there probably can never be, to the major codification statutes like the English Law of Property Act 1925. The law of contract no longer contains within itself the possibility of endless growth because there is no equivalent to the tort law doctrine that 'the categories of negligence are never closed'—that is, judges will always be free to find new obligations and duties of taking care of each other. (There are attempts to reduce tort to a code, contained, for example, in the various Model Codes and Restatements, but no common law state has ever seriously attempted to make these statutory). It is perhaps because of this logical open endedness that negligence remains so intrinsically political. Some lawyers actually see the law of negligence as *the* base or foundation law, from which individuals may by agreement in contract partially withdraw. One thing in particular that makes negligence fascinating to the political theorist is that its principles tend to clash with most ideas of economic efficiency—often, and especially during the period covered here, the law of negligence has to be reined in. Case after case shows the curtailment of the *natural* implication of the principles of the law of negligence by cautious judges imposing 'policy' constraints in the name of economic or commercial necessity. Judicial ideology, and the very notable lack of consensus therein, shows at its clearest when these policy arguments are wheeled in. Perhaps ideology shows even more when attempts are made to hide the very fact that an obvious extension of negligence principles is being prevented, or a major advance in those principles is being overturned for economic and commercial convenience.

Land law and the law of contract, originally created by the common law for the needs of unregulated economies in their earlier stages of development, have been brought under control and fine tuned for the mixed economies of the late twentieth century. Law governing other aspects of the economy like labour relations and industrial injury has from a developmentally much earlier point been essentially statute controlled, largely because of the failure of judges to accept the political necessities. Specific areas of modern concern like social welfare were from the beginning the creation of statutes, though, as shown in Chapter 8, the judiciary have had to take on new managerial roles within the resulting schemes. The growth areas of law, the areas of greatest and, as it were, legitimate judicial freedom and therefore of judicial ideology, are either the areas that control the State itself, public law, or this last and vast area of negligence. Negligence is the area concerned with the very general problem of the consequences of individuals living increasingly interconnected lives in which anyone's chances of hurting another are very high.

What perhaps makes the law of negligence of ever pressing importance is the breakdown of non-legal norms enforcing a private sense of obligation to take care of each other. One cannot but be struck by stories behind some recent cases that have caused controversy because the law of negligence has been forced to step in where those with a restrictive judicial ideology would not wish to tread. Two of the most recent and most controversial are to point. In *Spring* v. *Guardian Assurance,* which we have discussed earlier, the problem was caused by someone's employment chances being blighted by a negligently written reference.[3] Is it entirely idealistic to think that an institution as powerful as Guardian Assurance could not have perfectly easily made up for its carelessness towards Mr Spring voluntarily, and perhaps more directly than by cash payment, and indeed that in an earlier day it would have done so? A failure of a voluntary acceptance of fault that seems even more out of keeping with what one might have thought to be a professional ethic lay behind *White* v. *Jones* in 1995. A solicitors' firm, by rank carelessness in processing a client's will, ended up depriving a family member the client had wished to bequeath £10,000 to of their rightful inheritance. The law of negligence had to be stretched beyond what many lawyers think is breaking point to compensate the deprived relative. (This was the case in which Lord Mustill, as quoted earlier, savaged his colleagues for being determined to do justice if they could find any argument whatsoever to support their value judgment.) While £10,000 was perhaps a large amount to the intended beneficiary, it hardly seems an enormous sum for the solicitors' firm, which may well have made a good deal of money from a long-term client during his life, to have paid over *ex gratia*. For whatever reason, the courts have been asked increasingly to enforce a generalized duty of care over the last half century, and the account of the ebbs and flows in their willingness to do so is the core of this chapter. One further factor, political or perhaps better, sociological, suggests the importance of ideology here. The story of the development and counter development of negligence is not just an English story, because this is an area of law where precedents are freely inter-quoted between the common law jurisdictions. And there are clearly discernible national differences—Canada, and even more New Zealand, are notably more 'plaintiff friendly' than are Australia and the USA, with English judges, depending on their predilections, borrowing more from one side than the other. It is improbable that such a difference does not stem from general ideological factors in the different political

---

[3] *Spring* v. *Guardian Assurance plc* [1993] 2 All ER 273.

cultures. In the chapter that follows we try to describe a process of revolution and counter-revolution in judicial thinking about negligence which
seems closely to parallel some of the account of scientific revolutions
developed by Thomas Kuhn and now widely followed in the social sciences. This parallel is revisited in the concluding chapter. But we could
not have written this account of ideological battle in the law of negligence
without establishing, in the first half of this book, that the judges were,
always, free to do what they wanted within the field.

1. A Revolution in the Law of Negligence

The classic beginning of the story of modern negligence is *Donoghue* v.
Stevenson,[4] from which Lord Atkin's quotation, at the head of the chapter
is taken. Before 1932, when this case came to the Lords from the Scottish
Court of Session, there was no generalized conception of a single tort of
negligence. English law recognized a set of situations when one had to be
careful not to inflict accidental harm of one sort or another, which had
developed piecemeal over the centuries. If a plaintiff wanted damages to
make up for some harm he had suffered, he had to show that what had
happened to him fell into one of these existing, and rather restrictive,
recognized categories. The categories themselves had largely developed
from a recognition that particular trades or callings had to be exercised
with great care, or from noting the inherent risk in some commodity.
Thus, for example, those who manufactured intrinsically dangerous
items, guns, say, would be liable if faulty workmanship led to someone
being hurt. Horses were seen as intrinsically dangerous, and a rider could
be liable for accidents his mount caused. The dangerously faulty manufacture of a normally harmless product would not, however, render the
maker liable for his carelessness. An example used by one of the majority
in *Donoghue* itself makes the point clear. A baker who allowed arsenic to
be mixed with flour might commit a criminal offence, but the customer of
a shop to which he provided such tainted bread would have no civil case
for damages.[5] The way to gain rights in such contexts was via contract,
because nothing stopped a baker voluntarily accepting obligations to
customers as part of a bargain. But this depended on the bargain being of
value; the baker had to get something in return, the famous 'consideration' of contract law. The contract between the shopkeeper and the baker
might, though it equally might not, make the baker liable to the shopkeeper—that would depend on the negotiated terms of the contract for
bread supplies. But by the doctrine of 'privity of contract', a third party

---

[4] *Donoghue* v. *Stevenson* [1932] AC 562.
[5] After Lord Macmillan, *Donoghue* at 620.

outside the contractual chain, the final purchaser of the poisoned loaf, could not claim. It is frequently said today by the Law Lords when grappling with modern problems of English negligence law that the problems are all caused by English law having a defective theory of contract. In the thirties, even more than now, contract was seen as supreme.

Donoghue was a case directly like this. Mrs Donoghue was bought a bottle of ginger beer by a friend in a café. After some of it had been poured and drunk, the rest was discovered to contain a partially decomposed snail. Either the effect of what she had drunk or the shock or both, caused her to be very ill. There are three aspects which turn out to be significant in the arguments over the development of the law. It is important to the story that the bottle was made of coloured glass and sealed so that, once it had left the manufacturer, it could not be inspected. It is also important, in a way that will not be apparent until later, that Mrs Donoghue was suing for actual physical harm from drinking the ginger beer, not because, once she saw the snail, she could not drink the rest. Finally, it is an obvious question to ask why she sued the manufacturer, if there was a legal problem about her claim, rather than the café which sold it to her. (In fact Mr Minchella, the café owner, was originally one of the defendants, but was dropped by the plaintiff.) Under various Acts governing the sales of goods she probably would have a claim against the seller. But the seller almost certainly did not have enough money to make it worth suing him. There is a concept in American legal practice of a defendant being 'judgment proof', meaning that whether you win in court or not, you will never get your money or expenses. It is a tendency, and a continual problem, in the law of negligence that the cases are frequently brought against someone further down the causal chain than the immediate contact with the plaintiff precisely because a simpler legal liability is, in this sense, judgment proof. So, for example, a vitally important case in negligence, *Anns* v. *Merton* in 1977, established crucially that local authorities could be liable for faulty construction of houses even though they were built by independent contractors, and the authorities' role was only to inspect the early stages of the building.[6] This case was much later overturned in the clearest example ever of an ideological reaction against the principles of negligence that stem from *Donoghue*, which we discuss at length later. The importance of *Anns* and the decisions in its train was precisely that local authorities always could afford to compensate the owners of the faulty houses, and the builders, if they had not already gone bankrupt, almost never could.

The whole art of plaintiff litigation in negligence consists in showing that responsibility for *any sort of loss* incurred to a *plaintiff of any description*

---

[6] *Anns* v. *Merton London Borough* [1977] AC 728.

by *carelessness of any sort* can be placed at the feet of *someone any distance back* in a causal chain and involved in *any capacity whatsoever*—who can afford to pay for it. All of these italicized points cause judges to rebel against the spirit of *Donoghue*—different judges rebel with greater or less passion in different jurisdictions at different times. The essence of the rebellion is always the same—judges feel that somehow it just can not be right to throw liability for negligence so widely. That instinctive position is never attacked in the pages of law reports. No one ever commits the sin that Mustill half accused his colleagues of in *White* v. *Jones*:[7]

> I do not of course ascribe to those who support the plaintiffs' claim the contemporary perception that all financial and other misfortunes suffered by one person should be put right at the expense of someone else. Nobody argues for this. Even under the most supportive of legal regimes there must be many situations in which the well founded expectations of a potential beneficiary are defeated by an untoward turn of events and yet he or she is left without recourse. Nobody suggests otherwise. What is said to take the present case out of the ordinary is that the plaintiffs' disappointment resulted, and resulted foreseeably, from what is called 'fault'.[8]

However obvious it may be to a lawyer, it may be less obvious to others— why, in principle, should one not be responsible for all the consequences of one's voluntary actions? This, at heart, is the value clash that runs through the Law Lords crafting, a crafting almost unimpeded by Parliament, of the most basic of all our common law, the tort of negligence.

Mrs Donoghue won her legal point, of course, otherwise there would be no story. The manufacturer was held to be liable for her physical suffering from drinking snail impregnated ginger beer.[9] It was how Lord Atkin for the majority gave her the victory that has caused the conflicts over negligence ever since. There were really three ways the plaintiff could win in *Donoghue*. One of them would have caused little trouble, because it was a route already available, and another argument would have been assimilable to the existing legal position, though with less comfort to the conservative position of the time. Atkin could have argued, though perhaps it would have been fanciful, that modern carbonated drinks were, like horses and guns, inherently dangerous—something to do with large-scale production processes made it, perhaps, both likely that dangerous foreign bodies would get in, and virtually impossible to check on this. Such a ruling—its empirical improbability does not matter here—would have been legally very safe. The actual number of winnable negligence cases

---

[7] *White and another* v. *Jones and others* [1995] 1 All ER 691.

[8] *White* v. *Jones* at 215.

[9] See, in particular, Richard A. Posner, *Overcoming Law*, Cambridge, Mass., Harvard University Press, 1955.

would go up, probably quite sharply, but nothing would have changed in the law. Alternatively Atkin could have created a new category of negligence to cover the narrow facts of the case. Perhaps the non-inspectability of consumable goods sold in sealed coloured containers, where because of the carbonation the drinks could not be decanted ahead of time, would provide enough to make producers liable. With this tack the range of liability would be extended both logically and empirically, but the overall structure of the tort would not be changed, because no broad change would have been made to the justification of holding some people liable for other people's misfortunes when highly specific acts were done. This approach, of adding a particular category, is how later judges have at times tried to characterize Atkin's argument in *Donoghue*, to limit its scope.

It is not what he did. Lord Atkin took neither route. What he did, or what he said he did, was to survey the existing categories of negligence to find what they had in common, on the grounds that the true basis for liability would be a rule derived from this commonality. Atkin is fully aware of the existing nature of law of negligence:

It is remarkable how hard it is to find in the English authorities statements of general application, defining the relations between parties that give rise to the duty . . . the courts have been engaged upon an elaborate classification of duties as they exist in relations to property . . . and distinctions based on the particular relations of the one side or the other, whether manufacturer, salesman or landlord, customer, tenant or stranger, and so on. In this way it can be ascertained at any time whether the law recognises a duty, but only where the case can be referred to some particular species which has been examined and classified. And yet the duty which is common to all the cases where liability is established must logically be based on some element common to the cases where it is found to exist.

This is not the lawyer's normal argument by analogy, where a case is held to be similar to the ones in which a rule has been established, and thus covered by that rule. This is argument by induction, essentially a matter of telling a story about the cases that makes sense of them. All such stories are ideological, because it is a feature of induction games that there is no one right answer—and indeed there may theoretically be an infinite number of rules that account for all of the facts. Hence induction involves choice, and it is clear, in the following quotation, perhaps the most familiar in modern English law, what are the ideological underpinnings of Atkin's inductive choice. After recognizing that liability for wrongdoing is based on 'a general public sentiment of moral wrongdoing', he admits that the positive law can only give force to morality in a restricted and limited way:

The rule that you are to love your neighbour becomes in law, you must not injure your neighbour; and the lawyer's question 'Who is my neighbour?' receives a restricted reply. You must take reasonable care to avoid acts or omissions which you can reasonably foresee would be likely to injure your neighbour. Who, then, in law, is my neighbour? The answer seems to be—persons who are so closely and directly affected by my act that I ought reasonably to have them in contemplation as being so affected when I am directing my mind to the acts or omissions which are called into question.

The New Testament language is neither accidental nor irrelevant. Lord Atkin was a devout and very prominent member of the Church of Wales, and at this time in history he could safely expect his readers to be fully equipped with an understanding of the specific moral code he was evoking. In fact at the end of his judgment when he states the specific proposition of law in the case—that manufacturers are liable for products they put out knowing they will be received by the customer with no chance of intermediate inspection—he goes on to say:

It is a proposition I venture to say no one in Scotland or England who was not a lawyer would for one moment doubt. It will be an advantage to make it clear that the law in this matter, as in most others, is in accordance with sound common sense.

Obviously there were technical details to iron out in the ensuing cases, largely about the degree of 'proximity' that had to exist between the careless actor and his victim—proximity being a concept Atkin borrowed from an earlier attempt to provide a rule rather like his. But by and large, as long as the issue involved *physical harm* to person or property by a *physical act or omission* Atkin's revolution worked, and has not seriously been eroded. If a particular sort of harm can in principle be expected as an at least fairly probable consequence of carelessness, in the sense that I would have realized this had I thought about it, I will be liable. The essence is this abstract, idealized sense of foreseeability. Foreseeability imposes on me a duty that covers anyone, a duty that follows from my basic moral obligations to humanity in general, and has nothing to do with any contract or other special agreement between me and the person I hurt. It is a very powerful and very general principle, which is why it was opposed so strongly. In one of the earliest reported cases on the issue the judge, refusing to allow a third party injured by negligence in construction of a coach, made the point that still worries those with restrictive attitudes to negligence:

The only safe rule is to confine the right to recover to those who enter into the contract; if we go one step beyond that, there is no reason why we should not go fifty.[10]

Lord Buckmaster, whose minority opinion in *Donoghue* quotes this, also quotes with approval a Scottish decision on almost identical facts only

---

[10] Alderson B in *Winterbottom* v. *Wright* 10 M & W 109.

three years before *Donoghue* where the idea of a decision like Atkin's was described as 'little short of outrageous'.[11] So tender were the judges to the concerns of manufacturers that Buckmaster even agrees with a dictum from one of the immediate precursor cases to *Donoghue*. There a proposition like Atkin's was seen as: 'impossible to accept . . . and indeed it is difficult to see how, if it were the law, trade could be carried on. No prudent man would contract to make or repair what [his purchaser] intended to permit others to use.'[12]

In other words, a morally embracing duty is seen as economically irrational, which is roughly what current problems in the law of negligence revolve round. Now so far we have been considering old history, though a necessary piece of history both to see the value laden nature of this branch of law, and to establish the bench line. Naturally it took some time, rather a long time, in fact, and further judicial decisions, fully to enshrine the *Donoghue* principle as a relatively automatic formula in English law. In textbooks and judicial opinions, references are often made to *Donoghue* as one of a trio of cases, the others being *Hedley Byrne* and *Dorset Yacht*. *Hedley Byrne* can easily enough be seen as a necessary extra step because it recognizes two aspects completely outside the 'physical damage caused by physical action' range of *Donoghue*—liability for 'words', in that case advice, and liability for monetary loss.

2. The Revolution Consolidated

Dorset Yacht, however, can seem an unnecessary case, because for three of the Lords who formed the four-man majority for the plaintiff it was basically a willing application of the general principle Lord Atkin had established. Nonetheless the complete acceptance, in a formulaic way, of the *Donoghue* principle in *Dorset Yacht* marked the full coming of age of Atkin's approach to negligence. Several borstal boys, working on an island under the supervision of three officers, escaped from their supervision one night and stole a yacht which they damaged in an attempt to make good their escape. The yacht owners sued the Home Office for damage caused by the negligence of the prison officers in allowing the escape, there being no point, as so often in these cases, in going after those directly responsible. Lord Dilhorne, in dissent, fought a last-ditch battle against the whole Atkin approach, and one can easily imagine him siding with Buckmaster had he been in the Lords in 1932. Dilhorne makes two points. The first, often argued, is that Atkin's 'foreseeability' test cannot be taken literally, because there are too many cases where we would not

---

[11] Lord Anderson in *Mullen* v. *Barr & Co.*, 1929 SC 461.
[12] Matthew LJ in *Heaven* v. *Plender*, 11 QBD 503.

expect the law to hold someone liable for action, and even more for omission, which allowed an entirely foreseeable accident to happen. He gives an often used instance—that the law would not hold liable someone who fails to go to the help of a child in trouble in a pond. (It is curious that examples of this sort are so often used because they are seen as undeniable—yet most continental legal systems in fact treat failure to attempt rescue in such a situation as a criminal offence.[13]) This part of Dilhorne's argument—over-generality—takes the 'Why not fifty steps' approach—if the prison officers are liable here, why would not the Home Office in general be liable for crimes committed by escaped prisoners anywhere and whenever? The tougher part of his argument, though, is to insist that *Donoghue* simply does not establish a principle that a duty of care arises from foreseeability. According to Dilhorne, Atkin's 'Who then in law is my neighbour' test is a test not to establish whether a duty of care exists, but only to whom the duty is owed, if the duty exists independently. The duty must be shown to exist by looking at precedents to demonstrate that the courts have regularly seen similar fact situations to have led to a duty. His analysis of the cases convinces him that there is no recognition of the duty claimed by the plaintiff, and that it would therefore be a breach of Parliament's prerogative for the courts to create a new duty. Dilhorne's conception here of the legitimate growth of judge made law is very carefully defined:

We are being asked to create in reliance on Lord Atkin's words an entirely new and novel duty and one which does not arise out of any novel situation. I, of course, recognise that the common law develops by the application of well established principles to new circumstances, but I cannot accept that the application of Lord Atkin's words . . . suffices to impose a new duty on the Home Office and on others in charge of persons in lawful custody of the kind suggested . . . we are not concerned with what the law should be but with what it is. The absence of authority shows that no such duty now exists. If there should be one, that is, in my view, a matter for the legislature and not for the courts.[14]

This is one of the best definitions of the restrictive conception of judicial creativity—the law is actually fixed, we have left the heroic age of judicial law creation. Now all that can be done is to adapt fixed law to changed situations, as opposed to adapting the law to new expectations. Dilhorne was a conservative, of course, but it is still remarkable that so basic a methodological change as Atkin's was being so forcefully resisted nearly forty years after *Donoghue* was decided.

Naturally the majority see problems in applying the foreseeability test.

---

[13] Legal thinkers sometimes argue that there is a crucial difference between what might justify the creation of a criminal offence in this area and what justifies the creation of a civil duty. See J. C. Smith, *Legal Obligation*, 1976.

[14] *Dorset Yacht* at 1045.

It cannot give an automatic answer because of what lawyers call the remoteness problem—just how closely connected must the tortfeasor be? The Home Office probably should not be held liable for a burglary committed days after an escape miles from the prison. In the instant case though, there is nothing remote about what happened. The boys were, after all, on an island from which a natural, maybe the only, mode of escape was to steal a yacht. This was too obviously foreseeable, and easily prevented had the prison officers been doing their job properly. Such policy decisions worry the majority not at all—it is just part of the judicial function for them. Indeed Lord Morris, who called the liability here 'glaringly obvious' and said it would be 'contrary to the fitness of things' were there to be no duty, does not even fully accept that the judicial decisions involved in applying *Donoghue* are policy decisions:

I doubt whether it is necessary to say, in cases where the court is asked whether in a particular situation a duty existed, that the court is called upon to make a decision as to policy. Policy need not be invoked where reason and good sense will at once point the way. If the test as to whether in some particular situation a duty of care arises may in some cases have to be whether it is fair or reasonable that it should so arise, the court must not shrink from being an arbiter. As Lord Radcliffe said . . . the court is 'the spokesman of the fair and reasonable man'.[15]

Perhaps the most revealing opinion in this case, from our point of view one of the clearest statements anywhere in English law of what judges do, is Lord Diplock's speech. He was in no doubt that a policy decision was being taken—describing what they were doing as carrying out a function 'which judges hesitate to acknowledge as law-making'.[16] He cites approvingly Lord Pearce from the other case in the trio, *Hedley Byrne*, who gives an explanation of the process:

How wide the sphere of the duty of care in negligence is to be laid depends ultimately upon the courts' assessment of the demands of society for protection from the carelessness of others.[17]

Diplock himself justifies this essentially legislative role:

The justification of the courts' role in giving the effect of the law to the judges' conception of the public interest in the field of negligence is based upon the cumulative experience of the judiciary of the actual consequences of lack of care in particular instances.[18]

In fact Diplock goes on to construct an extremely elaborate methodology, which he too describes as induction, for handling situations like *Dorset*

---

[15] *Dorset Yacht Co.* v. *Home Office* [1970] AC 1039.
[16] *Dorset Yacht* at 1058.
[17] Lord Pearce in *Hedley Byrne & Co. Ltd.* v. *Heller & Partners* [1963] AC 465 at 536.
[18] *Dorset Yacht* at 1058.

Yacht. What is important here, apart from the frank acceptance of judicial legislation, is that Diplock does see himself as legislating, and accepts that a policy-making instance has occurred precisely because he does not, like the rest of the majority, see *Dorset* as a straightforward application of *Donoghue*. It is always difficult for a commentator to guess when judges will perceive a case as falling outside the range of a previously agreed principle. For whatever reason, Diplock did so regard this case. The important difference between *Donoghue* and *Dorset Yacht* is, for Diplock, that the second case raises the legal question of whether a person can be liable for another person's act. Lords Morris, Reid, and Pearson, the rest of the majority, were not unaware of this aspect of the case—they just did not see it as mattering. Diplock thought it required a completely new legal creation, though one he was happy to share in. Although Diplock's decision here is substantively the same as the rest of the majority, and though he is every bit as willing to extend liability for negligence, the fact that, unlike Morris or Reid, he does not see it just as doing justice by applying a broad principle heralds the way in which much less generous judges were later to mount a counter-attack.

At least *Dorset Yacht could* be seen by some as an automatic extension of *Donoghue*, but one further case was needed before the Atkin approach to liability for negligence could be fully developed. This is the last of the famous trio, *Hedley Byrne & Co.* v. *Heller & Partners Ltd*.[19] Each of the Law Lords specifically rebuts the plaintiff's argument here that the issue is covered by *Donoghue*, though all of them say that *Dongahue* supports what they see themselves as doing, which is opening up a whole new branch of lability. Hedley Byrne, an advertising company, asked for a credit reference on one of their customers from Heller & Partners, a merchant bank, which was given negligently, though by honest mistake, leading them to lose a good deal of money when their client went bankrupt. Everyone was agreed that *Donoghue* did not apply because the law had always recognized important differences in the way that mis-statements could function in a modern society. Lord Pearce, who produced the explanation for judicial law making in negligence quoted earlier, describes the legal problems of words rather poetically:

Negligence in word creates different problems from those of negligence in act. Words are more volatile than deeds. They travel fast and far afield. They are used without being expended and take effect in combination with innumerable facts and other words. Yet they are dangerous and can cause vast financial damage.[20]

In fact Pearce goes on, after the earlier quotation, specifically to comment that 'economic protection has lagged behind protection in physical

---

[19] *Hedley Byrne & Co.* v. *Heller & Partners* [1963] AC 465.
[20] Lord Pearce, *Hedley Byrne* at 534.

matters', attributing this leg to the deterrent effect of the sheer range and size of possible economic claims. Nonetheless he like all the others is prepared to make this extension. They are all influenced, notably, by foreign cases, particularly in America, where the extension of liability to cover, for example, negligently drawn up certificates had already been made. Their Lordships varied somewhat in their justifications, but what they all had in common was an acceptance of the general principle of liability, along with a search for some limiting principle which could restrict the dangers of imposing liability for what the famous American judge Cardozo had characterized as liability in 'an indeterminate amount for an indefinite time to an indeterminate class'.[21]

With the trio of cases in place by the early seventies English negligence law seemed established as a far-reaching and principled doctrine based on a general proposition of liability for what one could foresee, where an adequate 'proximity' (*Dorset Yacht*) or some voluntarily accepted special relationship (*Hedley Byrne*) existed. Subsequent cases were decided on this simple basis. Lord Wilberforce describes this test, and his words demonstrate how thoroughly the cases had been integrated into such a principle:

Through the trilogy of cases . . . the position has now been reached that in order to establish that a duty of care arises in a particular situation, it is not necessary to bring the facts of the situation within those of previous situations in which a duty of care has been held to exist. Rather the question has to be approached in two stages. First one has to ask whether, as between the alleged wrongdoer and the person who has suffered damage there is a sufficient relationship of proximity or neighbourhood such that, in the reasonable contemplation of the former, carelessness on his part may be likely to cause damage to the latter, in which case a prima facie duty of care arises. Secondly . . . it is necessary to consider whether there are any considerations which ought to negative, or reduce or limit the scope of the duty or the class of person to whom it is owed or the damages to which a breach of it may give rise.[22]

In many ways this approach could be seen as radically 'de-legalizing' the whole negligence issue, pushing most of the emphasis onto quasi-factual questions. Certainly it seemed this way to critics from a traditional perspective. In an article published in 1983 to commemorate the fiftieth anniversary of *Donoghue* two Canadian scholars issued a blistering attack, avowedly from what they called a 'rights-based' approach:

The prima facie duty doctrine created from Lord Atkin's 'neighbour principle', first authoritatively pronounced by Lord Reid in *Dorset Yacht* and restated . . . by Lord Wilberforce in the *Anns* case, enacts a fundamental change in the basis of tort liability, which inevitably will have important economic, social and political

---

[21] This is very frequently quoted and comes from *Utramares* 255 NY 170.
[22] Lord Wilberforce in *Anns* v. *London Borough of Merton* [1977] 2 All ER at 498.

consequences. It is part of a wide shift in post-liberal society from formalistic law to an 'ad hoc balancing of interests'. It is a device whereby courts are enabled to exercise a discretion as to the creation of legal liability, in that the existence of a duty, since it is assumed, need not be justified in terms of precedent or principle relating to well-recognized grounds of civil obligation. Instead the ultimate cost-bearing issue is shifted from the legal question of the existence of a duty, to the factual questions of standard of care.[23]

Similarly the authors complain that this approach means the judge:

> need then only show in terms of a utilitarian calculus, economic analysis, political ideas of fairness or a religious sense of right and wrong, dressed up in the amorphous language of public policy, that the defendant ought to have done what he failed to do.

Earlier, and revealingly, they accuse Lord Atkin, and judges involved in subsequently developing his approach, of failing to accept the fundamental difference between law and morality which they regard as 'essential for the autonomy of law as a social institution'. Such a phrase could well be used to stand symbolically for the opposite of our legal realist perspective. Unfortunately for anyone who thinks autonomy either non-existent or undesirable, they were wrong in their predictions, because the two cases they particularly attack in their article, *Anns* in 1977 and *Junior Books* v. *Veitchi Co. Ltd.* in 1982, were the high water mark of negligence law. A new generation of judges, several still in the Lords, have been at work ever since pushing back the frontiers of negligence liability.

3. The Revolution Established

Both were cases which non-lawyers find it hard to see as exceptional at all. In *Anns* the London Borough of Merton was sued by the owners of maisonettes which had been built with inadequate foundations and were now in danger of collapse. The council had not built the maisonettes—the actual builder was not being sued, presumably because he could not pay or could not even be found. But the council had, years before the block was built, passed by-laws requiring adequate foundations, requiring the deposit of building plans, and providing for inspections to be made. The council had approved plans for this two-storey block which showed foundations 'three feet or deeper to the approval of the local authority'. The foundations were actually only taken down two feet six inches, and within ten years of construction structural movement had taken place. Though the case was complicated by doctrines about the nature of discre-

[23] J. C. Smith and Peter Burns, 'Donoghue v. Stevenson—The Not So Golden Anniversary', *Modern Law Review*, 1983, vol. 46, pp. 147–163.

tion when carrying out a statutory duty, the main point was clear, and the Law Lords had no problem in finding liability. Indeed it is hard to see what point there is in having local authorities empowered to regulate building if those who suffer because of the authority's negligence cannot recover damages. Why *Anns* later came to be seen as wrong, at the beginning of a much less plaintiff friendly era in the Lords, we will see in due course. It is important though to see that although *Anns* was a complex case for a variety of technical reasons, the Law Lords who heard it did not for a moment doubt the general idea that the law of negligence had now become broad and essentially simple. The very simplicity of the case in this sense is suggested by a powerful paragraph in Lord Salmon's opinion:

The council are given these statutory powers to inspect the foundations and furnished with public funds to enable the powers to be used for the protection of [amongst others] prospective purchasers of the buildings . . . If, when the council exercises these powers they do so negligently, it must be obvious that those members of the public in the position of the present plaintiffs are likely to suffer serious damage. *The exercise of power without responsibility is not encouraged by the law.* [My emphasis.][24]

The thrust of opinion in the Lords remained expansionist on liability for some years, steadily removing traditional barriers to plaintiffs, expanding the range of hurts covered by the simple idea that we are responsible for the consequences of our carelessness. Even in the cases where liability was expanded, there were increasing signs of tension, however. One of the most revealing of these cases is one that, even read in the Law Reports, has a profound emotional effect, and where the separate speeches, though mainly admirable, do not hide the tension between restrictivist and expansionist lawyers. *McLoughlin* v. *O'Brien*[25] was a case concerning what English law still quaintly calls 'nervous shock'—that is, psychiatric illness brought on by death or injury caused, negligently, to another. Mr McLoughlin and three of his children had been involved in a crash with a lorry and taken to hospital, where Mrs McLoughlin arrived, alerted by a neighbour, within a couple of hours. The husband suffered bruising and shock; George, his seventeen-year-old son, suffered, *inter alia*, cerebral concussion; Kathleen, his seven-year-old daughter, suffered concussion and various fractures; and the three-year-old daughter died. It is so important to grasp the reality behind dry discussion of restricting liability for 'policy reasons' that I quote Lord Wilberforce, always a writer to be admired, in full in his terse description of Mrs McLoughlin's experience:

[24] *Anns* at 511.
[25] *McLoughlin* v. *O'Brien* [1983] AC 410.

Mr Pilgrim told her he thought George was dying, and that he did not know the whereabouts of her husband or the condition of her daughter. He then drove her [to the hospital]. There she saw Michael [her eleven-year-old son, who had not been in the car] who told her that Gillian was dead. She was taken down a corridor and through a window she saw Kathleen, crying, with her face cut and begrimed with dirt and oil. She could hear George shouting and screaming. She was taken to her husband who was sitting with his head in his hands. His shirt was hanging off him and he was covered in mud and oil. He saw the appellant and started sobbing. The appellant was then taken to see George. The whole of his left face and left side was covered. He appeared to recognise the appellant and then lapsed into unconsciousness. Finally the appellant was taken to Kathleen who by now had been cleaned up. The child was too upset to speak and simply clung to her mother.[26]

Mrs McLoughlin subsequently suffered not only severe shock, but organic depression and a personality change accompanied by 'numerous symptoms of a physiological character'. The judge at first instance held for the defendant on the grounds that these consequences were not foreseeable. Even the Court of Appeal, which upheld his decision in favour of the defendant, could not believe that, holding that it was 'readily foreseeable that a significant number of mothers, exposed to such an experience might break down under the shock of the event and suffer illness'. However, the Court of Appeal found instead that though the driver of the lorry could perfectly well be expected to foresee Mrs McLoughlin's suffering were he to be careless, there was still no liability. Either: (1) it was foreseeable, and there was a duty of care to Mrs McLoughlin, but policy considerations prevented her winning (Stephenson LJ); or (2) it was readily foreseeable but there was no duty of care, the duty being limited only to those on the road nearby, again for policy reason (Griffiths LJ). It makes no difference which of these formulations one takes—indeed, despite their apparent difference, the third member of the Court of Appeal, Cumming-Bruce LJ, claimed to agree with *both* of them! The so called 'policy arguments' were really restricted to the ever repeated floodgates argument, that opening up the duty of care in contexts like this would lead to thousands of cases. In fact the Lords all treated this with some degree of scepticism, though the lead opinion by Wilberforce does accept the basis of the policy argument, and he claims to be 'impressed' by both the arguments in the Court of Appeal. This includes the argument by Stephenson LJ that the duty of care should not be enforced because it crosses a line 'indicated by the barrier of commercial sense and practical convenience', and the patronizing claim by Griffiths LJ that it was not even in the litigants' interest to accept that they were owed a duty because 'to do so would quite likely delay their recovery by immersing them in the

[26] *McLoughlin* at 417.

anxiety of litigation'.[27] Nonetheless Wilberforce himself does find that Mrs McLoughlin's case, by analogy to previous situations where damages for nervous shock have been allowed, is an acceptable extension. He is very keen to limit this extension, describing her claim as 'upon the margin of what the process of logical progression would allow'. Wilberforce thinks indeed that the line could be drawn excluding her case more easily than it could have been drawn in earlier cases, for example one where a child had a fatal accident within earshot of his father who then came upon him,[28] or where a mother on one side of the road saw a terrible accident happening to her family picnicking on the opposite side,[29] 'but so to draw it would not appeal to most people's sense of justice'.[30] The general drift of the cited cases, mostly from other common law jurisdictions, had been to impose restrictions along three dimensions—how nearly related the plaintiff had to be to the injured, how physically and temporally near the plaintiff was to the incident, and how directly the plaintiff experienced the incident— merely being told of the event would never do. All Wilberforce is doing, all he even pretends to do, is to extend each dimension at the margin. If this was all that was to be said about the case it might not be worth discussing. However, it is characteristic of the period, because it represents the furthest the law has gone. Specifically a later, restrictivist, House of Lords refused in a further case to take up Wilberforce's suggestion that watching an event of similar horror on television could constitute adequate proximity.

Where the case is crucially important is for containing the two most extreme rejections of policy arguments we are aware of, rejections virtually never cited in future negligence cases. These occur in the speeches given by Lords Scarman and Bridge, and come very close to asserting not just a principle of judicial decision making, but a constitutional position. More than any argument quoted so far these two speeches show how deeply political is the entire matter of negligence, both in substance and in methodology. Nor does one have to be a social scientist rather than a lawyer to see them as highly significant. Lord Edmund-Davies, who otherwise simply agrees with Wilberforce's arguments and method, and has no great patience himself with the 'floodgates' thesis from the Court of Appeal, delivered a speech almost entirely dedicated to expressing his horror at the Bridge–Scarman approach. Scarman's argument he describes as '. . . as novel as it is startling' and as running 'counter to well-established and wholly acceptable law'.[31]

---

[27] I take these summaries from Wilberforce, *McLoughlin* at 418.
[28] *Boardman* v. *Sanderson* [1964] 1 WLR 1317.
[29] *Hinz* v. *Berry* [1970] 2 QB 40.
[30] *McLoughlin* at 418.
[31] *McLoughlin* at 427.

Both arguments are similar, though Scarman deliberately discusses policy arguments in general while Bridge writes entirely about this particular branch of negligence, though at no point does he say that his logic should be restricted to similar cases. Bridge takes the history of extension of liability for nervous shock, including cases from Ireland and Australia, and attaches especial importance to a Californian case, *Dillon* v. *Legg*[32] which opened up the area enormously. What he shows is that every time a line has been drawn it has had to be abandoned under the pressure of a new tragic case and progress in psychiatry. Effectively Bridge is suggesting that Wilberforce's acceptance of the need to draw a line just cannot work. For Bridge it is inherent in the uncertainty of psychological illness caused by traumatic shock that adjudication must always be piecemeal, extending from fact situation to fact situation. The lines will always be artificial, and therefore always unjust. Here at least the law of negligence must use 'foreseeability simpliciter'. A reasonable man would realize he might cause great psychological harm. As Bridge points out, we are talking about a defendant who is, *ex hypothesi*, guilty of fault in causing death or serious injury. Here, if anywhere, what we could foresee we really must compensate. A very clear call to courts not to shirk their duty, obviously referring to the Court of Appeal in this case, is made:

> To attempt to draw a line at the furthest point which any of the decided cases happens to have reached, and to say that it is for the legislature, not the courts, to extend the limits of liability any further would be, to my mind, an unwarranted abdication of the court's function of developing and adapting principles of the common law to changing conditions.[33]

Just how much Bridge accepts the whole thrust of Atkin's-style negligence argument is shown in his peroration:

> My Lords I have no doubt that this is an area of the law of negligence where we should resist the temptation to try yet once more to freeze the law in a rigid posture which would deny justice to some who, in the application of the classic principles of negligence derived from *Donoghue* v. *Stevenson* ought to succeed in the interests of certainty where the very subject matter is uncertain and continuously developing, or in the interests of saving defendants and their insurers from the burden of having sometimes to resist doubtful claims.

And, finally:

> To put the matter in another way, if asked where the thing is to stop, I should answer . . . 'where in the particular case the good sense of the judge enlightened by progressive awareness of mental illness, decides'.[34]

[32] *Dillon* v. *Legg*, 29 ALR 3d 1316.
[33] *McLoughlin* at 441.
[34] *McLoughlin* at 443.

There is no clearer acceptance anywhere in English law of the principled application of Atkin's good neighbour argument. Of course it is presented as necessary for this particular problem. But Bridge's argument rests on the need to accept legal uncertainty rather than imposing certain but arbitrary policy constraints where the uncertainty comes from the very nature of the issues. It is not easy to find many areas where this is not exactly the general situation. Lord Scarman's speech associates him entirely with this position, and puts a fascinating constitutional twist on Bridge's exhortation to courts to fulfil their role. To Scarman, and this is the point that Edmund-Davies found 'startling', policy arguments are literally 'non-justiciable'. In a very short opinion he sketches a powerful and unusual constitutional doctrine which, had it become widely accepted amongst his colleagues, would have transformed much of the common law and, in particular, have prevented the wholesale onslaught on negligence doctrines that have characterized the last ten years or more of English law. After explicitly concurring with both the approach and conclusion in Bridge's speech, he admits sharing the anxieties of the Court of Appeal as to the possible practical consequences of Bridge's fully principled solution—but Scarman completely inverts the conclusions the Appeal Court came to. He starts by a fairly routine description of the inevitability of judge made law through the development and extension of basic principles, noting that the common law covers everything not covered by statute, and allows no 'casus omissus'—the courts must always find an answer. But he goes on to argue:

The distinguishing feature of the common law is this judicial development and formation of principle. Policy considerations will have to be weighed: but the objective of the judges is the formulation of principle. And, if principle inexorably requires a decision which entails a degree of policy risk, the court's function is to adjudicate according to principle, leaving policy curtailment to the judgment of Parliament. Here lies the true role of the two law-making institutions in our constitution. By concentrating on principle the judges can keep the common law alive, flexible and consistent and can keep the legal system clear of policy problems which neither they, nor the forensic process which it is their duty to operate, are equipped to resolve. If principle leads to results which are thought to be socially unacceptable, Parliament can legislate to draw a line or map out a new path. The real risk to common law is not its movement to cover new situations and new knowledge but lest it should stand still, halted by a conservative judicial approach. If that should happen . . . there would be a danger of the law becoming irrelevant to the considerations, and inept in its treatment, of modern social problems. Justice would be defeated.[35]

Here Scarman thinks the logic of previous cases requires the application of the 'reasonably foreseeable test . . . untrammelled by spatial, physical, or

---

[35] *McLoughlin* at 430.

temporal limits'. He insists that he is by no means sure the result so achieved will be desirable from a policy viewpoint. 'Social and financial' problems may well arise if no restrictions are placed on who can claim for nervous shock, or where limits are not imposed in terms of requiring the claimant personally to have witnessed the accident, and he presses for legislation of the type that had been enacted in Australia. (Though it is worth noting Bridge's point: that legislation was itself the result of dissatisfaction with what he called 'manifestly unjust' restrictive court rulings in nervous shock cases.) Then comes the blunt conclusion that shocked Edmund-Davies, and would have transformed English judicial behaviour had it been accepted:

Why then should not the courts draw the line, as the Court of Appeal manfully tried to do in this case? Simply, because the policy issue as to where to draw the line is not justiciable. The problem is one of social, economic and financial policy. The considerations relevant to a decision are not such as to be capable of being handled within the limits of the forensic process.[36]

And, of course, if the policy issues are not justiciable here, it is unclear where and why they would ever be. The argument is the complete reverse of the normal one, which is that some proposed extension of the law can only be made on the basis of expertise that the courts do not have, and value choices they are not entitled to make. Rather, for Scarman, and he is surely right, the extension of legal principle is the only thing the courts are capable of, and it is the curtailment of principle that requires resources and rights only Parliament has. Though *McLoughlin* is cited less than other cases from the heyday of negligence law, it could have been the most important. As it is it stands pre-eminent, and as yet not overruled, in a modern trio of cases. *McLoughlin*, along with *Anns* and the final case in this section, *Junior Books* v. *Veitchi*, make up the end point trilogy, as *Donoghue*, *Dorset Yacht*, and *Hedley Byrne* stand at the beginning. *Junior Books* is again a case the non-lawyer struggles with in an effort to see why it could be regarded as a dangerous extension of negligence liability, though here at least, because it is the last great extension case, the consensus is crumbling and an outspoken dissent by Lord Brandon gives at least some clues as to the nature of the restrictivist backlash to come.

It is necessary to understand one legal concept which arose also in both *Hedley Byrne* and *Anns* if any sense is to be made of the objections to *Junior Books*. This is the idea of 'pure economic loss'. Like many legal terms of art, pure economic loss, or just economic loss, means something other than it might seem, though in fact even in legal contexts it is not always used with precision. It does not mean just an alleged loss of money or monetary value. If one of the maisonettes in *Anns* had fallen down and crushed a

---

[36] *McLoughlin* at 431.

car, there is little doubt that the owner of the car could sue for the cost of replacing it, though his loss is economic or financial. If the liquid in Mrs Stevenson's ginger beer bottle had been corrosive, and when spilt out had burned a hole in her dress, she could probably have had the cost of a new dress. As long as physical damage is done to one's possessions by an offending negligently made product, the loss does not count as pure economic loss. And, of course, physical injury to a person caused by the product is recoverable. The problem in *Anns* is that the subsiding maisonettes caused no damage because they had been repaired, and it was this loss, the loss of money involved in making safe the defective building that is termed 'economic loss', and about which the law is unsure. Similarly had Mrs Stevenson seen the snail in time to avoid drinking the polluted ginger beer, the money she had wasted on the fizzy drink, were it to be legally recovered, would be, if anything, pure economic loss. Basically *Donoghue* has not been seen as precedent for that sort of recovery. This version of economic loss is essentially what has come to be known as 'product liability', and in the UK nowadays is largely covered by statute. Many judges have not liked accepting liability in negligence for this type of economic loss because they see it as a trespass on contract law, with which they are happier, because it fits into a neat model of rational actors coming to a mutually beneficial deal, where the role of the law is to ensure the strict terms of the deal are kept to, and moral judgements do not enter. In fact some writers treat contract as a way for two parties effectively to suspend the rest of the common law as it would otherwise touch on their dealings together. More practically economic loss of this sort is feared as being economically dangerous. A manufacturer of a product, if he is to be held liable to anyone who comes into possession of it and feels it is substandard, can be at risk of an unknowably large potential number of lawsuits by an unknowable class of litigants for an unknowable time span. To some judges this means that the potential risk cost is so high that no one would ever take the risk of making anything at all. In contract the risks can be known, controlled, quantified, and taken account of in the contractual terms. Economic loss *per se* is less worrying to these judges, who are largely happy to accept *Hedley Byrne*. There, after all, only financial loss was involved—the money the firm had lost by trusting a negligent credit rating—but the risks were quite different because the class of potential litigants and at least the rough boundaries of potential losses were known or knowable. To say anything more at this stage would preempt later discussion of the opposition to widely defined negligence liability, but with this background the otherwise curious fact that *Junior Books* was seen as controversial should be clearer. The fear in such cases is the interrelated fear that contract law will be sullied and that 'commerce' will become risky.

The story of *Junior Books* is easy to tell. The firm, Junior Books, had a factory built in 1969, the specially designed floor of which was put down by a subcontractor nominated by the firm's architect, but which only had a contract, as is usual in building deals, with the main contractor. The floor, negligently constructed, was faulty from the beginning, developing cracks and imposing a high maintenance cost on the firm, to the point that they decided it would be cheaper to replace it than keep on repairing it. They sued the subcontractor, Veitchi & Co., for the costs of replacement and the indirect costs they would incur by having to close the factory while the work was done. It is germane that there was no allegation that anyone had been or was in danger of being hurt, nor that any other property was in danger, nor that the production process in the factory had been interfered with. Simply, the floor was not as good as it should have been. They could not, of course, sue in contract because there was no contract between them, so they sued in tort. As an aside it is notable that no one knows why they did not sue the main contractor with whom they did have a contract. As noted earlier, it is a perennial feature of this whole area of law that building contractors go bankrupt and evade contractual liability, which is one reason we need a negligence law with as long an arm as possible. The 1988 product liability legislation, necessitated by European Union requirements, intentionally allows almost anyone in the chain from original producer to final retailer to be sued precisely because it is felt unjust to force the consumer to track down some specified link in a chain he has no control over but which collectively delivered an inadequate product.

Was Veitchi to be held liable? For what, and under what theory? A majority of three, Lords Fraser, Russell, and Roskill were prepared to go the whole way and impose complete liability, despite the inevitable floodgates argument. Lord Brandon took up the fight against the entire idea of imposing this sort of liability on the poor subcontractor which could not defend itself by waving a contract allowing it to build inadequately. Significantly Lord Keith, until recently the senior Law Lord but then fairly junior, was somewhere in between. It is significant because Keith, as the rest of this chapter will show, became the standard-bearer of the restrictivist legal troops. In his lead opinion Lord Roskill immediately dismisses the relevance of policy argument, coming close indeed to Scarman and Bridge in insisting that policy no longer had a legitimate role to play, and that if principle pointed to a conclusion, so be it. On the floodgates argument he forcefully notes that: 'I see no reason why, if it be just that the law should henceforth accord that remedy, that remedy should be denied simply because it will, in consequence of this development, become available to many rather than to few.'[37] He also quotes

---

[37] *Junior Books* at 209.

approvingly from the New Zealand Court of Appeal, which has increasingly come to seem the most pro-plaintiff and expansionist of common law courts. Cook J there had described the floodgates arguments against decisions like *Anns* as 'specious' and 'in terrorem or doctrinaire'. After surveying the various, usually limiting, cases mainly from abroad, Roskill defines the question to be faced in a way that makes no attempt to hide the breadth of its implications. Should they 'extend the duty of care beyond a duty to prevent harm being done by faulty work to a duty to avoid such faults being present in the work at all'? Describing the 'contract is special' approach, Roskill says of it:

... that approach and its concomitant philosophy ended in 1932 and for my part I should be reluctant to countenance its re-emergence some fifty years later ... I think today the proper control lies not in asking whether the proper remedy should lie in contract or instead in delict or tort, not in somewhat capricious judicial determination whether a particular case falls on one side of the line or the other, not in somewhat artificial distinctions between physical and economic or financial loss ... (it is sometimes overlooked that virtually all damage, including physical damage is in one sense financial or economic for it is compensated by an award of damages) but in the first instance in establishing the relevant principles and then in deciding whether the particular case falls within or without those principles. To state this is no more than to restate what Lord Reid said in the Dorset Yacht case and Lord Wilberforce in *Anns*.[38]

Wilberforce's test is the familiar two-stage test: (1) was there 'sufficient relationship of proximity' for foreseeability; (2) if so, are there any special reasons for negativing or reducing the scope of the duty, limiting the class to whom it is owed or restricting the level of damages. Roskill then sums up the facts to make the answer to the Wilberforce test obvious: Veitchi were deliberately selected as specialists to do the job, they knew they were being relied on, they knew that if they messed up it would cost Junior Books, and no one got in their way while they were doing the job. If no other aspects matter, and Roskill has thrown them all away, the answer really is as automatic as that. Veitchi made a bad floor and must pay to have it put right, including paying for the consequent dislocation.

Given the general description, in Chapters 3 and 4, of arguments just passing each other by it is hardly surprising that Lord Brandon's argument in dissent completely ignores Roskill's dismissal of the primacy of contract. Brandon has no problem with economic loss *per se*, and insists that is not what the case is about. Nor does he doubt that the relationship between the subcontractor and Junior Brooks is close enough to pass the first part of Lord Wilberforce's test. He specifically says 'it is difficult to imagine a greater degree of proximity, in the absence of a direct

[38] *Junior Books* at 213.

contractual relationship'.[39] And that, for Brandon, is the sole point—there was no contract, and to give the sort of rights that Junior Books is seeking would be to give contractual rights in tort. As far as part two of the Wilberforce test goes, there is indeed a 'consideration which ought to limit' the duty. In fact Brandon is not applying the test at all. He says that because there is no case in which such a claim has been granted before, granting it now would 'involve a radical departure from long-established authority', and presents this as a ground under part two. But part one of the test specifically rests on the position that one does not, any longer, have to show previous cases, but need only apply the foreseeability principle. That is the whole point of Wilberforce's attempted revolution. It is quite clear that Brandon in fact has no sympathy with the Wilberforce position, or indeed with much of the change in liability from the great trilogy onwards, when he gets to what he presents as the second 'part two consideration'. This is the argument that there is no policy reason for making the change, for accepting the implications of the principle. According to Lord Brandon, no policy arguments have been adduced at all. It is worth reading in full Brandon's reasons for rejecting the implications of the principle, because they amount, though hardly meant that way, as a splendid justification precisely for doing what the majority wants to do:

The effect of accepting [the plaintiff's] contention with regard to the scope of the duty of care involved would be, in substance, to create as between two persons who are not in any contractual relationship with each other, obligations of one of those persons to the other which are only really appropriate as between persons who do have such a relationship between them. In the case of a manufacturer or distributor of goods, the position would be that he warranted to the ultimate user or consumer of such goods that they were as well designed, as merchantable and as fit for their contemplated purpose as the exercise of reasonable care could make them. In the case of sub-contractors [such as Veitchi, they would warrant] to the building owner that the flooring, when laid, would be as well designed, as free from defects of any kind and as fit for its contemplated purpose as the exercise of reasonable care could make it.[40]

There can be no doubt that this is exactly what all the judges who had laboured since *Donoghue* to extend the tort of negligence aimed at. Lord Brandon's only reason for not joining that group is that such a move is 'contrary to any sound policy requirement'. Yet Brandon's was the voice of the future. *Junior Books* has never, quite, been overturned, but it has never been followed, and Brandon's dissenting speech or Keith's very

[39] *Junior Books* at 217.
[40] *Junior Books* at 218.

limited concurrence, not Roskill's bold argument for the majority, has been held to be the proper response in the case.[41]

4. The Counter-Revolution

Anns was decided in 1978, *Junior Books* in 1982. Almost immediately the protest launched by Brandon's dissent in the latter case began. From the mid-eighties onwards there was a series of cases throwing doubt on Wilberforce's two-stage test. *Anns* was the usual immediate target but it was the whole idea of a general principle of negligence that was really at stake. The case that finally ended the revolution came in 1991, when the Lords took the highly unusual step of overtly overruling *Anns*, a power they had only had since they gave it to themselves in 1966, and which is very seldom used. It is a measure of how great a step it is to specifically overrule a precedent that instead of the normal five-man bench, seven Law Lords, headed by the Lord Chancellor, Lord Mackay, heard *Murphy* v. *Brentwood*. (The only other case with a seven-man panel discussed in this book is *Pepper* v. *Hart*.) The others were Lord Keith, by then the senior Law Lord, and Lords Bridge, Brandon himself, Ackner, Oliver, and Jauncey. Apart from Brandon they all served for several more years, during which what has become known as 'the retreat from *Anns*' pro-ceeded apace. Lords Keith and Jauncey still served at the time of writing, and still regularly vote for the defendant in negligence cases. The Lords were at pains to show how reluctantly they were forced to overturn Wilberforce's position, Lord Bridge, after depicting an apparently terribly confused state of the law following from *Anns*, agonizing that:

Sooner or later, in this unhappy situation, a direct challenge to the authority of Anns was inevitable. Perhaps it is unfortunate that it did not come sooner, but the House could not, I think, have contemplated departing from the decision on an Appellate Committee so eminently constituted unless directly invited to do so.[42]

The 'unhappy situation' in question was brought about almost entirely by their Lordships' continuous attempts to restrict the rule in *Anns*, as Lord

[41] Keith argued that, because continually repairing the floor was costing the firm money, this cost was necessarily reducing their profits, and they were therefore suffering economic loss. Therefore they were entitled to compensation for replacing the flooring not because there was an obligation not to build a shoddy floor in itself, but because of the economic loss. In later cases, notably *Murphy* v. *Brentwood*, to be discussed shortly, he claims that his opinion is the proposition of law for which *Junior Books* stands. Roskill and the two Law Lords who concurred with him made no mention whatsoever of this argument. (Keith in *Murphy* v. *Brentwood* [1991] 1 AC at 466.)

[42] *Murphy* at 474.

Bridge admits by implication at the beginning of his speech, decisions which more or less invited counsel to ask for the overruling of the precedent. The picking away at the Wilberforce test began with Keith in a 1985 case,[43] and was contributed to by Brandon[44] and Bridge[45] over the next two years, culminating in a complete dismissal of the test by Keith in 1988 and 1989 in cases we shall look at shortly. These cases, it should be noted, did not necessarily refer to the situation in *Anns*, though some did. They were much more general attacks on the methodology which yielded liability for negligence in a wide variety of situations. As far as the specific problem of *Anns* itself—local authority liability for bad building practices—for many of the judges the real start to the campaign was not an English case at all. The issues in *Anns* were the sort that any modern State is likely to have had to cope with, and legislation giving local authorities either the duty or the right to control building plans is common throughout the common law world. Consequently courts in Australia, Canada, and New Zealand have all had to face up to the same issues. Most of the judges in *Murphy* and related earlier cases have made much of the Australian decision in *Council of the Shire of Sutherland* v. *Heyman* in 1985 which specifically refused to follow *Anns*.[46]

Bridge is open about the way this represents one of two opposing policy choices. In New Zealand and Canada the *Anns* doctrine was not only accepted but developed further. There, presumably, the awful confusion that English law experienced never happened. In fact the New Zealand courts anticipated the House of Lords, by deciding an earlier case in the way that Wilberforce was to decide *Anns*, largely on the basis of the same opinion by Lord Denning that later influenced the Lords.[47] For example, in the leading Canadian case a local authority, discovering a house was being built with inadequate foundations, issued a 'Stop work' order. This was ignored and the completed house was subsequently sold, without the required occupancy certificate. When the new owner discovered the deficiencies he sued, *inter alia*, the council for negligence. Although their only failure was to not enforce the stop order, they were held to be liable for the pure economic loss involved in repairing the foundations.[48] In a case that Bridge describes as 'no less striking' a New Zealand local authority was

---

[43] Lord Keith in *Governors of the Peabody Donation Fund* v. *Sir Lindsay Parkinson & Co. Ltd.* [1985] AC 210 at 240.

[44] Lord Brandon in *Leigh and Sillavan Ltd.* v. *Aliakmon Shipping Co. Ltd.* [1986] AC 785 at 815.

[45] Lord Bridge in *Curran* v. *Northern Ireland Co-Ownership Housing Association Ltd.* [1987] AC 718.

[46] *Council of the Shire of Sutherland* v. *Heyman*, 157 CLR 424.

[47] The New Zealand case was *Bowen* v. *Paramount Builders (Hamilton) Ltd.* [1977] 1 NZLR. The earlier Court of Appeal case of which *Anns* was in many ways an affirmation was *Dutton* v. *Bognor Regis Urban District Council* [1972] 1 QB 373.

[48] *City of Kamloops* v. *Nielsen* (1984) 10 DLR (4th) 641.

found liable because exterior weatherboarding of an inferior standard to that required by building by-laws had been fitted without the council's inspectors noticing. Even though no risk of damage to person or property was even alleged, damages were awarded to the plaintiff against the council.[49] It was thus perfectly clear that respected courts with a wide variety of experience were capable of seeing *Anns* as very good law. Bridge, noting that in the UK 'we have shown a marked inclination to confine the *Anns* doctrine within narrow limits' , faces the choice of path squarely. It is between following the Australians and rejecting *Anns* altogether or following the other Commonwealth path and:

carrying the *Anns* doctrine a large legislative step forward to its logical conclusion and holding that the scope of the duty of care, imposed by the law on local authorities for the negligent performance of their functions . . . embraces all economic loss sustained by the owner or occupier of a building by reason of defects in it arising from construction in breach of building byelaws or regulations.[50]

Bridge's particular characterization, with its reference to 'a large legislative step' is, of course, intended to suggest that only the Australian path can safely be taken. It may well not have followed that supporting *Anns* involved throwing local authorities entirely to the mercy of discontented home owners, but this was a natural rhetorical strategy to follow. Bridge had already described the underlying Court of Appeal decision by Lord Denning not only as without precedent, but 'widely regarded as judicial legislation', going on to say that if one reads Denning's opinion 'it is difficult to think he would have demurred to that criticism'. Lord Denning, of course, would only have demurred at the idea that it was a 'criticism' to describe his work as 'judicial legislation'. What Denning actually said, Bridge quotes later. His quoting, and the passage itself, sums up perfectly one of the things the 'retreat from *Anns*' is about:

Mrs Dutton has suffered a grievous loss. The house fell down without any fault of hers. She is in no position herself to bear the loss. Who ought in justice to bear it? I should think those who were responsible. Who are they? . . . in the second place the council's inspector was responsible . . . in the third place the council should answer for his failure. They were entrusted by Parliament with the task of seeing that houses were properly built. They received public funds for the purpose. The very object was to protect purchasers and occupiers of houses. Yet they failed to protect them. Their shoulders are broad enough to bear the loss.[51]

Bridge takes a very firm line here. There may be good social policy reasons for making authorities liable, but only if Parliament says so in legislation. After all, the only reason the authorities have the money is because of

---

[49] *Stieller* v. *Porira City Council* [1986] 1 NZLR 84.
[50] *Murphy* at 474.
[51] Lord Denning in *Dutton* at 397–8, quoted by Bridge in *Murphy* at 481.

taxation. It is 'pre-eminently for the legislature' to decide if these social arguments are strong enough for 'imposing on the public the burden of providing compensation for private financial loss'. If Parliament does think this 'it is not difficult for them to say so'. What a rhetorical gap there is between 'Mrs Dutton has suffered a grievous loss' and 'providing compensation for private financial loss'. Those who support the retreat from *Anns* would, naturally, say that it is precisely the function of judges to look coldly at such cases and see only 'private financial losses'.

There are several arguments in *Murphy*, all long, all complex, all subtle, because here we have a deliberately assembled united front to put down, as firmly as possible, an entire approach to negligence. It is not for us to try to argue that the assembled Law Lords in this case are fundamentally 'wrong'. There may be some sense, deep inside the logic understood only by lawyers, in which *Anns* was a terrible legal error which had to be put right. It remains the case that the way *Anns* was put down foreclosed an approach with obviously far-reaching implications in favour of what cannot but be seen as a return not to a decade or so earlier, but to a position before *Donoghue*. Without getting involved in more detail than absolutely necessary, we do need to see briefly how this was done. The basic facts in *Murphy* are similar to *Anns* in that a house was built on inadequate foundations which had been passed as satisfactory by the council, and a few years later serious cracks developed in the walls and consequently in assorted pipes, including a gas pipe, and plumbing, including the soil pipe, when the foundations fractured, to an extent the judge at first instance found to constitute an imminent danger to the health and safety of occupants. The owner could not get full coverage from his insurance, and sought damages to cover the loss he made when forced to sell the house in its unrepaired condition. (He had to sell at what was estimated to be about half of the market value the house would have had if undamaged.)

The best way to begin analysing the arguments is to note that the following point is accepted by both sides. Had the damage remained undetected, and the gas pipe fractured causing physical hurt to an occupant, the council would have been liable. Some of the judges also agree that the council would have been liable if this undetected defect had caused physical damage to property in or near the house. This much is allowed on the grounds that it was a ruling of this form that was specifically authorized in *Donoghue*. The analogy is to the dark glass bottle that cannot be opened and inspected ahead of time, and the fact that it was for personal injury that Mrs Donoghue sought compensation. But, the argument goes, as soon as a latent defect—the cracks underground in the foundations—become manifest, steps can be taken to prevent danger or damage, either by repairing or selling on the house. Consequently the damages sought in *Murphy* are for pure economic loss—the cost of repair or, in the actual case, the loss from selling cheap. This, recovery for loss because the manufactured object, house here, ginger beer in *Donoghue*, is unusable, was never intended to follow from that case in 1932. Consequently there is no prior justification for the decision in *Anns*, it is innovation with no supporting case law, constitutes judicial legislation, and was simply wrongly decided. Furthermore it is judicial legislation in a field, consumer protection, which the Lords, with no obvious justification, claim is peculiarly suitable only for Parliament.

A good deal of effort was spent destroying an ingenious theory, the 'Complex Structure' theory, in which cases like *Anns* do involve damage to property other than the defective property itself, by claiming the foundation is somehow or other separate from the house. In fact the absurdity here is not of Wilberforce's making—he never used any such argument. The complex structure theory was created by Lord Bridge in one of the post-*Anns* cases, the difficulty of which is held to justify overruling *Anns*. But the counter-revolutionaries want, if at all possible, to show that *Anns* was 'mistaken' rather than just a rival policy choice, so Lord Keith and others concentrate on Wilberforce's alleged mistake in thinking that he was dealing with physical damage following from a latent defect. In fact all that Wilberforce ever said was that: 'To allow recovery for such damage to the house follows, in my opinion, from normal principle. *If classification is required,* the relevant damage is in my opinion material, physical damage.'[52] (Our emphasis.) The truth is that Wilberforce and his colleagues in *Anns* were neither ignorant of the fact that *Donoghue* in its exact application was about damage to a person or a piece of property by a latent defect in another object, nor were they concerned about it. It was not the finding in *Donoghue per se* that they relied on—indeed they did not solely rely on *Donoghue*. They relied on an approach which *Donoghue*, along with other cases, was said to exemplify. This crucial aspect of Wilberforce's opinion in *Anns* was fully understood by the attackers. Lord Keith gives this away in a curious statement which shows just how determined some of the Lords had been, for some time, to oppose the very methodology of *Anns*:

I think it must now be recognised that it did not proceed on any basis of principle at all, but constituted a remarkable example of judicial legislation. It has engendered a vast spate of litigation, and each of the cases in the field which have reached this House has been distinguished. Others have been distinguished in the Court of Appeal. The result has been to keep the effect of the decision within reasonable bounds, but that has been achieved only by applying strictly the words of Lord Wilberforce and by refusing to accept the logical implications of the

---

[52] Lord Wilberforce in *Anns* at 759.

decision itself. These logical implications show that the case properly considered has potentiality for collision with long-established principles regarding liability in the tort of negligence for economic loss.[53]

What this actually says is that some time after Wilberforce's membership of the Lords their Lordships started systematically to oppose his approach, and have deliberately never tried to apply *Anns*. What one judge calls judicial legislation is what another calls deciding according to principle, unless he happily accepts the characterization anyway, as Diplock did in *Dorset Yacht*. To say that *Anns* was decided not on 'any basis of principle at all' is to ignore the lengths Wilberforce went to in setting out the relevant methodological principle. The extent that there were at this stage *any* clear principles covering economic loss is dubious, but that we turn to shortly. But the quotation implies, and Keith elsewhere is open about this, much more. We have noted that the first rejection of *Anns* was by the Australian High Court. Lord Keith was particularly attracted to this because of the methodological position taken up in the lead opinion there, by Brennan J:

It is preferable, in my view, that the law should develop novel categories of negligence incrementally and by analogy with established categories, rather than by a massive extension of a prima facie duty of care restrained only by indefinable 'considerations which ought to negative, or to reduce or limit the scope of the duty' . . .[54]

Keith had already used this in an earlier attack on Wilberforce's test in a Privy Council case where he had gone on to say that, because of the direction the law seemed to be taking, 'their Lordships consider that for the future it should be recognised that the two-stage test . . . is not to be regarded as in all circumstances a suitable guide'.[55] In *Hill* v. *Chief Constable of West Yorkshire*, in 1989, Keith had gained support for a definite statement that Brennan's incrementalism was correct, and the two-stage test was to be abandoned. Given all this, it is not surprising that he and others could detect nothing but unprincipled judicial legislation in *Anns*. The wheel had turned full circle, because it is quite impossible to detect any difference between the Keith/Brennan approach and the approach that Atkin had been opposing in *Donoghue*. From now on there was to be no generalized approach to negligence. Atkin's good neighbour principle, the entire doctrine of responsibility for what you should be able to foresee, had gone. Effectively the law on liability had hardly developed from the 1932 position. Or rather, it could develop now only where a coalition of judges found an analogy to an already established duty and where they

---

[53] *Murphy* at 472.
[54] *Council of the Shire of Sutherland* at 481.
[55] *Yuen Kun Yeu* v. *A.-G. of Hong Kong* [1988] AC 175 at 191, and similarly at 193.

found no impassable policy objections. The irony is that this situation is seen as somehow less replete with 'judicial legislation' than one where a principle is generally available and policy arguments are seen as, if not completely 'non-justiciable' as with Scarman, but at least to be employed only *in extremis*. A little reflection is needed to realize just why the Wilberforce test approach to negligence is so different—it does not, after all, outlaw policy considerations completely. What it does is to make it very clear that policy is being used to curtail a right. The first part of the test, applying proximity to foreseeability, is the part that identifies a duty. Policy can only come in at the second stage, and cannot be camouflaged— it is overtly then a refusal to do what principle requires. With a pre-*Donoghue* approach, the existence of the duty can be denied, on the grounds of no suitable analogy, and policy arguments can then be seen protecting principle. Or, as with Brandon's dissent in *Junior Books*, it can be argued that there are no policy grounds for interfering with principle. At least rhetorically there is a major difference between admitting that a duty exists which the world cannot afford to instantiate, and denying that there is a duty. In this sense the two Court of Appeal grounds for rejecting Mrs McLoughlin's claim for nervous shock discussed earlier are not, in fact, equivalent.

The counter-revolution was not contained in just this one case. We have already noticed the stream of cases in which the Wilberforce two-stage test was slowly undone. It seems fair to say that, at least until very recently, the Lords have set their face against extensions in liability of almost any kind. So complex has this branch of law become of recent that it is hardly appropriate for a non-lawyer to say very much, though it is uncontroversial at least to say that most experts believe the field to be in a terrible mess. Nor can we afford the space, even had we the nerve, to try to make sense out of recent developments. However, it follows from the analysis of this chapter that one would expect increasing conflict, and increasing evidence of value choice, that is, of 'policy arguments', in such a situation. Consequently we conclude this chapter with an overview of some of the leading negligence cases since the retreat from *Anns*, though it is really a matter of gilding a legal lily. The brute fact of an ideological/ methodological conflict in the development of common law is established by the preceding history.

5. After the Counter-Revolution

There are two ways of seeing the generality of negligence cases in the post counter-revolutionary age. The brute fact is that plaintiffs have had a hard time in such cases, and 'policy' has apparently very frequently run against

claims. Between 1987 and 1995 thirty-nine negligence cases came before
the Lords, and the plaintiffs succeeded in only 38 per cent, compared with
an overall plaintiff/prosecution success rate of 55 per cent. But has this
been simply that the counter-revolution established that there should not
really be any new 'heads of negligence', or is it an unwillingness to extend
the tort of negligence even within existing categories, and where there
seem natural growth points? Not surprisingly, the answer is probably
both, and that it depends on which Law Lords one is considering. Thus
the overall success of plaintiffs mentioned above needs to be set against
the fact that the success rate for plaintiffs since 1992 has been 50 per cent.
Some of the Lords sitting mainly in the earlier cases do seem to have been
particularly hard for negligence plaintiffs to impress. Lord Keith has
found for the plaintiff in only 5 of 20 such cases, Lord Bridge in 5 of 18,
Lord Griffiths in 4 of 17, Lord Ackner in 3 of 18, Lord Jauncey in 4 of 15.
The members of the House appointed since 1992, unfortunately, have not
heard enough cases to make individual comparisons fair, but none of
them, with the possible exception of Lord Mustill who has only found for
the plaintiff once in the five such cases he has heard, seem set to follow the
lead of judges like Keith. The sort of distinction we suggest between a
generalized unwillingness to find for plaintiffs, and a more theoretical
intention to uphold the counter-revolution even where new categories or
subcategories seem possible, can be demonstrated with a few cases.

We spent some time on an analysis of *McLoughlin* v. *O'Brien*, the
nervous shock case where their Lordships, albeit in varying degrees, were
deeply impatient with floodgate-style policy arguments that would
prevent claims against careless people who caused psychological harm to
the relatives of those they injured. In his opinion in that case Lord
Wilberforce, while accepting that the shock in question must come
through 'sight or hearing of the event or of its immediate aftermath',
specifically raised, as something that might later have to be considered
'Whether some equivalent of sight or hearing, e.g. through simultaneous
television, would suffice'. Lord Bridge, in his more sweeping desire to
remove policy blocks in this area, closed his argument with two hypothetical cases where he thought liability would lie. And Lord Bridge, as
noted above, is not prima facie, a plaintiff friendly judge; he was, after all,
an important member of the panel that, deciding *Murphy*, established the
counter-revolution. Bridge first hypothesises a woman whose family is
staying in a hotel. In her morning paper she reads that the hotel has burnt
down, and sees a photograph of unidentifiable victims trapped on the top
floor and waving for help. She learns soon after that all her family have
died and suffers an acute psychiatric illness. 'Is the law to deny her
damages', asked Bridge, 'simply on the ground that an important link in
the chain of causation of her psychiatric illness was supplied by her

imagination of the agonies of mind and body in which her family died rather than by direct perception of the event?'[56] His other example was to combat the restriction that Wilberforce does insist on, that liability only extends to very close relatives of the deceased. On this point Bridge noted an exception the law does allow, that a voluntary rescuer at such a scene of tragedy could have a case, because it is foreseeable that people will rush to help. But Bridge insisted that it was impossible to stop there. Why should not another uninjured passenger in a train crash suffer awful psychiatric damage from seeing complete strangers in agony? Such a case inevitably came, years after the counter-revolution, in 1991, as a result of the disaster at the Hillsborough football stadium. The facts are straightforward. Just before the beginning of a major football match the police responsible for crowd control allowed an excessive number of spectators into one section of the ground. Panic in the ensuing crush led to ninety-five deaths and four hundred plus injuries. Scenes were broadcast live from time to time on both television and radio, and repeated on the news. In keeping with broadcasting regulations no pictures were broadcast in which dying or injured individuals could be recognized. Though the Chief Constable accepted liability for those actually killed or injured, he denied liability for nervous shock. Ten nervous shock appeals reached the Lords, eight from those who had seen the tragedy on television and who had lost close relatives or, in one case, her fiancé, two from people who had suffered such losses and had themselves been at the match, though in a different section of the stadium.

Unfortunately for the plaintiffs, Lord Bridge was not one of the five who heard the appeals, which came before Lords Keith, Ackner, Oliver, Jauncey, and Lowry. Bridge could have been, he was still serving. This second nervous shock case, *Alcock* v. *Chief Constable of the South Yorkshire Police* is one of the starker examples of a disturbing phenomenon we have pointed out several times—the way law can be established by a subset of Law Lords when a differently constituted committee might well have found otherwise. In this case the replacement of any one of those who did hear the appeals by Bridge would at least have forced a further serious debate. Suppose the two with the strongest arguments for denying liability in this case, Lords Keith and Oliver, had been joined by Bridge, omitting either Lord Ackner or Lord Jauncey but leaving Lowry. Lowry, though concurring in the result, said nothing himself and, as demonstrated in Chapter 4, he is known to be generally not well disposed to policy arguments, which were all that were available to Keith and Oliver. It is at least possible, and probably likely, that liability for nervous shock would have further developed in *Alcock*, instead of being

[56] *McLoughlin* at 442–3.

very firmly restricted. Because it was very firmly restricted—Oliver goes out of his way to mention that the ruling he was supporting meant that several recent Court of Appeal cases, in which the extensive aspects of *McLoughlin* had been built on, must now be regarded as wrongly decided.

In the light of the counter-revolution the plaintiffs probably had no chance of success, because, basing themselves on Bridge's opinion in *McLoughlin*, they argued straightforwardly that all they needed to establish was reasonable foreseeability. As even Wilberforce had flagged the possibility of television replacing direct personal observation as the intervening mechanism, there is absolutely no reason the Lords could not have treated *Alcock* as an almost routine extension of an established category, even if they were still insisting on a 'category by category' application of the tort of negligence. Unsurprisingly, both this part of Wilberforce's speech, and Bridge's expansion of the idea, were almost completely ignored. Oliver does, it is true, briefly mention Bridge's general argument for foreseeability, but only to replay the entire counter-revolutionary argument by going back to the originating nineteenth-century opinions and taking up their dire warnings about over wide acceptance of liability. For the rest it is simply asserted that seeing the events on television is not immediate enough, in part because broadcasting rules had prevented the broadcasting of shots with identifiable victims. Bridge's hypothetical example of the newspaper had, of course, specified that no one was identifiable in the photographs. The other, perhaps even more gratuitous basis for their Lordships' finding for the defendant Chief Constable was to deny that the family relationships were close enough. Here they did, in fact, rely on Wilberforce, who had insisted that no precise rule on how closely related one had to be to suffer nervous shock could or should be given. But he had done so in a context where his point has to be taken as intended not to be restrictive. *McLoughlin* involved a wife, and no one doubted that spouses were sufficiently 'close'—to mention the possibility of other relationships could only be to invite a broader range. Yet in *Alcock* a man who had been present at the game, and had lost two brothers, was held not to have suffered nervous shock in a foreseeable way. Apparently it is now necessary to demonstrate an unusually strong filial bond. In one of the less sensitive passages to be found in a speech, Lord Ackner, who accepts in general that close familial ties may produce liability for nervous shock, nonetheless delivers himself of the following view:

. . . one of the plaintiffs . . . was at the ground. His relatives who died were his two brothers. The quality of brotherly love is well known to differ widely—from Cain and Able to David and Jonathan. I assume that Mr Harrison's relationship with his brothers was not an abnormal one. His claim was not presented upon the basis that there was such a close and intimate relationship between them as gave rise to that very special bond of affection which would make his shock-induced psychiatric illness reasonably foreseeable by the Chief Constable.[57]

Opinions like this make one wonder if, whether or not *Hansard* can be quoted in court, the Bible ever should be. Ackner's estimate of the quality of brotherly love is all the more remarkable given that he had earlier cited approvingly the way legislation in New South Wales had extended the coverage in such cases to include brothers and half-brothers.[58] This determination to rule out all the plaintiffs in *Alcock*, not only those depending on allowing TV as a medium, shows how important it was to the Lords to mark *McLoughlin* as the very far limit of nervous shock. Lord Keith had also held brotherhood not to be close enough, though he had accepted a fiancé as sufficiently close—only to rule out the fiancée's claim because she had seen the events only on television. The argument about closeness of relationship does not even work within the restrictive context of their approach. Foreseeability is still crucial—in the counter-revolutionary approach it becomes a necessary, rather than a sufficient, aspect of liability. Yet if brotherhood itself is not enough, how could a specially intense feeling of brotherly love make any difference? It was entirely foreseeable that a brother would be in the stadium to see his sibling die. But how could the Chief Constable foresee that this apparently unusual, needing of extra proof, condition of sibling bonding be exemplified amongst the fans?

Not all the cases where extension of liability is denied are like *Alcock*, obviously. Some would clearly involve creation of new categories of negligence, now that categories are back and the general foreseeability rule is relegated. It may be, though it is not stated, that the real problem, or at least an additional problem that some of the Lords had with *Alcock*, was quite different from the stated ones. One can discern a thread linking many of these later negligence cases. Though described as a policy argument, the consideration is rather broader. It is a question of whether the civil law of negligence is ever suitable as a tool to be used against public authorities. We return to this as the final section of the chapter, and an extension of the thesis occupies much of our discussion on public law in later chapters. We cannot entirely ignore the possibility, of course, that some of their Lordships do have, on top of any policy views, a basic unwillingness to take negligence liability an inch further than they have to. Before pursuing the question of some form of protection for public institutions, this can be demonstrated easily with another case somewhat arbitrarily labelled 'nervous shock'. In 1995 the Lords heard an appeal arising from a minor automobile accident, an utterly routine case which

---

[57] *Alcock and others* v. *Chief Constable of the South Yorkshire Police* [1991] 4 All ER at 919–20.
[58] Law Reform (Miscellaneous Provisions) Act 1944 (NSW) s. 4(5).

would never normally rise above the Crown Court. One car, carelessly driven, collided with another at so low a speed that no one suffered more than trivial bruising as an initial result. However, the plaintiff driver was at the time in remission from a debilitating disease, and the shock of the accident initiated a recurrence so severe that he was never expected to be able to work again. What brought the case to the Lords was the disease he was suffering from—ME. Everyone was at pains to agree that the labelling of 'nervous shock' was misleading, and to insist that they did not at all doubt the finding of fact by the judge below, that ME really does exist, and really is an organic disease, and really was triggered by the accident. Nonetheless the court split 3:2. The majority, under Browne-Wilkinson, had no difficulty—there is no source of difficulty—in finding a duty of care. Yet Keith and Jauncey still could not see that a consequence so odd, in their eyes, could possibly be foreseeable. A minority position like this betokens nothing but an obdurate refusal 'to do anything for the first time lest it become a precedent', in the famous words of the *Micro-Cosmographica Academica*. Whether this case could have been won by the plaintiff a few years earlier may be in some doubt, but by 1994 new members of the Lords were grappling with the need to find some way of fashioning a law of negligence that was prepared to move beyond the frontiers to which it had been pushed back by the counter-revolutionaries. Unfortunately several of the counter-revolutionaries were still around to make this process difficult. This delaying action has been called by one of the newcomers a process of 'turning "the retreat from *Anns*" into a rout'.[59]

These and other cases dominated by the restrictive approach of Lord Keith and others from the generation that started the move back from *Anns* towards the 'category' approach to negligence, whether one thinks of it as retreat or rout, are not representative of the more creative thrust of the Lords in this latter period. There have been around a dozen cases in which the Lords have struggled to construct a new, though narrower, 'general formula' to make sense at least out of those cases involving economic loss, with possible extensions outside this concern. The actual decisions have gone some to the plaintiffs, some to the defendants, and the doctrine is very far from clear as yet. Our only concern with it, and it can be no more than sketched here, is to note the basic nature of the sort of answer the Lords may be able to settle for, in contrast to Atkin's good neighbour approach. What one might think of as this search for a new general formula goes for its roots to the second of the old trilogy, *Hedley Byrne* v. *Heller*. In various ways it has been brought up to stand as the basis for liability in negligence cases where some conception of one party rely-

---

[59] Lord Lloyd in *Marc Rich & Co.* v. *Bishop Rock Marine* [1995] 3 All ER 307.

ing on the actions or advice of another, with or without that other's knowledge, can be shown. We have discussed one of these cases in a different context earlier. In *Spring* v. *Guardian Assurance plc*, in 1994, Lord Goff's version of why an employer is liable for damages when he hurts the job opportunities of a past employee by a negligent reference was based on the principle in *Hedley Byrne*. Whether *Hedley Byrne* is specified or not, many judges seem happier with an approach along these lines. Thus in 1990 a bench of Lords Keith, Brandon, Templeman, Griffiths, and Jauncey, the core, it might be said, of the pro-defendant group in the Lords, unanimously found for the plaintiff in *Smith* v. *Bush*.[60] Here a house purchaser had relied on the surveyor's report commissioned by his building society in buying a house which later turned out to need repairs not mentioned in the survey. Even though both the mortgage application form and the surveyor's report contained disclaimers of liability, it was held that the surveyor was a professional man who knew that prospective purchasers would, in fact, rely on his reports, and so he could not deny a duty of care. Where professionals accept responsibility in return for a fee, they are now very likely to be held liable, even if the responsibility is not obviously one they directly accepted to the specific plaintiff.

So in 1995, in *White* v. *Jones*, which we mentioned briefly earlier, possibly the most controversial negligence case since *Donoghue* v. *Stevenson* itself, a majority of the Lords under Browne-Wilkinson found a solicitors' firm liable for negligence. Their negligence, it will be remembered, lay in drawing up a will which had the result of cutting out a man's daughters after he had changed his mind and let everyone know he wanted to include them as beneficiaries. What startles professional lawyers about this case is the very remote sense in which the firm can be said to have known that anyone but the dead man would be thought to be relying on them, and the obvious lack of any real act of reliance on the part of two passive potential beneficiaries who probably did not even know of the solicitors. Lord Keith and Lord Mustill made up the minority, pointing out forcefully that the majority was acting beyond any known principle of the common law, and, indeed, apparently completely denying the sanctity of privity of contract. These were, of course, precisely the arguments always used against Atkin's position in *Donoghue*, and against the majority in *Junior Books*. This conception of reliance is even less robust as a predictive norm than foreseeability had been before, and *White* v. *Jones*, with its apparent radical indifference to traditional contract law, is an extreme application. More typical of how the doctrine is likely to work in practice is the contrast between two cases which have for the non-lawyer a surface similarity, but for judges none at all. In *Caparo Industries* v.

---

[60] *Smith* v. *Eric S. Bush* [1990] 1 AC 831.

Dickman a firm of auditors who prepared an audit on a company of a form required under the Companies Act was sued for negligence by Caparo because they had relied on the audit in making a successful takeover and had ended up with a firm worth much less than they had expected.[61] Four years later in 1994 came the financially biggest negligence case in British legal history, *Henderson* v. *Merrett Syndicates*, in which Lloyd's names sued their underwriting agents for negligence which had led them to be disastrously overexposed on the insurance market.[62] Both cases are about people losing money because they relied on professional expertise. They are fascinating and, given infinite space, we could profitably look at the detailed arguments. Here all we can say is that Caparo did not win money from the auditors, and Henderson et al. did win money from their agents. The difference in the eyes of the Lords—there was no overlap of membership between the two committees—was about the immediacy of the connection. The auditors held no duty of care to investors in the company they were auditing because they had no control over who might read their public report, or the purposes it might be put to in decision making. This was not an inevitable conclusion, because there was an unchallenged High Court ruling in a very similar case where the opposite had been held, and indeed Caparo had won in the Court of Appeal. The High Court ruling was by Woolf J, but he did not reach the Lords until several years later.[63] But the arguments in 1990 were still very much concerned with the dangers of wide liability, the concern that professionals should not be laid open to claims unknowably extensive in time and source. In other words they were still concerned with the warning in *Hedley Byrne* itself that 'if the mere hearing of words were held to create proximity there might be no limit to the persons to whom the speaker or writer could be held liable'[64] or in Lord Oliver's words in the instant case:

To apply as a test of liability only the foreseeability of possible damage without some further control would be to create a liability wholly indefinite in area, duration and amount and would open up a limitless vista of uninsurable risk for the professional man.[65]

In truth most of the argument in *Caparo* is still fighting the counter-revolution, going over and again the reasons why incremental expansion of existing categories rather than formulaic application is the proper way forward. Indeed it is now *Caparo* that judges tend to use as a shorthand for the 'ordinary rule of negligence'—the threefold requirement of proximity, foreseeability, and fairness. Even if assumption of responsibility is a pref-

---

[61] *Caparo Industries plc* v. *Dickman and others* [1990] 2 AC 605.
[62] *Henderson and others* v. *Merrett Syndicates Ltd. and others* [1994] 3 All ER 507.
[63] *J.E. Fasteners Ltd.* v. *Marks, Bloom & Co.* [1981] 3 All ER 289.
[64] Lord Pearce in *Hedley Byrne* at 534.
[65] *Caparo* at 643.

erable formula, it is still a formula and therefore suspect. By 1994 the considerably different case of people who were indisputably agents for others, and therefore could not hide behind the notion of limitless risk, produced a much tougher ruling that assumption of responsibility coupled with reliance gave rise to a duty of care.

From our point of view it is clear that some version of this assumption of responsibility argument is easier for the law to accept because it brings the entire matter much nearer to the idea of a contract, of an intentional relationship for mutual benefit, and away from impersonal duty. It does not really matter that the solicitors in *White* v. *Jones* did not have a contract with the daughters—at least they had a contract with someone. The agents did have contracts with the names in *Henderson*, even though the case is one in tort; both the building society and the surveyors were in quasi-contractual relationships with the house purchaser in *Smith* v. *Bush*. (Quasi-contract here is not used in its technical legal meaning, but connotes individualistic, voluntary commercial relations.) Even in the negligent reference case, *Spring* v. *Guardian Assurance plc*, much of the argument revolved round the fact that Smith had a contract of employment, and was owed special care because of this. Those cases where the argument has not worked, and there were several earlier on, have been about setting up the boundaries of this sort of relationship. Furthermore, they might well have been resolved otherwise had they occurred later, once the Lords had started looking for this new formula. So in a much earlier case before the Privy Council in 1971, *Mutual Life* v. *Evatt*,[66] the dissent by Lords Reid and Morris in favour of the plaintiff might well have won—the rest of the committee then being influenced by the fact that the advice given was outside the normal scope of Mutual Life's business and therefore could not be seen as having this contract-service aspect. Contract and contract-like activities the English law can understand; the judges, as fine tuners of commercial relationships can cope. The preference is still for contract, and, on the whole, negligent actors can hide behind the need to avoid damaging contractual systems. We quoted above Lord Lloyd in despair on the notion that the retreat from *Anns* was turning into a rout. This came from his dissent against the familiar pair, Lords Keith and Jauncey, abetted by Browne-Wilkinson and Lord Steyn in *Marc Rich & Co.* v. *Bishop Rock Marine*.[67] A merchant ship, a bulk carrier, developed a crack in its hull. A marine surveyor acting for the ship's classification society (part of the complex institutional network of marine insurance) originally certified that the ship required permanent repairs in dry dock. Under pressure from the ship's owners he changed his report to allow them to proceed after temporary repairs, but these proved

---

[66] *Mutual Life and Citizens' Assurance Co. Ltd.* v. *Evatt* [1971] AC 793.
[67] *Marc Rich & Co.* v. *Bishop Rock Marine* [1995] 3 All ER 307.

inadequate and the ship sank, with complete loss of cargo, after a week at sea. The cargo owners sued the classification society for that part of their loss they could not get out of the ship owners. The classification society won in the Court of Appeal and then in the Lords almost entirely on the basis that they were a part of a complex web of contracts, and this claim in tort had no place—there was no tortious duty of care at all. Lord Lloyd, after surveying the whole history of the retreat from *Anns*, sums up his sense that this is a terribly simple and obvious case of negligence under the assumption of responsibility doctrine thus:

We are not here asked to extend the law of negligence into a new field. We are not even asked to make an incremental advance. All that is required is a straightforward application of *Donoghue* v. *Stevenson* ... where the facts cry out for the imposition of a duty of care between the parties, as they do here, it would require an exceptional case to refuse to impose a duty on the ground that it would not be fair, just and reasonable. Otherwise there is a risk that the law of negligence will disintegrate into a series of isolated decisions without any coherent principles at all.[68]

But the pressure of contract won out, despite Lord Lloyd's point that 'the function of the law of tort is not limited to filling out gaps left by the law of contract', when he cited *Henderson* v. *Merrett*, saying that in it the Lords had 'rejected an approach which treated the law of tort as supplementary to the law of contract', i.e. as providing for a tortious remedy only where there is no contract. On the contrary: the law of tort is the general law, out of which the parties may, if they can, contract.[69] A large number, perhaps a majority, of Lord Lloyd's colleagues do not yet seem to share this faith in tort. Where this 'contract like' requirement does seem to be indispensable is where a public official or public body's agent is involved. We conclude by thus picking up the point made earlier about the possible underlying thread in many of these cases that public institutions will almost never be found to have a duty of care, whether their scope is purely economic or more broadly social. This more or less has to follow, because, if judges are only happy with negligence when it is restricted to a quasi-contractual status, the 'duty at large' aspect of negligence by a public official negates the conditions they require. An alternative way of saying much the same is that a public official is, often anyway, producing what economists would describe as a public good rather than a stream of separate private goods. One of the strongest policy reasons, in their Lordships' eyes, for restricting negligence has always been the horror of a duty owed to an unknowably large group—in the public official case this is taken to the extreme. Indeed there appear to be very few cases before

[68] *Marc Rich* at 321–2.
[69] *Marc Rich* at 315.

the Lords or the Privy Council where such a body has been found liable, and it is hard to believe this is either an accident, or not connected to the strong preference for making tort into something philosophically like contract.

Sometimes, especially with economic loss cases which involve the rich complaining that failure to carry out a public duty has made them less rich, it is hard to sympathize with the plaintiff—how much this affects the judgments is something their Lordships themselves probably do not know. There are two ruling cases in this area, one from the Lords and one from the Privy Council, both of them being amongst Lord Keith's proudest achievements. In the 1989 case, *Hill* v. *Chief Constable of the West Yorkshire Police*,[70] the plaintiff was the mother of one of the victims of the serial killer known to the press as the 'Yorkshire Ripper'. Mrs Hill tried to sue for damages on behalf of her daughter's estate on the grounds that incompetence in the police operation to catch Sutcliffe, the murderer, had led to her daughter's death as she was the last of the victims. Had the police properly collated and evaluated the information they had, it was alleged, they would much earlier have strongly suspected Sutcliffe.

Lord Keith had two grounds for refusing to see the police as under a duty of care to Ms Hill. The first was based on the narrowest possible reading of the *Dorset Yacht* case—entirely from Lord Diplock's speech rather than the broader majority opinions. In Keith's words 'it has been said almost too frequently to require repetition, that foreseeability of likely harm is not in itself a sufficient test of liability'. There must be a special proximity between plaintiff and defendant to create this duty of care, not just that Ms Hill was in the category—young females—at risk. This argument, and a fuller version is developed by later cases, would seem inevitably to rule out any possibility of negligence arising in the exercise of a general public duty, and Keith does insist the argument is sufficient to dispose of the appeal. Despite this sufficiency he goes on to stress a second reason, deriving it from his slightly earlier Privy Council ruling in *Yuen Kun Yeu* v. *Attorney-General of Hong Kong*.[71] This second strand is pure policy—Keith claims to rest it on Wilberforce's two-stage test in *Anns*—which refers to the justice of allowing the claim, but it amounts to no more than saying that there are public interest reasons for making the police immune from this sort of challenge, no matter how careless they may be. In essence the argument is that such litigation would be costly and time consuming for the police and would distract them from getting on with the job. It may be more significant that Lord Keith clearly does not think police forces require the goad of potential liability. He accepts, in theory, that liability might in general be in the public interest

[70] *Hill* v. *Chief Constable of the West Yorkshire Police* [1989] AC 53.
[71] *Yuen Kun Yeu* v. *A.-G. of Hong Kong* [1988] 1 AC 175.

by forcing a higher standard of care in carrying out duties. But not the police:

I do not, however, consider that this can be said of police activities. The general sense of public duty which motivates police forces is unlikely to be appreciably reinforced by the imposition of such liability so far as concerns their function in the investigation and suppression of crime. From time to time they make mistakes in the exercise of that function, but it is not to be doubted that they apply their best endeavours to the performance of it.[72]

Indeed, he goes on to argue, such a pressure may make them carry out their duties 'in a detrimentally defensive frame of mind'. No one is likely to believe the police would be made more careful in pursuit of a serial killer, but the ruling, unfortunately, will be taken to cover many areas where vulnerable members of the public do indeed think the police care little enough to be fairly sloppy. Many of the points raised here have to be dealt with in the next chapter, because they involve public law doctrines of justiciability, but there is nothing in Keith's ruling that depends on these—the opinion is a blunt refusal to allow negligence to be used against public authorities. It is a point worth remembering that in the Hillsborough football stadium case the South Yorkshire police accepted liability for the deaths and injuries. This was never ruled on. What would Keith's doctrine in *Hill* have been taken to imply if it had been litigated?

Lord Keith's Privy Council case of a year earlier had involved economic loss, but that was not in itself the problem. Hong Kong had an ordinance setting up a Commissioner for Deposit Taking Companies whose duties included registering such companies 'to regulate the taking of money on deposit and to make provisions for the protection of persons who deposit money. . . .'[73] The plaintiffs deposited money with one such company which had been registered. It shortly afterwards went bankrupt, and they lost their money. They claimed the company had been fraudulently and speculatively managed, that the Commissioner either did know this or should have done, and that he should either never have registered it, or suspended it. In particular it was claimed that the Commissioner had access to much more information than a private depositor could have. Because he did neither, the plaintiffs relied on him to their detriment, and his negligence in performing his public duties cost them a large amount of money for which he should be held liable. Lord Keith was in no doubt about the significance of the case:

The issues in the appeal raise important issues of principle, having far-reaching implications as regards the potential liability in negligence of a wide variety of regulatory agencies carried on under the aegis of central or local government.

---

[72] *Hill* v. *Chief Constable of West Yorkshire* at 63.
[73] Quoted in *Yuen Kun Yeu* at 187.

... Such agencies are in modern times becoming an increasingly familiar feature of the financial commercial, industrial and social scene.[74]

Furthermore, in one of those curious circularities that sometimes happen, Keith is able to use the *Hill* case in making his argument here, by giving his approval to the result in the Court of Appeal which was already out before argument in *Yuen Kun Yeu*. The two cases are in fact one general statement of what is effectively a hidden constitutional doctrine—policy reasons make it impossible to allow negligence claims against public authorities. The details of why it would not be in the public interest to hold the Commissioner liable are not worth going into, being, as such policy arguments always are, a ragbag of amateur assumptions about institutions the judge can know no more about than any other layman. Much of the argument in Keith's opinion is, in any case, part of the, at that time unfinished, attack on *Anns*. Perhaps it is a desirable constitutional rule that these 'increasingly familiar features' of modern society should not be held liable when they are incompetent, but it is not for the Lords to say so. Yet unless they do say so, they have no obvious way of limiting liability in negligence in general. But it is not simply that public authority liability would push negligence away from the quasi-contractual version the judges are comfortable with. There really is a deep-seated unwillingness to see those conditions of 'special proximity' now held necessary when public authorities are involved, even where, had the authority been a private actor, liability could be found without going back to a generous *Anns*-like doctrine. This can be seen in the last case to be discussed here. We should repeat that this section necessarily touches on public law doctrines to be discussed later. In some ways this last section could have been placed entirely within the next chapter. We have put it here because it is concerned with an important implication of the post counter-revolution theory of negligence, but also to help make the point that, where judicial ideology is concerned, law is a seamless web, and the standard subdivisions largely irrelevant.

Even though not all public duty cases would require the creation of a constitutional duty in order for liability to be found, it still seems exceptionally difficult for the Lords, even under their assumption of responsibility doctrine, to find for the plaintiff. This last case serves very well to demonstrate the suggested limit. It is actually a bundle of cases heard as a consolidated appeal, where county or borough councils are sued for alleged breach of educational and welfare duties. A recent, 1995, case, with a single, lengthy opinion by Lord Browne-Wilkinson, under the collective name of *X and others (Minors) v. Bedfordshire County Council*,[75] it

---

[74] *Yuen Kun Yeu* at 190.
[75] *X and others (Minors) v. Bedfordshire CC; M (A Minor) and another v. Newham LBC and others; E (A Minor) v. Dorset CC and other appeals* [1995] 3 All ER 353.

may or may not be representative of current thinking of the Lords. Browne-Wilkinson is certainly a leader in the new attempt to find a formula for negligence, but three of the panel either represent the counter-revolution itself (Lord Jauncey) or had already retired from full duties in the Lords (Lords Ackner and Lane). However, it is the most powerful recent statement of where liability for negligence stops. The cases are typical of the problems citizens experience, or feel themselves to have experienced, at the hands of public authorities. Two of the cases refer to decisions by the social services to take children into care—one a complaint that the social services wrongly took into care a child not at risk, one that several children in a family were left far too long in danger. The education cases all deal with children whose parents felt they were not provided adequately with special educational provisions for dyslexia—in two cases the complaint is that the children were forced to stay in ordinary schools, in the third that he was offered only special school provision when an ordinary school would have been preferable.

Browne-Wilkinson's opinion starts with a lengthy theoretical section on the law as it applies to breaches of statutory duty—all of these cases involve local authorities acting under particular duty-imposing Acts: the Children and Young Persons Act 1969, the Child Care Act 1980, the Children Act 1989; and the Education Acts of 1944 and 1981. According to Browne-Wilkinson there are three levels at which the plaintiffs might hope to gain redress. First, failure to carry out a statutory obligation in itself might cause liability, but he holds that breach of a statutory duty does not confer a private law cause of action. This seems to be established law, and is deeply rooted in public law doctrines we must leave until later. Secondly, carelessness in carrying out a statutory duty might more obviously produce a claim in negligence because of harm caused to the children by negligence. Thus continually failing to consider the children's plight, or continually insisting that they did not need help which later turns out to have all along been necessary is surely harmful negligence in some sense, and, absent any other remedy, one might think the plaintiffs entitled to damages. This is the core area of disagreement in all five cases. Finally, several of the cases involve the actions of professionals, doctors, social workers, educational psychologists, who arguably did their jobs very badly. In this case there is a failure of professional duty which would, in a non-public context, be the basis for a negligence claim. As all these professionals were acting for the local authorities, it would, as a matter of ordinary law, be possible to hold the authorities vicariously liable. What about such professionals when employed by public authorities?

Browne-Wilkinson's treatment of the core issue can be summarized in the following way. Such complaints all relate to carrying out duties where there is a great deal of discretion—nice judgements have to be made about when to separate children from their parents, when to decide a child is best educated with his age group as opposed to in a special school. These are essentially 'policy' questions where a wide latitude of judgement must be allowed, and can only be handled by the institutions the statutes have set up—they are essentially non-justiciable. They also involve resource allocations—school places and children's homes are scarce and so on—and clearly courts cannot make substantive allocation decisions. Consequently the courts cannot handle claims of negligence, because it would be impossible to distinguish between a wrong but rational decision to intervene or not in a family or to allocate or refuse a special school place, and a negligent decision with the same effects. Only, and this comes from a classic standard in public law, only where the authority acted in such an extreme way that no rational authority that was not being negligent could have come to the conclusions it did could a court intervene. Even given such an 'absolute' meaning to negligence, though, Browne-Wilkinson will not allow the educational claims:

. . . a common law duty of care in the exercise of statutory discretion can only arise in relation to an authority which has decided an issue so carelessly that no reasonable authority could have reached that decision. Why it may be asked, should such a grossly delinquent authority escape liability? However I have reached the conclusion that, powerful though those considerations may be, they are outweighed by other factors.[76]

The specific reasons given for protecting even such grossly delinquent authorities are not very convincing. Indeed the main reason given is that the statute has its own appeals machinery. It was, of course, precisely the failure of the parents to get satisfaction from this machinery that led them to the courts. Secondly, and it is the familiar argument against the police being liable in *Hill*, 'many hopeless (and possibly vexatious) cases will be brought, thereby exposing the authority to a great expenditure of time and money in their defence'.[77] This is one of the most common substantive contents of the generic 'policy reasons' argument. It is worth pointing out that no one willingly undergoes administrative bad treatment and then seeks compensation. In all five cases under the umbrella of *X v. Bedfordshire* very long periods of maladministration are alleged to have been suffered, and in all but one case the latest of the actions of the local authorities involved accepting the initial claims of the plaintiffs, at least a year, in two cases several years, late. People turn to the court because they want redress against institutions, and because they do not trust them. A doctrine based on the proposition that the courts should not look underneath the cover of administrative discretion cannot satisfy.

[76] *X (Minors)* v. *Bedfordshire* at 391.
[77] *X (Minors)* v. *Bedfordshire* at 391.

Why, after all, have courts? Yet if the Government were to try to exclude the courts by an ouster clause, the judges would be up in arms. (This point is developed properly in later chapters.) Nor is it fair to object that damages are an inappropriate remedy. Often, as Templeman noted in *Hills*, the plaintiff does seek damages only for symbolic reward, but frequently enough, as in two of the education cases here where parents had been forced to buy private education, there is real financial harm to be recompensed. In any case, financial awards just are the currency of judicial reparation for wrongs done in this legal system. Much more revealing is Browne-Wilkinson's general conception of welfare and educational legislation, from which an indifference to the rights of what one might think of as 'consumers' of the statutorily provided goods can easily flow. Several times he alludes to this conception. In the opening theoretical section comes the powerful statement:

Although regulatory or welfare legislation affecting a particular area of activity does in fact provide protection to those individuals particular affected by that activity, the legislation is not to be treated as being passed for the benefit of those individuals but for the benefit of society in general.[78]

The legislation relevant to the child abuse cases 'are all concerned to establish an administrative system designed to promote the social welfare of the community'.[79] Finally, in summing up his opposition to private rights arising from negligence in making educational discretionary judgements he rounds off the theory:

In my judgment, as in the child abuse cases, the courts should hesitate long before imposing a common law duty of care in the exercise of discretionary powers or duties conferred by Parliament for social welfare purposes. The aim of the 1981 Act was to provide, for the benefit of society as a whole, an administrative machinery to help one disadvantaged section of society.[80]

The argument, or rather stance, because no argument is provided at all for this, highly unusual, doctrine of welfare schemes, brings the five cases here conveniently into the same logical category as the disappointed investors in *Yuen Kun Yeu* and the bereaved mother in *Hill*. That is, they are all simply consumers of a public good, and have no special right to be protected. It is, in all but name, a doctrine of standing; just as a mere taxpayer has no special right to be heard in court about government action, a mere schoolchild or abused child has no special redress against a local authority because it only dealt with him for the public good. This further withdrawal of negligence to a quasi-contractual context is heightened by Browne-Wilkinson's position on the third level defined above—

[78] *X (Minors)* v. *Bedfordshire* at 365.
[79] *X (Minors)* v. *Bedfordshire* at 378.
[80] *X (Minors)* v. *Bedfordshire* at 392.

liability for the direct actions of the servants of the authority, the educational psychologists in the latter cases. This is very important to Browne-Wilkinson, because he partly defends the refusal to allow a claim against negligence in the statutory duty on the grounds that there will often be 'an alternative remedy by way of a claim against the authority on the grounds of its vicarious liability for the negligent advice on the basis of which it exercises its discretion'. For Browne-Wilkinson it is somehow or other more acceptable to hold a professional employed by a local authority negligent, even when vicarious liability transfers the actual responsibility back to the local authority. In his terms we are then dealing with negligent *advice* on which a decision is made, rather than a negligently made *decision*. Tortuous though the idea is, it might seem sufficiently generous to make our earlier analysis unfair and grudging, but this is not so. The apparent protection offered here may be at best partial—what happens where good advice is still used to reach an absurd decision? In any case there are reasons to think the Lords would very seldom allow the only route Browne-Wilkinson left open. He himself points out that if a trial discloses that the authority's educational service was just part of the machinery established to carry out its statutory duties, any duty of care would have to be excluded or limited 'so as not to impede the due performance by the authority of its statutory duties'. And he had so held earlier. In one of the abuse cases a quite flagrant mistake by a psychiatrist and social worker over the identity of the abuser had led to a child being unnecessarily parted from its mother for over a year. Liability still did not hold, because as a matter of policy (per Lord Nolan) such liability would get in the way of the service's functioning. Even more tellingly (per Lord Browne-Wilkinson), liability did not hold because the contractual relationship was between the psychiatrist and the authority. The doctor, apparently, had no more of a duty to the young child than a doctor working for an insurance company has towards the would-be insuree he examines. Back, at every chance, to a quasi-contract situation.

6. Conclusion

Does all of this lengthy chapter add up to anything that matters? We have shown, beyond any reasonable doubt, that a major area of judge made common law is entirely controlled by judicial views on entirely substantive matters. This could have been demonstrated by telling almost any other story from common law. What makes the story of negligence crucial for our purposes is that it might have been, nearly was, another story. Even when one has demonstrated, or the judge has admitted, that a particular decision was taken for policy reasons, it is sometimes hard to show that it was a choice, as our legal realist position requires. Legal argument, and the methodology of legal argument as shown in Chapters 3 and 4, is particularly adept at giving the impression that there was never a choice. Somehow or other the policy matters are so self-evidently right or necessary or inevitable that the decision is correct, legally correct, and not really a policy choice. But in the case of negligence we know this is false, precisely because so many judges, often the most distinguished of their day, have seen other possibilities. Indeed whole jurisdictions have followed those other possibilities. Furthermore the same fight goes on and on. In 1996 the Privy Council had to uphold a decision by the New Zealand Court of Appeal which they would have struck down sitting as the Law Lords on an appeal from the English Court of Appeal, because the New Zealand courts were still holding local authority building inspectors liable for faulty construction of private houses. Lord Lloyd:

In truth, the explanation for divergent views in different common law jurisdictions . . . is not far to seek. The decision whether to hold a local authority liable for the negligence of a building inspector is bound to be based at least in part on policy considerations.[81]

But the 'policy considerations' are, for once, spelled out honestly, in a quote from a 1995 Australian judgment as 'the court's assessment of community standards and demands'. Commenting on there being a difference, apparently, between New Zealand and the UK, Lloyd goes on to say: 'Whether circumstances are in fact so very different in England and New Zealand may not matter greatly. What matters is the perception.' But this is the core problem. Whose perceptions? Why the Law Lords' perceptions? And through what set of assumptions are these perceptions filtered, other than those that are sometimes, very crudely, ideological? And anyway, if in fact community concerns are to be the basis for judicial 'policy' decisions, should there not be some sense in the dozens of opinions canvassed here that this is the basis? Instead all we are treated to is a clear, though only majority, judicial preference for limiting the tort of negligence to an auxiliary role in contractual-like situations.

[81] *Invercargill City Council* v. *Hamlin* [1996] 1 All ER 756 at 767.

7

Imposing Rationality on the State

This is a land, in the words of the poet: 'Where a man may speak the things he will. A land of settled government. A land of just and old renown where freedom broadens slowly down from precedent to precedent'.

Lord Denning, quoted by Lord Browne-Wilkinson in
Wheeler v. *Leicester City Council*

Far from being the point at which public law woke up, the *Wednesbury* case is a snore in its long sleep.

Sir Stephen Sedley in 'The Sound of Silence;
Constitutional Law without a Constitution'

1. The Rights of the Executive

I. Preliminary Remarks

Public law, the subject of the next three chapters, is both hard to characterize in general, and a difficult area on which to assess the Law Lords. Obviously it is the area where political and other attitudes will have major consequences because it deals with the courts' abilities to exercise control over the executive. There are several reasons for the difficulty, which is probably more acute in the nineties than for some time. First, there are important, perhaps still dominant strands in the British constitutional approach which tend against the very legitimacy of curial interference with the executive. The old views of unquestioned parliamentary supremacy held for much of this century, as expressed in the quotation below, are not, perhaps, fashionable any more:

Parliament is supreme. It can enact extraordinary powers of interfering with personal liberty. If an Act of Parliament is alleged to curtail the liberty of the subject or vest in the executive extraordinary powers of detaining the subject the only question is what is the precise extent of the powers given . . . In the constitution of this country there are no guaranteed or absolute rights. The safeguard of British liberty is in the good sense of the people and in the system of representative and responsible government which has evolved.[1]

---

[1] *Liversidge* v. *Sir John Anderson* [1942] AC 206, overruled in *R* v. *IRC, ex parte Rossminster* [1980] AC 952.

The quotation is from Lord Wright, in *Liversidge* v. *Anderson*, a notorious Second World War case which upheld the right of the Home Secretary to incarcerate enemy aliens with no need to demonstrate any evidence to back his judgement. It has long embarrassed English judges, though it was not technically overruled until 1980. But the quotation is taken from an article by the then Lord Irvine of Lairg QC, now Lord Chancellor, attacking what he saw as a recent and unjustified burst of judicial activism in public law, published in 1996.[2] Without doubt many judges, and much of the 'political class', believe that courts should be very circumspect in interfering with executive freedom, despite the recent burst of public statements by some judges and Law Lords which either call for greater judicial assurance, or congratulate the English system precisely on a renaissance in the power and confidence of public law. There probably have been more extrajudicial pronouncements, in lectures and articles, appearing to herald a period of judicial activism in the protection of individual rights than for a very long time. On the whole we ignore this literature, preferring to stick with the methodology of this book, which is to rely almost exclusively on the output of the judges—their formal opinion—than their private expressions. In any case only two of the current Law Lords have spoken in this sort of arena at any length, the more interesting opinions being expressed, on the whole, by men lower down the judicial hierarchy. Part of the difficulty in assessing the Law Lords at this time is that they are themselves, perhaps, going through a process of change. It is not just that there is no single entity intelligently to be looked for called 'the Lords', or 'the view of the Law Lords', a point made in the first chapter. It goes beyond the facts, pointed out earlier in this book, that the appeal committee is always in flux, and much constituted by individualists. It is more that while there may be no clear consensus, nor is there any obvious polar debate. This leads to the second problem, that the case record is very mixed, hard to assess, and intellectually very hard to categorize. Part of this problem, as we try to show in the first section of this chapter, is that the recent cases on which doctrinal development has had to stand are pragmatically difficult ones for any judiciary to take an assertive stand. That is, they are cases where there is a strong 'common sense' drive to leave the executive alone. Such a drive might not prevail against a judiciary whose training and instincts were more absolutist in terms of human rights protection, but that is the last thing that can be said of the English judiciary. Because the whole of English law is imbued with a pragmatic, 'problem solving' approach, as clearly demonstrated in the last chapter, only the clearest cases with the strongest factual basis will suffice for the development of the sort of 'rights' approach needed for a

[2] Irvine of Lairg QC, 'Judges and Decision Makers: The Theory and Practice of *Wednesbury* Review', *Public Law*, Spring 1996, pp. 59–78.

powerful public law. It remains to be seen whether the recent Government proposal to incorporate the European Convention on Human Rights into English law will change this. Little in the analysis to follow suggests the Law Lords will be very energetic in making use of any new powers they receive.

The problem of categorization is very great for the analyst, because public law, in a loose and non-technical sense, is very broad, but also somewhat inchoate. There is always a great temptation to find the one great case, or line of cases, and tell the story from that, to find one, simplifying theme, even just one paramount subject area. It was possible to discuss the politics of common law development, though obviously not exhaustively, by taking a single main theme, the law on liability for negligence. No such approach can really work for public law, so there is an inevitable untidiness in accounting for it, or in trying to draw together a series of judicial pronouncements into one analysis. Consequently this and the next two chapters lack a single narrative drive, and cannot provide a single main analytic conclusion. We start this chapter with the nearest there is to the story of the one great case, the underlying thrust of much, though not all, public law as far as the exercise of control over the executive goes. But the last section of the chapter is much more of a ragbag, because there simply have been a small number of vitally important cases where the Lord have essentially 'stuck their necks out' and produced quite brave public law results. The analytic trouble is that these cases do not very easily follow from the 'single great case' and its story, told in the first two sections. This is because that story is most certainly not one in which the Lords feature as champions of the individual against the State.

It is by no means only our view that the record displayed by cases on the main doctrine have been less than adventurous. The Hon. Sir Robert Carnwath, for example, says of the 1980s that they 'cannot be regarded as a very distinguished chapter in the development of the law'.[3] Chapters 8 and 9 approach public law from a very different angle. We have suggested earlier that the Lords can only be understood if it is accepted that they actually play several very different roles. One we characterized as 'managing the welfare state'. This is *par excellence* public law, but it is law carried out in a quite different manner from the way in which a court may be seen to engage in an *ad hoc* protection of major values. At the same time the record of the courts in managing the system tell us every bit as much about the realities of their views of executive power as the grandstand protection of, say, the freedom of expression. Similar to the management of the welfare state, which is described in the penultimate chapter of the

---

[3] The Hon. Sir Robert Carnwath, 'The Reasonable Limits of Local Authority Powers', *Public Law*, Summer 1996, pp. 244–65.

book, is the long-term control over the rights of individuals in a structured, institutionalized relation to the State. This is the theme for the next chapter where we again look at public law as a relatively routine process of checking on the State versus individual relationship, by considering a complex of immigration, deportation, and prisoners' rights cases. These three different approaches will give us three rather different assessments of the politics of public law, but the differentiation, as well as being imposed by the variety of judicial business, may well reflect a reality of the judicial mind, which is not always as consistent as the legal drive to appear consistent can sometimes suggest. One thing is clear, however. The judiciary itself, as shown by very frequent self-congratulatory obiter in cases, as well as increasingly common extrajudicial pronouncements, think the state of public law is massively better than it used to be. This is not necessarily a view that this rather complicated multi-stranded approach to analysing their work will bear out. Because this chapter is necessarily without a single theme, we offer the following 'plan' and capsule statement which we believe the cases analysed demonstrate. First, public law can be seen as falling into two basic parts. There is that part which is governed, in a very loose sense, by a dominant case. This case, which we go on shortly to discuss, is probably not best seen as a traditional precedent, but somewhat more like a paradigm in the natural sciences. We develop this idea of law as governed by paradigms in the last chapter. What we mean here is that the governing case acts to help judges organize the issues, provides a set of starting points for decision, and, above all, provides a vocabulary with which to announce a decision. It does not function as lawyers think precedents function because, as we show, radically different positions can be presented in the same case as equally validly following from the paradigm case. On the whole this paradigm produces decisions in the State's favour, because it provides more ways of finding for the State than for the citizen-plaintiff. However, this paradigm does not always apply—we suggest that it is rather voluntary on the part of the judges whether to find it applicable or not. Where the paradigm can be escaped from, where it does not govern, common law is much more likely to result in decisions in favour of the citizen than the State. As noted above, the cases in this chapter are all high-salience cases, dealing usually with major constitutional issues. The two chapters that follow deal with the more routine application of public law. In all three chapters, however, the role of this paradigm, and the freedom the courts experience in its absence, are very similar.

II. The Basic Test

The paradigm, the great guiding case in public law, is an oddity in many respects. First, the case, *Associated Provincial Picture House Ltd.* v.

Wednesbury Corporation from 1948, is not itself a judgment of the House of Lords, but only of the Divisional Court of the then King's Bench Division, given by the Master of the Rolls of the day, Lord Greene.[4] Thus it could at any time since then have been overruled by the Lords, even before they gave themselves permission to overrule their own precedents in 1966. Yet difficult though *Wednesbury* (as it is always known) is to understand, interpret, and apply, it remains semi-sacred. In all probability no one has tried to overrule it because the difficulty of actually crafting a new and equally complete rule in public law would be horrendous. This landmark case involved the right of a council to stop children going to the cinema on a Sunday, and Greene's judgment in support of the council lays down tests whereby executive action can be held to be illegal on the grounds of being unreasonable. What Greene did, in very simple terms, was to repeat first the standard doctrine of public law. A court cannot overturn a decision by a public body acting under statutory authority because the court believes the decision to be substantively wrong. There are only two grounds upon which administrative action can be challenged. The first is that the authority never had the power to do what it did—the statute in question does not thus empower it. The second ground, which is what *Wednesbury* is famous for setting out, is that the executive can, in principle, be thought to act so unreasonably in using a power it does have as to be effectively acting illegally, and could thus be overturned. It must immediately be grasped that the level of irrationality implied by Lord Greene is exceptionally high—it amounts to the notion that the authority, whether a single decision maker or a council, has acted in a way which is virtually insane. It is this acceptance of one limited substantive ground for annulling administrative action that gives *Wednesbury* its fame, and it is an overvaluation of this aspect that has led some critics to react as Sir Steven Sedley does in the quotation at the head of this chapter. *Wednesbury* has, aptly, been described not so much as a case as 'an epithet',[5] 'Wednesbury unreasonableness is a code-phrase. What precisely it means has never been clear, and indeed even Lord Greene emphasised its ambiguity.' Another commentator has claimed that 'Lord Greene uses the term in almost as many senses as one could imagine'.[6] The reaction of any political scientist is more likely to be that *Wednesbury*, like so many ruling cases, does not in fact tell a judge what to decide at all. It tells him how to enunciate what he has decided, what code language to use. In a sense the definitional problems inherent in the *Wednesbury* rule, which are largely about the concept of 'discretion', and the range of different problems it is said to cover, make its utility even greater for this rhetorical purpose. But they make it even less useful if it truly is to be an objective test to be

---

[4] *Associated Provincial Picture House Ltd.* v. *Wednesbury Corporation* [1948] 1 KB 233.
[5] The Hon. Sir Robert Carnwath, op. cit.
[6] Paul Walker, 'What's wrong with irrationality?', *Public Law*, 1995 at p. 570.

conscientiously applied. The best way to demonstrate the sheer incoherence of *Wednesbury* as a rule is to give a recent example. The one we have chosen has the great virtue of showing a council being convicted of unreasonable behaviour so extreme as to justify its being overruled by *Wednesbury* doctrine. In fact it shows two different versions of how *Wednesbury* can convict the council, one in the Court of Appeal and one in the House of Lords, which rejected the Court of Appeal's version of why the council was 'Wednesbury unreasonable'. But what makes the case a sheer delight for our purpose is that the majority opinion in the Court of Appeal also used the *Wednesbury* doctrine, to show that the council acted perfectly reasonably, and thus could not be overturned.

In 1984 Leicester City Council, whose electorate was 25 per cent Afro-Caribbean or Asian, asked Leicester Rugby Football Club to do everything in its power to dissuade three of its members from joining a tour of South Africa, and to press the English Rugby Football Union to call off the tour. The tour had been condemned by the Government, and was in breach of the Gleneagles Agreement made in 1977 between Commonwealth Heads of Government. The Gleneagles Agreement recorded it as an 'urgent duty' to take 'every practical step to discourage contact or competition by their nationals with sporting organisations, teams or sportsmen from South Africa'. When the Leicester RFC refused to do what the council asked, the latter used what it claimed were its legal powers under various Local Government Acts to ban the club from using a council owned sports field. In doing so it claimed to comply with its duties under the Race Relations Act 1976, especially clause 71(b) which establishes a 'general statutory duty' to 'make appropriate arrangements with a view to securing that their various functions are carried out with due regard to the need . . . to promote good relations between persons of different racial groups'. In the words of a council official:

The council considers it appropriate, in order to encourage racial harmony, to be seen publicly to distance itself from bodies who occupy an important position in the city, which may be seen to be representing the city and which do not actively discourage or condemn sporting contacts with the South African regime which discriminates against and oppresses people of the same ethnic origins as a substantial proportion of Leicester's population.[7]

The High Court agreed that the council had acted within its powers, and it was upheld by a divided Court of Appeal which contained two men, Ackner and Browne-Wilkinson LJJ, who were shortly to become Law Lords. (We use here for the first time a tactic that is used throughout these latter chapters, which is to choose cases where the range of opinions amongst Law Lords is demonstrated by quoting some of them before they

---

[7] *Wheeler* v. *Leicester City Council* (CA) [1985] 1 AC 1054 at 1059.

actually got to the Lords. In many ways one can tell more about a judge's views when he is not sitting in a panel with some felt need to go along with his fellow peers.) Ackner and Browne-Wilkinson disagreed with each other. Ackner supported the city council's right to freedom of administrative action under statute. Browne-Wilkinson supported what he saw as the club's right to freedom of speech. The House of Lords a little later reversed the Court of Appeal, also supporting the club, but specifically distancing themselves from Browne-Wilkinson's argument. There were, in other words, three completely different interpretations of what this great rule of public law meant, offered by three men who were all soon to be colleagues in the Lords.

The Ackner/Browne-Wilkinson conflict on the Leicester City Council case is a prime example of what we have demonstrated at arduous length in Chapters 3 and 4. The same legal building blocks are used to establish antithetical positions because when both use the *Wednesbury* test all they are really doing is to use the same label to describe what they are doing. The reason they come out with different results, almost without actually disagreeing with each other's argument, is because the questions they separately ask about the council's decision are so different. Ackner, who accepts that the council was doing no more than trying to distance themselves from a racially insensitive amateur sports club, has no doubt that they can only do this if their actions pass the *Wednesbury* reasonableness test:

Can it be said in the circumstances of this case that no reasonable local authority could properly conclude that temporary banning from the use of their recreational grounds an important local rugby club, which declined to condemn a South African tour and declined actively to discourage its members from participating therein, could promote good relations between persons of different racial groups? (The well-known *Wednesbury* test.) . . . to accept the mere existence of such a school of thought [that the club had done enough] does not establish that the council's decision was perverse, and that is what the club is obliged to do to succeed under this head. . . . In my judgment it would be quite wrong to categorise as perverse the council's decision to give an outward and visible manifestation of their disapproval of the club's failure, indeed refusal, 'to take every practical step to discourage the tour'.[8]

Browne-Wilkinson's concern is simple. The council decided how to use their statutory powers as a result of the club's response to the request to oppose the tour. Making their decision in this meant falling below *Wednesbury* standards of reasonableness.

It is now clearly established that the exercise of a discretionary power is unlawful if those exercising the discretion had regard to legally irrelevant matters or failed

[8] *Wheeler* at 1064.

to take into account legally relevant matters. Those are two instances of what, [in *Wednesbury*,] were held to constitute unreasonable decisions which could be quashed. There is another type of such 'unreasonableness' constituted by the decision being so perverse that no reasonable body properly directing itself could have reached such a decision: in my judgment that kind of consideration does not apply to the present case.[9]

To make our point about the huge unclarity of *Wednesbury* even stronger, the main opinion in the House of Lords, by Lord Roskill, used yet another version of the *Wednesbury* test to find for the club. In fact Roskill thinks that even Browne-Wilkinson's dissent in the Court of Appeal did not go far enough. Roskill claims that none of the judges in the Court of Appeal 'have felt able to hold that the action of the club was unreasonable or perverse in the *Wednesbury* sense', and goes on 'respectfully' and 'with great hesitation' to differ 'and to say that the actions of the council were unreasonable in the *Wednesbury* sense'. Indeed he thinks they were 'perverse'. However, the perversity does not exhaust the council's failure under *Wednesbury*, because Roskill prefers to overrule it on yet a third version of the rule, based on the argument that 'the manner in which the council took that decision was in all circumstances unfair'.[10] Roskill does not, however, then go on to detail procedural irregularity or some breach of natural justice as one might expect from such a judgment. Instead the council's 'unfairness' turns out to depend on the fact that it was unsatisfied with the statement the club was prepared to make, and was only going to be satisfied if the club said precisely what they wanted it to say. It was this obstinacy on the part of the council that constituted a degree of unfairness adequate to make the entire decision illegal.

We have three stories here. For Ackner LJ the council was trying to carry out its duties under the Race Relations Act by using its powers under other Acts, and thus could only be overturned by the courts if what they were doing was so unreasonable that no sane council would do it. Manifestly their actions were not unreasonable in this sense, and public law could not touch them. Browne-Wilkinson LJ thinks they are being 'unreasonable' in a special sense—they are misusing powers they were given for mundane purposes to achieve something quite different which they were never authorized to do. Lord Roskill thinks they were unreasonable, indeed perverse, to be trying to do what they were doing at all, but attaches more importance to the way they were being excessive, and therefore unreasonable, in the actual demands they made. (This actually has shades of a quite different doctrine we will come across soon, which is not supposed to be acceptable in English public law, the doctrine of 'proportionality'.)

[9] *Wheeler* at 1064–5.
[10] *Wheeler* at 1079.

It is worth noting one other opinion in the Lords, because it shows how easily a Law Lord can intervene against the executive if he wishes, without relying on *Wednesbury*. Indeed it is refreshing to find Lord Templeman, in the only other opinion, failing to mention *Wednesbury* at all, contenting himself with a somewhat more direct, if rather extreme claim that the council was acting illegally because it was trying to punish the club when the club had done no wrong. The council continually denied that it was into punishment, of course, and always talked of distancing itself, but Templeman had a quite different image in his mind: 'The laws of this country are not like the laws of Nazi Germany . . . a private organisation cannot be obliged to display zeal in the pursuit of an object sought by a public authority and cannot be obliged to publish views dictated by a public authority.'[11] Templeman's own way with public law will be noted more than once in the following pages.

Wheeler v. *Leicester City Council* is in one crucial respect unlike most applications of the *Wednesbury* doctrine. The brute fact of the history of public law is that the executive, whether a local authority or a central government department, is only very rarely indeed found to have failed the *Wednesbury* standards. It is typical in another respect, for it is another fact that the rare cases of the executive being found wanting are all where, in something pretty close to a 'right/left' clash, the ultimate appeal decision has meant a victory for the more conservative side. The two great classics of this kind, the Tameside education case and the GLC transport policy case, are discussed in the next section. We refer here, of course, to major 'one-off' clashes of a constitutional nature, not to the routine application of public law of the type we discuss in Chapters 8 and 9.

In the rugby club case Templeman, as so often, tells us what is really going on. The clash between the Leicester RFC and its council engages very deeply felt political positions and in such a context the very permeable walls of doctrine enshrined in *Wednesbury* are quite inadequate to prevent a decision based on the judge's own reaction to the merits of the substantive fight. But it is this separation between the substantive and the procedural that public law, in England but not always elsewhere, regards as crucial. It is the judges themselves who insist over and again that they will never substitute their own judgement about the correct substantive policy or administrative act—they will merely check to see that the administrator had the power to do what he did. Even unreasonable behaviour is only a ground for quashing a decision because it cannot be thought of any statute that it intends to authorize extremely irrational administrative conclusions. The case we have just used to display the incoherence of *Wednesbury* concerned a local authority. But of course

---

[11] *Wheeler* at 1081.

central government also makes administrative-style decisions under statutory or other grants of authority. We turn now to consider three such cases to investigate how, if at all, the courts apply doctrines of rational behaviour to central government. In so doing we shall see *Wednesbury* becoming ever less coherent. One point that it is useful to understand ahead of the cases, because it enters much of the judicial argument, is this. The classic way in which English law has sought to understand administrative behaviour has been to consider what matters the decision maker took into account, and what conclusions he drew from them when making up his mind. This is in many ways what irrationality, or any other aspect of the *Wednesbury* rule amounts to—did the decision maker think about the wrong things or fail to think about the right things in making up his mind. The Law Lords prefer this sort of approach because it sounds more like a typical legal evidentiary question. It also allows them to continue insisting that they cannot be, and need not be, concerned with the substantive decision. They must be content as long as the process of decision making was rational. This, in a variety of phrasing, is what much of the rest of this section is about.

What Roskill claimed to depend on in *Wheeler* was a reinterpretation of *Wednesbury* which is now often cited as one of the two standard and authoritative readings of the basic rule in public law. The case was *Council of Civil Service Unions* v. *Minister for the Civil Service,* *(CCSU)* from 1984, which we analyse momently. If *CCSU* had indeed managed to impose order on the confusions arising from years of attempting to use *Wednesbury*' it would have been invaluable. Anyone trying to learn public law from a textbook will indeed rapidly come to think, as the authors of the books always do, that the whole doctrine of court interference with executive decisions is enormously complicated and difficult. For lawyers struggling to discover detailed objective rules of law to describe and account for all the decisions of the courts it is, no doubt, tremendously difficult. For political scientists a rough and ready account will do. We are interested in what sort of arguments counsel will think might influence a judge to overturn a decision. We are interested in what sort of rhetoric the judge will then engage in. Actually hoping to find a set of definitions which went further, and predicted how the judge would decide, is vastly too ambitious. Nor, of course, has it been achieved by any legal academic. At its most basic, the *Wednesbury* doctrine, in either its original or its refined versions, rests on the simple fact that what passes for a constitution in the UK more or less follows the tripartite separation of powers model. As such the power to execute the laws is granted to the State in one of its manifestations by Parliament (technically, 'the Crown in Parliament'). Then, as we have said, the State's practical decisions and applications cannot be restricted, altered, challenged or second guessed on their merits. (Parliament could take away the grant of power, or change the relevant law, possibly with retrospective effect, of course.) The question is, where does the third branch in the separation of powers, the court system, come in on this arrangement? And the answer is that, in a fundamental way, it does not. The courts become involved when a state agency has broken the law, just as when anyone else breaks the law. This is the way public law works. It treats an executive decision which is deemed to be capable of being challenged not as an executive decision at all, but as something the executive has done which it never had the power to do—and which hence is illegal. In some ways this can be seen as an extremely powerful doctrine, and some of the conflicting recent trends in public law thinking certainly trend towards a powerful curial control on the executive. What we have just said in a rather cumbersome way was put most pithily in a potentially momentous case we discuss later, by the then Lord Justice Nolan, now a Law Lord (and the Law Lord thought best fitted to chair the first inquiries into parliamentary ethics):

... the proper constitutional relationship of the executive with the courts is that the courts will respect all acts of the executive within its lawful province, and that the executive will respect all decisions of the courts as to what its province is.[12]

On the face of it this is an incredibly powerful doctrine—what greater power could a court have? But that is indeed the essence of the problem. In a country without a fixed written constitution it seems impossible to give an account of public law control over the executive which does not end up either making the courts seem quite powerless, or making them seem potentially leviathan like. Everything depends on self-restraint. The executive, with its ability to get almost anything through Parliament, must exercise self-restraint not to wipe an irritating judiciary off the map. To prevent the executive dropping self-restraint requires judicial self-restraint. It is clear from the record that English judges have been noted for enormous self-restraint. If, as its supporters like to believe, there has been a renaissance in public law, it is because the self-restraint is wearing increasingly thin. The cases we discuss in this chapter tell a somewhat ambiguous story on this point. The restraint rests on this repeated refrain of never making the substantive judgment oneself, of operating only to check procedure. Thus the 'irrationality' aspect of *Wednesbury* tends to be buried under the more procedural aspects, though it never vanishes. In truth it is an impossible test to formulate. Perhaps Sir John Laws, a man with lengthy public law experience as Treasury Counsel before going on the bench, has it right: 'Irrationality is monolithic, and is for that reason an

---

[12] Nolan LJ in *M* v. *Home Office* [1992] QB 270 at 314.

imperfect and inappropriate mechanism for the development of differential standards in judicial review.'

A huge amount of legal writing, academic as much as judicial, has gone into trying to define, and thus to justify overturning, an inherently irrational or unreasonable (the two words are often treated as synonyms) decision, or a decision so odd as to be perverse. No very obvious progress has been made, and judges themselves often give up and go for homely touchstones, like Mr Justice May's idea that this sort of illegality, *Wednesbury unreasonableness* properly and fully so called, can only be identified as when the judge feels 'my goodness, that is certainly wrong'.[13] We will learn something about what sorts of things the English judiciary find to be unreasonable, irrational or perverse as we look at the cases. But we look at them for the far more general purpose of discovering how, and what sort of, judicial ideology breaks through into their oversight of the executive, rather than in some hopeless search for an objective definition of administrative irrationality. All that can be said generally is that while the judges could never agree openly with the definition of rationality offered by moral philosopher Charles Taylor they actually seem to operate by it. Taylor makes the apparently trivial but fundamental point, if ironically, that 'this means that the criterion for rationality is that one gets it right'.[14] For a judge the last thing they can do is to ask if a local council, or the Secretary of State, 'got it right', because that would be putting their own judgment in place of that of the executive. But what else can they actually do?

We shall look then at three crucial cases where major government policy has been sought to be challenged in public law, all three of interest substantively, but also as judicial attempts to make *Wednesbury* and related doctrines actually work. They are examples of the development of doctrine, and the mere fact that the Government won each case in itself should not lead one to write them off as faltering steps towards a public law with rather more teeth than Lord Greene's.

III. Development of Public Law Doctrine

The *CCSU* Case

This first is the civil service case on which Roskill relied, *Council of Civil Service Unions* v. *Minister for the Civil Service* in 1985. Despite the modesty of the title, the minister in question was, in fact, the Prime Minister who caused an announcement to be made in the House of Commons on 22 December 1983, out of the blue, that henceforth no civil servant working

---

[13] Quoted by Donaldson MR in *R* v. *Devon CC, ex parte G* [1988] 3 WLR 49, discussed later.
[14] Charles Taylor, *Sources of Our Selves*, p. 83.

at the Government Communications Head Quarters (GCHQ) would be allowed to be a member of a national trade union. They would instead only be allowed to join a special departmental staff association approved by the Director General of GCHQ. GCHQ is Britain's main electronic intelligence gathering body, the equivalent of America's famous National Security Agency. Civil servants from GCHQ had joined in various industrial actions taken by civil servants nationally but sporadically between 1979 and 1981 in pursuit of generalized grievances against their employer, the Government, though these had not been specific to GCHQ. The terms on which civil servants work for the Crown do not preclude a unilateral withdrawal of the right to join a trade union, but it was commonly accepted that union members would normally have a 'legitimate expectation' that their unions would be consulted on something like this, and that they would have a chance to argue against the decision, and to suggest special agreements that might alleviate whatever the Government's anxieties were about union membership. It gives a flavour of the politics involved here when it is remembered that the incoming Labour Government of 1997, honouring a long-term commitment, lifted this ban during its first week in office. Such a legitimate expectation would, again a matter of common agreement, make the withdrawal without such consultation something that could be quashed in public law by the application of judicial review. The CCSU sought such review and were successful in the High Court. But on appeal the Crown introduced a new argument they had never addressed to Glidewell J in the High Court. Initially the argument was a very broad and unspecific claim that considerations of national security precluded consultations. This was enough for the Court of Appeal to grant the Crown's appeal, but was still too vague and the House of Lords forced the Crown to a much more specific claim. The specific claim was that consultation was impossible because the Government feared disruption of the vital intelligence work in GCHQ. To engage in consultation would have the direct effect of alerting the CCSU to how they could best hurt national security. Thus consulting them risked directly causing the sort of disruption that the union ban was intended to prevent in the future. This final version convinced even the Law Lords, and the CCSU lost their appeal. In one way it is obvious why the Government was not eager to press this detailed argument. It amounts to saying that the reason the unions were not consulted about the removal of ordinary industrial relations rights from the workers is that the workers might use ordinary industrial relations rights. In any ordinary case such an admission would be fatal to the Government's case. Only the spectre of a breach in national security allowed them to use the argument, reluctantly and belatedly, in *CCSU*.

Despite the fact that the unions ultimately lost is believed by many that the case represents a real achievement for public law control over the executive, because the Law Lords held the Crown to a relatively tough test. In particular it is thought important that they did not simply accept the bald statement that the case concerned a matter of national security and therefore public law could not intervene. Instead they insisted that it be demonstrated that the decision really had been made because of the sort of national security consideration the Prime Minister complained of, and not just that it might have been so made. Lord Scarman, probably the judge least likely automatically to accept the mere waving of the security umbrella, puts it this way:

I have no doubt that the respondent refused to consult the unions before issuing her instruction . . . because she feared that, if she did, union-organised disruption of the monitoring services of GCHQ could well result. I am further satisfied that the fear was one which a reasonable minister in the circumstances . . . could reasonably entertain. I am also satisfied that a reasonable minister could reasonably consider such disruption to constitute a threat to national security.[15]

Scarman's position applies a 'reasonableness' test three times here: the minister herself was a reasonable person; it was reasonable to fear that disruption might happen; it was reasonable to think this might be a threat to national security. Scarman's stance was agreed by Lords Diplock, Fraser, Roskill, and Brightman and is seen as setting some sort of limit to executive action. In fact the case could be said to turn on almost an evidentiary point—did the Crown adduce enough material to show that security considerations of an at least 'reasonable' nature really were the motives? Counsel for the CCSU tried hard to persuade the Lords that in fact such considerations were an afterthought, tacked on belatedly. The suggestion was fairly plausible, given that the Crown never thought to mention the fear of disruption during consultation when the case first came to trial, and the affidavit from the Cabinet Secretary, which was the only evidence of the motive, hardly mentioned the problem. Furthermore there was at least one good alternative reason—the Government had earlier given assurances that a routine use of polygraph testing, which the unions opposed, would only be introduced after consultations with them. These consultations had not as yet been held, and would no longer have to go ahead if the union branches at GCHQ ceased to exist. At the beginning of the case the main security concern held to preclude consultation was said to be the fear of disclosing official secrets. But Glidewell J had rejected this as enough to overcome the legitimate expectation of the unions. So the whole case, by the time it got to the Lords, had a rather rickety appearance.

The supposedly tough stance of the Law Lords was said to follow a

---

[15] *CCSU* v. *Minister for the Civil Service* [1985] 1 AC 374 at 404.

First World War case, one they themselves were eager to brand as very brave, when the Law Lords of the day had overturned an attempt by the Government to seize a cargo of copper carried by a neutral ship arrested by the Royal Navy which the Government claimed was urgently necessary for the war effort. In this case, known as *The Zamora*,[16] the Lords had held that the Crown could not win because it had not provided adequate evidence that the cargo really was vital for the war effort. Scarman calls *The Zamora*, 'Surely one of the more courageous of judicial decisions even in our long history'. It probably was, and, compared with the performance of the courts in the Second World War, it was amazing. The question for us is whether the Lords in 1985 came anywhere close to that degree of courage. The basis on which Scarman said he was so satisfied of the Government's reasonableness was the mere statement by the Cabinet Secretary—it was a Cabinet Secretary who later admitted in a security case to being 'economical with the truth'—that the Government had the concern described above. Was this really enough to establish the bona fides of the minister? It may well be that the nature of public law investigation means that the executive must be able to protect itself like that, but the Lords certainly could have taken a different stand. Scarman had in a previous case refused to take mere statements as enough. He had been in dissent in *Secretary of State for Defence* v. *Guardian Newspapers Ltd.* that same year[17] when he refused to rule for the prosecution in a Contempt of Court Act case that required him to accept an affidavit that some material published by the *Guardian* was security sensitive. The evidentiary base in *CCSU* simply was not as strong as that which the *Zamora* court would have required, and was less strong, if anything, than the evidence Scarman rejected in the *Guardian* case.

There are generalized reasons that can be given for judicial reticence about second guessing the executive. Lord Diplock sets these out in this very case, but they do not in fact apply to the situation in *CCSU*. *CCSU* concerned a procedural impropriety—whether the banning of the unions was carried out by legally acceptable procedures. This is what used to be called natural justice, something the judges are clearly competent to judge. The reason the case is seen as important to lawyers is that Lord Diplock's speech in part tidies up, and produces new nomenclature for the fuzziness of, the *Wednesbury* tests. (Or so it said—in fact judges continue to use the *Wednesbury* language and label to this day, often in the same opinions in which they pay lip service to Diplock's speech in *CCSU*.) Diplock argues that there are three heads under which judicial review can control administrative action. These are illegality, irrationality, and procedural impropriety. Illegality is the old test of properly understanding

---

[16] *The Zamora* [1916] 2 AC 77.
[17] *Secretary of State for Defence* v. *Guardian Newspapers Ltd.* [1985] AC 339.

the law and correctly applying it, and Diplock says, pointedly, that it is 'par excellence a justiciable question to be decided, in the event of dispute, by those persons, the judges, by whom the judicial power of the state is exercisable'. Even the most modest of judges could not dispute that. What is more interesting is his account of 'irrationality':

By 'irrationality' I mean what can now be succinctly referred to as 'Wednesbury unreasonableness'. It applies to a decision which is so outrageous in defiance of logic or of accepted moral standards that no sensible person who had applied his mind to the question to be decided could have arrived at it. *Whether a decision falls within this category is a question that judges by their training and experience should be well equipped to answer, or else there would be something badly wrong with our judicial system.* [Our emphasis.][18]

The italics are to stress Diplock's assessment of the judiciary, the boldness with which he does accept that the judiciary is perfectly well equipped to make the entirely substantive judgment that something is unacceptable, a stance that most of his colleagues are much more hesitant about. Unfortunately this fairly brave assessment of judicial competence and the definition of administrative irrationality has, as suggested, not much been used by judges. Indeed one eminent critic has dismissed Diplock here, noting that he is rarely followed, and saying, in a way which if true is ominous: 'Logic is a useful, but not normally the critical, criterion in public law decisions, which are more likely to depend on an aesthetic or policy judgment'.[19] But if Lord Diplock's restatement of *Wednesbury* had been followed fully, much of the idea that judges cannot overturn administrative action for substantive reasons would evaporate. Although it would remain an entirely subjective judgement whether some action was 'outrageous in defiance of logic'.

Diplock's third heading is, as noted above, really a retitling of accepted doctrines about fairness and natural justice. There is, almost, a fourth heading in Diplock's speech, because he excited some commentators by what might in political terms be called 'flying a kite' for a more full-blown public law approach. Having pointed out how much progress public law has made since 1945, before setting out his three heads he deliberately warns that the case by case basis does not preclude adding further grounds. 'I have in mind particularly the possible adoption in the future of the principle of "proportionality" which is recognised in the administrative law of several of our fellow members of the European Economic Community.' As we shall see, this suggestion has never been taken up, though it is still hinted at from time to time by their Lordships. It may be that the proposed incorporation of the European Convention on Human

[18] *CCSU* at 410.
[19] The Hon. Sir Robert Carnwath, 'The Reasonable Limits of Local Authority Powers', *Public Law*, Summer 1996, p. 244, at 265.

Rights will, though it need not, help the introduction of proportionality arguments.

CCSU falls under heading three, a case involving procedural irregularity, and only the security aspect saves the Government. Thus we are not supposed to see the case as an example of judicial passivism in the face of the executive. The Government merely had to satisfy an evidentiary hurdle. The most one might complain of is that the Law Lords set the hurdle in practice far too low. The problem is that categorization of cases into these three heads still seems a matter of choice, in the sense that a judge will place a case in whichever category helps him get the result he wants. In *Wheeler*, as we saw, the same facts were seen variously as falling into all three headings, by three judges, one of whom saw it falling into both the second and third! The trouble with *CCSU* is the suspicion that had the national security argument not been strong enough to work under the procedure category, the Law Lords would have considered it under the pure irrationality category instead. Diplock's definition of irrationality under this category was, to repeat, 'a decision which is so outrageous in defiance of logic or of accepted moral standards that no sensible person who had applied his mind to the question to be decided could have arrived at it'. If removing consultative rights had to be tested for Diplock-irrationality, rather than as a procedural irregularity, then it would be very easy to use the merest hint of a security problem to say the minister's decision could not be regarded as irrational. And this tactic would be no different from the one we saw in *Wheeler*, where Ackner did in fact measure the council's actions against a rationality test, while Browne-Wilkinson measured it against a procedural test with different results. Could any Cabinet decision ever be treated as 'Diplock-irrational'? Because, of course, *CCSU* was, as was admitted, Cabinet level policy?

Broadcasting Freedom—the *Brind* Case

The second of our major cases in this section is of interest not only because it replays these problems, but because there was an attempt to take up Diplock's invitation to proportionality. If *CCSU* may be seen, with a little charity, as a relatively strong affirmation of the courts' role in controlling the executive, no one could so describe *R v. Secretary of State for the Home Department, ex parte Brind*[20] from 1991. Only Lord Roskill sat on both courts, and he did make some limited effort to keep the spirit that may have shown in *CCSU* alive, but the main speech by Ackner was certainly no continuation of anything liberal in *CCSU*. In particular Ackner completely ignored Diplock's restatement of *Wednesbury*. Of the other Law

[20] *R v. Secretary of State for the Home Department, ex parte Brind* [1991] 1 AC 696.

Lords who heard *Brind*, Lord Lowry most clearly agrees with Ackner, though both Lords Templeman and Bridge have no problem with the result.

Brind and the others on his side were broadcast journalists and members of the National Union of Journalists who asked for judicial review of an order issued by the Home Secretary in October 1988 to the BBC and the Independent Broadcasting Authority (IBA). This was the order that prohibited the broadcasting of the actual voices of anyone claiming to represent, or to solicit support for, the IRA and other organizations proscribed by the Prevention of Terrorism Act 1984. This order led to the strange system whereby statements made even by IRA leaders such as Gerry Adams would be read by actors with Irish accents mimicking their styles over still photographs of the original speaker in a curious attempt to prevent the IRA winning what the Prime Minister responsible, Mrs Thatcher, called 'the battle of the airwaves'. The orders were issued under legislation and agreements between the Government and both the IBA and BBC in 1981 which clearly allowed the Home Secretary to issue notices 'to refrain from broadcasting any matter or classes of matter specified in the notice'. These orders, according to Brind et al., should be declared to be illegal because they were of a kind forbidden by the freedom of expression protection in Article 10 of the European Convention on Human Rights. Alternatively, the orders abridged the doctrine of proportionality, hinted at by Diplock in *CCSU*, which required that interference with so fundamental a right as freedom of speech could only be legal where it corresponded to a 'pressing social need'. Their Lordships were unanimous on this case, but there was a sense of regret in the speeches of Bridge, Templeman, and Roskill that left some hope that freedom of speech was one area where the English law might be capable of future judicial development. These three Law Lords clearly experienced difficulty crafting arguments which upheld the Home Secretary's order without shutting down such hope. That such a development did come, in a rather roundabout way, later, is discussed in section three. *Brind* was in many ways a case that could have developed public law in a liberal human rights direction. It did not do so. Part of the problem was the facts of the case. In all jurisdictions with active courts there is a problem of waiting for the case where the facts are stark enough to carry public sympathy. The very odd, to many plain silly, nature of the restriction on broadcasting freedom involved in *Brind* loaded the case for the Government. Ironically, instead of making the Government look foolish, the complainants were held to be themselves odd to object to something so trivial. As Lowry was to say with obvious impatience:

Indeed the issue which seems to arise is whether the disadvantage of exposing the government to the misrepresentations of its attitude of which your Lordships have seen examples may outweigh the advantage to be derived from the directives themselves.[21]

Similarly Ackner dismisses the claim by Brind's counsel that the Home Secretary 'had used a sledgehammer to crack a nut' by quoting Lord Donaldson MR from the Court of Appeal. 'The Home Secretary has used no sledgehammer' because the IRA are no worse off than if they had newspaper publicity with the huge circulation of BBC and IBA news broadcasts. Furthermore the effect could be shown to be minimal, affecting only 8 minutes and 20 seconds of ITN's 1,200 hours of broadcasting. Of course these minimalist arguments should have been contrasted with a 'slippery slope' argument, one judges are usually happy with. The rhetoric of human rights is full of elegant versions of 'give a government an inch and it will take a mile', but for one reason or another the Lords were more impressed with the triviality of the actual impact. Four of them make the point. Lord Bridge, 'what is perhaps more surprising is that the restriction imposed is of such limited scope'; Lord Templeman, 'But the interference with freedom of expression is minimal and the reasons given by the Home Secretary are compelling.' At least most of their Lordships did express sympathy with the broadcasters, and stress their conviction of the bona fides. The true flavour of the case might more properly be seen, however, in Lord Ackner's clear distrust of the media's impartiality. He dismissed an affidavit from the broadcaster Jonathan Dimbleby, who had argued for the truth seeking power of broadcasting by talking of 'cross examination in the full and merciless glare of the television lens', with words that reveal clearly his own views:

Your Lordships will, I am sure, need no persuading that all cross-examinations are not thorough. Indeed there are occasions where someone may wonder whether an incompetent cross-examination is the product solely of lack of preparation.[22]

Not one of their Lordships even hint at a concern at a breach in the sanctity of this civil liberty. But then, absolute rights have little place in English judicial thinking. This matters particularly because, given the logic of English public law, to admit that rights cannot be absolute is in danger of admitting massive executive discretion. The structure of this implication is perhaps shown best by Lord Bridge's speech. He starts by insisting that the European Convention cannot directly apply in the UK, not even to test a discretionary executive decision. To allow this would be 'a judicial usurpation of the legislative function'. Nonetheless the courts are not impotent to prevent exercise of discretion in a way that infringes on 'fundamental human rights'. After all, even the Convention recognizes most rights are 'less than absolute'. English judges, exercising judicial

[21] *Brind* at 764.
[22] *Brind* at 759.

review have 'neither the advantages nor the disadvantages of any comparable code'. It leaves one to wonder what hope there is for the Convention,
once incorporated, if it is seen as full of disadvantages. However, Bridge
does at first seem to want English courts to be able to protect fundamental
freedoms, and to think the common law powerful enough as it is:

But again this surely does not mean that in deciding whether the Secretary of
State, in the exercise of his discretion, could reasonably impose the restriction he
has imposed . . . we are not perfectly entitled to start from the premise that any
restriction of the right to freedom of expression requires to be justified and that
nothing less than an important competing public interest will be sufficient to
justify it.

So far so good, but the crunch comes with the introduction of *Wednesbury*
in the next sentence:

the primary judgment as to whether the particular competing public interest
justifies the particular restriction falls to be made by the Secretary of State to
whom Parliament has entrusted the discretion. But we are entitled to exercise a
secondary judgment by asking whether a reasonable Secretary of State, on the
material before him, could reasonably make that primary judgment.[23]

And there is the rub, because all the courts are going to allow themselves
to do is to ask, in effect, does the Secretary of State really promise he
thought about all the implications? As long as the executive goes through
the motions, he is going to be safe. The test is whether the Secretary of
State could come to the conclusion he reaches without being massively
irrational, not whether he should have come to those conclusions. Bridge
probably agrees with Templeman who seems to think that this approach
is more or less equivalent to the European Court of Human Rights'
practice, which is to allow 'a margin of appreciation' to the executive in
such decisions. But there is a world of difference between simply
allowing some leeway and the English practice which is to say that as
long as a reasonable Home Secretary could reasonably think his decision
necessary then the courts cannot interfere.

Templeman's very short speech in this case in fact contrasts rather
sharply with all the others. Were one not carefully schooled in English
public law, one might think that he did not know the European Convention cannot be applied by English courts. It was just that as far as
Templeman could see, the Government was in accord with it. He discusses the aspect of *Wednesbury* that stresses that decision makers must
take account of all relevant matters. Templeman insists that the Home
Secretary passes the 'taking into consideration' test because there was
'evidence from the Home Secretary himself that he took the Convention
into account'. As far as the 'irrationality' aspect of *Wednesbury* is con-

[23] *Brind* at 748.

cerned, Templeman actually seems to ditch the test on the grounds that it is out of date and inadequate. Instead he seems to establish some new sort of test which may even be intended to be a form of European Convention, or a general proportionality, test. Indeed the first part of Templeman's comments may be the most negative judgement on *Wednesbury* ever given in the Lords:

The subject matter and date of the *Wednesbury* principles cannot in my opinion make it either necessary or appropriate for the courts to judge the validity of an interference with human rights by asking themselves whether the Home Secretary has acted irrationally or perversely. It seems to me that the courts cannot escape from asking themselves whether a reasonable Secretary of State, on the material before him, could reasonably conclude that the interference with freedom of expression which he determined to impose was justified. In terms of the Convention, as construed by the European Court, the interference with freedom of expression must be necessary and proportionate to the damage which the restriction is designed to prevent.[24]

In other words Templeman wants to differentiate the gross irrationality sense of *Wednesbury* and replace it with a much weaker reasonable connection test. It might almost be better to treat Templeman's speech as a dissent, despite his agreement to the actual result. In fact what one gets from combining Bridge and Templeman is a fairly obvious desire to develop the law on freedom of expression, and considerable *de facto* agreement with at least the spirit of European jurisprudence. Nonetheless, even for them, what the Home Secretary had done was too trivial, compared with what he thought he would achieve, to trigger even their proposed tests.

Such a relatively strong position *vis-à-vis* the Home Secretary is not Lord Ackner's, and his is the major speech, presenting what must be taken as the legal ruling in *Brind*. Ackner has no truck with any shade of the 'proportionality argument', accepts no role for the European Convention whatsoever, and countenances no weakening in *Wednesbury* rationality. Ackner divides his attack on the appellants' case into three main sections: allegations of *Wednesbury* irrationality; failure to take account of the Convention; and the claim that the ban is so disproportionate that it must be *ultra vires*—outwith the powers the Broadcasting Act grants the Home Secretary. Ackner at no stage uses Diplock's arguably more plaintiff-oriented redefinition of the overall *Wednesbury* doctrine. He deals instead with *Wednesbury* as forbidding a 'perverse' decision by showing how much parliamentary support there was for the decision, and by stressing the minimal nature of the impact. He deliberately puts the 'taking note of the Convention' aspect into a separate section of his speech.

[24] *Brind* at 751.

Though Ackner admits in this second section that the Convention may be used where a problem of statutory construction arises, his view is very restrictive. The relevant sections of the Broadcasting Act are not at all ambiguous or uncertain for him—they intentionally confer an unrestricted discretion, discretion only restricted by the overall purpose of the Act, and thus the Convention cannot be used. However, the really important, and very negative, part of this argument is different. Counsel for Brind had argued that it was not enough for the minister simply to have considered the Convention, 'but that he should have properly construed it and correctly taken it into consideration'. Not doing so is, according to counsel, how the Home Secretary failed under *Wednesbury*. It is indeed hard to see how taking note could not imply at least giving it a reasonable interpretation, else evidence only that he opened the covers would suffice. Had this argument been accepted, *Brind* would have been a stronger civil libertarian case than *CCSU*. Both of them would then require some proof that the Government had taken certain matters seriously. The argument in *Brind* would have been that the Home Secretary not only had to read the Convention, but that his reading had to be at least plausibly accurate, just as *CSSU* was thought to insist that there really should be a rational connection to national security, rather than only a government statement that there was. But for Ackner this is a crucial fallacy. Because no one doubts that the Convention has some effect in England, that the Government must consider it along with other matters, it does not, for Ackner, follow that any particular reading of the Convention is necessary:

If the Secretary of State was obliged to have proper regard to the Convention, i.e. to conform with Article 10, this inevitably would result in incorporating the Convention . . . by the back door. It would oblige the courts to police the operation of the Convention and to ask themselves in each case . . . whether the restrictions were 'necessary in a democratic society . . .' applying the principles enunciated in the decisions of the European Court of Human Rights. The treaty, not having been incorporated in English law, cannot be a source of rights and obligations, and the question 'did the Secretary of State act in breach of Article 10?' does not arise.[25]

This argument need never have been made, were Ackner prepared to allow a sympathetic influence to Convention arguments, like Templeman. And indeed, why should the Government stress that the Home Secretary had considered the Convention, why should Ackner even take note, earlier, of that claim, but for fear that it would be proper to have such marginal influence? By drawing out the implications in this particular way, by making it appear blatantly unconstitutional to ask about what the Home Secretary thought the Convention meant, the Convention is safely put out of count. The recent attempt by the counsel in question, now Lord,

---

[25] *Brind* at 762.

Lester, to introduce a Bill in the Lords specifically allowing the use of the Convention was directly a response to Ackner's position in *Brind*. That Bill was supported by several members of the current Law Lords. Lord Ackner could have contented himself, as did the other Law Lords, with insisting that the Secretary of State had said he had looked at the Convention—but the extra sentences actually make *Brind* a very strong authority against use of the Convention in English law.

Lord Ackner's final section, on proportionality, is hardly surprising, given the above. He asserts bluntly that a proportionality test must always involve specifically 'balancing the reasons, pro and con, for his decision, albeit allowing him a margin of appreciation . . .'. Ackner says this follows from the definition offered of the proportionality test, which was simply 'Could the minister reasonably conclude that his direction was necessary?' It is true that any commentators have understandable difficulty working out how the proportionality test is actually different from existing *Wednesbury* doctrine. What is clear is that if Ackner's argument against the proportionality test is valid, then *Wednesbury* rationality could also never be applied. Perhaps the point is that *Wednesbury* irrationality almost never is applied, and this failure would be all the more obvious if couched in proportionality terms. Whatever, Ackner rules proportionality out of court by making it directly dependent on the Convention, indeed by equating the two. As he has so completely rejected the Convention as unconstitutional, he disposes completely of the proportionality test as well. Effectively condemning Diplock's kite-flying for proportionality in *CSSU*, Ackner states categorically that unless the Convention is incorporated, proportionality, which he describes as a doctrine of the European Court, has no basis on which it can be followed by the English courts. Proportionality is, in fact, a general public law doctrine in Europe, and existed long before the European Court of Human Rights.

Is *Brind* 'the law'? If it is, any steps towards allowing courts to assess the actions of the executive against some standard less permissive than ministerial lunacy were stamped on hard. In fact it is unclear what *Brind* really does stand for. Lord Ackner's leading opinion was simply too strong to carry the Lords, many of whom, if not going as far as Templeman seemed to, certainly did not wish to ignore the Diplock initiative completely. Bridge, for example, clearly wanted to sharpen up *Wednesbury* in areas approaching fundamental human rights. What *Brind* does show strongly is that positions like Ackner's, sympathetic to executive independence, are always going to be easier to argue, and especially when the fact situation is not compelling. It shows, surely, also that any tendencies towards a human rights perspective are most timidly held. Unfortunately the non-Ackner speeches in *Brind* and aspects of *CCSU* are the most liberal an English court has yet managed to be, because the other important *Wednesbury* case cited nowadays is, within its own sphere, even more strongly pro-executive.

Super Wednesbury

The case in question, *Nottinghamshire County Council* v. *Secretary of State for the Environment* caused Lord Templeman, in exasperation that the council had come to court at all, to produce one of the more memorable lines in the jurisprudence of public law—'Judicial review is not just a move in an interminable chess tournament'—and to offer the tactical advice 'persuasion should be offered not to the judges who are not qualified to listen, but to the department, the minister, all members of parliament and ultimately to the electorate'.[26] This was 1986, and the issue was the legality of the Secretary of State's 1986 setting of expenditure targets for local authorities under the 1982 Local Government Finance Act and the Local Government Planning and Land Act 1980. This was, of course, the time when the Conservative Government, first elected in 1979, was fighting a protracted battle to control local government expenditure. The primary weapon was to set target expenditures in an annual exercise. Though later the Government took powers directly to set maximum levels of local authority expenditure, at this stage control was exercised by varying the central government's block grant to councils. Councils which exceeded the Government's expenditure targets were given proportionately lower block grants than those which obeyed the targets, thus forcing them to raise more of their annual expenditure through the rates, which at that time were the primary source of local government financing other than central government grants. It was, in Lord Bridge's words, a 'carrot and stick' method. Nottinghamshire (and Bradford Metropolitan City Council) appealed against the setting of targets in the Act which would penalize them, by forcing them to levy a higher local rate than other councils, because they were planning to spend at a level higher than that set by the Government in its annual 'Rate Support Grant Report'. They had two legal arguments by which to claim the Secretary of State was acting illegally in setting the targets in this discriminatory way.

The first objection specific to this particular legislation, was that the empowering legislation, the 1980 Act, required that the Secretary of State's 'guidance' (as it was euphemistically termed) must be 'framed by reference to principles applicable to all local authorities', and the discriminatory element in the 1985/6 guidance was therefore illegal. If the Lords had accepted this there would have been some outcry, but it was, in the end, a straightforward application of statutory interpretation, if a very sensitive one, and on a hideously complicated statute. The second argu-

---

[26] *Notts. CC* v. *Secretary of State for the Environment* [1986] 1 All ER 199 at 217.

ment was broader, and if accepted by the Lords would have constituted a much more powerful incursion into executive independence by the judiciary. The second claim was a straight *Wednesbury* argument, from the 'irrationality' or 'perverseness' part of the test. The councils claimed that even if the guidance complied with the words of the statute, then, to use Lord Scarman's summary:

it is so disproportionately disadvantageous when compared with its effect on others that it is a perversely unreasonable exercise of power conferred by the statute on the Secretary of State. . . . The respondent's case is that the guidance is grossly unfair, some authorities doing disproportionately well and others being hit undeservedly hard. Your Lordships . . . have been invited to hold that no reasonable Secretary of State could have intended consequences so disproportionate in their impact as between different local authorities. The House is invited in its judicial capacity to infer from these consequences that the Secretary of State must have abused the power conferred on him by the 1980 Act.[27]

The councils had won in the Court of Appeal, but, unsurprisingly, on their first argument, not on this wider one. The Lords practised a slightly unusual division of labour, with Bridge disposing of the argument from statutory interpretation, leaving Scarman to do all the work on the 'perverseness' argument. It must be admitted immediately that this argument could never have been accepted by the courts. This is because, *de facto* if not *de jure*, it would have been to strike out legislation, and therefore to deny parliamentary sovereignty, not simply to control the executive. Much of the ability English courts do have to produce results which do not really follow from legislative language is because the judges know as well as any commentator that the hallmark of British political life is party discipline. This has come to produce a real 'democratic deficit' in the UK, because most of the time when any reference is made to parliamentary intent one knows that the only intent involved is the executive's, and that the executive will be able, if necessary, to force its backbenchers, whatever they really think, to back them. Only rarely will a Law Lord say this quite so bluntly in an opinion, though it does happen. (Lord Goff, in an opinion exceptionally rare for its honesty, does so in a case discussed in the concluding chapter.) Here though we are dealing with an issue right at the very forefront of the partisan clashes of the time. Here the Government's backbenchers really would have intended the executive to discipline high-spending authorities, and here they would genuinely and individually 'intend' the legislation to mean whatever the Secretary of State said they intended it to mean. The councils could have won on the first argument, only to have a parliamentary draftsman produce blunter language. But to win on the second would mean that the Lords were, in effect, telling

---

[27] *Notts. CC* at 202.

Parliament itself that it was being irrational and perverse. So what is of interest to us here is how Scarman can establish the Secretary of State's immunity without actually giving up the core idea that some decisions can be so unfair as to constitute, for legal purposes, 'irrationality' that implies illegality.

Scarman's opinion, though not lengthy, falls short of his usual elegance, verging on the repetitive, largely because the line he must draw, the impossibility, indeed the unconstitutionality, of the Law Lords intervening here, must be said in such a way as not to seem to remove any of the more usual powers of judicial review, including the idea that there might be some circumstances where a minister acting very closely with Parliament could still be seen to be committing an abuse of power. An important factual aspect of this case was that the annual decisions of the Secretary of State were not only authorized by the Act initially, but could only take effect when presented to the Commons in an annual report and after this report had been approved by the House. Thus, again quoting Scarman:

That House has therefore a role and a responsibility not only at the legislative stage when the Act was passed but in the action to be taken by the Secretary of State in the exercise of the power conferred on him by the legislation.[28]

Scarman then set down a new, higher version of *Wednesbury* which has come to be called '*Super Wednesbury*' in the public law literature, and which ought to be, but has not necessarily been, restricted to the constitutionally most sensitive applications. Scarman takes as central to the whole idea of *Wednesbury* illegality that the decision maker has committed an 'abuse of power', giving *Wheeler*, incidentally, as an example of abuse of power arising from an improper motive. (As the main speech in *Wheeler* actually held it on the grounds of procedural impropriety, this is an interesting, though very common, example of slippage in the use of precedent.) He refuses even to consider the detailed evidence produced by the plaintiffs to suggest irrationality, and politely reprimands the judge at first instance for 'giving more attention to the detailed arguments as to the financial consequences of the guidance than they were strictly entitled to receive'. There is a lingering unwillingness to give up the courts' potential power even here. Scarman is very careful to limit the freedom implied by the test he proposes to situations where it is the unfairness of the policy consequence that is complained of. His suggested test is indeed put in terms of what would justify such an investigation of the evidence:

Such an examination by a court would be justified only if a prima facie case were to be shown for holding that the Secretary of State had acted in bad faith, or for an

[28] *Notts. CC* at 204.

improper motive, or that the consequences of his guidance were so absurd that he must have taken leave of his senses.[29]

Because of Parliament's own involvement in approving the annual report, he adds one further branch to the test—that Parliament would have to be shown to be misled, where the minister has 'to put it bluntly, deceived the House'. Obviously if the House has been deceived, then parliamentary sovereignty would not be challenged—Parliament cannot have intended something it did only because it had been lied to. Scarman is crafting the opinion with great care so as to surrender as little potential curial power as possible—he goes on to say the courts could rule:

that a minister has acted unlawfully if he has erred in law as to the limits of his power even when his action has the approval of the House of Commons, itself not acting legislatively but within the limits set by a statute.

This is a necessary limitation, otherwise it would not have been possible for the councils to make the argument from statutory construction that Bridge deals with. It is also clear evidence of how careful Scarman was being to limit the scope of his ruling. It does, after all, imply that Parliament, though required to approve a report, can do so without realizing that it is going against its own intention. Anyone who has sat on committees in the real world is familiar with the role of the secretary pointing out to the committee that it is ignoring its own general policy statement at some earlier meeting, and it is presumably this reality which Scarman would point to in reserving to the courts this escape from '*Super Wednesbury*'. The speech in *Nottinghamshire CC* can be seen in several different lights. It is, on the one hand, a clear-cut acceptance that, constitutionally, public expenditure is a matter for Parliament. It is a carefully crafted restriction on the courts, but it is more remarkable for its limitations on that restriction, rather than as a restriction. All it really does is to recognize that certain types of acts, where Parliament takes on itself an unusual degree of supervision of the executive, cannot be brought within the courts' ambit. In many ways the problem is actually caused by the all-pervasiveness of *Wednesbury*. As a stand-alone constitutional doctrine on the division of powers *Nottinghamshire CC* would be unremarkable, or even, perhaps, remarkably restrictive on the executive. But cast in the language of *Wednesbury*, from which the courts cannot seem to free themselves, it is potentially dangerous. Because, whether labelled '*Super Wednesbury*' or not, there is nothing to stop other courts using its doctrine that administrative decisions are safe unless taken in bad faith or 'irrationality to the point of lunacy' to allow other decision makers far too great a leniency. For better or worse, these three cases largely represent current

---

[29] *Notts. CC* at 202.

doctrine on judicial control of the State, though they may not at all well represent the reality of how the Lords will, when they see a chance outside the doctrine, impose their views. This we turn to now.

2. The Lords at Their More Adventurous

One possible theory about the House of Lords when it deals with clashes between the State and its citizens on issues touching fundamental rights is that their apparent bowing to the executive really is enforced by the *Wednesbury* doctrine, and that when they find a case that lies outside those very restrictive walls, they are a good deal more responsive to a 'rights' orientation. One may still ask why, if this is so, they do not make greater efforts to amend *Wednesbury*, or whether or not the doctrine, whatever they think of it intellectually, produces results in accord with a set of pragmatic managerial values, as their record in certain policy areas suggests. For example did *CSSU* really depend on their Lordships' sympathy with the difficulties of civil servants managing complex institutions when unions get in their way? Was *Brind*, at least for Templeman and Bridge, largely the result of the sheer exasperation of sensible men with journalists complaining about trivia? Often in the less dramatic cases this sense of empathy with hard-pressed administrators trying to do their job comes across strongly, as the next two chapters show. However, there are good examples of the Lords being far stronger against the executive where they seem to wish to. We discuss four main cases in this section, three of them quite recent. There are others like this, and indeed in some *Wednesbury* technically applies, but these are also reserved for the next chapter because of their subject matter—what may roughly be called 'liberty of the person'. What we discuss here are broader issues that can properly be called 'constitutional'.

Our thesis is roughly as follows. First, that the Law Lords do, in an important way, hold to a core principle of the British Constitution, the supremacy of Parliament, and that this has an absolutely determinant force. Much of the time they see this supremacy as delegated—to a minister or a local authority imbued with discretionary power—and wherever they do find that a case involves a delegation of supremacy, they absolutely will not intervene. This is what is meant by much judicial discussion on discretion. Unclarity arises, however, because the discretion attributed to the State is of two kinds, only one of which fits the delegated supremacy model, but both of which are covered by *Wednesbury* and other public law doctrines. Full policy discretion refers to the making of value judgement choice—the belief that the governance of the country in some area be carried out with acknowledged costs to be borne by some to provide intended benefits for others or for the common good. Basically the courts accept, in the language of political theory, that these are 'essentially contested concepts', though they are prone to describe the matter in phrases like the oft quoted one of Lord Diplock's from *Secretary of State for Education* v. *Tameside Metropolitan Borough*. This is itself a case, discussed briefly later, which can be read in several different ways depending on one's prior sense of what the judges are about. There Diplock asserts that:

The very concept of administrative discretion involves a right to choose between more than one possible course of action on which there is room for reasonable people to hold differing opinion as to which is to be preferred.[30]

Administrative discretion is also granted, however, in a narrower sense. Parliament usually sets some limits to discretion. It may require certain conditions to be present or absent, it may require certain matters to be taken into consideration, statute may imply or state situations which have to exist before an agency is even entitled to consider acting, or prohibit action under some other conditions. Are these matters, the restricting conditions, to be assessed only by the executive? If they are assessed by the executive, may the courts not check on that assessment? There is no reason that the strong sense of delegated power to make the ultimate value choice need imply unfettered discretion as to the conditions.

It does not follow from any basic principle of our constitution that such discretion is outwith the courts' competence, because it is not in a direct way a delegated supremacy. The courts often say that they are not competent to remake the first type of discretionary decision even where they disagree with the executive. This may be. But their claim, made equally often, that they are less capable than the executive of the second type of assessment is shallow, because they do it all the time in other contexts, and find pretexts to do it in public law cases when they wish to. The record of the Lords in policing this narrower sense of discretion is the subject of the next two chapters. For the rest of this chapter we are dealing with two questions. How do the Lords handle the fully constitutional matters where parliamentary sovereignty, delegated or direct, is in focus? Secondly though, we have to note another matter. Where the central guiding principle of a constitution is that of parliamentary sovereignty, where political decisions are all inherently contestable, that parliament exists in a world of radical freedom. It is part of our essentially Hobbesian constitution that the 'Crown in Parliament' may do no wrong. What happens in such a world where parliament has not spoken? What happens, according to the Lords, is that we inhabit an almost Hobbesian state of nature. The Lords sometimes admit this, especially when they contrast other countries governed by constitutional codes, and particularly when drawing a

[30] *Secretary of State for Education* v. *Tameside MBC* [1976] 3 All ER 665 at 695.

contrast between the way common law answers questions where legislation does not cover, and the way such questions would be handled if the European Convention on Human Rights applied fully in this country. This orientation shows particularly when the Lords discuss fundamental rights such as freedom of expression, which we turn to later. Thus Goff in one freedom of speech case says of the Convention that it:

in accordance with its avowed purpose, proceeds to state a fundamental right and then to qualify it, we in this country (where everyone is free to do anything, subject only to the provisions of the law) proceed rather upon an assumption of freedom of speech, and turn to our law to discover the established exceptions to it.[31]

Browne-Wilkinson made a very similar argument in defence of Leicester RFC's common law freedom of speech in *Wheeler*. This raises quite a serious problem because the common law seen against this view would seem to be without any generative capacity, without any guidelines, yet the Lords not only frequently state their faith in it as the repository of the Englishman's hallowed rights, but indeed have to use it to control the executive at what amounts to a constitutional level where Parliament is silent. When doing this, they do nothing but implement their own values in the ways shown in the chapter on negligence, and more generally in Chapter 4 on common law methodology. Of course the reliance on parliamentary sovereignty is usually hollow, given the democratic deficit of the British system imposed by party discipline and executive dominance in Parliament. The Law Lords are not ignorant of this. Our discussion of the new interpretation doctrine in *Pepper* v. *Hart* shows their open acceptance that, for interpretation purposes, Parliament intends what the Government front bench says. They seldom openly admit to this hollowness, but it does come out, especially when they are attempting to exert common law control of the executive. Because then, of course, the Lords need to remove the legitimacy of Parliament from the executive. Thus Lord Goff, always one of the more open of judges, gives one of the clearest admissions of the democratic deficit in a case where the Lords changed common law doctrine to prevent the unjust enrichment of the Inland Revenue:

I fear that, however compelling the principle of justice may be, it would never be sufficient to persuade a government to propose its legislative recognition by Parliament; caution, otherwise known as the Treasury, would never allow this to happen.[32]

Where Parliament is involved, however slightly, the Lords can always take this as a complete block to their right to intervene in the executive's decisions. For example, in *Brind* Lord Ackner prayed in aid of the argu-

[31] *A.-G.* v. *Guardian Newspapers (No. 2)* [1990] 1 AC 109 at 283.
[32] *Woolwich Equitable Building Society* v. *Inland Revenue Com'rs.* [1993] AC 70 at 176.

ment that the Secretary of State was not acting irrationally the fact that there had been supportive speeches in both Houses of Parliament; in *Ex parte Nottinghamshire* the fact that the annual rates support report was presented to Parliament was decisive in establishing the *Super Wednesbury* standards that required bad faith before judicial involvement. The fact that actual involvement by the members of the House of Commons is usually fictional can make parliamentary involvement as an argumentative token somewhat unpredictable, as we shall shortly see. However, that same doctrine can, when the Lords so wish, be quite fatal to ministerial discretion. Thus if Parliament has delegated its supremacy elsewhere than to a minister, the minister may find himself quite without protection and deprived of help from the courts. The classic case here, from which the Diplock quote used earlier comes, dates from the seventies. A Labour Secretary of State tried to intervene to stop a newly elected Conservative council, in Tameside, from stopping dead their predecessors' plans to comprehensivize secondary education, even though the detailed comprehensive plan was due to go into effect only a few months after the local government elections. The Secretary of State (ironically Roy Jenkins, later one of the 'gang of four' who split the Labour party only four years later) attempted to use his reserve powers under the 1944 Education Act to stop a hastily constructed new plan of selection and order the implementation of the original comprehensive policy. He claimed that it was unreasonably disruptive and educationally unwise to reverse the plans in such a hurry, and he relied on what would seem, prima facie, a very strong grant of supervisory powers in section 68 of the 1944 Act:

If the Secretary of State is satisfied . . . that any local authority . . . are proposing to act unreasonably with respect to the exercise of any power conferred or the performance of any duty imposed by or under this Act, he may, notwithstanding any enactment rendering the exercise of the power or the performance of any duty contingent upon the opinion of the authority . . . give such directions as to the exercise of the power or the performance of the duty as appear to him to be expedient.[33]

There can be no doubt at all that a grant of supervisory power in this form could be taken to be absolute. Wilberforce admits so directly: 'The section is framed in a "subjective" form—if the Secretary of State "is satisfied". This form of section is quite well known, and at first sight might seem to exclude judicial review.' Had the case involved anything to do with national security, or probably national economic policy, the whole tenor of *Brind, CCSU,* and *Ex parte Nottinghamshire* would surely seem to imply victory for the Government—especially as the new tide in public law some claim to discern had hardly started at that time. But in fact, for subtle

---

[33] *Tameside* at 681.

and complicated reasons, Wilberforce and his fellow Lords find no difficulty at all in making the test quite different. Here, the Secretary of State is required to be *correct* in his assessment of the various facts—it is not enough that there was material on which he *could* come to the conclusion that the local authority was behaving unreasonably. Or, which amounts to the same thing, 'no reasonable man could be satisfied that no reasonable authority on the evidence could take the view that . . . [the new council's policy would work]'. There was absolutely no deference to the usual idea that it is up to the executive to assess facts—the Lords themselves made an overt judgement of the credibility of his claim that the council was acting unreasonably by themselves assessing the conflicting affidavit evidence—something they would usually absolutely refuse to do on the grounds that it was outwith their expertise. What they were doing was treating the Secretary of State as though he was in the position plaintiffs try to put the court into when appealing against a council's decision, and refusing to allow him to exercise the powers they refuse to themselves. This they did even though section 68 in general seems entirely apt to allow the assessments of the education authorities to be overruled—the section after all contains the words 'notwithstanding any enactment rendering the exercise of the power or the performance of any duty contingent upon the opinion of the authority'.

The ways in which the Lords manage to persuade themselves that the Secretary of State's power was not 'subjective' are intellectually fascinating but irrelevant here, except for two aspects. The first is that the 1944 Act does clearly give the local education authorities the primary job of deciding what system was necessary and appropriate in their area—there was a delegation of supremacy in the strong sense, but not to the minister. The second was the political factor—the Lords stressed that the Secretary of State and his government colleagues have a political preference for comprehensive education, and that the voters of Tameside can be seen to have rejected precisely this. As Wilberforce again says, 'the authority—this is vital—is itself elected'. The *Tameside* case can perfectly well be interpreted as one where the Lords made a political choice. That was unavoidable. Comprehensive education was a very conflictual issue in British politics at the time, and the Lords could not but come down on one or other side of an openly acknowledged policy fight. In contrast, in cases like *Brind* and *CCSU* the anti-government side could hardly be seen to be politically powerful or popular. What is important for our purposes is the way Tameside is clear evidence that major executive power plays can be thwarted, in the name precisely of this supremacy of elected representatives. The crucial factor here was that there was no legislative statement in favour of comprehensive education. The 1944 Act, as the Lords carefully point out, was passed by the war-time coalition Government and expressed no preference for any type of secondary education. There was a Bill going through Parliament at the time which would express such a preference, but the Lords were not going to let this pre-empt the existing expression of legislative supremacy—though there could be little doubt that the Commons would pass the Bill in due course. (This type of argument from local election mandate, however, only works when the Lords want it to, as witnessed by the famous 'Fares Fair' case, *GLC* v. *Bromley*.) The *Tameside* case is well known, and also some time ago, with a rather different generation of Law Lords. To show that this technique for turning parliamentary sovereignty against a minister is still fully available we next discuss a quite amazing example of its use, which came quite close to being the nearest a court has ever got in the UK to overturning legislation as unconstitutional.

I. The Executive Ignoring Legislation

Any view of the Lords as supine cannot withstand a careful look at a case innocuously titled *R* v. *Secretary of State for the Home Department, ex parte Fire Brigades Union*, from 1995. The case requires considerable precision in analysis, because, as so often happens, the result reached by a Law Lord depends very much on exactly what question he treats it as raising, and the two dissenters here, Lords Keith and Mustill, do not really answer the same question as the majority, Lord Browne-Wilkinson, who gave the main speech, and Lords Lloyd and Nicholls. The Divisional Court had supported the Home Secretary, and the Court of Appeal had split, with Bingham MR and Morritt LJ finding for the plaintiff unions, though for different reasons, and Hobhouse LJ dissenting. This variety of judicial opinion was commented on by Lord Mustill as evidence of the difficulty of the case. From our point of view it is, rather, evidence of the range of choices that could be made with equal plausibility. The case is difficult to present, because although the ultimate point of difference between the majority and minority is narrow, the speeches are incredibly rich with statements about the nature of public law and the proper role of the courts. Though they are often not strictly necessary to the decision, and some are clearly *obiter dicta*, that is, general judicial pronouncements without any precedential role, they are no less vital for us as indicators of judicial attitudes to the whole question of judicial intervention in political matters. Fortunately the facts at least are fairly simple. In 1964 the Labour Government introduced a scheme for compensation of those who suffered injury as a result of crime—the Criminal Injuries Compensation Scheme. It was organized to run as though the injured had been successful in a civil case, and damages were based on what someone could have expected to be awarded in tort. The scheme was never legislated—it was simply announced in both Houses of Parliament, and operated under the executive's residual prerogative powers, though the money for it was provided by specific votes in the Commons. In 1978 a Royal Commission recommended that the scheme be continued on the same basis of comparison with civil law damages, but be put on a statutory basis, so that the injured would actually have a legal right to compensation, rather than receiving, as with the prerogative scheme, *ex gratia* payments. Though it took ten years to come about, the recommendation was finally embodied as part of the Criminal Justice Act 1988. The Act was somewhat of an omnibus, covering many areas of criminal law. Certain parts of the Act were not scheduled to come into force the day the Act did; some had specified dates for their coming into force, but others, including the compensation scheme, were left for the Home Secretary to choose the starting date. Section 171 of the Act covered these arrangements, and that section itself did, naturally, come into force immediately. (The compensation scheme was contained in sections 108 to 117, and in Schedules 6 and 7.)

The compensation scheme had already proved to be expensive, and increasingly so; by 1984 the annual cost was £35 million, and the backlog of claims had reached 50,000. In fact the backlog may well have caused the problem, because the original reason for not bringing the statutory scheme into place soon after the Act was passed was the request by the Criminal Injuries Compensation Board to delay it to avoid interruption of their existing workload. As the statutory scheme was in all important ways the same as the prerogative scheme this must have seemed harmless and sensible. The Government of 1993, however, were both determined to reduce public expenditure, and clearly less sympathetic to the claimants. They announced in a White Paper that the old prerogative scheme was to be abandoned and replaced by a new one, still a prerogative scheme based on *ex gratia* payments, which would be much cheaper because it would seriously reduce the levels of payment. This was to be done by replacing the equation to civil law tort awards with a flat rate scheme. Not only was the amount assessed for each type of injury much less than in the old scheme, but the elements of compensation for pain and suffering and loss of earnings which the equation to civil damages provided were dropped completely. Obviously such a scheme would not only be different from the existing prerogative scheme, but it would be incompatible with the statutory scheme that had been passed in 1988 but never implemented. Several trade unions and other associations whose members were unusually likely in their work to be victims of criminal injuries therefore asked the Divisional Court for a declaration that the Home Secretary was abusing his powers in introducing the new scheme, and also for an order to bring the statutory scheme into effect.

One can identify the single sentence, in this instance from the White

Paper, which fuelled the Law Lords' attitude. The White Paper refers to the statutory scheme, saying: 'With the impending demise of the current scheme the provisions in the 1988 Act will not now be implemented. *They will accordingly be repealed when a suitable legislative opportunity occurs*'[34] (our emphasis). This seemed to some readers an incredible arrogance—it is Parliament, and not the executive, which repeals legislation. It was, as it were, acknowledging the 'democratic deficit' too openly. Even Lord Mustill, who found for the Home Secretary, agrees that 'The tone of the White Paper and of the utterances in Parliament can be presented as a defiance of the will of Parliament.'[35] But, he is insistent, it is a matter of 'Parliamentary practice, expectation and courtesy, not of public law'. In the same vein Lord Keith had insisted that if the Home Secretary was in breach of any duty, 'it may be a breach of a duty owed to Parliament, but that is a matter for Parliament to consider'. But for the majority it really was a legal red rag to a constitutional bull, though technically a mere sentence in a White Paper obviously could not constitute the argument. Lord Browne-Wilkinson was clearest: 'it is not for the executive . . . to state . . . that the provisions of the 1988 Act "will accordingly be repealed when a suitable legislative opportunity occurs". It is for Parliament, not the executive, to repeal legislation.'[36] This is where the problem of how one conceives of the Home Secretary's actions comes in.

There is a legal doctrine, known as the *De Keyser*[37] principle that while the Crown (for which one can read the government of the day) retains traditional prerogative powers in areas which legislation has never touched, such powers vanish once there has been legislation. The old scheme could be brought in by the Royal Prerogative, because it was entirely new and there had never been any form of State compensation for the victims of criminal assaults. As long as there remained no legislation, such schemes could be altered, replaced, or just abandoned, and no one could complain, because, as they consisted of *ex gratia* payments, no one had a legal right to any payment. This is how Lords Keith and Mustill, and Hobhouse LJ in his Court of Appeal dissent, saw the matter. All the Home Secretary was doing was acting in a legislative void, just as the Home Secretary of 1964 had done. If there was a duty to do anything else, it was a political duty, a duty to Parliament. As Keith has it, 'The fact that the decision is of a political and administrative character means that any interference by a court of law would be a most improper intrusion into a field which lies peculiarly within the province of Parliament', and 'to

[34] *Compensating Victims of Violent Crime: Changes to the Criminal Injuries Compensation Scheme*, (Cm. 2434), Dec. 1993, para. 39.
[35] R v. *Secretary of State for the Home Department, ex parte Fire Brigades Union* [1995] 2 All ER 244 at 264.
[36] *Ex Parte Fire Brigades Union* at 254.
[37] Developed in *A.-G. v. De Keyser's Royal Hotel Ltd.* [1920] AC 508.

grant the applicants the relief which they seek, or any part of it, would represent an unwarrantable intrusion by the court into the political field and a usurpation of the function of Parliament'.[38] This position depends on treating the statutory scheme in the 1988 Act, because it had never been brought into operation by the Home Secretary's decision, as though it had 'no legal significance of any kind' (Browne-Wilkinson's summary of the dissent in the Court of Appeal).

The majority of the Law Lords had a completely different sense of what the Home Secretary was doing. This is well summarized in Lord Lloyd's account of how a voter would see the issue:

It might cause surprise to the man on the Clapham Omnibus that legislative provisions in an Act of Parliament, which have passed both Houses of Parliament and received the Royal Assent, can be set aside in this way by a member of the executive. It is, after all, the normal function of the executive to carry out the laws which Parliament has passed, just as it is the normal function of the judiciary to say what those laws mean.[39]

Similarly Lord Browne-Wilkinson speaks of it as 'most surprising if, at the present day, prerogative powers could be validly exercised by the executive so as to frustrate the will of Parliament expressed in a statute . . .'. There is, inevitably, a good deal of hollowness in this outrage on behalf of Parliament. The Parliament which passed the 1988 Act had been replaced at the General Election of 1992, and as the minority pointed out, the new Parliament had already voted funds for the new scheme in the 1994 Appropriations Act. Indeed some time after the case Parliament passed a watered down version of the Home Secretary's plans. In truth there was probably more real parliamentary backing for the minister in this case than there usually is in those cases where the Law Lords defer to a largely imaginary 'parliamentary intent'. But in this case some of the Law Lords found it convenient to be outraged on behalf of Parliament. Certainly they thought the idea of parliamentary supremacy was enough, if they could show that the 1988 Act was somehow or other being flouted. There were some initial steps that had to be taken before this could be directly addressed, of which the most important was the question of the plaintiffs' standing. If the *ex gratia* scheme provided no legal entitlements, how did anyone get standing to sue? There was an attempt to argue that the Act conferred a right on members of the public to have the statutory scheme passed, but even the majority could not go that far, though Bingham in the Court of Appeal had so found as one of his alternative arguments on behalf of the Fire Brigades. One might jump over this point in analysing the political importance of the case but for the way it throws light on the

---

[38] *Ex parte Fire Brigades Union* at 247–8.
[39] *Ex parte Fire Brigades Union* at 269.

implications of an earlier decision that may, in fact, be more supportive of public law rights than we have earlier argued. Lord Browne-Wilkinson used *CCSU* to give the Fire Brigades Union standing, despite the fact that they had no legal rights to receive any payments. The Civil Service Unions had had no 'rights' to be consulted either, but Diplock had been very careful to assert that this did not matter, because they had, from prior practice, a 'legitimate expectation', and also that such legitimate expectations allowed judicial review over prerogative powers as well as statutory ones. Here, the absence of private law rights too is held not to matter because, as it is a public law case, there was a legitimate expectation that the existing scheme would not be scrapped for one inconsistent with the statutory scheme at that stage lying in legislative limbo. As the unions were never going to win in *CCSU*, it had never been technically necessary for Diplock to stress this point, and it is open to us to wonder whether *CCSU* was a case some of the Lords really would have liked to decide in another way, and, if so, whether they did not quite deliberately lay down stepping stones for future action.

With the standing point settled the disagreement narrows very sharply. None of the Law Lords were going to go so far as to issue an order to the Secretary of State to bring in the scheme. Section 171 simply says the scheme shall come into force 'on such a day as the Secretary of State shall appoint'. This cannot be turned by the courts into a requirement to do so at any specific time. No one denies that one prerogative scheme could, under the prerogative, and in the absence of legislation in force be altered or scrapped. So what has the Home Secretary done that flouts Parliamentary Supremacy? Obviously for the dissenters, the answer is nothing, and they spent a good deal of time insisting that the only way to disapprove of the Home Secretary's actions would be to make a completely inadmissible substantive judgement that he is just wrong. Lord Mustill, in fact, produces a new and extremely restrictive definition of administrative irrationality worth quoting as an indication of how far some of the Law Lords are from being prepared to intervene on what they see as policy decisions:

A claim that a decision under challenge was wrong leads nowhere, except in the rare case where it can be characterised as so obviously and grossly wrong as to be irrational, in the lawyers' sense of the word, and hence a symptom that there must have been a failure in the decision making process.

Though no such claim was attempted here, and the remark is simply obiter, it is noteworthy because it amounts to saying that even a grossly wrong decision is only wrong because of some procedural matter, and takes the courts away from the notion of a 'perverse' or 'immoral' decision as one that could be quashed for reason of perversity or immorality—this narrows *Wednesbury* rationality to vanishing point. Lord Keith effectively says that there is *no* general principle under which the Home Secretary's decision could be impugned, and that any attempt to do so would require separate legislative provision—that the Act itself would have had to authorize the courts to control the Home Secretary:

The first question for consideration is whether, by the terms of s. 171(1) of the Criminal Justice Act 1988, Parliament has evinced an intention to confer upon the courts an ability to oversee and control the exercise by the Secretary of State of the power thereby conferred on him to bring into effect [the statutory scheme], at the instance of persons who claim an interest in that being done.

This extremely passive view of the courts, along with his idea that there could be a duty owed to Parliament but not to members of the public was strongly criticized by Lord Lloyd. He felt it necessary to remind his colleagues that:

the duty of the court to review executive action does not depend on some power granted by Parliament in a particular case. It is part of the court's ordinary function in the day to day administration of justice . . . [in doing so the court] is not acting in opposition to the legislature or treading on Parliamentary toes. On the contrary: it is ensuring that the powers conferred by Parliament are exercised within the limits and for the purposes which Parliament intended.[40]

To highlight how strongly he feels, Lloyd shortly after says of the Government's argument 'I fear that it would, if accepted, put the clock back 30 years or more'. In this area Lloyd, then, is using the parliamentary supremacy argument, as we earlier discussed, against a minister. The majority had to chart a very careful course, given the minority's warnings and their own protestations of innocence. The core argument is this. The statute left it to the Home Secretary to bring in the scheme whenever he felt like it. (There had been an attempt to suggest that he had a duty to bring it in as soon as practicable, but though in the Court of Appeal Bingham MR seemed to agree with this, no one else felt that there could be a justiciable duty of such a nature.) So if there was no particular date, if indeed the Home Secretary would not be in breach of any duty to the public if he never brought the scheme in, what justiciable duty was there? All the Lords had to admit that the power to introduce a scheme when he thought fit must also mean that the policy context might change so much that it became pointless to establish the scheme. What the majority settled for was the idea that the Home Secretary was under a duty as far as the sections of the Act went 'to keep the question whether they should be brought into force under review', and that it was 'an abuse or excess of power for him to exercise the prerogative power in a manner inconsistent with that duty'. (Taken from the headnote to the case.) This seems, at first

---

[40] *Ex parte Fire Brigades Union* at 272.

sight, a very weak obligation indeed. Lord Mustill made a strong point about this weakness. He claimed that if that is the only duty, and a declaration ordering him to abide by the obligation all the court could do, then the Home Secretary could discharge the duty very simply. All the Home Secretary would have to do is to say that he had reviewed the matter, and he had decided not to do anything; he promised to keep on reviewing it, but he did not expect ever to have to change his mind. As Mustill says, 'Such a reply would in practice be impregnable, and for my part I would not be prepared as a matter of discretion to grant a relief so empty of content.' The fact that the White Paper said the scheme would not now be implemented and made the (perhaps improper) promise to repeal it when convenient Mustill brushes aside in the notion of a mere 'duty to Parliament', and not legitimately the stuff of judicial review.

In the end the difference between the majority and the dissenters comes down to a disagreement on a quasi-factual matter. Will the dismantling of the old prerogative scheme and the imposition of the new 'tariff' scheme, with its own administrative machinery, make it in practice impossible to bring in the statutory scheme? If so, the Home Secretary is abusing parliamentary supremacy, because he is deliberately making it impossible to carry out the duty imposed on him by the Act. Mustill and Keith understand the argument, and rely on a very literal approach. It cannot be said that the Home Secretary's actions will make it absolutely impossible to change his mind and carry out the statutory duty at some later date. Lord Keith insists that 'if a political decision were made to bring in the statutory scheme then there is no reason to suppose that the political will would not be found . . .'—the repetition of 'political' to describe the whole process—the word occurs twice more in the paragraph—being intended to underline the sense that the courts have no business trespassing here. Similarly Mustill dismisses the practical argument. 'The new scheme is not in tablets of stone'; it would be feasible to change 'just as it proved feasible to pull down the original scheme'; 'nothing is certain in politics'. Nothing the Home Secretary has done could prevent this; 'his words have no lasting effect, he has not put an end to the statutory scheme; only Parliament could do that'.

Such a literalist approach cannot, in a sense, be faulted, and it suits well the tenor of that whole approach to public law which distances the courts from facts, from assessing evidence, from any substantive decision except where the decision implies certifiable insanity. But such an approach also requires a deliberate blindness, and the majority, understandably, perhaps, spent little time on it. Lloyd is the most terse:

I regard this as little short of fanciful. Ministers must be taken at their word. If they say that they will not implement the statutory scheme, they are repudiating the power conferred on them by parliament in the clearest possible terms.

Lord Browne Wilkinson, who had already described any argument that gave the Home Secretary unfettered discretion in this context as 'not only constitutionally dangerous but flies in the face of common sense', puts the legal nature of the Home Secretary's act very clearly. Of course a situation could occur where it would become impossible or wrong to implement the statutory scheme:

> But if the power is conferred on the Secretary of State with a view to bringing the sections into force, in my judgment, the Secretary of State cannot himself procure events to take place and rely on the occurrence of those events as the ground for not bringing the statutory scheme into force. In claiming that the introduction of the new tariff scheme renders it undesirable now to bring the statutory scheme into force, the Secretary of State is, in effect, claiming that the purpose of the statutory power has been frustrated by his own act in choosing to introduce a scheme inconsistent with the statutory scheme approved by Parliament.[41]

The facts are stark. But should the Lords be taking note of the facts? Lord Nicholls is clear about this, admitting that the whole division between their Lordships is a factual one, but saying of the minority view 'it seems to me that such an evaluation of the facts is detached from reality'. By this we can fairly take the view that the factual nature of the debate is largely a matter of scene setting, a contrivance to bring into judicial play the real 'fact' which is that the Home Secretary's White Paper demonstrated an indifference to the rules by which Parliamentary Supremacy works as a constitutional theory. No one doubts that Parliament, by which we can only mean the majority, has no choice but to let the Home Office have its way. What the Lords are doing is not so much protecting Parliament's interests as forcing them to have their interests protected. One is struck by a deep inconsistency between this decision and that in *Pepper* v. *Hart*, because the latter effectively relaxed the protection of a notional parliament in favour of an outright acceptance of executive power. There is no fully convincing way of explaining why the Lords will sometimes make such a major effort to protect the main thrust of the constitution and yet so often will allow the executive its way. There is, though, a hint at why they do not do it more often in a most unusual, very revealing, but also perhaps rather alarming, codicil to Mustill's speech. Mustill starts, admirably, by being far blunter about what we have called the 'democratic deficit' than is usual from the Lords. Having rehearsed the usual division of labour between the courts and Parliament in checking the legislature he admits:

> In recent years, however, the employment in practice of these specifically Parliamentary remedies has on occasion been perceived as falling short, and sometimes well short, of what was needed to bring the performance of the executive into line with the law and with the minimum standards of fairness implicit in every

[41] *Ex parte Fire Brigades Union* at 253.

Parliamentary delegation of a decision-making function. To avoid a vacuum in which the citizen would be left without protection against a misuse of executive powers the courts have had no option but to occupy the dead ground in a manner, and in areas of public life, which could not have been foreseen 30 years ago.

One way of seeing the case then is to contrast Lord Lloyd, who thinks the minority would be putting the clock back thirty years, with Lord Mustill who thinks he is protecting thirty years of improvement. Many writers on public law would have found it extremely useful had Mustill given examples of the failures in the system he had in mind. Those less impressed than the judges seem to be with their own record of the last thirty years— a period of time frequently referred to—would have found it even more useful to have a list of the leading 'occupations of dead ground'. Nonetheless Mustill's statement sounds most like a very powerful reason to join with the majority. So why dissent? There is a school of thought amongst commentators on the English judges that they are acutely aware of the role as restricted to the classic 'art of the possible', and that they actively fear that the executive might take steps to remove all judicial review powers were they to go too far.[42] This fear may lie behind an interesting point in a public lecture by Lord Woolf (before he became Master of the Rolls) in which he suggests that an attempt to cut down judicial review would be a situation where the courts would not be bound by parliamentary sovereignty. Though Mustill never quite admits to such a fear as the reason for supporting the Home Secretary in the *Fire Brigades* case he comes very close indeed to doing so. His speech continues with a statement of support for the thirty years of judicial activism, but adds this warning:

Nevertheless it has its risks, of which the courts are well aware. As the judges themselves constantly remark, it is not they who are appointed to administer the country. Absent a written constitution much sensitivity is required of the parliamentarian, administrator and judge if the delicate balance of the unwritten rules evolved (I believe successfully) in recent years is not to be disturbed, and all the recent advances undone. . . . some of the arguments addressed would have the court push to the very boundaries of the distinction between court and Parliament established in, and recognised ever since, the Bill of Rights 1688. Three hundred years have been passed since then, and the political and social landscape has changed beyond recognition. But the boundaries remain; they are of crucial significance to our private and public lives; and the courts should, I believe, make sure they are not overstepped.[43]

But, of course, the Parliament of 1688 had not become the party-disciplined rubber stamp that many think it is today.

---

[42] Joshua Rosenberg, the BBC Legal Correspondent and legal journalist, who has an unusual degree of familiarity with senior judges, has argued this on several occasions.
[43] *Ex parte Fire Brigades Union* at 268.

II. Protecting the Authority of the Court

If *Ex parte Fire Brigades Union* was a strong statement, by the courts, of Parliament's supremacy, *Re M*[44] from 1993 shows them very directly defending their own position in the separation of powers. Though the result of the case is of undoubted importance, it need take little time here because the Lords were quite unanimous. Perhaps because of this the sole full speech, by Lord Woolf, though a masterly treatment of legal history, contains little of interest to us, unlike the rich veins of political theory contained in the speeches in the previous case. The facts are enormously confusing—part of the problem was that several main actors in the story were very confused about both events and legal powers, but a simplified version will suffice here. M was a citizen of Zaïre who entered Britain in 1990 seeking political asylum. His claim was rejected as was his application for judicial review to challenge the rejection. On 1 May 1991 he was told he was about to be removed to Zaïre, and on the same day he made a second unsuccessful application for judicial review. Still determined to stay, and still on 1 May, M, now represented by new lawyers, made a third application, claiming new evidence and that his previous solicitors had incompetently failed to produce it. The judge hearing this third application wished to delay his decision by a day and asked that M's departure be postponed. He thought that counsel for the Home Office gave him such an undertaking. Counsel, as it transpired later, did not realize he had been so understood and did not intend to give a complete undertaking (the Home Office solicitor was at that very moment trying to contact the Home Office to stop M being put on the plane). The Home Office managed neither to take him off his plane, nor to intercept his journey to Zaïre, even though he had a stopover of several hours in Paris, and even though they knew by then of the requested undertaking. In the middle of the night the judge, when told of this, issued an order to the Home Secretary requiring him to return M, though the order also gave him leave to appeal the next morning, 2 May, for leave to discharge the order. The Home Office initially made arrangements to fly M back on the evening of 2 May, but did nothing immediately. By the time the Home Secretary was finally told about all of this personally it was the afternoon of the 2nd. He decided to cancel the return arrangements, both because he was convinced the original decision on asylum was correct, and because his legal advisers told him the judge had no jurisdiction to make the order, so that rather than obeying it, he could just request that it be discharged. When, on 3 May, the Home Office finally asked for the order to be discharged the judge accepted that he had no authority to make an injunction against an officer of the Crown, and discharged it. M was told he was not needed for a court

[44] *Re M* [1994] 1 AC 377.

appearance in London, and has never been heard of again. (It was part of his claim for asylum that he was in danger of persecution in Zaïre, from where he had been smuggled out on a false passport because of his trade union activities.) M's lawyers attempted committal proceedings against the Home Secretary in person as well as the Home Office, and though they lost in the court of first instance, the Court of Appeal held that the Home Secretary was guilty of contempt of court.

The core issue was whether or not a court can issue an injunction against the Crown or one of its officers, and secondly whether the usual method for enforcing an injunction, a finding of contempt of court with consequent punishment, could be used against such an officer of the Crown. The Home Office was doubtless as indifferent to M's welfare, and as heavy-handed as it usually is to asylum seekers. (The note taken by the Home Secretary's private secretary, at the meeting referred to, records that they were unwilling to bring M back because if they did so it would involve giving him a visa, and then 'it would be very difficult to remove him if, as was expected, we won the case'.) Nonetheless there appears to have been no intentional villainy—the Home Office was certainly not eager to accept the intervention of the courts, but the advice the Home Secretary acted on—that a court could not issue an injunction against the Crown—seems to have accorded with the professional consensus until the Lords themselves decided otherwise in this very case. After all both High Court judges, Garland J who issued the initial order, and Simon Brown J in the committal proceedings against the Home Secretary, thought there had been no such power, and the Court of Appeal was split. Simon Brown, now in the Court of Appeal, would be regarded by most as one of the more active and assertive public law judges. Thus the Home Secretary probably was obeying the law as well as he could at the time. The main problem is almost a linguistic one by now, the traditional English doctrine of political legitimacy: 'the Crown can do no wrong'. (And hence cannot be sued in its own courts.) No modern State could possibly really believe, or certainly could publicly admit to believing, that the State was above the law in this sense, yet there was heavy enough a weight of precedents to force any court below the Lords to accept the doctrine. Furthermore there was a relatively recent case which seemed, with a very odd consequence, to support the general idea that courts could not make mandatory orders against the Government. This is a 1989 case known as *Factortame*. Here an injunction had been sought to force the Government not to bring into operation a UK statute which the plaintiffs claimed breached their rights under European Union law. The Lords had initially refused to grant an injunction though the substantive issue itself was being sent up to the European Court of Justice, on the grounds that it had no such power. That question was also referred. Did the UK courts have a duty to make a temporary restraining order against the Government while the ECJ considered the substantive matter? The ECJ insisted they should. So by the time M's case came along there had come about what Lord Woolf described as 'the unhappy situation' ... that a citizen could get an injunction to protect[45] his Community law interests but not his English law interests.

Lord Woolf found no particular difficulty in 'distinguishing' *Factortame*, and in explaining away the cases that seemed to back up the tradition of a Crown, and therefore a Government, that was above the law. The fact is that the Lords had very much more reason to 'discover' that there was a power of injunction in *M* than they had in *Factortame*. The injunction power had to be found to exist, otherwise the contempt power did not exist, and the Home Office would be in a position virtually to ignore the court, something that, of all Departments of State, it might well feel inclined to do at times. *Factortame* was a clash between English and European law, and was a case pressed by foreign economic interests against legislation intended to protect English interests. *M* was a case about the interests of the courts themselves, and a logically necessary step. The whole language of 'the Crown' has increasingly come into dispute amongst legal thinkers, including Lord Woolf himself in an extrajudicial context, and the case provided a perhaps needed opportunity to make some strong statements about the respective role of the courts and the executive in a rare context where there was no need for the defensiveness usually found. One of the more powerful statements has already been cited above, from the then Lord Justice Nolan to the effect that 'the executive will respect all decisions of the courts as to what its province is'.[46] Here, of course, it was still possible to rely on parliamentary supremacy. Indeed it was necessary to rely on Parliament here, as Lord Woolf did, to sort out the tricky question of what the courts could have done if the Home Secretary ignored a contempt finding:

> The Crown's relationship with the courts does not depend on coercion and in the exceptional situation when a government's conduct justifies this, a finding of contempt should suffice ... It will then be for Parliament to determine what should be the consequences of that finding.[47]

Whether this is a very safe reliance is unclear, but it avoids the famous American situation of President Andrew Jackson's reaction to a Supreme Court decision: 'John Marshall has made his decision, now let him enforce it!' The case clearly is very important. One academic commentator has said of it that it was 'a great loss to the government', primarily because it

---

[45] *R v. Secretary of State for Transport, ex parte Factortame Ltd.* [1990] 2 AC 85.
[46] Nolan LJ in *M v. Home Office* [1992] QB 270 at 314.
[47] *In re M* at 466.

'established the law of remedies in a way that no government would have allowed in legislation'.[48] The whole tenor of the case is best set by a quotation from Templeman's very short speech, which could almost have been written as a response to Mustill's conclusion in *Ex parte Fire Brigades Union*. Powerful though this is, it is also characteristic of the cautious methodology of public law, because Templeman's vision is of a rule that has always been in existence, rather than one that perfectly clearly was created, against the consensus that the Lords' own rulings in previous years had shored up. But here is a classic piece of Templeman prose:

My Lords, the argument that there is no power to enforce the law by injunction or contempt proceedings against a minister in his official capacity would, if upheld, establish the proposition that the executive obey the law as a matter of grace and not as a matter of necessity, a proposition which would reverse the result of the Civil War.

III. The Limit to Parliamentary Supremacy

There is, of course, one restriction nowadays to the doctrine of Parliamentary Supremacy, which is the undisputed supremacy of European Union legislation over Acts of the UK Parliament. Constitutionally there is no problem here—the right of British courts to impose this European supremacy depends itself on a UK Act, the European Communities Act 1972. What the UK's membership does, however, is to present UK courts with a problem when they are asked to consider a complaint that the Government is failing to carry out duties under European legislation. The duty in question might imply that they must modify their own relevant UK legislation. Whatever critics may make of the Lords' public law performance in some areas, it has a more or less perfect record of obedience to rulings of the European Court of Justice. It also has, and this may be more surprising, a very good track record when it comes to interpreting UK legislation in all areas of equality of opportunity and anti-discrimination. Consequently one recent ruling hated by Eurosceptic circles ought not really to be a surprise, though it demonstrates one very useful point for us. This is the famous 1994 case, *Equal Opportunities Commission* v. *Secretary of State for Employment*[49] where the Law Lords upheld a request from the Equal Opportunities Commission (EOC) for a declaration that UK legislation was discriminating against women in its treatment of part-time workers. Though there was a dissent in the case, by Lord Jauncey, the dissent cannot be said to stand for a principled rejection of the general position. (Jauncey dissented because he disagreed with the

[48] M. Gould, '*M v the Home Office*: Government and the Judges', *Public Law*, 1993, pp. 568–78.
[49] *Equal Opportunities Commission* v. *Secretary of State for Employment* [1994] 1 All ER 910.

majority on whether the EOC could have standing to bring a case against the very Secretary of State they were set up to advise and counsel.) The majority brushed aside Jauncey's concerns, as well as other possible but highly procedural barriers. Indeed the only reason Lords Browne-Wilkinson and Lowry added speeches of their own in support of Lord Keith was to use the case as a vehicle to remove these other possible barriers to judicial activism. Consequently we need only concern ourselves with Keith's speech. It is worth noting immediately the fact that here we have Lord Keith trouncing the same Government he had so staunchly tried to defend in the *Fire Brigades Union* case. Nor is his support for the EOC here to be interpreted as a result of a personal strong EuroFederalist position—he is fairly well known to be rather negative about Brussels. Thus the case stands as a strong warning against any automatic categorizations of the judges. In all probability Keith found as he did in this case simply because he thought that was what the law required—nothing in the thesis of this book denies that such events happen. We are concerned only to stress how voluntary it is for a judge to decide a case simply because of his view of the law. The case resolves itself very rapidly therefore to what became not even a matter of interpretation, but a straightforward clash between the Secretary of State's economic theories and the court's assessment of evidence about them. The issue is familiar from current political debates. European Union legislation from the Treaty of Rome onwards has always sought to remove pay differentials made on a gender basis, and includes in this ban 'indirect discrimination'. Indirect discrimination comes about when a distinction is drawn on some ground other than gender, but which has a gender discriminatory effect because a differential proportion of men and women are covered by the discriminating factor. UK employment legislation, the Employment Protection (Consolidation) Act 1978 requires part-time workers to be employed for five years, but full-time workers for only two years before they become entitled to various redundancy and related benefits. The great majority of full-time workers (more than sixteen hours per week) are men, and the great majority of part-time workers (between eight and sixteen hours per week) are women. There is therefore an indirect discrimination, and unless this can be shown to be 'objectively' justifiable by factors unrelated to sex, the pattern is breach of clear European Union legislation.[50] The EOC, which is charged under the legislation setting it up '(a) to work towards the elimination of discrimination; (b) to promote equality of opportunity between men and women generally . . .'[51] wrote to the Secretary of State for Employment asking him to review the matter urgently,

[50] Particularly Art. 119 of the EEC Treaty and Council Directives 75/117/EEC and 76/207/EEC.

[51] Sex Discrimination Act 1975, s. 53(1).

and to inform the EOC whether the Government would be willing to introduce the necessary legislation to remove the discrimination inherent in the 1978 Act, giving reasons if he was not prepared to. In order to make sense of Lord Keith's ruling one needs to know the text of the Government's reply to the EOC, which he quotes in his speech:

[We do not accept that] statutory redundancy pay and statutory compensation for unfair dismissal constitute 'pay' within the meaning of Article 119 . . . or . . . that they fall within the equal treatment directive . . . we believe that our current statutory thresholds are entirely justifiable. These thresholds have existed in one form or another ever since employment protection legislation was first introduced. Their purpose is to ensure that a fair balance is struck between the interests of employers and employees. We have no plans to change the thresholds.[52]

The 'definition of pay' issue was dispensed with as easily as the procedural matters. The Lords did not even bother to refer the question to the European Court of Justice for clarification, even thought they admitted that the matter had not been resolved at the European level. Instead they are happy to assert that if compensation for unfair dismissal is carried out on a discriminatory basis, this is unfair in itself. The case law of the European Court of Justice involves a grant of power to courts in member states that one might have thought an English court would be unhappy to have, because the ECJ has insisted that the core question of whether an indirect discrimination is justified by objective factors is a question that the national courts themselves must answer. 'It is for the national court which has sole jurisdiction to assess the facts and interpret the national legislation to determine . . . [such indirect discrimination] is justified by reasons which are objective and unrelated to any discrimination on grounds of sex'.[53] Yet so much of what we have discussed and continue to discuss in the rest of this book shows English courts shying away from such substantive judgments. Here, however, the English courts have no choice but to undertake the sort of policy evaluation that they so often claim to be quite incompetent to handle. They cannot escape these duties towards the ECJ by hiding behind '*Super Wednesbury*'—although the policy problem is in no way simpler than the one Scarman rejected in *Nottinghamshire*. The legal texts seems to be very little help in interpreting the concept of 'a criterion which is objective and unrelated to any discrimination related to sex', so the Lords would seem to have a pretty free hand. The ECJ's caseload provides only one legal example of policy discrimination in a German case which is not very helpful. German legislation had restricted part-time workers' rights to sick pay, and had justified this on

---

[52] *EOC* at 916–17.
[53] *Rinner-Kühn* v. *FWW Spezial-Gebaüdereinigung GmbH & Co. KG* Case 171/88 [1989] ECR 2743 at 2760–1.

the grounds that such workers were not 'as integrated in or as dependent on, the undertaking employing them as other workers'. The ECJ, before insisting that it was a matter for the national courts, had commented only as far as follows:

those considerations, in so far as they are only generalisations about certain categories of workers, do not enable criteria which are both objective and unrelated on any discrimination on grounds of sex to be identified. However, if the Member State can show that the means chosen meet a necessary aim of its social policy and that they are suitable and requisite for attaining that aim, the mere fact that the provision affects a much greater number of female workers than male workers cannot be regarded as an infringement of Article 119.

The British Government would appear to have at least a slightly better defence than this, because they claimed the discrimination was necessary to increase employment, because employers would not take on as many part-time workers if they had to carry these indirect labour costs and, by implication, would not replace them with full-time workers in any great number. (The court may well have been influenced by the fact that this seems to be a second thought by the Department of Employment—the reason given to the EOC in answer to their request was a different one, as Keith notes.) Accepting that it is both a 'beneficial' and a 'necessary social policy aim' to increase the amount of part-time work available, Lord Keith stresses that the question, nonetheless, is whether the threshold provisions in the 1978 Act 'have been shown by reference to objective factors to be suitable and requisite for achieving that aim.[54] *Wednesbury* is not available, so the Lords cannot argue, as they surely would have done otherwise, that it was not actually perverse to think cheaper part-time workers means more of them, and thus the Government must be left alone. Indeed the burden of evidence was clearly against the Government. The Lords were forced to evaluate the evidence submitted by the Government and the contradictory material provided by the EOC. 'Evaluate' is a rather strong word to describe what Lord Keith actually does in the mere page and a half of the Law Reports that it takes for him to settle the question. The first step is very simple. He points out that it would be even simpler if part-time workers got a lower basic rate than full-timers, and that there is no legitimate distinction between direct and indirect costs. He then asserts that such a policy 'would surely constitute a gross breach of the principle of equal pay and could not possibly be regarded as a suitable means of achieving an increase in part-time employment'. This is an admirably neat way of dealing with the matter, but the idea that one cannot distinguish between direct and indirect labour costs is not so self-evident as to force itself upon the court. The approach is entirely a judicial

---

[54] *EOC* at 922.

choice of description in order to get a particular result. Indeed it should be regarded as begging the question, because we are given no discussion at all of what range of matters can be regarded as 'suitable'. Lord Keith then goes on to deal with whether the Government has proved that the policy is 'requisite' to achieve the aim. Here we really are in the thick of a serious macro-economic debate, and the Lords express no anxiety at all in acting as an Economic Referee. Their answer, of course, was 'No'. Various statistics are quoted. For example—the French used to have a similar threshold, dropped it, and yet part-time employment increased over the next few years by more than it did in Britain. Or, The Netherlands and Denmark each have over 25 per cent of their workforce in part-time work and do not have similar thresholds. Ireland has just dropped similar thresholds. But Lord Keith merely comments: 'While various explanations were suggested on behalf of the Secretary of State for these statistics, there is no means of ascertaining whether these explanations have any validity.' The affidavit and published research evidence submitted by the two sides revealed, unsurprisingly, that employers' organizations supported the thresholds as helping provide employment, and trade unions 'and some academics in the industrial relations field' took the opposite view. This (our paraphrase in not much shorter than Keith's original) is enough. 'The conclusion must be that no objective justification for the thresholds in the 1978 Act has been established.'

It may well be that the case was one of the worst argued by government counsel in history. Quite probably they were astonished that the court insisted on reviewing the evidence at all. Nothing in the Law Lords' recent history can have prepared them for such a decision. Their decision may be right—we have no idea how a headcount of professional economists would decide the matter. Their decision cannot be seen as a usurpation by the judiciary of someone else's authority—the ECJ is quite clear about the courts' duty here. What is so unusual about the case is that the Lords could so easily have avoided the conclusion they came to. There is no appeal from the Lords in this situation, so had they decided for the Government, the EOC could not have taken it further. Thus the Lords were not just bowing to the inevitable on the assumption that the ECJ would find against the UK Government. They were the judge of fact of last resort. The ECJ's own jurisprudence would have precluded them from overruling the House of Lords on the all-important national scene aspect. The Lords need not have decided as they did. They could so very easily have supported a main plank of government policy and did not. There was no substantive dissent. Yet three of the Lords on the panel, Keith, Jauncey, and to a lesser extent Lowry, have more usually tended towards accepting executive expertise. Notably there is no discussion at all about what would constitute adequate standards of proof in such an unusual factual disagreement, no comments on the difficult evidentiary problem, no recognition, indeed, that it was an unusual or difficult or uncharacteristic role for the Law Lords. All one can say of the case is that it must rank along with the *Fire Brigades Union* case (in which Keith did dissent) as powerful evidence that when not restricted by *Wednesbury*, when there can be no question of a delegated Supremacy of Parliament, the current generation of Law Lords have no problem at all about exercising policy-determining powers. But, as always, they do such a thing only when they choose to, and will always be prepared to treat vastly simpler technical matters as beyond their expertise.

3. Freedom of Expression

Where the Lords are at their freest, of course, is where they can have a clear common law run at a problem, and the final case for this chapter, though there are several others that could be canvassed, is common law at its purest. But it must be remembered that English lawyers have always indulged in the boast that, left to itself, common law can do anything a Bill of Rights can do. We have seen this hinted at, for example, in *Brind*. Freedom of speech cases in English law over the last thirty years have nearly all occurred in ways involving either security matters or the very inner workings of government, with consequent constraints on the courts. Even if one feels privately that cases like *Brind* were decided with excessive deference to the executive's claims of national security, such claims inevitably muddied the pure consideration of the value of freedom of speech—national security being, perhaps, the only ground that even the most dedicated liberals will accept for restrictions on self-expression. Freedom of speech, is a value some Law Lords have taken seriously. This is shown by cases like *Wheeler*, although only in Browne-Wilkinson's Court of Appeal opinion, and Templeman's short supporting speech, is the value overt. And it needs to be remembered that the main House of Lords' speech in *Wheeler* expressly distanced itself from Browne-Wilkinson's argument. Once recently, though, the Law Lords had a clear common law run at the issue of freedom of speech, untrammelled by high policy considerations. In *Derbyshire County Council* v. *Times Newspapers Ltd.*[55] the Lords heard an appeal from a county council which had sued for libel after *The Times* had published two articles alleging impropriety in the way the council was managing its workers' superannuation fund. The Law Reports do not contain any details, but the flavour is given by the headlines of the articles: 'Revealed: Socialist Tycoon's Deals with a Labour

---

[55] *Derbyshire CC* v. *Times Newspapers Ltd.* [1993] 1 All ER 1011.

Chief'; 'Bizarre Deals of a Council Leader and the Media Tycoon'; 'Council Share Deals under Scrutiny'. *The Times* settled the tycoon's action by an apology and payment of damages and costs, but fought and lost the action against the council. The newspaper, however, appealed against the decision on the grounds that a local authority did not have the right to bring a libel case at all. It seems to be settled law that corporate bodies, and a county council is such a body as much as any commercial company or a trade union, can in principle be libelled, and not just for identifiable financial losses. The council's claim shows that it was presenting itself as capable of the same sort of hurt from false accusations as a living person:

By reason of the words published . . . the Plaintiff Council has been injured in its credit and reputation and has been brought into public scandal, odium and contempt, and has suffered loss and damage.[56]

There were very few precedents—only twice had the direct issue of whether a council could sue for libel been before the courts at all, once in 1891 and once in 1972. There are those, like Steven Sedley, who think that the passivity of the courts in public law for much of this century has actually been a retreat from a much more active nineteenth century past.[57] For them there is some support in the fact that the Manchester Corporation was found not capable of mounting a defamation case when accused of corruption in 1891, but Bognor Regis UDC was found capable of doing so in 1972. The judge then distinguished the *Manchester* case, and actually called for it to be overruled by the Court of Appeal, insisting that:

just as a trading company has a trading reputation which it is entitled to protect by bringing an action for defamation, so in my view the council, as a local government corporation, have a 'governing' reputation which it is equally entitled to protect in the same way.[58]

If this really was the law of England, the consequences for freedom of expression in the political arena would be severe, because, as Lord Keith points out in his speech, many central government departments are organized as corporations, and would have a similar right to use defamation suits to stifle the media. The point is that the well-known 'chilling effect', a phrase Keith himself uses, of merely facing the risks of a libel case and all that can go wrong in litigation can be enough to frighten off even a critic quite sure of the veracity of his allegations. The Lords had no difficulty with the case at all. Rather than developing the rather special logic of the old *Manchester* case, they asserted outright that local

[56] *Derbyshire CC* at 1013, quoted in Lord Keith's opinion.
[57] Sir Steven Sedley, 'The Sound of Silence; Constitutional Law without a Constitution', *Public Law*, 1996, pp. 265–85.
[58] Browne J in *Bognor Regis UDC* v. *Campion* [1972] 2 All ER 61 at 66. The earlier case was *Manchester Corp.* v. *Williams* [1891] 1 QB 94.

government is different, and simply cannot be expected to have all the rights an ordinary citizen has. Keith does not doubt that there may be something similar to a 'governing' interest. He accepts that, just as a trade union may suffer membership loss or a charity a drop in subscriptions if unfairly attacked, a local authority might, for example, find it hard to borrow money or even attract good staff if traduced. It is the very fact that he accepts this, and still goes on to reject the right to sue for defamation that makes the ruling such a powerful defence of freedom of speech, and the justification goes directly to the nature of competitive politics:

There are, however, features of a local authority which may be regarded as distinguishing it from other types of corporation . . . The most important of these features is that it is a governmental body. Further, it is a democratically elected body, the elected process nowadays being conducted almost exclusively on party political lines. It is of the highest public importance that a democratically elected governmental body, should be open to uninhibited public criticism. The threat of a civil action for defamation must inevitably have an inhibiting effect on freedom of speech.[59]

Lord Keith relies on an interesting range of citations from other jurisdictions, including South Africa and the USA, to support this approach. He also cites a Privy Council case where a law penalizing the publishing of a false statement 'likely to undermine public confidence in the conduct of public affairs' was struck down as incompatible with the written constitution of Antigua. (Ideally we would consider the Privy Council jurisdiction here, because much of the Law Lords' overtly constitutional consideration occurs under this guise, but their record in that role is not sufficiently clear cut to justify the extra length. Certainly it is not the case that they regularly use written constitutions so effectively that there is good reason to believe that they would maximize the impact of one in the UK. No one should be optimistic that their Privy Council experience will lead them to use an incorporated European Convention with especial energy.) It is noteworthy that Lord Keith has a very realistic view of defamation as a restriction on political discourse, and the nature of that discourse itself:

What has been described as 'the chilling effect' induced by the threat of civil actions for libel is very important. Quite often the facts which would justify a defamatory publication are known to be true, but admissible evidence capable of proving these facts is not available. This may prevent the publication of matters which it is very desirable to make public.[60]

It is a powerful demonstration of the Lords' ability, and desire, to establish at least some liberal public law values, and it is worth speculating whether, given their common law freedom, they might in the future take

---

[59] *Derbyshire CC* at 1017.
[60] *Derbyshire CC* at 1018.

a further step and adopt something like the American doctrine that public figures need to prove malice before they can succeed in a defamation case, even where the publisher cannot prove the truth of his allegations. Lord Keith closes his speech with a refrain that has become almost repetitive from many judges, which increasingly sounds defensive, and which acts to limit the possible impact of decisions like this. It is the claim that the case shows, yet again, the power of the common law. The Court of Appeal had come to the same decision as the Law Lords. They, however, had based their decision almost entirely on the European Convention on Human Rights, claiming that the uncertainty in English law, given the clash between the two existing precedents and the absence of a Lords' decision on the issue, allowed them this recourse. Consequently Balcombe LJ had used the much clearer legal technology of the Convention's Article 10, which upholds freedom of expression subject only to those restrictions which 'are necessary in a democratic society', where 'necessary' requires 'the existence of a pressing social need', and involves the familiar 'proportionality' assessment rejected in *Brind*. Lord Keith is eager to stress that he did not need this approach:

My Lords, I have reached my conclusion upon the common law of England without finding any need to rely upon the European convention . . . and can only add that I find it satisfactory to be able to conclude that the common law of England is consistent with the obligations assumed by the Crown under the treaty in this particular field.

The trouble with this position is that the same common law of England was compatible in 1972 with the opposite conclusion—then it recognized a local authority's right to protect its 'governing interest'. Yet at that date the UK was already a signatory of the European Convention, and Article 10 would then have been in conflict. The common law will always yield liberal results with liberal judges. But every time such an issue reoccurs, it has to be debated again, under whatever terms seem pressing or suitable at the time. The convention short-circuits all this. In general, rights trump, and circumscribe debate, cutting off much discretion. In a way, the contrast between the *Wednesbury* cases in the first part of this chapter, and the those cut free from that restraint in latter sections are all about this. *Wednesbury* acts as a powerful rights guarantee to the State, and needs to be combatted with a citizen rights guarantee. *Wheeler*, of course, was a *Wednesbury* case, and it was a case which, in substance, upheld a claim to freedom of expression. But it did not uphold that claim on those grounds. Instead a rather dubious and far from clear argument about procedure had to be engaged in. For the rest, it can be argued that the cases in the first part, as long as the court accepts the initial *Wednesbury* context, could not be decided in another way. But all four cases in the second half of the chapter could so easily have turned out differently. At other times, with different panels, they probably would have resulted in victories for the Government. Lawyers may see a coherent pattern in the cases discussed in this chapter so that there is no contrast, but such patterns can always be invented—that is what counsel are trained to do. For our purposes it is very hard to see anything going on here other than collective personal choice. Of course *Wednesbury* binds when judges wish it to. But in fact it can be made to do almost anything. It remains bluntly the truth that the liberal decisions are those achieved when *Wednesbury* has not been available. *Wednesbury* is much more common, and much more powerful in cases of a more routine administrative nature, rather than those that invoke central government or constitutional questions, and these we now turn to.

8

Public Law and the Liberty of the Person

I view with apprehension the attitude of judges who on a mere question of construction when face to face with claims involving the liberty of the subject show themselves more executive minded than the executive.... In this case I have listened to arguments which might have been addressed acceptably to the Court of King's Bench in the time of Charles I. I protest, even if I do it alone, against a strained construction put on words with the effect of giving an uncontrolled power of imprisonment to the minister.

Lord Atkin in Liversidge v. Anderson

This whole business is another warning against bureaucratic 'discretion'. When the facts are known, it will be realised that this terrible power has been used neither wisely nor justly, and that thumping lies have been told about it in Parliament.

A letter from C. K. Allen, Warden of Rhodes House,
to Lord Atkin in November 1941[1]

Everywhere in the civilized world courts have two functions which can often seem to be in conflict. They are, on the one hand, the machinery which legitimizes the use of coercive force over the very body, rather than only the property, of the individual. Courts, and only courts, can ultimately sanction the forcible movement, removal, and detention of an individual. On the other hand those same courts are charged with protecting those individuals both from invalid application of those sanctions, and misbehaviour by authorities while being sanctioned. The vibrancy of public law, which we claim is largely a consequence of the values held by the judges, is nowhere better tested than in cases regarding what European lawyers tend to call 'the liberty and security of the person'. In the English context two types of case particularly test the public law of personal liberty—questions about the rights of prisoners, and questions about the rights of those caught up in the web of immigration and deportation rules. Immigrant rights are probably no more controversial in the UK than in the rest of Western Europe, but they are everywhere politically troublesome, and in England have always been at the centre of executive/court conflict. This is demonstrated statistically by the fact that immigration related

---

[1] Geoffrey Lewis, *Lord Atkin*, Butterworths, 1983, p. 53. The case referred to is *Liversidge* v. *Sir John Anderson* [1942] AC 206.

issues account for around 35 per cent of all applications for judicial review against central government. The importance of those which do get to the courts is enhanced by the fact that fully two-thirds of these applicants are denied leave. The importance of what little control the courts do exercise is further enhanced by the fact that there is an utterly appalling variance in individual judges' tendency to grant leave, such that some judges grant leave only 21 per cent of the time, while others grant it in more than 80 per cent of cases. These figures apparently cover great constancy by individuals, and are not explicable in terms of the subject matter.[2]

Rights of prisoners are much less salient, though they too account for a sizeable, though apparently declining, part of the total judicial review application statistics. Prisoners' rights are peculiarly important, because prisoners are almost the paradigm of those most needing the courts to make up for their powerlessness in the face of a State which has, by definition, been given authority to treat them almost as though they were no longer fully human.

1. Immigration Rights

The immigration code has tightened in many respects since its main framework, the Immigration Act 1971, was put in place. The originally quite generous internal appeal mechanisms in the Act have been severely restricted by the Immigration Act 1988. We are not here concerned with appeals against an original refusal of leave to enter at all. The public law rights of such persons are virtually non-existent. Because they are not allowed to enter even long enough to initiate appeals, the Home Office is virtually outwith the supervision of the courts in its treatment of original applicants. The cases available to us concern those who are facing deportation after managing to enter the UK. There are three principal types— those alleged to have entered without ever gaining any valid form of leave to do so; those it is claimed have overstayed a limited term leave to enter; those who appear to have broken the conditions attached to a leave to enter, almost invariably by taking paid employment. Although there are many cases where the Lords have dealt with immigration issues, we want to concentrate on a few cases selected to bring out constitutional issues. These cannot necessarily be treated as a random sample of immigration cases, and thus this chapter does not purport to say anything about judicial attitudes to immigration *per se*. Unfortunately the immigration laws are complex and a certain amount of general description is unavoidable.

[2] M. Sunkin, L. Bridges, and G. Meszores, 'Trends in Judicial Review', *Public Law*, 1993, pp. 443–5.

Perhaps the case with greatest general constitutional relevance is the 1991 case *Ex parte Oladehinde.*[3] The case demonstrates, *inter alia*, the impact of the 1988 Act, which severely restricted the appeal rights contained in the original 1971 Act. The restrictions were intended, quite transparently, to reduce the chances that the courts would interfere with Home Office decisions. In fact they have, in one way, put much more pressure on the courts. Absent the sympathetic substantive appellate consideration which the 1971 Act required and its internal appeals process, first to an adjudicator and then the Immigration Appeal Tribunal (IAT) largely provided, advocates for immigration rights, and public law judges sympathetic to them, have been forced to use any plausible public law argument they can invent.

The main thrust of these reforms, which it is important background information to have in mind, is that before 1988 the adjudicator could decide not only on whether the immigrant was someone who the Home Secretary had the discretionary power to deport, but whether he had used this power properly. While this may seem an unusually generous and broad appellate function, seen against the background of the *Wednesbury* approach in the last chapter, the whole approach of the 1971 Act, which was not *overtly* altered by the 1988 Act, required it. The point is that Parliament has never expressed the immigration law in words as tough as the Home Office's actual policy. Indeed the Immigration Acts have always been noted for a certain woolliness in language, and parliamentary statements have made much play with ideas like 'full and sympathetic consideration'.[4] The immigration rules on the face of them are indeed thorough and generous. After saying that deportation will normally be the proper course for illegal immigrants, they go on to stipulate that 'Before a decision to deport is reached the Secretary of State will take into account all relevant factors known to him . . .'. These factors include: age; strength of connections with the UK; personal history, including character and conduct; domestic circumstances; compassionate circumstances. Such considerations, it has been suggested, would in any case follow from 'the principles of administrative law relating to the exercise of discretionary powers', and were in fact imposed by House of Lords and Court of Appeal decisions before the 1988 Act.[5] As long as adjudicators and the IAT could take these matters into consideration and replace the Secretary of State's decision the Act contained a serious element of mercy. The removal of these powers, and the restricting of the appeal to purely factual

---

[3] *R v. Secretary of State for the Home Department, ex parte Oladehinde* [1991] 1 AC 254.

[4] Ann Dummett, 'Immigration and Nationality' in C. McCrudden and G. Chambers, *Individual Rights and the Law in Britain*, Oxford, The Law Society & Clarendon Press, 1995.

[5] S. H. Bailey, D. J. Harris, and B. L. Jones, *Civil Liberties: Cases and Materials* (4th edn.), London, Butterworths, 1955, p. 720.

matters, for example of whether an immigrant had worked when his leave
to enter forbade that, has not surprisingly cut massively the success rate of
appeals under the Act. It has also, in the eyes of counsel for immigrants,
meant that any avenue which might work will be tried. The importance
for us of *Oladehinde* is to see to what extent the Lords are capable of taking
the same stance—will they be generous in considering imaginative ways
round the Home Office's decisions, or will they restrictively interpret the
Act in support of the Home Office? While it might not be something that
could ever be written down in a constitutional code, there is an underlying concept shared by many that, the more stringent legislation is, and the
more extensive powers over the person are, the more legitimate it is to
press very hard indeed on any conceivable procedural impropriety on
the part of the State. Do the Lords agree that constitutional benefit of the
doubt should be given to immigrants, especially since the 1988 Act?
Oladehinde represents both the 'yes' and 'no' to this question. The Law
Lords, Lords Keith, Brandon, Templeman, Griffiths, and Ackner were
unanimous, along with the Court of Appeal, in refusing to read a constitutional power of the Home Secretary very narrowly where so doing
would, at least slightly, restrict the Home Office's undoubted tendency
to deport whomever they can. But the Divisional Court in this case
had found for Oladehinde, and it was presided over by the then Woolf
LJ, some of whose judicial work we have seen in the last chapter—he was
the author of *M* v. *The Home Secretary*. So highly respected was he even
then as an expert in public law that one senses real sincerity, and not
formal politeness, in Donaldson MR's words when overturning him: 'We
would always hesitate to differ from Woolf L.J. in a matter such as this in
which he has such vast expertise and experience but . . .'. The majority in
the Court of Appeal go on, indeed, to say that they would have agreed
with him entirely but for the omission of two words in his conclusion!
We cite this here for an obvious reason. We are going to argue that it
was entirely possible for the Lords to have found for Oladehinde, and
there were very good contextual reasons for doing so. Thus having
Woolf's credentials stressed so by the Court of Appeal supports the contention that the Lords quite freely chose, from two courses, the one most
respectful to the executive and ignored the one more supportive of human
rights.

    We need to set down the facts carefully. Part of the argument depends
on one crucial aspect of the story. But also the deportation process
happens by stages which need to be understood. Shamusideen
Oladehinde, a Nigerian, had been given leave to enter the UK as a student;
this leave was extended once, and he applied for a further extension. He
was arrested shortly before his existing leave to remain in the UK would
have expired, and when interviewed in a police station by an immigration

officer he admitted that he had been doing part-time work in contradiction of the terms of his entry. The man in the other case heard at the same time, Julius Alexander from St Vincent, had overstayed his leave to enter by nearly three years when he was arrested. Both were treated in the same way, which is germane to the case. As soon as they had given the immigration officers the information they wanted, the officers telephoned immigration inspectors, recounted the interviews, and on the basis of these accounts were immediately given oral authority to serve notices of intention to deport on the men. Serving such a notice is the first stage of the deportation procedure for such cases, and may only be done with the authority of a chief immigration officer or immigration inspector. The next stage, if the immigrant avails himself of the chance, is to appeal to an immigration adjudicator, and from there to the Immigration Appeal Tribunal, both now restricted, as described above, as to what they can take into account. Where such appeals fail, as they did for both Oladehinde and Alexander, the matter is reviewed by the Deportation Department at the Home Office which then advises the Secretary of State who makes the final decision as to whether or not actually to deport. Both Oladehinde and Alexander applied for judicial review to quash the unfavourable decisions of the IAT and the original notices of intention to deport.

It must be admitted that there is an air of contrivance about the argument for Oladehinde and Alexander. Their application for judicial review depends on one part of the account. Immigration officers cannot themselves issue notices of intention to deport—under the rules as issued by the Home Secretary in August 1988 the power to do so, which the statute gives to him, was to be 'delegated' or 'devolved' to members of the Immigration Service of a rank not less than inspector—the third rank up, equivalent, it is said, to a senior executive officer in the Civil Service. The applicants' contention is that this delegation is improper, because the Home Secretary is not authorized to let others carry out his decisions except under a particular constitutional doctrine, known as the *Carltona* principle, which, they claim, does not apply here.

What lies behind this rather abstract complaint makes good substantive sense, but is only hinted at here and there in the various arguments of the three courts which heard the case. It is the idea that the Immigration Service should not be entrusted with sensitive decisions of such crushing impact on anyone's life—they are akin, as it were, to the police rather than the magistracy, intent only on the result. As counsel for Oladehinde put it before the Lords, 'The system is analogous to a situation where an accused person is required to mitigate against sentence to the arresting officer at the police station.' In contrast before August 1988, which is, of course, also before effective appeal powers were stripped out of the system, immigration officers required the authority of a civil servant in the Deportation

Department of the Home Office. The Home Office's evidence speaks for itself, though possibly not in the way it was intended. In the words of a Home Office official:

I am satisfied that the change has created greater efficiency with no loss of fairness or consistency. The number of people removed under section 3(5)(a) has increased from just under 200 a year in 1985 and 1986 to 393 (including 84 supervised departures) in 1987 and 871 (including 584 supervised departures) in 1988. In the year ending June 1989 1,440 (including 1,169 supervised departures) persons were removed under these powers.[6]

Woolf LJ clearly accepts this understated pragmatic reason for concern. Of the above boast he drily remarks that 'it is not surprising that the advocates . . . in these cases contend that the same standards are not being exercised . . . as existed prior to the changes'. He made the point that the legislation had always expected immigration officers to make the point-of-entry decision about leave to enter, but this was a very different matter from deciding to deport some one who had originally gained leave:

The two applications which are before the court disclose that in practice the way the decision to deport is being handled by the immigration service is very much in accord with the way in which contested applications for leave to enter are dealt with. Instead of focussing on the importance of the decision to deport, in his evidence even the Secretary of State seems to attach greater importance to the consequence of that decision.

Woolf in fact goes on to make considerable play with the somewhat less than clear statements that had been made to the House of Commons on the whole matter, which seem to have been an attempt to hide the fact that these very sensitive decisions had been handed over to the Immigration Service. He even notes how belatedly the Home Office disclosed the change to the House—not until five months after it took effect. Woolf comments sharply on another related practice—the Immigration Service no longer allows the immigrant to see the form on which the immigration officer records his reasons for recommending deportation, on the grounds that, as the matters can no longer be considered on appeal, there is no reason for the immigrant to see it. Woolf comes as close as can be to ordering the Home Office to change this practise, on the basis that judicial review is still allowed, and thus the immigrant can still use the material.

All of this is scene setting, though we have presented these points out of the order of Woolf's judgment for expository purpose. They explain why there might be very good pragmatic reasons, and indeed principled reasons, for stopping the delegation of the Home Secretary's powers. But can the courts do that?

---

[6] *Ex parte Oladehinde* at 268.

The *Carltona* principle, so named after a judgment by Lord Greene MR of *Wednesbury* fame in *Carltona Ltd.* v. *Commissioners of Works* in 1943, states that where legislation requires a minister to make a decision he can allow a responsible civil servant in his department to do it instead, on the grounds that such officials are, as public law pleasantly describes them, 'the alter ego' of the minister, who remains entirely responsible to Parliament for any decision they make in his stead.[7] The precise legal point then on which *Oladehinde* comes down to is whether immigration inspectors and chief immigration officers who are now allowed to make the Secretary of State's decisions are just a subset of Home Office civil servants, not constitutionally different from the senior and higher executive officers in the Deportation Department who used to do it before August 1988. There is obviously no correct answer to this question, except in some special legal sense of a 'correct answer'. Neither the 1971 nor the 1988 Acts say openly whether the Immigration Service is a special and separate service, or just an administrative compartment of the main Civil Service. It is an issue no one seems ever to have considered within the administration. It is entirely a matter of inference drawn from various aspects of the Act, and the general scheme by which the Act separates discussion of deportation, treated as the Secretary of State's business, from descriptions of specific functions for the Immigration Service. If, by such inference, the service can be shown to be a creature of statute, it is then a creature of Parliament, and not something created by the prerogative powers of the Secretary of State to be his agent. If so, arguably, he could not delegate his authority because none of its members could be seen as his *alter ego*.

There is little point addressing the arguments on either side in any detail. They cannot be conclusive. The flavour of the argument can be given fairly quickly. Sometimes the Act specifically says that the Secretary of State himself must do certain things, which implies that there must be some decisions he can delegate. But nowhere in the Act are there examples of the Secretary of State being allowed to devolve decisions to members of his department who are given clear statutory duties or functions. The whole structure of the Immigration Service, and its pre-legislative existence going back to 1920, suggest that it is a special service, not part of the generality. Woolf's general position is that 'The Carltona principle is therefore, in my view, more correctly regarded as an implication which is read into a statute in the absence of any clear contrary indication by Parliament that the implication is not to apply.[8] Woolf finds by inference that 'the Act of 1971 recognises the independent status of immigration officers', and thus applying *Carltona* to them 'would amount to an

---

[7] *Carltona Ltd.* v. *Commissioners of Works* [1943] 2 All ER 560.
[8] *Ex parte Oladehinde* at 264.

extension of the principle beyond its present accepted limits'. The Court of Appeal, while being very curt about the other judgment in the Divisional Court, regarded Woolf's argument as one of 'outstanding clarity'. That may be. We have no intention to be disrespectful, but it is hard to see the bundle of inferences and references to the *pre*-legislative history of the Immigration Service as forcing beyond doubt the conclusion he comes to:

In the end the case comes down to the question of what was the intention of Parliament? Was it the intention of Parliament that the power to take the important decisions to deport could be taken by immigration inspectors on behalf of the Secretary of State in the manner that I have indicated these decisions were taken? In my judgment only one conclusion is possible, that Parliament did not and would not have intended the decisions to be taken by the immigration officers who have been given expressly by that Act completely different functions, those functions being the functions which they had performed in general terms prior to the introduction of the new regime under the Immigration Act 1971.[9]

What Woolf may really have meant is that Parliament could not possibly want (or admit to wanting) hurried telephone calls after an interview in the intimidating conditions of a police station (and under caution) to sew up a matter calling for impartial consideration of complex factors. He may well accept counsel's suggestion that the immigration inspector does no more than rubber stamp the immigration officer, and he may think the immigration officer and his inspector probably have an eye on the statistics the Home Office so proudly produced in its affidavit. If he had thought this he would probably have been right. There is no shortage of evidence against the Home Office's Immigration Service, not least a damning report by the Commission for Racial Equality published in 1985.[10] For whatever reason Woolf finds it 'beyond doubt' that the *Carltona* principle does not apply. To many it is perfectly respectable to allow suspicions about the behaviour of an administrative agency to lead to setting the executive very tight tests on the constitutionality of their practice. It might not have hurt at all to have said this more openly, if only to force the courts above to explain either why this was not a suitable maxim of constitutional interpretation, or why it was quite unfair to be so suspicious of the Immigration Service. Because, by not pushing the point, Woolf left it altogether too easy for the Court of Appeal, and then the Lords, to reverse him.

Even as it is, Woolf's argument almost carried the day with the Court of Appeal which so admired him. They got out of following his argument in an extraordinary way. They accept Woolf's conclusion as stated above expect, they say, for the omission of two words. Had he written that

---

[9] *Ex parte Oladehinde* at 269.
[10] Commission for Racial Equality Immigration, *Control Procedures: Report of a Formal Investigation*, 1985.

'Parliament did not and would not have intended the decision to be taken by immigration officers *as such*' (my emphasis), they would have upheld his decision. Donaldson goes so far as to say, with an admirable casualness about legal niceties, 'Whether we would have upheld his decision upon the grounds that Parliament had impliedly limited the *Carltona* principle in this context, or upon grounds of *Wednesbury* unreasonableness, we need not pause to consider. It would have been on one or other or both grounds'.[11] But, for the Court of Appeal, the immigration inspectors to whom the Home Secretary has devolved his powers are not, *as such*, immigration officers. They are 'part-time' immigration officers, whose duties are mainly managing immigration officers:

'Members of the immigration service at not less than inspector level' and 'a senior member of [the Secretary of State's] staff in the immigration service' do not necessarily connote an immigration officer *acting as such* and the authority in fact conferred has not been upon any immigration officer *acting as such*. It can be, and in context is, merely descriptive of particular Home Office officials. (Emphases added.)

It is improbable that Donaldson MR believes that the officers in question change their very natures when not acting as immigration officers *as such*. But then, as the real argument was never made by the Divisional Court, it is an easy way of being gentle to a much admired public law judge. What is never clear is why this very odd distinction is made by the Court of Appeal at all—why save the Secretary of State? In the Lords there is clear impatience with the entire argument, but the Court of Appeal does not seem to feel such. In any case they certainly give Woolf far more consideration than he got in the Lords, and they do, by implication, accept that there is something constitutionally improper in allowing the Immigration Service to decide, even if it is only the provisional decision, on deportation. It is only because they persuade themselves that immigration inspectors are not, as it were, *really* members of the Immigration Service that they allow the Home Office's appeal. It needs also to be said that the Court of Appeal shows itself, as English courts so often do in public law contexts, suitably impressed with arguments from administrative convenience to the exclusion of worries about conceivable unfairness. Donaldson's conclusion:

There are clear advantages and no unfairness in the (provisional) decision to deport, which does not of itself affect the status of the immigrant but which gives him the right of appeal, albeit of a very limited nature, being taken by civil servants who are readily available and have considerable experience and expertise in immigration matters. The operative decision, in the form of a deportation order, comes later and is a personal decision by a minister.

[11] *Ex parte Oladehinde* at 285.

So completely to disregard the uselessness of the appeal, and to disregard the importance of the initial stage because later a busy minister will complete the ongoing process of deportation, means effectively that administrative convenience rather than constitutional suspicion becomes the trump. This is a hallmark of English public law judging, even more apparent in the next chapter. It stems, we feel, from the lack of a 'rights' perspective in English legal thought. Immigrants, prisoners, welfare recipients are much more prone to be seen as the beneficiaries of government largesse than the holders of vital rights. Only in this way can a judge believe it is any business of his to care in the slightest about administrative convenience.

The Lords refused to entertain any of the background reasons that may have influenced Woolf, and possibly led to the half-hearted stance of the Court of Appeal. As often, it is useful to go first to Templeman's short speech to get the main thrust. He takes exactly no notice of the inferential argument on the *Carltona* principle—for Templeman the legal position is very simple: 'There is no express or implied statutory prohibition on the employment of immigration inspectors selected by the Secretary of State with due regard to their seniority and experience to authorise the service of a notice of intention to deport'.[12] More importantly, he refuses to take the point that influenced Woolf, and again which the Court of Appeal accepted, that there is something vitally different about the routine refusal of leave to enter and the much more crushing effect of being deported after living in the UK for some time. To Templeman the decisions are on a par—if it is acceptable for the Immigration Service to make the first decision, there is no reason why they should not make the second. Typically of Law Lords who, basically, trust administrators, either at central or local level, Templeman discards any sense of impropriety:

Some attempt was made to equate the members of the immigration service (including immigration inspectors) with the role of policemen and to equate members of the deportation department with the role of judges. In my opinion the analogy is false. All members of the Home Office who are concerned with entry or deportation, or both, are bound to use their best endeavours to ensure that persons lawfully seeking to enter are treated fairly, that persons lawfully entitled to remain are permitted to remain, and that persons who have acted unlawfully are nevertheless permitted to enter or allowed to remain if in all the circumstances their unlawful conduct ought fairly to be excused.

Such protestations of faith may well be sincere, but one wonders whether they are an appropriate backdrop to the making of constitutional law. Neither view of immigration officers is easily susceptible to empirical proof—ought there not, therefore, to be an accepted onus of proof built

---

[12] *Ex parte Oladehinde* at 295.

into constitutional adjudication? And if there were, would it not have to be an onus on the State to prove that a power may safely be put in its hands? Such an argument is, after all, only a refinement of the separation of powers doctrine. But it is not one that many Law Lords seem to entertain. Finally Templeman acknowledges the fact that with the removal of appeal rights, the position of such immigrants 'is said to have been weakened', but 'this possibility does not affect the present question'. The self conception of a constitutional law judge who can write that last sentence is, to say the least, extremely restrictive.

The main speech, by Lord Griffiths is different only inasmuch as he takes time to mount his own inferential argument as to why *Carltona* does apply here, and it is no more persuasive than Woolf's for the other side. Where Griffiths' speech also differs slightly from Templeman's is that by giving more recognition to the substantive anxieties of the immigrants, his dismissal of them marks even more strongly this sense of 'constitutional trust' in the executive. Griffiths notes, for example:

there was a suggestion that because immigration officers were primarily concerned with control of entry and policing functions in respect of illegal immigrants there might be an ethos in the service that would lead too readily to a decision to deport.[13]

This is perhaps the clearest statement anywhere in the case of the real anxiety, yet Griffiths 'can see no reason why senior members of the service should be tarred with this image'. Nor is he unaware that the initial stage is crucial, even though the final decision is made by the Secretary of State: 'I appreciate however that the initial decision is a serious matter setting in motion the deportation procedure which will gather a momentum that may be difficult to reverse.' But this appreciation leads nowhere. It hardly could, because Griffiths, most important of all, completely dismisses the idea that the immigration inspectors were doing nothing but rubber stamp their juniors' decisions, even though he admits, himself, to 'unease' about the process by which a mere telephone call can elicit authority to serve the notice. He thinks it would be much better to have a written report, including representations from the immigrant, before the decision is taken:

It is after all a grave decision affecting the future welfare of the immigrant and although it will be reviewed again in the deportation section, I have already commented on the momentum of the initial decision.

The justification for the procedure, which convinces Griffiths of its necessity despite the dangers, is a most striking example of the administrative convenience argument. There is no power of detention until the notice has

---

[13] *Ex parte Oladehinde* at 303.

been signed, so if time is taken to prepare a written report, the immigrant will have to be released, and 'may well have disappeared'. The argument that the State is entitled to restrict one right, that of natural justice, because it has not given itself statutory power to restrict another, that of freedom of movement, is quite extraordinary. But it seems completely to convince the Law Lords in this case. It needs only Lord Ackner's almost complete acceptance of the problems in the system, combined with his rejection of their relevance, to complete the picture. His speech, of only twenty-two lines, reads for the most part like a complete condemnation of the Home Office system, until the last sentence.

> The issue is *not* whether such immigration inspectors in the instant appeals broke the rules of natural justice in making their decisions. During the course of submissions I expressed concern both at the apparent failure to give the appellants any opportunity to make representations to the inspectors prior to their making their decisions and the apparent failure to ensure that the appellants knew precisely what material the immigration officers had put before the inspectors as the basis on which to decide whether or not to make the decision. The Immigration Act 1988 seriously restricted the immigrant's right of appeal. It has therefore become even more important that the decision-maker has all the relevant material before him and that this material is accurate. However the procedure which was or should have been adopted by the immigration inspectors is not the subject matter of this appeal. [Emphasis added.][14]

Indeed this prime concern that Lord Ackner describes so well was not formally the subject matter—largely because the only possible evidence were the affidavits of the inspectors—that, after all, is the nature of telephone authorizations. But, yet again, if the arguments on the highly technical question of the application of the *Carltona* principle (like *Wednesbury*, not a House of Lords decision anyway) are as even as it seems, what about the benefit of doubt? The juridical history of the immigration laws is very largely a history of repeated attempts to penetrate ever denser shields against judicial control. It is also a history which, while not entirely demonstrating the Law Lords at there most acquiescent, certainly demonstrates how much it has been a matter of individual, almost random, concern by particular Lords, with most of their colleagues unwilling to be adventurous in defence of natural justice. From time to time a Lord Woolf, a Lord Bridge, a Lord Slynn will voice concern, sometimes as leaders of a united or majority house, usually not. Most of the time their Lordships continue with legal readings which, though they are not necessarily 'wrong', never evince bias towards the immigrant. And always, as we have demonstrated throughout the book, so much depends on the random selection of the appeal panel.

---

[14] *Ex parte Oladehinde* at 305.

There have been victories for immigrants. One of the rare successes came as the second of a pair of cases which shows this haphazard nature. The first was *Zamir v. Secretary of State for the Home Department*[15] in 1980, which was effectively overruled only three years later in *Khawaja v. Secretary of State for the Home Department*,[16] although two Law Lords, Wilberforce and Fraser, were on both cases, and both had unanimous panels. In the second case, though, Wilberforce and Fraser were joined by two Law Lords with strong, if unpredictable, civil rights records, Lords Scarman and Bridge. Quite intentionally the immigration laws attempt to exclude appeals to the courts. One very effective way to do this is by requiring that appeals against refusal to grant entrance can only be pursued when the applicant is out of the country. This also very largely renders useless what internal appeal rights the scheme itself has. Parliament has, in general, largely given up on what used to be called 'ouster clauses', that is, attempts to prevent the courts being involved in adjudicating even illegal administrative behaviour, a practice that used to be widespread, though seldom successful. It is now more or less accepted that judicial review of such behaviour cannot be excluded. But judicial review, restricted usually by the *Wednesbury* principle, allows only the most limited control over what the administration actually does, as opposed to what it says it has done. *Zamir* represented an attempt to get away from *Wednesbury* restrictiveness, which we have seen in the last chapter is usually fatal to any complaint against the administration if it is held to apply to a case. On the facts of *Zamir* it is unsurprising that an unsympathetic court should side with the Home Office—all in, Mr Zamir was pretty clearly trying to cheat and nearly got away with breaching the immigration laws—and it was the relatively more generous 1971 Act that applied to him. But civil rights law is often made on the back of undeserving cases—it has often been remarked that the great advances in criminal civil rights of the US Supreme Court in the fifties and sixties would never have been made if the actual guilt of those whose names appear in the case lists was relevant.

Mr Zamir had gained leave to enter the UK in November 1975 in order to join his father, who had immigrated in 1972. At that time children over 18 in general had to qualify in their own right, but unmarried and fully dependent children under 21 could be admitted to settle with their family. Zamir was about 18 at the time he gained leave. He did not actually enter until March 1976. In the intervening few months he had married, a marriage he claimed had not been arranged until several weeks after the November granting of his entry permit. He was not asked, and did not volunteer this fact when he arrived at Heathrow—in fact he does not seem

---

[15] *Zamir v. Secretary of State for the Home Department* [1980] 2 All ER 768.
[16] *Khawaja v. Secretary of State for the Home Department* [1984] 1 AC 74.

to have been asked anything at all. Unfortunately for Zamir, in 1978 his wife applied for entry, along with the son who had by then been born to them, which triggered an investigation. After an interview in August 1978 in which Zamir could offer no explanation for how he could regard himself as dependent on his father when he was himself already married, and during which he admitted to having got a job shortly after arrival, he was detained. He still insisted that he had never been asked if he was married, and did not know that he should have volunteered this information. The Home Office decided to deport him on the grounds that his original leave was vitiated by his deception, and he was therefore an illegal immigrant.

Zamir applied for judicial review of this decision on the grounds that an applicant for leave to enter has only one duty—to answer questions honestly—and that he therefore had not deceived, and not vitiated his leave to enter. But the real problem and the one that makes this case a setback for immigrants was that the way the Home Office argued the case depended on the *Wednesbury* principle in an extreme way. As far as they were concerned the very question of whether he was guilty of deception was entirely up to them—it was an administrative conclusion, not a factual issue to be argued about in the courts. Applying *Wednesbury* the most the courts could do was to ask the familiar question—was there any material upon which a rational immigration officer could decide that he had been deceived. The Lords made it clear that such a hurdle would be very easily passed, because of the second issue they decided in this case. The second issue was whether silence about a matter that one ought to have known was relevant counted as deception, and Wilberforce here produced a very tough stance, deeming would-be immigrants to have 'a positive duty of candour'—they had a duty to volunteer anything that might count against them. Wilberforce's general attitude to immigration is perhaps well described by this passage in his speech:

In my opinion an alien seeking entry to the United Kingdom owes a positive duty of candour on all material facts which denote a change in circumstances since the issue of the entry clearance. He is seeking a privilege; he alone is, as to most such matters, aware of the facts: the decision to allow him to enter, and he knows this, is based on a broad appreciation by immigration officers of a complex of considerations, and this appreciation can only be made fairly and humanely if, on his side, the entrant acts with openness and frankness. It is insufficient in my opinion to set as the standard of disclosure that which applies in the law of contract; the relation of an intending entrant and the authorities is quite different in nature from that of persons negotiating in business. The former requires a higher and more exacting standard. To set it any lower than as I have described is to invite, as unhappily so many of the reported cases show, a bureaucratic and anti-bureaucratic contest with increasing astuteness, manouvering and ingenuity on one side, and increasingly cautious technicality and procrastination on the other. This cannot be in the interest of sensitive administration.[17]

While it is no answer to Wilberforce to point out that no one with personal experience of dealing with them would ever accuse the British Immigration Service, even in clear-cut cases, of 'sensitive administration', it is highly relevant that he should have used the word 'privilege'. It supports our general conception that English public law jurisprudence lacks any strong rights basis. Lord Wilberforce is technically correct. There is no positive law right of abode for aliens in this country, but so clearly to renounce the idea of rights here makes the colouration of his jurisprudence in the field very clear. To return to the main point—the Home Office position is that it is up to the immigration officer, applying the Secretary of State's powers, to decide if Zamir has deceived and therefore is 'an illegal'. Mr Zamir's failure in this duty of candour provides the *Wednesbury* minimal material to make that decision rational. Such is a potentially enormous power—if the courts can be so thoroughly excluded and can never themselves weigh evidence, almost no one could be guaranteed to have anything approaching a right of entry. Naturally there was an alternative approach Wilberforce (his was the only opinion in the case) could have taken. There already existed, as a meliorating doctrine to *Wednesbury's* pro-executive force, the idea of a 'precedent fact'. Instead of characterizing all factual bases for administrative discretion as wholly for the administrator to decide, the law is sometimes seen as itself insisting that a situation must be empirically valid before discretion comes into play. We touched briefly on this sort of distinction in the last chapter. Though apparently a refined constitutional nuance, it is vital to the whole idea of discretion. One can either say to an administrator—given a set of facts, make the value choice that has to be made. Or one can say—decide what you think the facts are, and then make the value choice that has to be made. Discretion is vastly wider—and potentially much more dangerous—in the latter case. In general *Wednesbury* seems to be taken to follow the latter mode. The doctrine of precedential fact is an attempt to turn discretion towards the former, more restricted, mode. We shall see attempts to get around *Wednesbury* using this doctrine in the next chapter on local authorities, but its modern establishment in public law is usually dated from the overruling of *Zamir*. In *Zamir* Lord Wilberforce flatly refused to believe that the courts could possibly be expected to treat the question of whether an immigrant had deceived the authorities as a precedent fact. Just as the decision of whether or not to grant an entry certificate was a purely administrative matter, this must be true also 'of a decision to remove on the ground that leave to enter has been

[17] *Zamir* at 773.

vitiated . . . It would be absurd to apply a different principle.' The whole scheme of the Act was against it:

It is true that it does not, in relation to the decisions in question, use such words as 'in the opinion of the Secretary of State' or 'the Secretary of State must be satisfied', but it is not necessary for such a formula to be used in order to take the case out of the precedent fact category. The nature and process of decision conferred upon the immigration officers by existing legislation is incompatible with any requirement for the establishment of precedent objective facts whose existence the court may verify.[18]

This, of course, is exactly what any state authority would want—the acceptance both that the fact finding is too difficult to be challenged in the courts, and that this presents no difficulties in public law. Wilberforce then goes on to justify this position, by describing graphically how difficult is the job of the immigration officer, and how inadequate would be the courts. We quote this at length because it is one of the most complete abdications of judicial competence, and one of the most powerful evocations of the difficulty of administrative decision making in the Law Reports:

The immigration officer, whether at the stage of entry or at that of removal, has to consider a complex of statutory rules and non-statutory guidelines. He has to act on documentary evidence and such other evidence as inquiries may provide. Often there will be documents whose genuineness is doubtful, statements which cannot be verified, misunderstandings as to what was said, practices and attitude in a foreign state which have to be estimated. So there is room for appreciation, even for discretion. The Divisional Court, on the other hand, on judicial review of a decision to remove and detain is very differently situated. It considers the case on affidavit evidence, as to which cross examination, though allowable does not take place in practice. It is, as this case well exemplifies, not in a position to find out the truth between conflicting statements: did the applicant receive notes, did he read them, was he capable of understanding them, what exactly took place of the point of entry? Nor is it in a position to weigh the materiality of personal or other factors present, or not present, or partially present to the mind of the immigration authorities. It cannot possibly act as, in effect a court of appeal as to the facts on which the immigration officer decided.

If all this is true and germane, it amounts to a confession that natural justice, of which the cardinal rule is that no one should be a judge in his own case, simply has no place in immigration law, and, therefore, possibly has no place in many areas of public law.

That was *Zamir*; had it stood it might have had a huge impact on British public law, because the doctrine of the precedent fact is a vital escape from *Wednesbury*'s rigours. But even though *Zamir* was rejected, as we shall

---

[18] *Zamir* at 772.

shortly see, the mere fact that arguments like those of Wilberforce in this case could carry a unanimous Lords' panel makes our point. The Law Lords demonstrate no vital urge to penetrate administrative convenience in the pursuit of a public law determined to impose natural justice standards. In fact *Zamir* and the other cases in this chapter testify to something else—just how important are the facts of cases and how crucial is the idiosyncratic role of individual judges. Because one curious fact about the overturn of *Zamir* is that two of the panel, including Wilberforce, were on the unanimous court which overruled it.

Khawaja was one of two cases heard together in the Lords, the other being an appeal on behalf of Bohar Singh Khera. (As a small interlude, it is one of the small ironies of the law that though the case is always known as *Khawaja*, Salamat Ullah Khawaja was actually found by the Lords to have lied, and lost his appeal, while the legal point for which the case is important only helped Mr Khera who won his appeal. The more famous irony is that the Midlands town of Wednesbury has gone down in legal history as an epithet for irrational behaviour when, in fact, the Wednesbury Council was found by Lord Greene not to have acted irrationally, but to have actually passed the *Wednesbury* test. But then, it is generally believed by legal historians that there never was a snail in the ginger beer bottle either, and *Donoghue* v. *Stevenson* would have turned out differently if it had ever gone to trial.)

Khera and Khawaja's cases also give us a useful reminder of the sheer chance involved in the setting of legal precedents. In Khera's case, the stronger of the two, leave to appeal was actually denied originally, and only granted when, a little later, a different Appeals Committee of the Law Lords granted leave to appeal in the weaker of the cases. Again we commented at the beginning of the book on this extra element of randomness built into the Law Lords' operations, in the selection of cases to be heard. The facts in Khera's case are very similar to those in *Zamir*. Khera's father entered the UK in 1972, and applied for leave for his wife and son, then aged 16, to join him. In January 1973 Khera married in India. Though the application for mother and son was originally refused—for some reason or other the immigration authorities at first decided they were not related to the father—they were successful in appealing to an adjudicator, and were granted leave and entered in January 1975. In 1978 Khera's wife applied for leave to enter, along with the children of the marriage, and from there the story is as with *Zamir*. Inquiries were made, Khera's situation discovered, and he was detained as an illegal immigrant pending deportation. Although he was released under conditions after a fortnight to await the outcome of appeals, Lord Fraser says, surely correctly 'the appeal has been dealt with all along as if the appellant was still detained, and I think that is right, because his personal liberty is undoubtedly restricted'. He lost his application for judicial review before the Divisional Court and the Court of Appeal, because, given *Zamir*, they had no choice. His only hope would be for a court to decide they believed his account of how he had not deceived the immigration officials rather than accepting the Home Office's version. But this would be to breach the line by doing more than deciding that there was enough material pointing to deceit for the decision to deport to be not irrational. The Home Office ultimately relied on only one instance where they claim they were deceived. During a medical examination in India on 15 December 1974 it was alleged that Khera falsely told the medical officer that he was not married, and that this lie was a material factor in the grant of a clearance certificate. The lie in question, however, was not mentioned in the affidavit evidence of the immigration officer who granted the clearance, and was denied by Khera, who also stated that he only spoke Punjabi, and could not communicate with the medical officer who did not speak it. In this case, as in the second, the written decision to detain states only that the detaining officer had 'reasonable grounds to conclude' that they were illegal immigrants, and never stated that the officers were 'satisfied' that they 'were illegal immigrants'.

The facts of Khawaja's situation were different and more colourful. He was a Pakistan citizen studying in Belgium. In August 1979 he applied for a visa to visit the UK for two weeks. The Embassy was instructed by the Home Office to refuse the visa, but before he knew of the refusal he flew to Manchester on 17 March 1980, said he wanted to visit a cousin and that he would return after a week, showing his return ticket. He was given leave to enter for a month. During that month he got solicitors to write to the Home Office saying that he had married on 10 April to a Mrs Butt, legally settled in the UK, and now wanted indefinite leave to stay with her. In fact inquiries demonstrated that he had married Mrs Butt in a civil ceremony in Brussels on 2 December 1979, and she had travelled with him to Manchester, presenting herself to another immigration officer as a returning resident, saying nothing about her husband. On 4 May an immigration officer, Mr Osborne, decided there were 'reasonable grounds to conclude' that he was an illegal immigrant, and ordered his detention pending deportation. The burden of the Home Office case was that, had the Manchester immigration officer known he was married and travelling with his wife who was seeking entry as a returning resident, he would have believed that Khera had no intention at all of returning to Belgium after a week but was actually trying to settle in the UK. Therefore the non-disclosure was a material factor in obtaining leave, because Khera had no legal right of entry as either spouse or fiancé of Mrs Butt.

We have presented the facts in the two cases fully because they show the very different nature of the evidence that immigration officers may use to decide someone is an illegal immigrant. In the latter case the Lords were clearly convinced that Khawaja had intentionally and quite deliberately set out to deceive. In Khera's case they are equally clear that the immigration officer 'was not entitled, on the evidence that was before him, to decide that the appellant had been guilty of deception'.[19] In other words, they have gone beyond *Wednesbury* and made up their own mind on the evidence. Though they do not make the point themselves, it was quite clearly no difficult job; they had the same material as the Immigration Service, and perfectly easily formed a conclusion, despite Wilberforce's dramatic description in *Zamir* of how impossible this would be.

Lord Fraser, in a short opinion, admits outright that the decision in *Zamir* was wrong, and gives no explanation for having then thought differently from the way he now does, resting content to adopt Lord Bridge's reasoning. Lord Wilberforce was entirely responsible for *Zamir* having delivered the only opinion. He now delivered a fairly lengthy speech, the burden of which—it is considerably less clear than his usual work—seems to be that *Zamir* never really stood for the propositions that were being rejected in the new cases, and in particular, the form of precedent fact argument tried by Zamir's counsel was still wrong. In other words, as far as Wilberforce was concerned, he was not really being overturned. But he was, and not just on the precedent fact issue. On the other point, the quite excessive statement of a 'duty of candour', he was resoundingly overturned. But Wilberforce himself remained interestingly stubborn, and even attempted to give the impression that objections to it were somehow unfair. As an image of a judicial approach it remains sufficiently interesting to quote:

The second line of thought was prompted by the great number and variety of cases of deception, often organised for money, which have come before the courts. I ventured the opinion that a system of consideration of individual cases for the privilege of admission to this country can only work humanely and efficiently on a basis of candour and good faith on the part of those seeking entry. If here I trespassed on the ground of moral judgment, I am unrepentant.[20]

No one objected to it being a 'moral judgment'; the objection was that it was legally wrong. For the sake of clarity, the author of the headnotes to *Khawaja* makes it clear the Lords found it appropriate specifically to hold '(4) That there was no positive duty of candour approximating to a requirement of utmost good faith . . .'. We can never know exactly what went on in the judicial discussions when counsel departed after oral argument in *Khawaja*, but it seems entirely appropriate to suggest that

---

[19] *Khawaja* at 95. The facts above are all taken from Lord Fraser's speech at this point.
[20] *Khawaja* at 99.

Lords Bridge and Scarman convinced Lord Fraser of the opposite of what Lord Wilberforce had convinced him three years earlier and Wilberforce preferred not to divide the court in a sensitive matter where a majority felt it necessary to use the rarely invoked powers of the House to overrule itself. From our point of view this case is a prime example of one which might never have happened. Lord Fraser sat on both the Appeal Committees in the Lords, the one that first rejected Khera's request to appeal, along with Lords Brandon and Roskill, and the second, this time with Lord Scarman and Bridge. Clearly as a result of that second decision Fraser's first committee changed its mind. There is nothing in the operating system of the Lords that guaranteed that Khawaja's request would come before two men who obviously felt that the *Zamir* decision must be overturned, and equally clearly Fraser did not think that initially. But for chance it might have been years before an appropriate opportunity to overrule *Zamir* came up again, and it might have come up before a group lacking either or both of Scarman and Bridge. This is not an over-pressed criticism—we raised the problem in the first chapter of the book. It is only because the main theme of this chapter is the randomness of constitutional decisions in an area like this that we return to it. Too much depends on individuality and chance in such areas. Unlike the material in our chapter on the law of negligence we do not find a lengthy battle, returned to over and again between shifting but coherent opposed sides which can ensure something like an orderly development of the law. There are probably no Law Lords who do not care strongly for civil liberties—the conflicts are not between liberals and illiberals. The conflicts are more procedural, conflicts even over constitutional values and the very role of courts. On such a dimension there is no obvious smooth progression of consensus over time, hence the back and forth movement on civil rights demonstrated in these cases, perhaps even more than in the major constitutional cases discussed in the previous chapter.

The speeches of Lords Bridge and Scarman in *Khawaja*, however providential their ever being uttered, are models of judicial assertiveness. Scarman spends very little time on the 'duty of candour' issue, which he patently thinks absurd, noting, with rather greater awareness of the realities of bureaucracy than judges sometimes display:

to allow officers to rely on an entrant honouring a duty of positive candour, by which is meant a duty to volunteer relevant information, would seem perhaps a disingenuous approach to the administration of control: some might think it conducive to slack rather than to 'sensitive' administration.[21]

Finding no express provision for such a duty in the Act, and thinking it impossible to imply one, he insists that non-disclosure, in the absence of

---

[21] *Khawaja* at 108.

fraud, is not a breach of the immigration laws. Lord Scarman is very clear about the importance of this case, not only for its own sake but for the future of public law:

My Lords in most cases I would defer to a recent decision of your Lordships House on a question of construction even if I thought it wrong. I do not do so in this context because for reasons which I shall develop I am convinced that the *Zamir* reasoning gave insufficient weight to the important—I would say funda-mental consideration that we are here concerned with, the scope of judicial review of a power which inevitably infringes the liberty of those subject to it. This consideration, if it be good, outweighs, in my judgment, any difficulties in the administration of immigration control . . . The *Zamir* construction [of the Act] deprives those subjected to the power of that degree of judicial protection which I think can be shown to have been the policy of our law to afford to persons with whose liberty the executive is seeking to interfere. It does therefore, in my view, tend to obstruct the proper development and application of the safeguards our law provides for the liberty of those within its jurisdiction.[22]

It is part of Scarman's approach very much to stress that the decision in *Zamir* depended on a gloss, a strained construction, by which extra words were read into the Act to justify ignoring the precedent fact rule. This makes it clearer what the court in *Zamir* had done, and consequently clearer what the relative standing of liberty versus administrative con-venience was. For Scarman, *Wednesbury* 'cannot extend to interference with liberty unless Parliament has unequivocally enacted that it should do'. It is not Scarman's court which is straining to get round parliamen-tary language. Rather it was the *Zamir* court, which reread a statute which did not require *Wednesbury* procedures in order to maximize executive convenience. In a very powerful defence of traditional liberties Scarman goes all the way back to the Habeas Corpus Act 1816, saying that section 3 of that Act displaces *Wednesbury*-style principles in cases of the liberty of the subject. In fact Scarman throws all the heavy ammunition going to discredit the whole style of the speech in *Zamir* including Atkin's famous dissent in *Liversidge* v. *Anderson* and even the reference to Blackstone obligatory whenever a judge really wants to insist on the age old truth of his argument. He concludes:

Faced with the zealous care our law traditionally devotes to the protection of the liberty of those who are subject to its jurisdiction, I find it impossible to imply into the statute words the effect of which would be to take [the relevant part of the Act] 'out of the "precedent fact category"' (Lord Wilberforce in *Zamir*'s case). If Parlia-ment intends to exclude effective judicial review of the exercise of a power in restraint of liberty, it must make its meaning crystal clear.

This is precisely the sort of constitutional benefit of doubt we discussed as present in Woolf's approach in the first case, but missing from the Lords

---

[22] *Khawaja* at 109.

then, and all too much of the time. Scarman to a large extent rests on the force of the constitutional principles and his characterization of the 'glossing' of the Act in *Zamir*. This is quite enough, but it leaves to Bridge the task of utterly destroying the administrative convenience argument in its own terms. He sets out the problem of *Zamir* and the preceding cases in language as strong as Scarman's, pointing out the consequence of the principle in *Zamir*:

It will be seen at once that this principle gives to an executive officer, subject no doubt, in reaching his conclusion of fact to a duty to act fairly, a draconian power of arrest and expulsion based on his own decision of fact which, if there was any evidence to support it, cannot be examined by any judicial process until after it has been acted on and then in circumstances where the person removed, being unable to attend the hearing of his appeal, has no realistic prospect of prosecuting it with success.[23]

Earlier Lord Bridge had noted that, by the Home Office's own evidence, only once in the twelve or so years from the inception of the Act had such an appeal been successful. The main point of Bridge's attack is the way in which Wilberforce, and others before him, had equated two different tasks carried out by immigration officers. One is the role of immigration officer in deciding whether or not to allow an alien initial entry, but quite separate, and to Bridge very different, is the officer's role in making the decision to detain and arrange the deportation of someone who was already in the country. While criticizing the same passage from Wilberforce that we selected above on the difficulty of the immigration officer's decision, he reserves his full scorn for an earlier example, which he describes as 'perhaps the most colourful expression of the argument which can be advanced in support of the prevailing doctrine'. This is from Lord Lane CJ in a 1980 case:

No distinction can properly be drawn between a person who is discovered at the airport trying to enter illegally and a person who by skill, fraud and deceit manages to get past the immigration officer at the airport and is then interviewed that night by the immigration officer in his hotel, the immigration officer by that time having gathered the necessary information of the fraud or deceit. There can be no possible distinction in principle between those two situations . . .[24]

Bridge describes this 'somewhat improbable illustration' (and, *a fortiori*, Wilberforce's argument as well) as intended to justify what he regards as an unacceptable assimilation between two quite different powers whose crucial difference, he says, the arguments are 'calculated to obscure and minimise'. It is rare that language as strong as this is used by one Law

---

[23] *Khawaja* at 120.
[24] Taken in Bridge's speech in *Khawaja* at 121. It is from an unreported case of 29 April 1980, R v. *Secretary of State for the Home Department, ex parte Pinky Badwal*.

Lord of others' argumentative techniques, and we would have chosen this case as an example of judicial methodology for Chapter 3 had it not been so important to discuss it in this substantive context. What previous cases have done, argues Bridge, is to equate powers for dealing with applicants arriving in the country with powers exercisable on those well settled. The former have to be essentially summary, because if unsuccessful applicants were allowed in just to make their appeals the system really would be unworkable. *Wednesbury* is entirely appropriate in this context:

> But the detention and removal of a non-patrial resident in this country, who may or may not be a British subject, who may have been here for many years and who on the face of it, enjoys the benefit of an express grant of leave to be here, on the ground that he is an illegal entrant, seems to me to be dependent on fundamentally different considerations . . . The established resident who entered with express permission enjoys an existing status of which, so far as the express language of the statute goes, the immigration officer has no power whatsoever to deprive him. My Lords, we should I submit, regard with extreme jealousy any claim by the executive to imprison a person without trial.

Lord Bridge too cites *Liversidge*, saying the majority opinion in that case is the only one on record where 'imprisonment without trial by executive order' has been justified, and referring to Lord Atkin's 'withering condemnation of the process of reading into the statutory language there under consideration the words which were necessary to sustain the decision of the majority' which begins this chapter. So *Zamir* was overturned, and in most passionate language. One is nonetheless left with the fact that it was good law once, and, indeed, was the end of a long chain of cases in the Court of Appeal where judges had no trouble in giving the executive the powers that Scarman and Bridge find so horrific. For that matter, every time a judge cites Lord Atkin's dissent in *Liversidge*, it is important to remember that it was only a dissent, and that the majority view was not formally overturned until 1980. If constitutional law followed a single line of development, *Khawaja* would be an important step along that path. But all it really stands for is evidence of the importance of individual judges. Bridge shows, not only here but in the next case we discuss, just how powerful a protection of rights English constitutional law *can* be. But Wilberforce was, throughout a very long career, one of the stars of the English legal stage. We are every bit as likely to get future Wilberforces as Bridges. Templeman was part of the unanimous court in *Khawaja* and thus shares in its rights-protecting force. But he was also part of the unanimous court in *Oladehinde*. There the Law Lords notably did not feel passionately that benefit of constitutional doubt should be given to imprisoned and deported aliens. Which Templeman might we get in the future? Let us for now continue with Lord Bridge's powerful sense of reality when examining executive powers.

A major problem for Western Governments wishing to operate very restrictive immigration policies is that they are also signatories of the Geneva Convention Relating to the Status of Refugees 1951 and its 1967 Protocol. These impose obligations in international law on the Government which, so far as they may clash with immigration policy, are given precedence by the Immigration Acts. This is the problem of political asylum which has much bothered both the courts and the Home Secretary in the latter half of the nineties, but which first came to the attention of their Lordships in a 1987 case called *Bugdaycay* v. *Secretary of State for the Home Department* while the 1971 Act was still the main legislation.[25] Under the Convention the UK guarantees not to return a refugee to a country where he has 'a well founded fear of being persecuted'. Three of the four applicants in the joined appeals that make up *Bugdaycay* can be dealt with here very quickly, as the Lords did. They had all entered on temporary permission with spurious reasons—one as a tourist, one as a student, one as a business visitor. All three later made new claims to be political refugees, one before, the other two after, their temporary permissions ended. The Home Secretary rejected all three claims to asylum, saying they were not genuine refugees, and ordered their removal as illegal immigrants. They were illegal on the grounds that they had lied to gain entry. Similarities to the *Khawaja* case are obvious, but there was no attempt here to claim that the immigration authorities were wrong, or had inadequate grounds for deciding that the applicants were illegal immigrants—they had clearly lied to gain entry. The basis of their appeal was instead against the Home Secretary's decision that they were not genuine refugees. Against this decision there was no provision for appeal. They tried to argue that the newly strengthened 'precedent fact' doctrine did apply to them, however, because, if they were refugees then they could not be deported, so the decision to treat them as non-refugees in this way must be outside the Home Secretary's power: 'the Secretary of State cannot give himself power to make a decision leading to a person's removal contrary to the rules by finding as a fact that he is not a refugee, if in truth he is'. If this argument is valid, the courts would not be *'Wednesbury* restricted' from examining the Secretary of State's decision. The practical reason for trying this argument was that appeals through the internal immigration machinery can only be made when the appellant is outside the country. If he is sent back to a country where he claims persecution awaits, and he was telling the truth, he is unlikely to survive long enough to launch an appeal. It has, indeed, some of the features of testing for witchcraft by the ducking-stool. A further strong moral, or political, but not legal argument here is that by Article 35 of the Convention 'contract-

---

[25] *Bugdaycay* v. *Secretary of State for the Home Department* [1987] 1 AC 514.

ing states undertake to co-operate with the Office of the United Nations High Commissioner for Refugees', whose 1979 Handbook on *Procedures and Criteria for Determining Refugee Status* stipulates both that a claimant to refugee status should, everywhere, not only be allowed some form of appeal against a negative decision, but that he should be allowed to remain in the country pending such an appeal. It is not a good legal argument, in this country anyway, because English law could never regard so indirect an international commitment as being justiciable, although there had been discussion of the issue in the Court of Appeal. According to Lord Bridge it was 'neither necessary nor desirable that this House should attempt to interpret an instrument of this character which is of no binding force in municipal or international law'.[26]

There might be ways round this if the Lords really wished to fight, but it is no part of the argument of this book that judicial discretion is total. As it must be admitted that there is a clash between the indirect imperative of the UN recommended practice and the clear words of section 13(3) of the 1971 Act which deny appeal as long as the claimant is in the country, one cannot take their Lordships' decision against the three as evidence that their commitment to human rights ran out at this point. Maybe they would have liked to find for the plaintiffs and simply could not find what Lord Mustill in another case called 'any intellectually sustainable argument'. Nonetheless this part of the case is interesting in showing how narrow the opening for human rights made by the decision in *Khawaja* really was. It takes a very fine legal appreciation to grasp the difference Lord Bridge relies on here.

For the reasons explained at great length in the speeches in *Khawaja*'s case the courts' fundamentally different approach to an order for removal on the ground of illegal entry is dictated by the terms of the statute itself, since the power to direct removal under [the Schedule to the Act] is only available in the case of a person who is in fact an 'illegal entrant'.[27]

The plaintiffs' argument was that the power to treat someone as not a genuine refugee and therefore to deny entrance is similarly something that can only be done to one who is, in fact, not a genuine refugee, but this is where the difference apparently lies, because:

all questions of fact on which the discretionary decision whether to grant or withhold leave to enter or remain depends must necessarily be determined by the immigration officer or the Secretary of State in the exercise of the discretion which is exclusively conferred upon them by section 4(1) of the Act. The question whether an applicant for leave to enter or remain is or is not a refugee is only one, even if a particularly important one ... of a multiplicity of questions which

---

[26] *Bugdaycay* at 524.
[27] *Bugdaycay* at 523.

immigration officers and officials of the Home Office ... must daily determine in dealing with applications for leave to enter or remain in accordance with the rules as for example, whether an applicant is a bona fide visitor, student, businessman, dependant etc. Determination of such questions is only open to challenge in the courts on well known Wednesbury principles. *There is no ground for treating the question raised by a claim to refugee status as an exception to this rule.* (Emphasis added.)

The grounds for so doing would be, of course, the extreme finality of sending someone back to a country he may die in. Certainly the real distinction between the two 'judgement calls' evades us. In one case *Wednesbury* does not stop the courts second guessing the Home Secretary, in the other it does. Nonetheless their Lordships clearly felt they could push *Wednesbury*-based deference to the executive too far out of the window, and chose to mark the limit at this point. However it may be, the Lords did draw a distinction between these three applicants, and the fourth, a Mr Musisi, and this distinction helps us towards understanding just what it is they do believe about refugees' rights. Musisi had arrived on 23 January 1983, to visit his sisters, but the immigration officer had doubts about his status and granted him only temporary leave to enter until the 26th, when he was interviewed by a different officer. This time the immigration officer decided not to grant leave, and his temporary permit was extended only until the next day when he was ordered to leave by the airline that had brought him to Heathrow. On the morning of 27 January he put in a claim for asylum from his home country, Uganda, though he had arrived in the UK from Kenya. This produced another temporary leave, which continued up to the appeal in the Lords.

Lord Bridge comments that he finds it very odd that counsel not only did not try, but expressly disclaimed, any *Wednesbury* challenge to the Home Secretary's decision, and essentially raises and answers the challenge himself, finding against the Home Office. It is clear, as in so many cases, that the actual details of the case triggered Bridge's sympathy. In particular the Home Office was clearly seen to have behaved in a very shabby fashion. It is a common factor this, the individual judge's perception of ill behaviour by the administration triggering a reaction which is simply not present in other cases. It is obvious, for example, that much of what inspired their Lordships in *Pepper* v. *Hart*, or in *Woolwich Equitable Building Society* v. *Inland Revenue Commissioners* mentioned briefly earlier, was simply outrage against the revenue authorities on the details of the case. Here the Home Office's behaviour was enough to make Bridge a defender of Musisi, even though he rejects all the arguments actually made on his behalf in the courts below. The details are quite complicated, but we must relate them briefly to show Bridge's attitude, to demonstrate the extent of misbehaviour the Home Office has to engage in to anger the judges, and, more generally, to demonstrate just why it is that the judges would do well to be less trusting of the executive than so many of them so often are. First, though, it is important to note something we have said several times about *Wednesbury*. As will become apparent, Lord Bridge did not formally stray from the *Wednesbury* rule when he rescued Mr Musisi. Instead he manipulated it to be less of a restraint than sometimes to get the result he wants. Here as elsewhere one gets the impression that *Wednesbury* can be a voluntary judicial restraint, easy to slip out of when a judge's reaction to the executive's behaviour makes him want to.

Bridge describes his approach as follows:

any issue of law and fact and the exercise of any discretion in relation to an application for asylum as a refugee lie exclusively within the jurisdiction of the Secretary of State, subject only to the court's power of [judicial] review. The limitations on the scope of that power are well known and need not be restated here. Within those limitations the court must, I think, be entitled to subject an administrative decision to the more rigorous examination, to ensure that it is in no way flawed, according to the gravity of the issue which the decision determines. The most fundamental of all human rights is the individual's right to life and when an administrative decision under challenge is said to be one which may put the applicant's life at risk, the basis for the decision must surely call for the most anxious scrutiny.[28]

This is still, just about, *Wednesbury*, but more or less the opposite of *Super Wednesbury*, the doctrine Scarman invented to deal with challenges to major government policy. We can call it, perhaps, by symmetry, *Minimal-Wednesbury*. It is echoed in the conclusion to Templeman's brief assenting speech: 'In my opinion where the result of a flawed decision may imperil life or liberty a special responsibility lies on the court in the examination of the decision making process'.[29] What allows their Lordships to apply this *Minimal-Wednesbury* test to Musisi, when they saw no reason to apply it, or any other check, in the other three related appeals, is unclear. It could be that the facts, which we are not given in the report of the case, were so strongly for the Home Office that there was no temptation, or point, in applying a *Minimal-Wednesbury*, though one has no reason to assume that. Certainly for the other three appellants the failure to avoid *Wednesbury* via the *Khawaja* route was final.

Musisi survived because of specific facts. The Home Office was intent on sending him back to Kenya from whence he had come to England. Musisi insisted that Kenya would immediately send him back to Uganda, where he was in danger. The Home Office left open the question of whether he would be in danger in Uganda, and simply insisted that this had no bearing on their decision to deport him to Kenya. Musisi had

---

[28] *Bugdaycay* at 531.
[29] *Bugdaycay* at 537.

arrived in the UK from Kenya, and it is to Kenya they wanted to deport him. The Convention only requires the UK to allow people entry as refugees from their home country. They were thus bluntly indifferent to anything but obeying the words and not the spirit of the Convention. In fact, with the Lords' unwillingness to ditch *Wednesbury* completely, had the Home Secretary insisted flatly that Musisi was not at all a refugee *vis-à-vis* any country, including Uganda, they might have felt unable to intervene. In fact, as we shall see, they were prepared to investigate evidence about Kenya's refugee policy in considerable depth, though it must surely be harder to assess that than the simpler question of whether someone is directly in danger in his home country. It was in this way that a mere *Wednesbury* analysis became indistinguishable from a thorough review of the facts. The evidence the Lords sifted and evaluated in Musisi's *Minimal-Wednesbury* appeal was considerably more complicated and called for far more judgement than the very simple claims involved in the, theoretically more extensive, 'precedent fact' appeal of Khera in *Khawaja*. Nonetheless as long as Lord Bridge strenuously announced that he was merely applying *Wednesbury* with a 'more rigorous examination, to ensure that it is in no way flawed, according to the gravity of the issue which the decision determines', he could produce the result he wanted without creating a constitutional clash. Unfortunately avoiding the clash meant failing to guarantee that people in Musisi's situation in the future can necessarily get the same consideration. Let us see what it was that made the Home Office's behaviour amount to Templeman's 'flawed decision'.

In part Bridge was obviously dissatisfied with the behaviour of the immigration officer who interviewed Musisi about his asylum request, which seems to have been deeply inadequate. Musisi's own story of his treatment and that of his family in Uganda is horrifying, yet the immigration officer wrote in his report in this vein: 'He would have me believe that Uganda is still a violent and turbulent country and should he return there he feels his life would be in danger . . . My feelings are that he is moving away from Uganda because a better life awaits him somewhere else. Perhaps our people in Kampala can give a report on the current political, social and law and order position at present pertaining in Uganda.' This was from the officer's contemporaneous notes. Eighteen months later in his affidavit he wrote: 'I formed the view that the applicant . . . was moving away from Uganda because a better life awaited him somewhere else, and that this was not a genuine application for asylum.' Bridge comments:

I find it strange that such an important interview as this should be entrusted to an immigration officer at the port of entry with no knowledge of the conditions in the country of origin of a claimant for asylum. It seems even stranger that having suggested that local conditions should be investigated, presumably with the object of assessing the background to the claim to asylum, the interviewer should later assert that he was in a position to, and did, reject it as not being genuine.[30]

Bridge goes on to say that although it does not matter, because the Home Office left open the Uganda aspect, 'It does little to inspire confidence in the procedure that the Home Office should have based their future consideration of the case on the immigration officer's report.' Lord Bridge is blatantly playing the advocate here. It makes absolutely no difference to the legal point he has to decide. What he is doing is to set the scene for a general distrust of the Home Office's procedures. Few would disagree with his implied criticisms—what is more remarkable is that, having 'judicial notice' of how immigration policy worked in this case, there appears to have been no felt need to look carefully at the other three applicants. As Lord Bridge continues his account, the Home Office Immigration and Nationality Department rejected Musisi's claim that he had been denied asylum in Kenya, and seem to have simply ignored the fact that his leave to reside in Kenya expired on 5 March 1983. As far as they were concerned, he had been living in a safe country, Kenya, and he could go back there. This formal rejection of his claim was delivered on 12 March 1983. An MP intervened with a lengthy account of his family's persecution in Uganda, but the Home Office reiterated their view, and gave new directions for his deportation. Again an MP intervened, forwarding a letter from a Law Centre. The point was made yet again that Musisi would not be allowed to enter Kenya and would sent on to Uganda. The Law Centre had contacted the Kenyan High Commission which confirmed that he would be removed to Uganda if he arrived without a visa, and that there was no chance of his getting a visa. Such might seem to be fairly conclusive. The Home Office continued to insist that Kenya, as a signatory to the Convention, would not deport Musisi. They did so despite information, gained by Musisi on their advice from the UN, which confirmed his danger, and despite further affidavits, one from a refugee who happened to be a former Attorney-General of Uganda, about Kenya's practice of removing people back there. At each stage the Home Office simply reiterated their faith that Kenya would abide by its Convention obligations. It is doubtful that anyone will disagree that the Home Office was acting with blatant disregard to their duties under the Convention, and that there was, at the very least, a real risk that Kenya would do to Musisi as they regularly had done to others in his position. But is this enough to produce a negative judicial review? Reading through Lord Bridge's speech one comes now to a paragraph, a quite orthodox application of *Wednesbury*, which would seem to doom Musisi. Describing a hypothetical situation:

---

[30] *Bugdaycay* at 528. The account of the immigration report is taken from the same passage.

. . . there may be varying degrees of danger that removal to a third country of a person claiming refugee status will result in his return to the country where he fears persecution. If there is some evidence of such a danger, it must be for the Secretary of State to decide as a matter of degree the question whether the danger is sufficiently substantial to [involve a breach of the Convention]. If the Secretary of State has asked himself that question and answered it negatively in the light of all relevant evidence, the court cannot intervene.[31]

Whatever else the Home Office had been doing, it had been in lengthy communication with Musisi's supporters and advisers, and had continually announced that they trusted Kenya. They may have been wrong, but they were undeniably thinking about the matter. One affidavit in particular should have shown that. This is from a senior Home Office official, taking up the burden of the complaints:

it is the respondents belief that Kenya as a signatory to [the Convention] would not knowingly remove a Ugandan citizen to Uganda if there was reason to believe he would be persecuted there . . . [the affidavit considers the evidence alleging Kenya's repatriation to Uganda and continues] . . . I can say that although it has been the case that Kenya has returned Ugandan nationals to Uganda in the past the respondent has no evidence that this continues to be the case and indeed earlier this year after representations had been made to it by the UN High Commissioner for Refugees the Kenyan Government confirmed its position as a signatory to the said Convention.

But this affidavit turned out to be fatal. Bridge savaged it, using it as evidence that the Home Secretary had made no effort at all to check that a situation he admits to knowing about in the past is not ongoing. Bridge reviews all the communications with the Home Office, and insists that the Secretary of State had been under a misplaced faith in Kenya, and comes back to the affidavit quoted:

The fact of such breaches must be very relevant to any assessment of the danger that the appellant, if returned to Kenya, would be sent home to Uganda. Since the decisions of the Secretary of State appear to have been made without taking that fact into account, they cannot, in my opinion, now stand.

One can only wonder what sort of evidence the Home Secretary would have to supply to the courts to satisfy them, remembering that, in the Lords' own words, it is up to him and not to them, to evaluate evidence. Lord Bridge was almost certainly right in his personal assessment of the Home Office's indifference, but it is also quite impossible to square what he does here with any normal application of *Wednesbury*, even at its most minimal. It is, in fact, a very intrusive judicial review which comes close to direct intervention in internal government department decision-making

---

[31] *Bugdaycay* at 532.

mechanisms. The Home Office behaved appallingly. There is no evidence that this was anything but par for the course. But why intervene here, and yet adumbrate doctrines that make it such a chancy and random matter as to when a refugee will get such curial protection? There is a very widely held view, expressed openly by some members of the Court of Appeal, as well as by criminal barristers, that the Lords' criminal law jurisdiction should be abolished. Law Lords themselves will admit, off the record, that their historical performance in criminal law is woeful. Often it is because of the random intrusion of sympathy or horror for the facts of particular cases. Something very similar appears to happen in immigration cases, and possibly in other public law areas where individual stories shock. The answer cannot be to strip the Lords of jurisdiction. It must be that they should fashion doctrines of constitutional protection for human rights which do not, because of an excessive formal trust in the executive, require them to twist their own doctrines to do justice when the facts do penetrate the formulas. Perhaps this would not matter if decisions like Musisi's and Khera's were a sign of a general shift towards a more intrusive orientation so that, whatever the doctrine, plaintiffs in human rights cases could expect, and the executive therefore automatically fear, extreme minimality even if *Wednesbury* was applied, or a greater willingness to slide out of *Wednesbury* by making far more use of the 'precedent fact' principle. After all what *Bugdaycay* really stands for is not a legal doctrine at all. It stands to demonstrate the complete permeability of either doctrine to judicial willpower. It really made no difference to Musisi whether *Wednesbury* was or was not the language in which Lord Bridge had to clothe his distaste for the Home Office officials (much of which, unquoted here, was scornful in the extreme). But there is no evidence at all that *Budgaycay* is part of a trend. This can be shown with a much more recent case involving very similar questions about asylum seekers and the need for adequate information for decision.

Unfortunately for the appellants in *R* v. *Secretary of State for the Home Department, ex parte Abdi*, Lord Bridge had retired by the time their case came up in 1996, though his paragraph in *Bugdaycay* which we have suggested defines a form of minimalist *Wednesbury* is often extensively quoted by those who argue, usually unsuccessfully, for immigrants' rights.[32] *Ex parte Abdi* is another political asylum case, and again it involves a general question of due process, or 'fair play in action', to use a phrase cited here by Lord Slynn.[33] By the time the case came up the statutory framework for asylum seekers had changed considerably,

---

[32] *R* v. *Secretary of State for the Home Department, ex parte Abdi* [1996] 1 WLR 298.
[33] The case, *Wiseman* v. *Borneman* [1971] AC 297, per Morris at 309, was relied on in all three courts to establish that common law could fill in necessary natural justice requirements where the statute failed to do so.

mainly through the passage of the Asylum and Immigration Appeals Act 1993. This Act, and the consequent Statement of Changes in the Immigration Rules (1993),[34] had taken on board the fact that many appeals could not truly be seen as involving any question of the UK's international law obligations under the Convention of 1951 and would therefore be, in the eyes of the executive, more or less hopeless. To dispose of such cases quickly, while still living up to the Convention's requirement that there be some right of appeal, a special fast-track process had been legislated, to be applied in cases where the Home Secretary issued what is known as a 'Without Foundation' certificate. In such cases no substantive assessment is made of the claim to be a genuine refugee. *Ex parte Abdi* is typical of such purported 'Without Foundation' cases. It involved an attempt by the Government, as in Musisi's case, to return someone not to his own country (Somalia) where he feared persecution but to the last country he had been in before arrival in the UK, which for Abdi was Spain. As Spain was a signatory to the Convention, the familiar argument is that he should have asked for asylum there, and even though he had not done so, Spain could be expected to listen sympathetically and not send him back to Somalia. The only differences at this stage were that Abdi had never tried to enter the UK illegally, and thus, unlike Musisi could not be treated as an illegal alien. The new legislation did allow asylum seekers into the country for the brief period of their application and appeal.

It is necessary to set out the Home Secretary's decision letter fully, because much depended on its wording. Having recited the facts of the application for asylum it notes that Somalia is not the only country to which he can be returned, because under paragraph 8(1) of Schedule 2 of the Immigration Act 1971, he can be returned to Spain which is a signatory of the Convention. It goes on to say:

> The Secretary of State on the basis of his knowledge of the immigration policies and practices of Spain, and on previous experiences of returning passengers to Spain, has no reason to believe that, in the circumstances of your particular case, the authorities there would not comply with their obligations under the Convention.[35]

In such a 'Without Foundation' case the applicant can appeal, as Mr Abdi did, to a special adjudicator against the validity of the certificate. The only issue raised in the appeal was a claim that there had been no chance to ask for asylum in Spain, which was rejected, and the certificate was upheld. There had been no evidence before the adjudicator that Spain was not a 'safe third country within the meaning of paragraph 180K of Statement of Changes in the Immigration Rules'.[36] Judicial review was sought and

---

[34] HC 725.
[35] *Ex parte Abdi* at 301.
[36] Taken from the headnote to *Ex parte Abdi*.

granted, and Steven Sedley J quashed both the decisions of the adjudicators and the original decisions of the Home Secretary. (Abdi was one of two appeals on almost identical facts heard together.) Sedley granted the applicants' requests for two reasons. First, he accepted their claim that the Home Secretary was under a duty to disclose all the material he had, on the basis of which he had made his decision that Spain was a safe country to which to return the applicants. Secondly, he accepted that the adjudicators had no evidence on which they could independently judge the Secretary of State's decision, because they were forced to rely on the bare statement in the letter cited above. Sedley was overturned by the majority of the Court of Appeal, but supported by the dissent of Steyn LJ, who shortly after the case was made a Law Lord himself. The Lords upheld the majority in the Court of Appeal. There was, however, a powerful dissent, supporting Sedley J and Steyn LJ on both points, by Lord Slynn who is, along with Lord Woolf, who did not sit, the most experienced public lawyer in the House. Lord Mustill was of two minds. He supported the majority on the disclosure point, and Lord Slynn on the evidence point. If nothing else, *Ex parte Abdi* is a fine example of happenstance. Had it occurred a year later, it might have come to the Lords during a brief period when Lords Steyn, Slynn, and Woolf could have heard it. There can be no doubt that had this happened, not only would Abdi be living in England, but an important public law doctrine would have been created on the executive's duty of disclosure. As it is, *Abdi* stands instead as evidence for our point that there is no developmental trend in public law—the decision was as negative, and as supportive of administrative expediency, as any case before *Bugdaycay*.

The essence of the special provision for 'Without Foundation' cases is speed. This is primarily done by cutting the timetable dramatically. Where normally an applicant has ten days to lodge an appeal, he now has only two, and whereas a normal appeal has to be completely dealt with in forty-two days, this period is shortened to only seven for these special appeals. One other change from the ordinary rules is that the special appeal rules do not have the requirement in the old rule 8(1) that the Secretary of State must serve a statement of the relevant facts related to his decision and his reasons for that decision. All he now has to provide is a copy of his decision letter, the notes of the immigration officer's interview, and any documents referred to in his decision letter. The timetable is for the convenience of the executive because, as Lord Lloyd for the majority notes, if the applicant stays in the UK for too long, the country he came to the UK from, which the Government is insisting is the appropriate place for a substantive asylum hearing, may itself refuse to grant one. If so, the only thing they could do would be to return him to the UK, which would then be stuck with him.

The crux of the legal argument is this. As the Act does now require some specific and very limited documents to be provided, and has dropped, to save time, the Home Secretary's obligation to give a reasoned decision, does it follow that it would be incompatible with the Act for courts to demand that he gives full disclosure of the information available to him? Sedley J thought not, because, he argued the special adjudicator could not possibly be an independent judge, as he was supposed to be, absent information. The courts had already established quite clearly that the adjudicator was to make up his own mind about the safety of the third country: 'The discipline which this system imposes upon the Secretary of State consists in the fact that the adjudicator must independently judge the merits of the certificate.'[37] This, interestingly, comes from Laws J, who had argued many public law cases for the Government until shortly before the *Abdi* case when he was promoted to the bench. (There is a curious constancy about one aspect of English public law. The last four Treasury Counsel, who represent the Government in public law cases, are Lord Woolf, Lord Slynn, Simon Brown LJ, and Laws J. They are well ahead of the field as the most active and anti-executive of senior judges now.) The Court of Appeal had also said of the special adjudicator: 'Clearly the special adjudicator is not bound by the Home Secretary's certificate. He must consider whether, on the material before the Home Secretary, and on any other material before him . . . the conclusion which the Home Secretary reached is justified.'[38]

Lord Slynn assembles these remarks, adds Bridge's by now famous dictum on the need for anxious scrutiny in asylum cases, and adds a further comment from Bingham LJ that 'asylum decisions are of such moment that only the highest standards of fairness will suffice',[39] and insists that it must follow that the applicant and the adjudicator must see the material the Home Secretary had, making the apposite back reference to *Khawaja*:

An applicant is required frankly to disclose relevant information to the immigration officer; on these appeals what is sauce for the goose is sauce for the gander and prima facie there is no reason why the appellant and the special adjudicator should not see the material on which the Secretary of State took his decision.[40]

He notes that there are said to be two reasons why this cannot be done—that Parliament has excluded such a duty, and that it is impractical. These arguments Slynn dismisses fairly quickly, noting that they could only apply if Parliament had deliberately laid down an exclusive, all embrac-

---

[37] Laws J in *R v. Secretary of State for the Home Department, ex parte Mehari* [1994] QB 474 at 490.

[38] Glidewell LJ in *Thavathevathasan v. Secretary of State for the Home Department* [1994] Imm. AR 249 at 254.

[39] *Secretary of State for the Home Department v. Thirukumar* [1989] Imm. AR 402 at 414.

[40] *Ex parte Abdi* at 305.

ing code' to cover the matter, and that the acknowledged independent role of the special adjudicator is incompatible with such an intention. On the impracticality question he notes something the majority never mention. The adjudicators are all equipped by the Home Office with special files on some twenty-four countries, each about fifty pages long, containing information supporting the 'safety' of the countries as destinations for would-be asylum seekers. Given that, Lord Slynn not surprisingly feels it cannot be claimed to be administratively impossible to provide the other side of the coin. (It is an important background fact of this case that Sedley J had personally known about, and cited, a report by Amnesty International showing that Spain had recently sent on two such asylum seekers to Columbia from which they had fled—the material not having been disclosed by the Home Office in the cases now in question.) As Slynn says:

If the Secretary of State has overriding or wholly dependable and consistent evidence that a country is a safe country then he is unlikely to have a lot of material the other way. If he does the evidence against the appellant's contention may be the less reliable. If there is little information in favour of the appellant it will not be difficult to produce it; if there is strong evidence in favour of the appellant's contention that the third country is not a safe country . . . the special adjudicator ought to be shown it by the Secretary of State . . . If there is a lot of strong material that a country is not safe then the Secretary of State is unlikely to find that it is so; if he does then it is patently important that the special adjudicator should have the material.[41]

Slynn also quotes the adjudicators themselves, who had been represented, noting that they were clearly very eager to do their job fairly, and unworried by the possible consequences:

If the result of requiring further material is that the particular appellant is less likely to be returned to a safe third country, that is the inevitable outcome of the need to deal with the appeals fairly.

On this point Slynn and Steyn LJ are very clear—Steyn LJ, in his conclusion, not only calling the process unlawful, but pointing out that it is, precisely, the habitual system:

For my part I am satisfied that the procedure in fact adopted is so unfair as to be unlawful . . . The consequence of the procedure in fact adopted in the cases before us and habitually adopted in all other similar cases is to render ineffective fundamental rights of asylum seekers.[42]

It would seem almost impossible not to accept this line of argument if one is to retain a working belief in the power of the common law to protect human rights. Yet the majority in the Lords, including on this point Lord

---

[41] *Ex Parte Abdi* at 306.
[42] Quoted by Lord Lloyd in *Ex parte Abdi* at 312.

Mustill, have no trouble at all. For them the mere fact that the legislation places some, limited, disclosure obligation on the Home Secretary, and had removed a greater obligation to give reasons (which still applies to other immigration appeals), is completely inconsistent with any implied duty to do more. They simply do not take up the fairness points, and ignore references to a general common law power to read into flawed procedures steps necessary for natural justice. Instead they stress the administrative need for speed, and de-emphasize the substance of the issue. Lloyd grants that the appellants' fairness argument is a strong one, but replies to it thus:

> This is a strong argument. But there are stronger arguments the other way. In the first place your Lordships are not now concerned with substantive rights to asylum. We are concerned with the procedural question whether the substantive hearing should take place here or in a third country.

For Lloyd the stronger argument is the one for speed lest Spain sends Abdi back to the UK. Lloyd's speech reads as though the case were a commercial case about where some contractual dispute should be legislated. It is not, from the point of view of Abdi, a question of where he gets his substantive hearing. If he is right, he may never get one if sent on to a third country the safety of which is in dispute. There is no obvious way of making sense of the clash between Slynn, Steyn, and Sedley on the one hand and the Lords' majority on the other. What could motivate the majority to be so unwilling to take the natural justice high road? Lord Mustill might have been of help here, given that he agrees, on different points, with both sides. He, of all judges, is prone to give very lengthy, often academically-styled speeches exploring the intricacies of both sides. Perhaps it says something about the essential indefensibility of the majority that all he says here is that, while sharing the 'hesitation' of the Court of Appeal majority, '[i]n the very special context of this abbreviated procedure no such duty can be implied'.[43]

Lord Mustill's reticence is all the more marked because the rest of his very brief dissent says all that there is to say about the other point, and says it with passion. The other ground for the appeal is that, whether or not there should have been disclosure, there was, in fact, precisely no evidence adduced that Spain was a safe third country. This is because of the curt language of the Home Secretary's certificate, quoted above. Four judges agree that this certificate does not begin to constitute enough evidence for the special adjudicators to reach their conclusions, and all express the same degree of horror. Mustill's language conveys it best. After quoting the certificate, he describes it thus:

---

[43] *Ex parte Abdi* at 300.

My Lord, to contend that such a statement is evidence sufficient to justify a finding favourable to the Secretary of State in his contest with the appellant before the special adjudicators amounts to this: that the Secretary of State knows what he is talking about and that the adjudicators should take his word for it. True the procedure was truncated . . . but the procedure was none the less adversarial. Plainly the Secretary of State cannot be contending that, in the absence of express statutory provision, a bare statement of honest belief by one party to an adversarial procedure is sufficient to prove the fact asserted, and equally plainly the Secretary of State would shrink from conceding that a similar statement would be sufficient to carry the day for the appellant, the other party to the issue. It must therefore be the proposition that there is something unique in the position of the Secretary of State which transmutes a statement of belief into an item of evidence. No authority was cited in support of this notion, which I find disturbing, the more so for its distant echo of *Liversidge v Anderson*. I do not accept it, and since in this case nothing other than the letter was adduced in support of the decision under appeal I agree in this respect with the judgment of Steyn LJ and with the opinion on this point of my noble and learned friend, Lord Slynn of Hadley.

And yet five judges, two in the Court of Appeal and three in the Lords, were unworried even by this aspect of the case, giving the Home Secretary victory at both levels of appeal. So unworried was Lord Lloyd that he spent only one paragraph on what he described as 'the subsidiary question'. And what he has to say is that the Home Secretary's statement about his past experience 'may not amount to much, but it is at least *some* evidence in support of the Secretary of State's certificate' (italics in original).[44] As fas as Lloyd is concerned, this minimal evidence was never challenged. But part of the argument, from Sedley upwards, was that asylum seekers, though they know quite enough about the countries they are fleeing from, are in no position at all to know about the third country, which is why they wanted disclosure in the first place.

There is little point giving further examples. This chapter has sought to demonstrate not that the Lords are always, or inevitably, executive minded where it comes to immigration questions, but that they most certainly can be so, and that there is no obvious predictability at all as to when they will be. Instead there is a huge randomness, with public law activism being sparked, as far as one can see, by accidental aspects of the stories would-be immigrants or asylum seekers happen to tell, by sheer chance about who hears the stories. There are cases, or sometimes just speeches within cases, of great liberality. These are high points in the protection of individual rights. Yet later cases show a falling away from what can be achieved, a failure to pick up and develop clearly enunciated principles. *Budgaycay* or *Khawaja* might just as well never have been decided for all the effect they had on *Abdi*. One model of constitutional

---

[44] *Ex parte Abdi* at 315.

law as found in other jurisdictions is that it develops via a ratchet-like process—once some position has been achieved, a case can never fall back below that point, even if most cases take the value in question no further for a long time. In the American experience, for example, control over executive and legislative policy in discrimination cases can never fall back below the standard of strict scrutiny now that doctrine has been enunciated. The French *Conseil Constitutionel* has explicitly accepted this ratchet approach in civil liberties. But British public law has structural features which makes this progressive establishment of levels of control impossible—impossible anyway in the sense of preventing judges who want to derogate from their predecessors' liberality from doing so. The main feature is that public law is very much concerned with statutes, and statutes which are altered frequently and radically, as with immigration control rules. Thus the cases are never, technically, more than examples of statutory interpretation, and high-sounding principles like Bridge's are 'only' obiter, and can gain little binding force over future generations.

2. Prisoners' Rights

It is useful to conclude this chapter with a very quick description of how a similar process of high principle with little consequence is exhibited in cases dealing with prisoners' rights, a subject matter analogous to immigrant rights. It should be noted that much of the actual law involved in the sorts of situations described in these cases has subsequently changed, either as a result of pressure from the European Court of Human Rights, or by government reform. Thus even more than usual, this section does not purport to describe the law at any particular time—it is concerned, as ever, with judicial argument.

Possibly the leading case on prisoners' rights, because it contains the requisite oft-quoted and high-sounding statement of principle, is *Raymond* v. *Honey*, heard in 1983 by a panel which held three of the Law Lords we have concentrated on, Lords Wilberforce, Bridge, and Lowry.[45] Colin Honey was the Governor of Albany Prison on the Isle of Wight at the time that Steven Raymond was serving a prison sentence for robbery and also facing committal proceedings in a magistrates' court for another offence. Raymond wrote to his solicitors about his forthcoming hearing. His letter included an allegation against an assistant governor, whose behaviour Raymond wanted to claim was relevant to the case he was trying to prepare. The Prison Service rules required what was known as 'prior ventilation', that any complaint about the behaviour of a member of the

---

[45] *Raymond* v. *Honey* [1983] AC 1.

service by a prisoner had to be dealt with internally before the prisoner was entitled to make any attempt to use external judicial machinery to help him. Consequently the Governor stopped the letter. He also stopped a subsequent communication by Raymond, which was his petition to the High Court alleging that the first stoppage of his legal communications, by interfering with his attempts to litigate, amounted to contempt of court. Raymond somehow or other managed to bring both issues to the courts. Lord Wilberforce gave the main speech. Despite anything his performance in some cases we have cited might make one think, Wilberforce was never automatically a supporter of the executive over individual rights—the Law Lords very seldom demonstrate such substantive consistency. Here Wilberforce starts his speech with what has become the prisoners' rights high principle. He claims that, 'under English law a convicted prisoner, in spite of his imprisonment, retains all civil rights which are not taken away expressly or by necessary implication'.[46] This proposition he drew, interestingly, from a Canadian Supreme Court ruling. It was clear to all the judges in the case, in the Court of Appeal as well as the Lords, that any attempt to 'inhibit suitors from availing themselves of their constitutional right to have their legal rights and obligations ascertained and enforced by courts of law could amount to contempt of court', a principle Wilberforce traces at least as far back as 1900. There was little need to construct complicated interpretative arguments in *Raymond* v. *Honey*, because the Prison Rules 1964 and the legislation they derived from, the Prison Act 1952, could not be interpreted as giving the Home Secretary the right to deny such a basic constitutional right. This was especially so because there had been a powerful adverse ruling by the European Court of Human Rights a few years before, when upholding the complaint of a prisoner against the UK, that access to a court was a basic right protected by Article 6 of the European Convention.[47]

Lord Bridge with his usual blunt acknowledgment of real executive intention characterizes the rules as being 'in their original form . . . intended to give the Secretary of State an absolute discretion whether or not to allow a prisoner to institute legal proceedings'. What moderation had been made in the rules after the ECHR ruling, according to Bridge, only concerned proceedings via a solicitor, and the rest of the rules were intended to maximally discourage a prisoner from instituting proceedings himself, and to give the impression that the Home Secretary could prevent such action. For Bridge, differing from Wilberforce only in the force of his language:

---

[46] *Raymond* at 12. But note that the principle was enunciated originally in *Solosky* v. *The Queen* (1979) 105 DLR (3d) 745,760 Canadian Supreme Court.

[47] *Golder* v. *United Kingdom* (1975) 1 EHRR 524.

The only statutory provision relied on as empowering the Secretary of State to make rules imposing such fetters on a prisoner's access to the courts as the rules ... purport to impose is the power in section 47 of the Prison Act 1952 to make rules for the 'discipline and control' of prisoners. This rule making power is manifestly insufficient for such a purpose ...[48]

Raymond v. *Honey*, then, is a clear-cut refusal of the courts to bend to administrative convenience, a splendid insistence that a basic human right cannot be taken away just because someone is, for precisely defined reasons, to be treated as lacking other rights. It is also, of course, a case which protects a jealously guarded prerogative of the courts themselves—though courts often, as we shall see especially in the next chapter, voluntarily shed themselves of chances to intervene in administration, they will never accept the right of other branches of the State to preclude them having the chance to hear a case. (And indeed, much of the force in the anti-government cases cited in the last chapter comes from this determination to protect the courts' own authority.) The Lords were more or less bound to take the position they did— the Prison Service's interpretation of its rules in this area amounted to the sort of ouster clause that the courts have not tolerated since *Anisminic*.[49]

Wilberforce's statement of the durability of human rights in prison has been quoted in many subsequent cases; in one crucial area the Lords have continued opening up access to justice. This was in the 1988 cases, heard jointly, of Leech and Prevot against the Governors, respectively, of Parkhurst and Long Lartin prisons.[50] The case is interesting because, though the Lords did change the law in a more libertarian way, they had to deal with arguments in the Court of Appeal of a very traditional nature, stressing the importance of administrative convenience we have seen so often in public law cases. Perhaps it will come as no surprise to the reader that the arguments in question were made by two men who later joined the Lords and have featured frequently in these pages—the then Lords Justices of Appeal Browne-Wilkinson and Griffiths. In fact the views of yet another future Law Lord, Lord Lowry, show by implication in this case, as will be seen. Lowry, in keeping with all we have seen from Chapter 2 onwards, is on the liberal side against Browne-Wilkinson and Griffiths. We again feel at liberty to use evidence about Law Lords from their prior career as evidence about Law Lords in general. It is, of course, precisely where one has a greater commitment to liberal principles in an older

---

[48] *Raymond* at 15.
[49] We have referred above to *Anisminic Ltd.* v. *Foreign Compensation Commission* [1969] 2 AC 147. It is the outstanding example of the Lords flatly refusing to accept that a statute actually said what it clearly said, because the Government of the day had clearly intended to keep courts out of a set of administrative decisions. The case would have been worth analysing in this book, except that it concerns a much earlier court.
[50] *Leech* v. *Governor of Parkhurst Prison* [1988] 1 AC 533.

generation of judges than amongst their replacements that the lack of a ratchet effect matters most. In this specific context a firmly liberal precedent was established which will not easily be unpicked later, but a future court would not be bound by any generalized implication of the decision. (Nor of course are they bound at all if they choose to use the 1966 Practice Statement.) The cases were both challenges to due process in that Leech and Prevot had been disciplined by prison governors for breaches of prison rules in such manner that natural justice and other procedural improprieties tainted the decisions. They applied to the courts for judicial review either of the Governor's decision (in Leech's case) or both the Governor's decision and the supporting decision of the Home Secretary (in Prevot's case). At the time prison discipline was handled by a two-tier system. Prison governors had the primary disciplinary role, but offences which the governors thought warranted sentences heavier than they could impose were referred to bodies known as Boards of Visitors. Both levels applied the same type of sanctions, with loss of remission of sentence as the most serious penalty, but the Boards of Visitors could award sentences of considerably greater severity within each category. (One feature that made the governor's jurisdiction sometimes more draconian was that the Boards often gave out suspended sentences. If a governor subsequently convicted a prisoner for something else under his own jurisdiction, he would effectively be deciding to trigger the other sentence, possibly one way above the level he could have applied himself.) The cases had added complexity because they presented the rare situation where a quasi-federal conflict had occurred. The ruling case for England and Wales was *Ex Parte King* in which the Court of Appeal had held the courts had no power to intervene in a governor's decision. Yet in the same year, 1985, the Court of Appeal in Northern Ireland, in *Ex Parte McKiernan* had decided the opposite, under the guidance of its Chief Justice, Lord Lowry, who at the time served occasionally on panels of the Law Lords, though not yet as a Lord of Appeal in Ordinary.[51] In order to find for the prisoners in the current case, then, the Law Lords had to overturn *Ex Parte King*, and bring the UK into line with Ulster. Some years earlier it had been accepted by the Court of Appeal that judicial review would lie against decisions of the Boards of Prison Visitors. Here a trenchant pro-administration line had originally been held by the Divisional Court under the Chief Justice, Lord Widgery. His argument requires citing, because it set the issue for all future cases, and in fact centres round an analogy from an even earlier case of Lord Goddard CJ in 1954. Having agreed that *certiorari* would normally, in non-prison contexts, allow courts

---

[51] R v. *Deputy Governor of Camphill Prison, ex parte King* [1985] QB 735; R v. *Governor of The Maze Prison, ex parte McKiernan* (1985) 6 NIJB 6.

to supervise disciplinary punishments analogous to those handed down by Boards of Visitors, Widgery finds an exception:

That exception is where the order under challenge is an order made in private, disciplinary proceedings where there is some closed body, and a body which enjoys its own form of discipline and its own rules, and where there is a power to impose sanctions within the scope of those rules donated as part of the formation of the body itself.

After citing from Goddard's earlier case, Widgery continues:

[Goddard's principle] that domestic discipline in the form of a disciplinary body is something for the officer charged with the duty of maintaining discipline and not something for the courts is a principle which in my judgment, we should adhere to and not allow to be wasted away ... At first I thought this was a principle which would apply only to the governor. I saw the governor equated with the commanding officer of the regiment in Lord Goddard CJ's judgment, and it was not until the argument had progressed some way that it seemed to me right that we should include in this principle the board of visitors. The reason why I think it is right to include them is because they are part of the disciplinary machinery of the prison. I reject entirely any suggestion that the governor's decision should be the subject of certiorari, and I cannot see myself how, if the governor is left out, the board of visitors can be put in.[52]

The Court of Appeal then overturned this judgment, but they did it by finding a way to make the distinction Widgery could not manage between the governors and the Board of Visitors, bringing the later into the scope of judicial review, but still not doubting the propriety of leaving the governor out. This distinction was to be upheld more clearly in *Ex Parte King*, especially in the opinion of Browne-Wilkinson and Griffiths LJJ. The opinions in *Ex parte King* ring with support for hard-pressed administrations. Prison governors are likened to line managers who need their discipline unchallenged if authority is to survive:

All prisons are likely to have within them a few prisoners intent on disrupting their administration. They are likely to have even more who delude themselves that they are the victims of injustice. To allow such men to have access to the High Court whenever they thought the governor abused his powers ... would undermine and weaken his authority and make management very difficult indeed. [Lawton LJ][53]

Griffiths LJ admits that it would be logical to extend curial supervision to governors now judicial review covers Visitors, but consoles himself:

But the common law of England has not always developed upon strictly logical lines, and where logic leads down a path that is beset with practical difficulties the

---

[52] *R v. Board of Visitors of Hull Prison, ex parte St Germain* [1978] QB 678 at 690. Widgery is relying on a point made by Lord Goddard CJ in *Ex Parte Fry* [1954] 1 WLR 730.
[53] *Ex parte King* at 749.

courts have not been frightened to turn aside and seek the pragmatic solution that will best serve the needs of society. I can think of no more difficult task in contemporary society than that of managing and maintaining discipline in our seriously overcrowded prisons, not a task more dependent upon the personal authority of the incumbent. I am convinced that we should make it very much more difficult to carry out that task if the authority of the governor is undermined by the prospect of every disciplinary award being the subject of potential challenge in the courts ... I wish I could find a logical way in which to distinguish between governors and boards of visitors, but I have not been able to do so and I think at the end of the day I must content myself by pointing to some of the differences that justify a different approach.[54]

And, logical or not, Griffiths does leave governors out of judicial review, as does Browne-Wilkinson. He also finds it difficult to distinguish between governors and Boards of Visitors, and is equally untempted by the solution that the governors should be under the same restraint as the Visitors:

I, too, can see no logical distinction between the disciplinary functions of prison governors and the disciplinary functions of boards of visitors which the House of Lords has held are subject to judicial review. On the other hand, the practical repercussions of holding that the disciplinary decisions of prison governors are subject to review by the courts are frightening. It would be to shut one's eyes to reality to ignore the fact that, if prisoners are able to challenge in the courts the disciplinary decisions of the governor, they are likely to try to do so in many unmeritorious cases and the maintenance of order and discipline in prisons is likely to be seriously undermined.[55]

Browne-Wilkinson found a way out to his satisfaction. It was one which may almost by itself have triggered the overturning of the Court of Appeal's decision, because it amounted to a willingness to see the courts as naturally limited in their powers, which Bridge could not tolerate. (As we have seen, the surest way to persuade the Lords to make a liberal decision is to link it to the defence of curial power and autonomy.) It involved the argument that the Prison Act 1952 imposed on prison commissioners the duty to ensure the Act and any rules made under it were complied with, and that this power had since devolved on the Home Secretary. Consequently:

Parliament has therefore by express enactment imposed on someone other than the courts a specific obligation to ensure compliance with the statutory provisions. In my judgment, where Parliament has so provided it would not be appropriate for the court to take jurisdiction to ensure compliance with such statutory provisions, at least in cases where the person entrusted with the duty has adequate powers to ensure that the statutory provisions are in fact complied with.

[54] *Ex parte King* at 750–2.
[55] *Ex parte King* at 753.

Browne-Wilkinson and Griffiths have not had occasion since their eleva-
tion to the Lords to decide a similar case on prisons, but it is to the point
that they formed part of the three-man majority in a case discussed earlier,
Page v. *University of Hull*, which denied judicial review against the decision on a university visitor, on very similar grounds. (One Law Lord, in
interview, saw that case as a conflict between the public law trained
minority, always eager to extend judicial review, and those with a private
law background eager to defend the autonomy of private institutions.)
However that may be, the argument backfired. Lord Bridge described
Browne-Wilkinson's theory, that if the Secretary of State is empowered to
police the Act the courts should not, as an attempt 'to stand the doctrine
by which the limits of jurisdiction in this field are determined on its head',
and insists that 'the allegation of a wrong of a kind recognised as remedi-
able by public law is sufficient to found jurisdiction in judicial review'.
None of the arguments in the Court of Appeal, or the previous cases,
persuaded either Bridge or Oliver (the other Law Lord who made a
speech). Many of the pro-administration arguments are dismissed with
something like scorn. The analogy to other (and more benign) disciplinary
systems are dismissed—by Bridge with, 'For my part I derive no assistance at all from the suggested analogies. The position of a commanding
officer or a schoolmaster differs in many obvious respects from that of a
prison governor.'[56] And from Lord Oliver, a rather more far-reaching
assertion of the scope of judicial review:

In common with Lord Lowry CJ [in the Northern Ireland case] I do not find either
analogy convincing. The quasi-parental relation of a schoolmaster to his pupil is,
in my judgment, no analogy at all, and as to the case of the commanding officer,
I entertain with Lord Lowry CJ some doubt whether it can be said to be either
firmly established by authority or universally self-evident that judicial review can
never in any circumstances lie in respect of his disciplinary adjudication.[57]

The policy arguments for administrative convenience, that judicial review
would be dangerous to a governor's authority, are similarly brushed
aside. Bridge comments on the way that the original difficulties Lord
Widgery CJ had found in distinguishing between governors and Visitors
has:

in the argument of the present appeals, been not so much abandoned as trans-
posed and adapted to sustain the alternative position that the system of internal
prison discipline, having survived and even benefited from judicial review of
decisions by boards of visitors, would nevertheless be totally undermined if the
court once crossed the threshold of the governor's province beyond which it could
not stop short of accepting responsibility for every facet of prison management.[58]

[56] *Leech* at 564.
[57] *Leech* at 582.
[58] *Leech* at 565.

Later in his speech Lord Bridge mounts what must be one of the most powerful attacks anywhere in English law on this sort of policy concern being used as a legal argument in public law. He characterizes the government counsel, Mr (now Sir John) Laws, as having 'held out the prospect, as one which should make our judicial blood run cold, that opening the door to judicial review . . . would make it impossible to resist an invasion by what he called "the tentacles of law" of many other departments of prison administration'. But Bridge notes:

> In a matter of jurisdiction it cannot be right to draw lines on a purely defensive basis and determine that the court has no jurisdiction over one matter which it ought properly to entertain for fear that it will make it more difficult to decline jurisdiction over other matters which it ought not to entertain . . . historically the development of law in accordance with coherent and consistent principles has all too often been impeded . . . by the court's fear that unless an arbitrary boundary is drawn it will be inundated with a flood of unmeritorious claims.[59]

Bridge's theory of legal history is therefore a complete contradiction of Griffiths'. Lord Griffiths cites inconsistency favourably, Lord Bridge sees inconsistency as the result of unprincipled decisions. In this Bridge comes much closer to the spirit of liberal constitutional jurisprudence. In some ways Lord Oliver's much curter summary of his arguments against accepting a policy restriction on jurisdiction is even more effective—he quotes Lord Atkin, 'Convenience and justice are often not on speaking terms',[60] and later talks of being unimpressed with Browne-Wilkinson's 'frightening' possibilities because the earlier decision to allow Boards of Visitors to be subject to judicial review had not proved a disaster. Though the speeches yield much more and equally rich material for a demonstration of how the Lords can ignore policy concerns when they wish to, enough has been quoted to make our point here. It is worth adding that Oliver did, indeed, also use the 'great principle' citation from *Raymond* v. *Honey*, though curiously from Lord Bridge's speech in that case, not Wilberforce's. Yet again, though, what the Lords were doing was to ensure their own capacity to intervene, and against the Court of Appeal's willingness to limit the courts. Nothing substantive emerges from either *Raymond* v. *Honey* or *Leech* in terms of prisoners' rights except their access to the courts. And we have seen that men who would wish not even to grant this were to go on to the Lords. What happens when the courts do hear substantive complaints? This is the concern of the only other major House of Lords' case on prisoners' rights, *Ex parte Hague*, 1992.[61]

---

[59] *Leech* at 566.
[60] *Leech* at 579. The Atkin quote is from *General Medical Council* v. *Spackman* [1943] AC 627 at 638.
[61] *R* v. *Deputy Governor of Parkhurst Prison, ex parte Hague* [1992] 1 AC 58, heard together with *Weldon* v. *Home Office*.

This again is a case with two appeals considered jointly. Hague was serving a fifteen-year sentence when in 1988 he was deemed by the Governor to be a troublemaker and, as a result, was transferred to another prison and there placed under twenty-eight days' segregation. He claimed procedural improprieties in this process. The Court of Appeal granted him a declaration to that effect, and the Prison Service changed the rules governing his situation for future cases. However, his further claim, that the result of the improprieties had been that he was falsely imprisoned *within* his imprisonment and therefore entitled to damages, was rejected, and his appeal to the Lords was on this question. Hague also claimed, in the Lords, that he was entitled to damages simply because the Prison Service was in breach of statutory duty, even if the false imprisonment claim did not work. This was, in a sense, always what the case was about, but binding precedent would have made it impossible for the Court of Appeal to agree with him, whatever they had thought, so the argument was delayed until the Lords' hearing. The other prisoner, Weldon, had been forcibly stripped and kept overnight in a strip cell in a manner he claimed was unjustified—he also alleged assault. He too claimed that as a result of this illegal treatment, his legal imprisonment was converted, *pro tem*, into false imprisonment. The Home Office asked the courts to strike out this part of his allegations, but both the judge at first instance and the Court of Appeal refused, against which decision the Home Office appealed.

On the core question of whether prisoners could claim damages for breach of statutory duty *Hague* ran straight into a principle the Lords were quite unwilling to alter. The principle, a general one, is that damages, being a remedy in private law, cannot be given in a public law case, or, at least, not unless the statute in question specifically authorizes them, which means, in effect, almost never. (This principle, which has been long and firmly held, will almost certainly have to be abandoned if the European Convention on Human Rights is incorporated into English law, because the European Court of Human Rights regularly awards compensation for administrative illegality.) Though it may seem a natural technicality, the rule is one which very largely removes any recourse from a prisoner except to have future ill conduct by the prison service prevented by a declaration. The public/private divide has always been a stumbling block for prisoners' rights, and indeed much of the current procedural law on judicial review stems from a landmark case, *O'Reilly* v. *Mackman*,[62] in which prisoners' claims against the Home Office were struck down by the Lords precisely because they had used public law procedures, which are quicker and easier for plaintiffs, to try to claim

---

[62] *O'Reilly* v. *Mackman* [1983] 2 AC 237.

private law remedies which would be more effective than anything available under public law. The argument there, in one of Lord Diplock's most famous and long-lasting judgments, had been that it was somehow or other unfair to the executive to make it put up with procedures that helped the plaintiff unless they were compensated by a restriction on what they could suffer if they lost the case. By coincidence, losing counsel in *O'Reilly*, the then Steven Sedley QC, now a High Court judge, was the loser also in *Hague*. Sedley offered the courts a way out of the long-standing public/private disjunction here, by suggesting a 'ground rule'. The rule would be that where a statutory provision exists specifically to protect a particular class of people, and someone suffers precisely the sort of detriment he was supposed by the rule to be protected from, then damages have to be available. This would not follow, however, if some other provision existed to enforce the performance of the duty. As there was no other enforcement machinery, as for example a criminal penalty, then without damages there simply is nothing to protect prisoners. Neither of the judges who gave speeches, Bridge and Jauncey, had any trouble in dismissing this argument, though their dismissal was, in a sense, perfunctory, consisting as it did in simply reiterating a principle that it was all a matter of statutory interpretation, and there would be no damages without explicit statutory intent. Neither made any attempt to answer Sedley's key point—if no damages, then what enforcement?

Given this, it is perhaps unsurprising that their Lordships were not moved by the alternative argument, on false imprisonment, as it was entirely an attempt to get round the private/public ban. Nonetheless it was a vital question, because it goes directly to the spirit of *Raymond* v. *Honey*, which insisted that prisoners retained all rights not expressly or necessarily removed. What was being argued was effectively that imprisonment, being a denial of legal freedom, loses its justification if it is carried out improperly or illegally. At several points Bridge, and others in the courts below, used as a form of argument against this proposition the *reductio ad absurdum* technique—if the argument were right, then a prisoner suffering such improper administrative action would be entitled to walk out of prison. The apparent absurdity of this conclusion is meant to show the proposition could not possibly be valid, and is a regular technique of judicial argument.[63] In fact this is not an argument *ad absurdum* at all—it is precisely the rationale of the not infrequent actions of American judges in ordering prison administrations to release a number of prisoners immediately when prisons become overcrowded. One of Weldon's arguments was in fact that the conditions under which he was held were intolerable. Though no one could begin to imagine an English judge

---

[63] See David Robertson, 'Logic, Language, Truth and Judicial Behaviour', University of Wisconsin Occasional Papers in Public Law, No. 51, 1976.

thinking it proper to order the release of someone because his conditions
were intolerable, the absurdity of the proposition depends on the culture
of legal deference to administration, not to some logical necessity.
Weldon's case was stronger than Hague's because Weldon could at least
try to make the 'intolerable conditions' claim. Weldon was also able to
claim that as the actions of the prison officers were deliberate assaults,
they were therefore not done 'in good faith', whereas Hague could not
plausibly assert personal bad faith on the part of the authorities. Consequently the Court of Appeal did find that, were his allegations proved to
be true, he had suffered false imprisonment—and therefore had suffered
a private law harm for which damages were procedurally available. The
arguments in the Lords are not easy to follow, largely because Bridge was
very unwilling to accept the notion of someone retaining a 'residual
liberty' when he was legitimately detained in general, and the more thorough argument, that the entire detention is made illegal was, as we have
said, treated simply as absurd. It is fair to say that neither of these arguments were, really, dealt with at all, and Bridge shows clearly why:

> In my opinion, to hold a prisoner entitled to damages for false imprisonment on
> the grounds that he has been subject to a restraint upon his movement which was
> not in accordance with the Prison Rules 1964 would be, in effect, to confer on him
> under a different legal label a cause of action for breach of statutory duty under the
> Rules. Having reached the conclusion that it was not the intention of the Rules to
> confer such a right, I am satisfied that the right cannot properly be asserted in the
> alternative guise of a claim to damages for false imprisonment.[64]

It is difficult to know quite how to characterize this argument, except
perhaps that it is not an argument at all. Bridge is careful to stop all
avenues that might lead to the conclusion that the overall detention could
become unjustified. Lord Bridge concedes that prison officers acting
wrongly from malice rather than in good faith could be *personally* liable for
false imprisonment, but this would not render the Home Office or Prison
Service vicariously liable, so the initial imprisonment would remain valid.
He insists that he is not being uncaring: 'I sympathise entirely with the
view that the person lawfully held in custody who is subjected to intolerable conditions ought not to be left without a remedy against his custodian . . .'. All he can suggest, in the end, is:

> The logical solution to the problem, I believe is that if the conditions of an other-
> wise lawful detention are truly intolerable, the law ought to be capable of provid-
> ing a remedy directly related to those conditions without characterising the fact of
> the detention itself as unlawful I see no real difficulty in saying that the law can
> provide such a remedy.

[64] *Ex parte Hague* at 163.

The remedy he had in mind was that causing suffering to a prisoner's health, or even 'just' causing him 'physical pain or a degree of discomfort which can properly be described as intolerable' would render the custodian liable for damages in negligent liability! Lord Jauncey's supporting speech makes our point about the essential irrelevance of the *Raymond* v. *Honey* principle for us. He quotes Ralph Gibson LJ, who had found for Weldon in the Court of Appeal:

It is apparent, in my judgment, from a consideration of those rules that the legislative intention is that a prisoner should, subject to any lawful order given to him and to any rules laid down in the prison, enjoy such liberty—his residual liberty—within the prison as is left to him.[65]

Jauncey notes that Ralph Gibson had used the Wilberforce quotation, and says of what he calls 'these observations': 'They are highly relevant to the protection of such rights as a prisoner retains but they do not assist in determining what those rights are.' Do they not? Not directly perhaps, but the quotation is clearly of meaning to those who use it, as Ralph Gibson did, to bolster a sympathetic position, and could obviously be used as the beginning of a theory of residual rights. No such creativity was allowed by Jauncey, however, who uses an argument to the effect that because prison is a highly organized and routinized experience: 'A prisoner at any time has no liberty to be in any place other than where the regime permits, he has no liberty capable of deprivation so as to constitute the tort of false imprisonment.' What the Wilberforce principle might at least be said to do is to forbid any such literalist approach to the whole question of residual rights.

This brief discussion of prisoners' rights may not lead to any clear conclusion about their Lordships' orientation to public law rights in this area. Nor was it ever intended to, because the main point is to demonstrate, as with immigration but in a different context, that clear orientations do not exist. It is particularly striking with these cases that the same man, Lord Bridge, is capable of both generous and surprisingly narrow interpretations, capable both of denying the relevance of policy fears in some cases and accepting as an absolute argumentative stop a policy implication in another. More directly, through the mouths of various judges in various courts one sees the complete inapplicability of anything shaped to be a general principle, an inability of public law to have more than procedural concerns and rules. It is a doctrine of public law that public law cannot provide private law remedies— yet offered at least two ways around this, the public law judges still refused to grant relief. The executive may not be able to bar the courts

---

[65] *Ex parte Hague* at 174.

from overseeing prison justice, yet seems to have little to fear from this weakness.

The next chapter demonstrates a much more consistent executive mindedness in a very different policy area, which has its own peculiar implications. But the main theme is related—as long as we are dealing with common law judges exercising discretion, there can be no strong safeguard against the pressures of executive convenience, no real sense of *rights* as opposed to occasionally granted *privileges*.

9

Judicial Review as Welfare Management

At various stages in this book we have referred to the way the Lords can be seen as exercising, amongst their various functions, the role of manager, or perhaps referee, of the welfare state. There are literally hundreds of cases one could select to show the way judicial review has been applied in this sort of highly routine context. Of course no case that gets to the House of Lords can really be seen as routine, but these cases involve only relatively straightforward interpretation of statutory duties, rather than calling for any common law creativity. They are routine also in the sense that they are mundane; indeed one problem is knowing why any particular case does make it so far in the litigation hierarchy, when others, presenting similar practical issues, do not. Certainly it is not that cases likely to win on appeal are selected, because the plaintiffs hardly ever do win. We have chosen to illustrate this role mainly through a linked series of cases on only one area of welfare. This is purely for heuristic reasons, and not because we believe this particular set of cases is anything but characteristic of the Lords in a self limiting mode. At the end of the chapter we briefly discuss cases arising in a very different sphere, education. These are chosen because, while welfare cases involve the poorest and most disadvantaged, the education system represents a form of social good offered as of right to the entire population. If, as we argue, the pro-administration bias of the Lords still pertains, it demonstrates an overall 'establishment' orientation, not simply an inegalitarianism.

1. Local Authorities as Housing Authorities

The obligations on local authorities to house homeless people was first put on a fairly secure basis with the 1977 Housing (Homeless Persons) Act, which changed the ineffective previous policy by which homeless people had some rights to help under national insurance and social security legislation. From 1977 onwards they had much clearer rights levied against the housing authority in their area. Furthermore the Act, passed by a Labour Government, was centred around the need to keep homeless families together, while the previous legislation had involved, at most, the right of each member individually to some form of shelter. The 1977 Act handled the issue by giving the housing authority a general duty to house, as in the past they had with traditional council housing, but to insist that some homeless people be given a special priority which had the effect of moving them instantly to the top of the housing authority's list. The subsequent legislation, the 1985 Housing Act passed by a Conservative Government, tightened up such entitlements, but changed no important conceptual or structural matter, so cases arising under both Acts can be treated together.

Central to the Acts and the cases to be discussed are three concepts—that of 'priority need', of 'intentional homelessness', and one part of the definition of when somewhere is fit for occupancy. Basically the right to immediate provision of permanent housing the courts have had to 'referee' is a right held by homeless people who are in priority need, not of their intentional causing, to housing fit for their occupancy. In the cases we are interested in this has mainly meant unintentional homelessness by parents with dependent children which gives priority need to housing fit for their joint occupancy. This latter is because the Act, intended as noted above to keep families together, defines suitable accommodation as such only when it is fit to be occupied by the applicant and those 'who might reasonably be expected to reside with him'. Thus in principle someone could be homeless even though he did have secure accommodation, where it was accommodation unfit also to be occupied by someone else, his wife or child, because they would reasonably be expected to reside with him, though if the child was clearly not a dependant—she was 22 and earning her own living, for example—he would not be regarded as homeless. This was the main logic and purpose of the Act, and it was deeply unpopular with those local authorities which were housing authorities because of its impact on their resources. At the same time it was popular with local authorities which were not housing authorities but were responsible for running social service departments which used to have the main emergency housing responsibility under the 1948 National Assistance Act. It is important to note that these responsibilities remained, though they became residual resources to tackle homelessness. Part of the whole story depends on the fact that, given the complexity of English local government, housing authorities and social services were sometimes merely different departments of one council, sometimes belonged separately to the district and county councils. But whatever the division, the courts became, *inter alia*, umpires between these two sorts of authorities in their fights to load responsibilities onto each other, as well as referees between applicants seeking housing and housing authorities seeking not to give it. The four cases discussed in this section give examples of all the major issues. It is a good quick summary of the way the Law Lords have acted, consistently over fifteen years or so, that in only one homelessness case which went to the Lords has the applicant ever defeated the local authority.

Not surprisingly much of the concentration has been on ways of showing that applicants were 'intentionally homeless', that is, had themselves to blame, because it is the loosest concept in the Act, and the one where applicants were most vulnerable. It is also, of course, the point of ideological clash. Very, very few people become homeless in a truly intentional way—throwing up housing they had, could afford, and which was suitable, just to make the housing authority give them something better. Instead it is those people either too inadequate to cope with their lives who run up too much debt to pay the rent, or the genuinely incredibly unlucky who become homeless in ways that authorities find 'intentional', and they are usually those least capable of managing and most in real need of help. Nonetheless intentionality, though essentially a subjective test, is one main aspect of the Acts where the cases crop up. It can only be said that the Lords have been deeply sympathetic about intentional homelessness—sympathetic to the authorities. The two earliest cases on the Housing Acts give ample material to demonstrate this. They also allow comparison between different judicial attitudes. Both cases to be discussed at this point have the added advantage that Lord Ackner, who had not yet reached the Lords, was on split Court of Appeal panels from which the cases came to the Lords. Taking the two cases together Lords Wilberforce, Ackner, Lowry, and Fraser thought one applicant aptly described as intentionally homeless, while Lords Bridge and Russell saw neither in this light. Furthermore the degree of willingness or unease that each Law Lord brought to his decision is itself of considerable interest.

The two stories involve the same problem, one which must have been common at the time, of immigrant men bringing their families to join them some years after settling in the UK and being unable to find suitable family accommodation, given that they had been prepared to live very cheaply and with minimum privacy while sending money home to their families for years. The only reason it is not so often a problem nowadays is that the immigration rules have been tightened so that such immigrant workers have to prove that they can provide accommodation now before their families are given right of entry. (Though even now similar problems can occur, as a latter case demonstrates.) It is hard to imagine a more politically uneasy situation than providing accommodation from council stocks to an immigrant who brings over his family, thereby putting indigenous UK citizens lower on the priority list. Certainly it is not an issue over which local authorities covered themselves with glory.

In Islam's case, which it is convenient to discuss first, the Court of Appeal had supported the local authority, the London Borough of

Hillingdon. Tafazzul Islam first entered the UK as a twenty-three-year-old immigrant from Bangladesh in 1965. On a visit to Bangladesh in 1968 he married, returning periodically to see his wife over the years, and she had four children from these visits. He always intended to settle the family in the UK, and applied for leave to bring his wife and children here in 1974, but she only received permission in 1980, the entry certificate only giving her six months in which to achieve this. (Such lengthy delays in the immigration process were common.) Mr Islam had been sharing a single room with another immigrant worker until he heard his family was coming, and he immediately arranged to take over another room for them as well as the continued share of his original room. When the family arrived in April 1980 his new landlord initially refused to allow them the room; after the council intervened he did give them occupation for a few weeks, but then summarily evicted them in September. They had nowhere to go, and the council put them up in temporary bed and breakfast accommodation as they were required to while deciding on their applications to be housed as homeless persons. The Act imposes on the council a duty to give this initial housing, but if the applicants are deemed unentitled to permanent accommodation, the council is only further obliged to provide such temporary accommodation for the period they judge adequate to allow the applicants to find something on their own, usually a maximum of six months. The application for permanent housing was denied, and they were told they would be accommodated only until 16 October. The council's decision is a fine example of how far housing authorities may be prepared to go to find reasons not to accommodate the homeless. They had two strikes against the Islams, using the familiar legal technique of the 'argument in the alternative'. It needs to be remembered that in order to get permanent housing from the authority the Islams would have to be in priority need by showing that Mr Islam had no accommodation 'which is available for occupation both by him and by any other person who might reasonably be expected to reside with him'.[1] The council would also have to be satisfied that he had not left such accommodation intentionally.

1. Mr Islam was homeless, but not in priority need, as his dependent children might not reasonably be expected to reside with him having lived apart for the past seven years.
2. Even if he were in priority need 'the applicant be considered to have become homeless intentionally, having deliberately arranged for his wife and children to leave accommodation which it would have been reasonable for them to continue to occupy'. The accommodation the housing authority meant was the accommodation in Bangladesh, which happened to be his father's house where his wife and children

---

[1] This formulation is taken from Lowry, *Islam* at 711.

had been living.[2] Even the council could not claim that his shared room in Hillingdon was accommodation suitable for the family.

The two arguments are not even compatible—if Mr Islam had not been residing with his family for seven years, he cannot have been occupying accommodation suitable for such occupancy. Even the two members of the Court of Appeal who sided with the council did not try to claim that the fact of separation overcame the clear statutory duty to keep families together. Instead in the Court of Appeal two different versions were presented by the judges. Lord Denning MR's opinion shows perhaps more honestly than was good for his reputation what he, and almost certainly the council, really thought about the obligation to house immigrants' families. Denning claimed, in a way that could only make sense by some legal fiction, that Mr Islam himself had always been truly resident in Bangladesh. Denning refers to the age of British imperialism when men went out to work abroad while leaving their families in their true residence in the home country, and bluntly says:

The moral of this case is that men from overseas should not bring their wives and children here unless they have arranged permanent and suitable accommodation for them to come to. Tafazzul Islam is homeless intentionally. He is not entitled to permanent accommodation. He will not take priority over young couples here who are on the waiting list for housing accommodation.[3]

Sir Denys Buckley in the Court of Appeal obviously did not feel able to maintain the fiction that Mr Islam had actually resided in Bangladesh during the twelve years he had been living in the UK. Instead he settled for the possibly even more far-fetched argument that the accommodation the Islams had been occupying and had left, thus rendering them intentionally homeless, was the *joint* accommodation of the shared room in London and the rooms in his father's house in Bangladesh. Buckley liked the point enough to suggest that it would also serve cases where an applicant's family had lived in the North of England and he had worked, and therefore had to live, in London. The fact that this would make the Act quite incredible was no problem. Neither Denning nor Buckley are relevant in a book about the Law Lords—they are cited merely to indicate the sort of efforts judges will go to in trying to help local authorities. Ackner LJ did dissent and support Islam, as his soon to be colleagues in the Lords unanimously did. Yet it is relevant in showing the unwillingness with which the Lords have treated the job of enforcing housing duties on local authorities that he did so very unwillingly, driven, as some of the Lords make it clear they were driven, by the sheer impossibility of accepting the council's tortuous logic. The peroration of Ackner's

[2] The council's letter from which the quotations are taken is reproduced in *Islam* at 710.
[3] *Islam* at 695.

judgement in the Court of Appeal may do credit to his sense of judicial restraint in carrying out the will of Parliament, but it does nothing to suggest any political sympathy for the Housing Act:

He may well have thus achieved, under the points system that operates, priority over a husband and wife and a smaller family who have for long lived in unsatisfactory accommodation in the respondent's borough. However open to criticism that situation is or may be, it seems to me to be the result of the absence of that immigration control to which I have referred . . . The Act is part of our social welfare legislation. It is concerned with homelessness in this country. One of its main purposes and functions is to keep the family unit together. *Much as I may regret the unanticipated advantages which the Act gives to persons in the position of the applicant, I cannot accept that the unrealistic approach to its interpretation, which the respondents seek to put forward, can be justified.* [Our emphasis.][4]

Ackner was, in fact, picked up with unusual directness for this expression of regret by Lord Lowry and Lord Bridge, who went out of their way to disassociate themselves. Bridge, for example, concurring with Lowry's speech, says:

I am not sure what prompted Ackner LJ to express regret and reluctance at having to reach the conclusion he did in his dissenting judgment. Like Lord Lowry I do not share that regret. On the contrary I should be hard put to it to formulate any defensible principle to justify denying the benefits conferred by the Act to immigrants who, like the appellant, have acquired under the relevant legislation controlling immigrants the unrestricted right not only to live and work in this country but also to bring their families to live with them.[5]

Lowry had expressed his view of both Hillingdon Council and the majority in the Court of Appeal with an elegant scorn, which makes the entire speech worth reading, as well as noting that he could not agree with Ackner's expression of regret.

The appellant must show that, on a proper construction of the Act and having regard to the facts, the panel had no right to be satisfied under s. 4(2) (b) that he became homeless intentionally. *This, I consider, is not a difficult task* . . . My conclusion is that by no artificial or other expedient, however ingenious, can a finding of intentional homelessness be legally sustained. It is therefore idle for the respondents to suggest that your Lordships ought not to interfere with the panel's decision unless it is plainly unreasonable . . . I cannot readily adopt a strained construction which would frustrate the policy of the Act and would promote the object, which is not to be found there either expressly or by necessary implication, of postponing the otherwise valid claims of homeless persons and families who have their origins outside Great Britain. [My emphasis.][6]

---

[4] *Islam* at 698.
[5] *Islam* at 718.
[6] *Islam* at 716–17.

In particular Lowry is the only judge to let the cat out of the bag about Hillingdon's real position, commenting that:

in the course of their argument they have still sought to restrict their liability to such people. I refer to what amounts to a submission which was ambivalently pursued before your Lordships and which I consider to be completely unsustainable, that a housing authority owes no duty under the Act to any family unit which has not previously occupied a family home in Great Britain.

Over the course of this book it must have become apparent that Lords Bridge and Lowry, as foreshadowed in Chapter 2, are amongst the most 'liberal' of Law Lords. The lack of regret they had for their decision was not felt by Wilberforce who certainly shares Ackner's attitude:

Not without misgiving, but without any doubt, I have reached the conclusion that the judgment of Ackner LJ is correct. Put very briefly, the case is four square within the Act . . . There is no answer to his claim. While the result in this particular case may be considered acceptable, in view of the appellant's long residence in this country and his efforts to unite his family here, and I entirely accept that immigrants as such are not intended to be excluded from the Act, I share the Lord Justice's misgiving whether . . . the Act is as well considered as it is undoubtedly well intentioned.[7]

It is, in fact, very rare for judges to make such outright criticisms of a fundamental result of a parliamentary statute, rather than just about technical problems in it. Such overt lack of sympathy for a whole category of complainants could not bode well for the scheme's judicial future, and it is hardly surprising in this light that the case was the last, as well as the first, that a housing plaintiff won. In the end, despite these reservations, and indications of an underlying disunity amongst their Lordships, Islam did win. Unless the Lords were expressly prepared to read in that exclusion of immigrant families the council wanted, which Lowry correctly says is not to be found in the Act either expressly or by necessary implication, Islam must be seen never to have occupied accommodation suitable for his family anywhere in the world, let alone in the UK. The subtexts of these opinions do not necessarily show anything like a block system of judges regularly grouped together, as might happen with, say, the US Supreme Court. On the whole Bridge has proved applicant friendly in public law cases and Wilberforce has not, but there is little predictability at the individual level.

The same group of Law Lords split over a second housing application case in the same session, *Din (Taj) v. Wandsworth London Borough Council*,[8] but here Lowry voted with Wilberforce and Fraser against Bridge and

---

[7] *Islam* at 708.
[8] *Din (Taj) v. Wandsworth LBC* [1983] 1 AC 657.

Russell, this time to uphold another split Court of Appeal, this time with Ackner, in the majority, favouring the council.

The issue in *Din* is simple on the face of it. In 1977 Mr Din, his wife and four children moved into a house in Wandsworth which had an attached shop. The lease on the house and shop was owned by his uncle, and the idea was that he would join the uncle in running the shop—an Asian food shop—though he also kept his job with the Airfix Company. In 1978 the uncle pulled out of the business leaving Mr Din trying to pay the rent on the premises, though unable to run the shop. A large rent arrears built up, and the Dins knew that sooner or later they would be evicted. It appears to be commonly accepted that this would have happened at the latest by December 1979, so in June of that year the Dins asked their local housing authority, Wandsworth London Borough Council, for help with housing. They were put on the usual waiting list, but told that they could not be treated as eligible for priority housing, though they were clearly entitled to such accommodation because of the dependent children, until the court order for possession had actually been made. (Because being evicted would make them involuntarily homeless.) In this situation it is hardly surprising that when a distress warrant for unpaid rates also arrived they panicked and left the Wandsworth accommodation to stay with relatives in Upminster, where Mr Din tried to get a new job. Failing to get one he returned to his old job in Wandsworth and got temporary lodgings adequate only for himself. The Upminster house was too small for the relatives to put the Dins up for long and they were asked to leave in December. At this time they asked Wandsworth Council for priority housing. This was refused on the grounds that Mr Din had made them intentionally homeless by leaving the original Wandsworth house before he was evicted. (It was common ground that he would have put himself even further into debt on rent and rates by staying there and trying to run the failing takeaway business, and that he would have been unintentionally homeless as a result of eviction by the time of his December application.)

The case revolved really round the question of whether the judges would support Wandsworth's policy of convenience. By the council's own admission they always insisted on people in Mr Din's position waiting until the last minute, whatever the legal and other costs thus imposed on landlords and applicants, simply to postpone as long as possible the date on which the council would have to start paying. And the council wanted to keep that policy going regardless of the impact on the Dins. Lord Bridge at least was aware of the social realities here, in particular the vacuity of the notion of 'intentional homelessness', as well as the attitudes of some of his colleagues:

Ackner LJ thought this a just penalty for what he called 'unfair queue jumping'. But I can detect no trace of any attempt to jump the queue in the circumstances in which these applicants left . . . I wonder what chance the class of homeless person in priority need who is driven to rely on the housing authority's assistance under the Act has of finding 'a settled residence' by his own efforts. If the respondent authority put the appellants on the street, as presumably they will if the appeal fails, the most likely outcome must surely be that the family will be broken up and the children taken into care.[9]

As far as statutory interpretation goes, the case could be, indeed was, argued with equal facility either way around. The theoretical point is what exactly a council must do when it makes the inquires it is obliged to make to satisfy itself whether an applicant has made himself homeless intentionally. Must they must concentrate on the reason he was homeless by the time of his application? Can they go back to an earlier time and, finding an intentional act that at that time rendered the applicant homeless, use it as a reason for finding him intentionally homeless at the later date of his actual application? For Lords Bridge and Russell in the Lords, Lord Donaldson in the Court of Appeal, and the original county court judge, this latter approach, favoured by the council, made no sense. Whether or not Mr Din had panicked in August, he would have been evicted before his application in December, so his homelessness cannot be put down to what Bridge called 'leaving prematurely'. The majority on both courts, however, claim to be interpreting the statute more literally, and insist that the only matter the council *can* look at is the actual intentional act of leaving on 28 August which then and there rendered the Dins homeless. To read the Act otherwise according to the majorities is both to add words to it which are not necessary and to complicate the council's job by forcing them to consider hypothetical matters. Lord Lowry, for once on the more restrictive side in a statutory interpretation case, puts the argument for the majority most succinctly, saying of the applicant's arguments that:

What would be required to sustain them is a reconstruction of the Act . . . the appellant's interpretation is not required by reference to the purpose of the Act . . . They then say that the real cause of their homelessness is not the act which caused it but something which did not cause it, namely the fact that they would have been homeless unintentionally by December.[10]

There is no inexorable logic to the majority's position and its implications. Lords Bridge and Russell both deal with it powerfully. Indeed Bridge's version was called by Lowry himself 'a thoughtful and challenging speech'. Bridge points out that the Act set out three questions for the authority to answer: (1) Is he homeless?; (2) Has he a priority need?; (3) Did he become homeless intentionally? Bridge then makes this argument:

[9] *Din* at 686.
[10] *Din* at 675.

In answering the first two questions the authority are clearly concerned with the applicant's circumstances at the date of the application. Is he *presently* homeless? Has he presently a priority need? It seems to me to be equally clear that the question whether 'he became homeless intentionally' imports an inquiry as to the cause of his *present* state of homelessness. To reach this conclusion I do not, with respect, find it necessary as was suggested in the Court of Appeal, to read any words into section 17 (1) which are not there . . . In construing the phrase 'whether he became homeless intentionally' in the context in which they are found in section 3 and section 4 it would be absurd to hold that the housing authority are at liberty to rely on any past act or omission on the part of the applicant which satisfies the section 17 formula but which is not causally related to the applicant's present state of homelessness.

Redefining the question as 'Is the applicant's present homelessness the result of a deliberate act or omission on his part in consequence of which he ceased to occupy accommodation . . . and which it would have been reasonable for him to continue to occupy?', Bridge then insists:

the housing authority must necessarily give it a negative answer. By the time he applies to the authority for accommodation, the fact that he left prematurely has no causal connection with his present homelessness. He would now be homeless in any event . . . It requires no profound philosophical analysis to demonstrate the fallacy in their proposition . . . it offends common sense to hold that the cause of his homelessness after that date was that he chose to leave of his own volition before that date.[11]

Ingenious though the technical arguments are, this case, even more than most, has little to do with what is the narrowly correct reading of parliamentary words. The case is a prime example of what American Legal Realists meant when they saw any high-level litigation as one involving two equally valid and mutually antithetical 'correct' legal positions. The case, perhaps all such cases, are straightforward policy choices by the Law Lords, every bit as much as a common law case on negligence might be, but one will never see an admission to that effect. At heart the issue is about the appropriate attitude of the courts to the role of local authorities in running a major, essentially new, welfare system. There are two very basic positions one can take on such a matter. One can, and the House of Lords always has, approach the administration of such a scheme as a highly 'operational' and intensely discretionary matter where well-intentioned and hard-pressed housing agencies must be, and can be, trusted to do the best they can in a difficult world of financial shortage. It is an approach which sees statutory schemes as though they were drafted in terms of targets—as though the parliamentary language decoded into something like 'OK, look, we want to do something about this homeless-

---

[11] *Din* at 682.

ness problem, we know you've already got a lot on your plate, but see what you can do about helping out the really deserving . . .'. The alternative is to see it as a matter of rights. In vain, in his argument before the Lords, did counsel for the Dins remind the panel of this:

Sedley in reply: 'It was the legislative intention of Parliament to give priority rights to families such as this, *rights in law*. It does not assist to refer to other alternatives which do not arise in the case in question.' [Our emphasis.][12]

Throughout this section the point will recur—the Lords, in their role as managers of the welfare system, do not seem, truly, to think in terms of rights, but of priorities, needs, of discretionary solutions. They cannot clear their minds of the practical consequences of their decisions, they cannot stop themselves acting as though they really were line managers, trying to make the best of a difficult situation, thinking always, in the words of Lord Templeman in a later housing case, 'But we've got to make this Act work!'[13] In this particular case, the Lords would not put aside the social policy context of London's housing problem. For example Lord Fraser:

As Wandsworth is in Inner London it is within judicial knowledge that housing in the respondents area was very scarce. For that reason the respondents determination that it would have been reasonable for the appellant to continue to occupy the accommodation at Trinity Road after July 1979 was, in my view, one that they were well entitled to make, although if the same issue had arisen in another part of the country where accommodation was under less pressure the position might have been different.[14]

This is management, not law. A homeless person's right to priority accommodation cannot be dependent on where they happen to live. All speeches from the majority have this style. Early in his speech Wilberforce points out that many other things can be done for the Dins apart from granting them the right to priority housing, and urges tolerance to local authorities in interpreting the Act:

The Act must be interpreted in the light of these matters with liberality having regard to its social purpose and also with recognition of the claims of others and the nature and scale of local authorities' responsibilities.

And, a little later:

As I have pointed out the Act reflects a complex interplay of interests. It confers great benefits upon one category of persons in need of housing, to the detriment of others. This being so, it does not seem unreasonable that, in order to benefit

---

[12] From the summary of argument, *Din* at 662.
[13] This was an oral interjection into counsel's argument during the hearing of *Garlick*, discussed later in this section.
[14] *Din* at 671.

from the priority provisions, persons in the first category should bring themselves within the plain words. Failure to do so involves, as Mr Bruneau pointed out, greater expense for a hard pressed authority, and greater pressure on the housing stock.[15]

But it should be seen that this approach, interpretation 'with recognition of the claims of others', this continual recognition of the 'detriment of others' , Fraser's taking judicial notice of Wandsworth's special problems, all amount to a judicial methodology which minimizes the sense of the Dins actually having something identified as a 'right'. Every attempt is made to remove any conception that what is going on is a conflict between the State and a citizen demanding his rights. Fraser specifically takes the point and insists that the case should not be seen as a conflict with:

on the one side a homeless person with a family including dependent children and, on the other side, a public authority . . . the true competition is between the appellant and the many other persons with families in the respondent's area who are homeless.[16]

And Lord Lowry gives almost the same description of what their Lordships are doing:

As in other cases the real contest here is not between the homeless citizen and the state: the duty of the housing authority is to hold the balance fairly among all homeless persons and to exercise a fair discretion according to the law, while your Lordships' task is to declare the law relevant to this case.[17]

One could very well argue that this sort of sympathetic understanding of an awkward situation for an agency of the State is never appropriate if indeed the task is 'to declare the law relevant' to the case, but in this context the understanding is simply misplaced. Housing authorities were not, in this legislation, charged with holding any balance at all. It was in part because they had failed to hold such a balance when urged to do so in earlier legislation that the Act was passed. The previous Act, the Housing Act 1957 had urged local authorities to ensure that the homeless were given proportional consideration along with other people with special problems like those in overcrowded conditions, but there had been no way of enforcing such a guidance. Counsel for Mr Islam had pointed out that the 1977 Act 'was a deliberate interference by Parliament with the way local authorities allocate housing stock', and had specifically admitted that the Act was controversial.[18] Effectively housing authorities were ordered to do something they did not want to do, and they tried hard to avoid doing it. By their attitude of managerial understanding the Lords

---

[15] *Din* at 667.
[16] *Din* at 672.
[17] *Din* at 674.
[18] Taken from the summary of the argument by Derek Wood QC, in *Islam* at 701.

were essentially undermining Parliament's effort in the guise of strictly reading legislation. This orientation continued throughout the case history of the Act, partly demonstrated in another judicial attitude fore-shadowed by Wilberforce in *Din*, an impatience with the very business of the courts being involved in the policy area, a sense that the local authorities should not have to be bothered. Wilberforce actually regards it as a defect in the applicant's argument that 'This approach almost invites challenge in the courts.'

This impatience with litigation getting in the way of good administration is common—we have seen it already in negligence cases aimed at public authorities, and it became even clearer in the next major housing case, *Puhlofer*,[19] heard again by Ackner LJ in the Court of Appeal and by Lords Keith, Roskill, Brandon, Brightman, and Mackay, with the Lords again upholding the Court of Appeal's support for the local authority. The question in *Puhlofer* was one that inevitably had to come up in a court at some time, given the living conditions of the homeless in many London boroughs—what standard need accommodation offered by the council under their section 17 obligations be? Mr and Mrs Puhlofer had been housed by the council as priority claimants being unintentionally home-less with a small child and a baby. They were given one room in a bedsit hotel used as a hostel which had three bathrooms between its thirty-six occupants. The hostel had no clothes washing or cooking facilities (the Puhlofers were allowed, as a special exception, to use the kitchen to warm the baby's milk). There was practically no room to move in the bedroom since, in addition to the double bed and single bed, there was the baby's cradle and a dressing table. The judge was told that the room was further crowded with a pram, sterilizer unit, toys, a baby walker for the elder boy, and disposable nappies. Though breakfast was provided all other meals had to be eaten out and this, plus the cost of doing all the washing in launderettes, effectively used up most of the Puhlofers' social security income. Mother and father were both unemployed and in their very early twenties. The Lords regarded as significant, and as an excuse for the council from providing anything better, that in the council's area there were 52 families in such accommodation, only seven of which had more than one room. Of these seven families four had more than three children. In all there were 437 families on the waiting list for two-bedroom units, and 44 of these had more priority points than the Puhlofers. Other inter-pretations of the council's housing efforts are, of course, possible given this data. In some jurisdictions the situation would have been used by a court to demonstrate how little sympathy the council was entitled to, if it had allowed such a situation to occur. At the very least it suggests that the

[19] *Pulhofer* [1986] 1 AC 484.

question of what standard of accommodation a council must provide was no idle one.

It might not be thought surprising that the county court judge who first heard the Puhlofers' request for judicial review upheld it. To be more precise he held two things. First, that where section 1 of the Act requires the provision of accommodation it must be taken to mean 'appropriate' accommodation. In fact this rather obvious point had already been established in a ruling by Lord Denning in 1982,[20] but the precedent was 'distinguished' , sometimes with rather elaborate effort, by every judge in the Court of Appeal. The Lords, not been bound by the precedent anyway, completely ignored the ruling.

Secondly, the judge rejected the council's preference for how 'appropriate' was to be measured. According to them the measure of appropriateness came from local conditions. If local housing conditions were so bad that it would be unreasonable of an occupant to leave somewhere he was living, that is, because he could not hope himself to find anything better, the council need only offer the same level of accommodation. The test comes from the Act itself. An applicant is not 'intentionally homeless' if he leaves accommodation so bad that he could not 'reasonably' be expected to live in it. As a test it imposes no standards whatsoever on the housing authority, because they are the sole judges of whether an applicant was reasonable in leaving accommodation he had, and the Act does indeed specify that local conditions can be taken into account in the overall administration of the Act. Inevitably *Wednesbury*-style arguments come in here, and inevitably that spells disaster for the plaintiff. Unfortunately for the homeless in London, the *Puhlofer* case came before a Court of Appeal and a House of Lords panel so determined not to second-guess local authorities that they took a position more extreme than the one the council itself sought to establish. Ackner, still in the Court of Appeal at this time, noted that the Act contained no definition of accommodation, and gave no help in determining what standard was required. Nonetheless he felt the test proposed by the council itself was too stringent. Ackner specifically rejected the council's standard. This amounted to saying that a council could offer accommodation so poor that, if one had found it oneself and then left it, one's leaving would not constitute becoming intentionally homeless. However, all Ackner was prepared to say was that some measure of 'habitability' must be implied by the very fact of the Act. Whatever that meant, and he and the others on the court offer no guidance, it is not Denning's 'appropriateness' test, and it was satisfied by the room the council had provided for the Puhlofers.

The Lords' decision is contained in only one main speech, by Lord

---

[20] *Parr* v. *Wyre Borough Council* 1982, apparently unreported.

Brightman. It is probably the most restrictive reading ever given to the Act, and must qualify for one of the narrowest and most pro-administration interpretations ever given to welfare legislation in this country. To put the issue firmly in the classic public law language of the reasonableness of the authority's actions, and thus to bring the power of the *Wednesbury* test into play, Brightman casts the applicant's argument in the following words:

No local authority properly directing themselves could have formed the view that the room allotted . . . was 'accommodation' within the meaning of s. 1, at least after the child of the marriage was born in April 1984, because it was then overcrowded in the statutory sense, and lacked both exclusive and communal facilities for cooking and clothes washing.[21]

That may be how Lord Brightman thinks the applicant defines the situation, but it is not at all how Lord Brightman does. Brightman points out that there is no statutory definition of homelessness in either the 1977 or any other Act, and argues therefore that more or less full play must be given to the council's discretion. Clearly only an extreme decision by a housing authority is going to trigger any sense of *Wednesbury* unreasonableness in Brightman's mind. As the case has never been questioned subsequently, we must take it that the same is true for any Law Lord. But it important to see just how far Brightman is prepared to go in rejecting any externally defined standards on local authorities. The quotation above shows that he was unconcerned that they were offering, in satisfaction of their legislative duty, accommodation statutorily defined as over-crowded. He goes on to insist that the fact that their room would be deemed unfit for habitation under Part II of the 1957 Housing Act is just as irrelevant as that it is overcrowded under Part IV of the Act: 'Those particular statutory criteria are not to be imported into the Homeless Persons Act for any purpose.' The courts seem to have absolutely no role to play for Brightman in applying this Act at all, and he could hardly be more blunt about it: 'What is properly to be regarded as accommodation is a question of fact to be decided by the local authority. There are no rules.' The idea that one function of a country's supreme court might precisely be to provide rules in such a situation never occurs to him. Later Brightman appears to relax this position, because he disagrees with Glidewell LJ in the court below who had suggested that overcrowding could not be taken into account in assessing the reasonableness of the authority's decision. It is a concession so limited that it is worth quoting to demonstrate just how far a Law Lord can be prepared to go in trusting those who know best to get on with the job of running the country's welfare system:

[21] *Puhlofer* at 513.

I do not however, accept that overcrowding is a factor to be disregarded as Glidewell LJ apparently thought. I agree that the statutory definition of over-crowding has no relevance. But accommodation must, by definition, be capable of accommodating. If, therefore, a place . . . is so small a space that it is incapable of accommodating the applicant together with other persons who normally reside with him as members of his family, then on the fact of such a case the applicant would be homeless.

There is no need to guess what Brightman would count as too small a physical space, because he answers this himself—Diogenes' tub is the example he gives of overcrowding that would be forbidden by the Act. What matters for our purposes is to see why it is that Brightman is prepared to take this extreme 'hands off' approach to housing authorities. The answer seems to be given rather clearly by his own understanding of what the entire Act is about: 'It is an Act to assist persons who are homeless, not an Act to provide them with homes.' This is simply false, and quite unsupported by anything in the Act itself. He goes on to inter-pret the Act in a way that cannot reflect anything but his own policy preferences but which, if true, would indeed justify a complete abdication of judicial responsibility for supervising authorities in their reading of the legislation:

It is intended to provide for the homeless a lifeline of last resort, not to enable them to make inroads into the local authority's waiting list of applicants for housing. Some inroads there probably are bound to be, but in the end the local authority will have to balance the priority needs of the homeless on the one hand, and the *legitimate* aspirations of those on their housing list on the other hand. [Our emphasis.][22]

Again we get this notion of balancing conflicting needs, and a clear sense of whose needs ought to be preferred. The Act simply has not such language in it. As a decision by itself *Puhlofer* is a very strong example of how a combination of judicial preferences and an overall belief in leaving state agencies alone characterize so much of English public law, and how very far from any model of 'rights jurisprudence' we really are. From a non-legal standpoint it seems barely credible that public law should really not feel a piece of legislation like the Housing (Homeless Persons) Act 1977 imposed no standards whatsoever by which an authority could be held up as failing to carry out its duties. But *Puhlofer*, because of other comments of Brightman, specifically adopted by Roskill, the only other Law Lord to give a speech, actually does stand for such a position, one in which it is very hard to see why public law in the UK is held in such high regard even by its practitioners. Brightman finishes his speech with a very tough warning about not involving the courts with these sorts of questions:

---

[22] *Puhlofer* at 517.

I am troubled at the prolific use of judicial review for the purpose of challenging the performance by local authorities of their functions under the 1977 Act. Parliament intended the local authority to be judge of fact . . . Although the action or inaction of a local authority is clearly susceptible to Judicial Review where they have misconstrued the Act, or abused their powers or otherwise acted perversely, I think that great restraint should be exercised in granting leave to proceed by Judicial Review. . . . it is not in my opinion appropriate that the remedy of Judicial Review, which is a discretionary remedy, should be made use of to monitor the actions of local authorities under the Act save in the exceptional case . . . Where the existence or non-existence of a fact is left to the judgment and discretion of a public body and that fact involves a broad spectrum ranging from the obvious to the debatable to the just conceivable, it is the duty of the court to leave the decision of the fact to the public body to whom Parliament has entrusted the decision-making power save in a case where it is obvious that the public body, consciously or unconsciously, are acting perversely . . . I express the hope that there will be a lessening in the number of challenges which are mounted against local authorities who are endeavouring, in extremely difficult circumstances, to perform their duties under the Act with due regard to all their other housing problems.[23]

It is particularly important that where in this quote he refers to exceptional circumstances he goes on to cite Scarman's view about the restrictions on courts overruling administrative decisions under the *Wednesbury* rules in his famous opinion in *Ex parte Nottinghamshire*.[24] But this version of the test, which we discussed in Chapter 7, often known as the '*Super Wednesbury*' test, was specially crafted to apply to a vastly different situation. Then county councils asked the courts to overrule the Secretary of State's application of a major cabinet policy—rate capping—which had been very specifically passed by Parliament. Scarman was at pains to restrict the use of his tougher *Wednesbury* test to situations where Parliament supported the administration. Here the Parliament of 1977 obviously wanted to help the homeless, and to force councils to help them. If standards of unreasonableness so elastic are to be applied to local authority welfare management, and Brightman's 'there are no rules' statement coupled with his effective denial of the applicability of judicial review suggests some Law Lords feel they should be, the model of curial responsibility for protecting public law rights in the UK would look unlike anything many jurisdictions would recognize. At bottom of course the approach does rest on a considerable trust in the bona fides of local authorities. But is it appropriate to have such a trust when the judge, at the same time, presents such a very personal interpretation of the whole purpose of the Act? Simply put, an authority which can be trusted to apply the 1977 Act as Brightman sees it probably cannot be trusted to

[23] *Puhlofer* at 518.
[24] *Ex parte Nottinghamshire* [1986] AC 240.

implement the Act as others could equally legitimately view it. Trust is not an applicable quality here.

As Brightman's argument in *Puhlofer* makes clear, these housing cases are necessarily contained within the standard judicial review net of the *Wednesbury* rules. The only reason the familiar reasonableness test did not show up earlier is that in *Islam*, as Lowry says, the council's case failed before it got to the stage where *Wednesbury* would apply. To repeat Lowry's words:

My conclusion is that by no artificial or other expedient, however ingenious, can a finding of intentional homelessness be legally sustained. It is therefore idle for the respondents to suggest that your Lordships ought not to interfere with the panel's decision unless it is plainly unreasonable.[25]

Normally, however, the steps in the decision, though apparently fairly tightly defined by the Act, are treated as matters of fact that cannot be appealed, with the result that any decision a council makes on the facts that it alone certifies can only be overturned under the extremely difficult irrationality standards of *Wednesbury*, or the even tougher restrictions that follow from Brightman's preference for 'Super *Wednesbury'*. This has, on the whole, made it very difficult to challenge housing authorities. But in fact the Lords have not been unwilling to help them even where decisions have been taken that could well have failed such a test. The best example of an apparent absolute determination not to allow interference with an authority's autonomy comes from a case where, as quite often happens, the plaintiff may have suffered from the company it was forced to keep when the Lords bundled together several apparently like cases on appeal.

The case, *Tower Hamlets London Borough Council* v. *Begum*, was heard along with an essentially unwinnable pair of appeals, and is collectively reported under the title *Garlick* v. *Oldham Metropolitan Borough Council and related appeals* in 1993.[26] What the appeals had in common was an attempt to push the courts into making the stress in the Act on protecting the whole family primary and conclusive. There is no doubt that a major thrust of the Act was to keep families together and avoid the splitting up of a family which had happened in the past. Then, because there was no single homeless persons Act, children of homeless parents were often taken into care under other legislation. Consequently the 1977 Act and its successor was organized round the notion of a homeless applicant who would get priority housing if he or she had dependent children (there were several other criteria for being in priority need) as long as the applicant was not judged to be intentionally homeless. This appears to leave a gap in the family protection aspect where, though in priority need

---

[25] *Islam* at 716.
[26] *Garlick* v. *Oldham MBC and related appeals* [1993] 2 All ER 65.

because of the children, a homeless person lost the right to such a status by being judged intentionally homeless. *Garlick* was an attempt to get round this by making the children themselves the applicants. In the other two cases in the bundle two mothers of four-year-olds, having lost their homes because of mortgage or rent arrears, and being judged therefore to be intentionally homeless, made new applications in their children's names. The councils in question rejected the applications on the grounds that four-year-old children could not be applicants. To be on the safe side one council added a finding that the child was not in priority need. The other bluntly wrote to the mother saying her application 'was a transparent device to get round the provisions of the Housing Act'. Which, of course, was one perfectly accurate way of putting it. It is hardly surprising that the Lords would have no truck with this strategy, especially given their general tendency to see the duties imposed by the Act in a narrow frame, as repeated here in Griffiths' words:

It is of the first importance to understand the nature of the duty imposed upon local housing authorities by Parliament. It is not a duty to take the homeless off the streets and to place them physically in accommodation. The duty is to give them and their families priority in the housing queue.[27]

It is not clear that this interpretation is even true and it certainly does not help very much. It appears, indeed, to be a fairly weak obligation, but in fact the language of the Act is much tougher. According to Lord Griffiths' reading, the Act might seem to allow a housing authority to put people first in a queue where nothing will be available for some time. In fact the Act requires the authority to 'secure' an eligible applicant housing, and to do so immediately. This is a clear cut right, and in fact comes much closer to the idea of taking the homeless off the streets than any right those who are not judged to be in priority need have. All that language like Griffiths' does is to remove some of the apparent aura of failure to provide for the weak that would otherwise cling to the authorities, and, presumably, makes it easier for the Lords to support the councils. It was, however, clear that a powerful argument, based as much on 'common sense' as on statutory interpretation, supported a block on what really was an end run round the Act. The statutory definitions of those in priority need are: pregnant women; someone with whom dependent children reside or might reasonably be expected to reside; a person who is vulnerable as a result of old age, mental illness or handicap or physical disability or other special reason, or with whom such a person resides or might reasonably be expected to reside. These manifestly do not include dependent children themselves. As Griffiths pointed out, 'old age' is included but 'young age' is not, and he is doubtless right in finding that:

[27] *Garlick* at 69.

Such a child is in my opinion owed no duty under this Act for it is the intention of the Act that the child's accommodation will be provided by the parents or those looking after him and it is to those people that the offer of accommodation must be made, not to the dependent child. If a family has lost its right to priority treatment through intentional homelessness the parent cannot achieve the same result though the back door by an application in the name of a dependent child; if he could it would mean that the disqualification of intentional homelessness had no application to families with dependent children. If this had been the intention of Parliament it would surely have said so.

A different court could have made a serious effort to handle what is a major policy problem with a different interpretation. After all, having an incompetent mother who loses one's childhood home by getting into rent arrears would make one a good candidate for having one of the 'other special reasons' the Act lists. We say this by way of pointing out the flexibility adventurous courts can have, not because it would be a sensible finding. There is a line between out and out judicial legislation and giving full effect to rights that are structured into legislation, and the line must not be crossed. The point of discussing Griffiths' ruling in *Garlick*, which was unanimously supported, is to contrast it with his much more arguable extension of this restriction on who can be an applicant under the Act in the case of *Begum*, covered in the same speech. Ms Garlick had no judicial support either in the House or the Court of Appeal, but Ms Begum won in a unanimous Court of Appeal which included Lord Donaldson, the Master of the Rolls, and gained Lord Slynn's dissenting support in the Lords. The comparison is extremely useful for sketching in the line referred to above between unwarranted legislation and rights-denial.

Ferdous Begum was a twenty-four-year-old Bangladeshi woman who arrived in England with her parents and four siblings on 17 December 1989. They approached their housing authority on arrival and were found to be intentionally homeless because they had left accommodation in Bangladesh. (How they were entitled to enter the UK without secured accommodation and what rights they should therefore have carried with them were never investigated in the courts.) Consequently the authority allowed them accommodation only up to 18 July 1990, the period judged adequate for Mr Begum to find his own place to live, which duty the councils may not avoid. Mr Begum then made a second application in his daughter's name. She could not do this herself, because she is deaf, almost completely mute, and can communicate only in a home-made sign language the family has worked out itself. (Psychological evidence not challenged nonetheless says she can function quite successfully within the family.) This application, on 17 July 1990, was made under section 59(1)(c) of the 1985 Act, for priority housing for herself on the grounds that she was 'vulnerable as a result of old age, mental illness, or handicap', and, as the Act specifies, also for her family on the grounds that they were persons who could reasonably be expected to reside with her. Not surprisingly the council initially tried a summary rejection on the *Garlick* line, writing to the father and saying 'the purported application was merely a device by which you sought to get around the unchallenged finding of your intentional homelessness'. They abandoned this, however, in the Court of Appeal.

The council clearly had a problem here, because an attempt to reject such an application could not be made on the grounds that Ferdous Begum herself had become intentionally homeless—she had never been the principal resident anywhere. Had they tried to claim that their investigations under the Act showed that a deaf mute was not in priority need, given the language of the Act, even the most council-friendly court would have had to rule the finding was perverse, and fail them under *Wednesbury*. Yet the original claim that the application was merely a device obviously coloured the approach of the authority's officer—a point that Butler-Sloss LJ in the Court of Appeal was clear about, as she attributed his 'falling into error' to this coloration. So an ingenious alternative approach was attempted. Ferdous Begum simply was not an applicant—she could not be counted as an applicant at all because she lacked the mental capacity to make the application, to understand the consequences of any offer made to her, or to abide by the terms of any rent agreement, and so forth.

It is at this point that the technology of public law comes into play. If a court wants to help the local authority, all it has to do is to hold that the very question of who can be an applicant is itself within the *Wednesbury* net—it is a question of fact, the authority is judge of fact, a factual determination cannot be appealed, the courts cannot interfere. But, of course, there is an escape from this remorseless logic, discussed earlier. Perhaps the question of whether someone is an applicant is not a *Wednesbury fact* at all, but comes under the alternative test, the *Khawaja* test, that is, it is a precedent fact which must be true before the council's discretion can come under the *Wednesbury* shield. In other words, it is not up to the council to decide whether someone is an applicant, only to assess an applicant's status. The latter question might be protected by *Wednesbury*, but the first is simply true or not, and the courts can rule which. If that approach is taken, then the court can make its own binding decision on whether someone like Ferdous Begum can be an applicant. The Court of Appeal did precisely that. The council had misdirected itself in law, and only its subsequent decisions on whether the application showed priority status and unintentionality of homelessness was up to them, matters they would have a very hard time disputing. The trouble, of course, is that to take the

Khawaja road rather than the *Wednesbury* route, quite simply is a decision a judge makes depending on whether he wants to find for the plaintiff applicant or the defendant council—there is absolutely no way the decision itself can be legally determined. So the Court of Appeal mounted an impressive argument from the language of the Act to show that the Act not only did not rule out applications from the mentally challenged, but specifically expected them, and that there was no precise form to be attached to the idea of an application itself. An application can be made by anyone on someone else's behalf or on their own behalf—it is more in the nature of an alerting of the council to someone's state of need. Donaldson MR puts the entire approach for those wishing to control the authority's decision very clearly:

I agree that reading s. 59(1)(c) with s. 62 makes it clear that no 'application' in the ordinary sense of the word is required of a homeless person as otherwise it would be quite impossible for some people who are 'vulnerable as a result of old age, mental illness, or handicap' to attract the attention which it is the clearly intended duty of housing authorities to provide . . . Accordingly s. 62 must be construed as contemplating only that the homeless person and his circumstances will be brought to the attention of the HA . . . In my judgment s. 62(1) of the Act contains a double barrelled threshold or precedent question of fact which has to be answered in the affirmative if the local housing authority's duties under Pt. III of the Act are to come into force. The first part of this question is whether a person has applied to it for accommodation in the sense which I have indicated. The second part is whether the authority has reason to believe that he *may* be homeless or threatened with homelessness. This is to be distinguished from the Pt. III duty which follows immediately afterwards in the same sentence, namely, to make such inquiries as are necessary to satisfy itself as to whether he *is* homeless or threatened with homelessness. I cannot believe that Parliament intended that whether or not a local housing authority became subject to the duties set out in Pt. III of the Act should depend on whether it happened to be credulous or incredulous, myopic or far-sighted. The intention must have been that an objective test should be applied. The authority's decisions on both aspects of this threshold question therefore falls to be reviewed not on *Wednesbury* grounds, but on *Khawaja* principles—does the evidence justify the conclusion.[28]

Donaldson's approach is just as much guided by his understanding of the nature of the Act as was Griffiths'. Griffiths' approach in *Begum* is characterized by the opening sentence of the relevant part of his speech: 'The Act is primarily about bricks and mortar and not with care and attention for the gravely disabled, which is provided for in other legislation.' Donaldson's view is instead: 'Such legislation is in accord with the expressed policy of government departments to accept within the community those who might in former days have been shut away.' How does a

---

[28] *Garlick* at 57.

judge choose in such a situation other than from personal political or moral preference?

However, given that Griffiths' overview is so different, the *Khawaja versus Wednesbury* choice must be inverted. Griffiths argues not from anything in the Act itself, but from a generalized position that legal obligations like taking on a tenancy require a particular degree of mental capacity. He has to find this from general principle, because the members of the Court of Appeal were quite clear that there is no such restriction in the Act itself. But according to Griffiths:

I can see no purpose in making an offer of accommodation to a person so disabled that he is unable to comprehend or evaluate the offer. In my view it is implicit in the provisions of the Act that the duty to make an offer is only owed to those who have the capacity to understand and respond to such an offer and if they accept it to undertake the responsibilities that will be involved. If a person is so disabled that he cannot do this he is not left destitute but is protected by the National Assistance Act 1948.[29]

More vitally, the discretion of the local authority is returned, because it is not enough simply for the House of Lords to come to a different decision than the Court of Appeal on the facts—the courts must be deprived of the right to decide on the facts:

If as the Court of Appeal decided, an application can be made on behalf of a totally mentally incapacitated person because a duty is owed to him or her under the Act it is understandable to regard the question of whether or not an application has been made to be a question of fact to be decided by the court. But if, on the true construction of the Act, Parliament only imposes the duty in respect of applicants of sufficient mental capacity to act upon the offer of accommodation then it seems to me it must have intended the local Housing Authority to evaluate the capacity of the applicant. In this field of social welfare all those concerned with the welfare of the victims must necessarily work closely together.

He pushes this argument further, using this concern that such helpless people be aided as well and rapidly as possible, by suggesting that the very need for urgent investigations and alerting of the social services means that a decision that the putative applicant:

lacks the capacity to make an application because he cannot understand or act upon an offer of accommodation can only be challenged on Judicial Review if it can be shown to be Wednesbury unreasonable.

There is little anyone can do faced with such a flat refusal. Slynn's dissent is quite clear. To define an applicant as one who ' has a priority need and who is capable both of being offered and accepting accommodation' is 'putting the cart before the horse'. For him '[a]ny person can be an

[29] *Garlick* at 72.

applicant', and indeed he shows that some parts of the Act expressly provide for situations where statements are made by someone other than the intended beneficiary. The Act obviously does cover people with mental handicaps because that is one of the specified grounds for priority housing, so the creation of some boundary line below which the handicap, instead of being a qualification, becomes a disqualification, if not included in the Act itself, is every bit as much judicial legislation as would be the introduction of housing rights for four-year-olds in the companion case. The difference is that Griffiths' judicial legislation deprives a category of people of a right, rather than granting one to a category not at all covered. He is perhaps the more able to do this because of the sense he creates that housing Ms Begum would be a form of social service—hence the reference to the 1948 National Assistance Act and the great urgency of making sure the right department gets to deal with her problem. All the National Assistance Act can do is to provide special accommodation for Ferdous Begum, when special assistance for her was not needed, and could only be a less happy resolution than housing her with her family. Counsel for Ms Begum tried hard to stress that she could cope very well inside her family home, and that what was needed was not social service provision but, precisely, a home. At no stage does Griffiths' speech take note of this point, because to do so would be to undermine the whole picture of the Act he has drawn in the 'bricks and mortar' description. Nor is the undeniable thrust of the Act to keep the family together mentioned at all.

Probably *Begum* was the most important of all the pro-council decisions on the Housing Acts, because it effectively reaches the extreme position of putting the whole working of the Act inside the barriers of administrative discretion. If the housing authorities not only get to say when an applicant is intentionally homeless, and what will constitute adequate accommodation when they do recognize a duty, but actually to define who may even count as an applicant there is very little scope left for judicial supervision. What would a council have to do that would result in a decision that it had behaved so irrationally that no council properly considering matters could have so acted, especially given the stress the courts have put on the 'local conditions' aspect of the Act?

This sense the courts have had that there is always another Act that can cope, that housing authorities must not be made to pick up anything but the clearest sort of rehousing task for the most legitimately needy, runs through all the cases, and has bedevilled any counsel trying to argue for this central thrust of coping with families whose overwhelming need is to get precisely the bricks and mortar Griffiths talks of. It is a common theme in these judicial pronouncements that the Housing Acts do not stand alone—there is always other legislation, other agencies who can help. These comments are not made for any reason of legal logic. They are in no way necessary to the judicial task of simply stating whether or not an applicant has a right to priority housing. The consequences of such a judicial investigation ought to be precisely the same if the alternative was, starkly, to put the families out on the streets. Yet Lord Bridge used this less sanguine prediction, that this probably would be the result in *Islam*, with the consequent splitting up of the family, as coloration for his more humane interpretation, presumably to stress the unpalatability of the majority view. The reason such reliance is placed on the alternative hopes is that the Law Lords cannot escape a sense of being managers of last resort to the welfare system, a system whose line managers they wish to trust to get on with the job of looking after the inadequate in whatever is the most efficient manner. There is a deep paternalism here, and a trust in a paternalistic welfare system which knows best, rather than an emotion-ally neutral rights-declaring orientation. But what happens when it is clear that the trusted line managers do not behave quite as the judges need them to, when the wonderfully supportive panoply of 'other agencies, other legislation' shows itself somewhat less caring? The last housing case we discuss here can be said, in a sense, to take up the invitation in Griffiths' speech to trust the co-operating agencies, the alerting to which of a problem is what, for him, an application really is.

R v. *Northavon District Council, ex parte Smith* in 1994 was precisely such a case.[30] Mr and Mrs Smith were gypsies who, along with their five children, all under ten, had been living in Housing Association accommo-dation in the St Paul's area of Bristol. They left this house, according to them because of problems of harassment and threatened violence arising from being a white gypsy family in a predominantly black area. There was enough alternative evidence mentioned in the case to suggest their story was at least one sided. Nothing, in any case, depends on the truth about their leaving the St Paul's house—we reproduce it here just to indicate the nature of the social problem the Smiths faced and represented. Initially they went to live in a relative's caravan, but were forced to leave, and asked the housing authority for accommodation, in October 1992. The housing authority in this case was the Northavon District Council. It is an important feature of the case that the housing authority and the social services authority were not, as is often the case, separate departments of the same council. The social services authority having responsibility for the Smiths was the Avon County Council. The Northavon District Council predictably held that though homeless and in priority need, the applicant, Mr Smith, was intentionally homeless because of leaving his St Paul's house. They were provided with temporary accommodation until 20 January 1993, and with advice about how to find somewhere themselves.

---

[30] *R* v. *Northavon DC, ex parte Smith* [1994] 2 AC 402.

Even before this the social services department of Avon County Council were already concerned about the Smith children. This was heightened when Shelter wrote to them early in January asking them to use their powers under the Children Act 1989 to pay the deposit and advance rent of private rented accommodation for the Smiths. The Children Act, and in particular section 17(6), gives them a duty to help where homelessness or impending homelessness is a problem that may make children a welfare risk. Avon County Council took the view that it was indeed their duty to help by providing in kind or cash, but that they had no duty to provide the sort of financial assistance Shelter was suggesting. Rather, says Avon CC, it was Northavon DC which had the 'primary responsibility for providing housing resources . . . This department's role is to liaise.' They promised to ask Northavon DC to reconsider their decision to evict the Smiths (from their temporary accommodation). In particular they decided to discuss Northavon DC's own duty under section 27 of the Children Act to assist vulnerable people. Accordingly they wrote to Northavon DC on 14 January saying:

I am requesting that, under s. 27 of the Children Act 1989 ('Co-operation between Authorities') that urgent consideration be given by Northavon DC to provide assistance for a full tenancy of a type and description commensurate with their housing needs.

In this letter they also accepted that extending the Smiths' current bed and breakfast arrangements might be adequate. Northavon District Council replied immediately in the following terms. (These letters are quoted because part of the legal argument depends on what was actually said. This is always a factor where judicial review is involved because of the idea of a duty to consider all relevant matters.)

I note that this section of the Act states that an authority to whom a request is made under the Children Act must comply with such a request unless it is not compatible with its own duties and does not prejudice unduly the discharge of its functions. But . . . [as the Smiths had already been considered the authority had fulfilled its duty by deciding not to help them] to offer them a tenancy would be a contradiction as the point of the process of assessing their homelessness application was to decide whether there was a duty to secure long term accommodation.

At this point, faced with imminent eviction, Mr Smith applied for judicial review on behalf of his children. It is important to remember by now that the children are the *de jure* applicants for help, via the Avon County Council. The important technical point here is that it was a judicial review application to consider whether or not Northavon DC had complied with its duties under the Children Act—it was not an appeal against their decision not to treat Mr Smith as entitled to housing. The duty in question is quite precise—it is a duty fully and fairly to consider Avon CC's request under section 27 of the Act. The court of first instance refused to grant judicial review, but the Court of Appeal overturned the judge and found for the Smiths.

The Court of Appeal was led by Sir Thomas Bingham MR, but also contained Lord Justice Steyn, who was shortly thereafter promoted to the House of Lords, so that his agreement with Bingham can fairly be treated as showing further the dissensus amongst the senior judges in cases of this kind. The dispute between the two authorities is relatively simple, but also unfortunately rather technical. Avon CC were asking Northavon DC to co-operate with them in solving the plight of the Smith children in as far as it involved homelessness, and cited the right to request such help under the Children Act. To be precise, they asked Northavon DC to consider the matter of the Smith children and to see if they could provide the suitable accommodation referred to in their letter. This accommodation would, inevitably, have to be suitable for the adult Smiths to live in as well, because the Act, of course, defines as suitable only accommodation capable also of taking those who could reasonably be expected to reside with them, i.e. their parents. In that sense it is logically the same as the sort of applications dismissed in *Garlick*, but here the request is not coming from a parent using their children as a way of carrying out an end run on the Act, but from the local government agency specifically charged with the welfare of the children, under a grant of authority allowing them to request such help from other agencies. It is therefore both procedurally, and surely substantively, very different. It is also precisely the sort of thing Griffiths ought to have had in mind when he justified his decision about Ferdous Begum on the grounds that there were other relevant coping agencies, all of whom ought to co-operate. Northavon DC was certainly entitled to provide housing in such a situation, as provided by section 65(2) of the 1985 Housing Act, if they thought it proper. When Northavon DC replied that they had already considered the case, and found Mr Smith to be intentionally homeless, it is suggested that they 'misdirected themselves in law', and thus made themselves subject to judicial review. The misdirection, carefully explained by Bingham in the Court of Appeal is that when Northavon DC claimed to have considered the case, they had, as their own Housing Act procedure requires them to, only considered their powers under section 65(3) of the Act to house Mr Smith and those who would normally reside with him. This is not the same question as whether, under section 65(2), they have a duty to house the children at risk, and those who would normally live with them. In that narrow but vital sense the issue they had been asked to consider had not been considered. For this reason Bingham granted the judicial review, saying:

It follows in my view that Avon's letter required Northavon to consider the Smiths' position afresh in the light of a new consideration, namely the judgment of the responsible authority that the children were in need and required to be housed.

He fully takes the point that Northavon had the discretion to refuse Mr Smith's application, and now to grant him housing under section 65(3) would be inconsistent. That might be a request 'not compatible with its own duties' and which would 'prejudice unduly the discharge of its functions'. But after analysing both Acts, Bingham says:

But if the conditions are fulfilled, the requested authority becomes obliged to comply even if compliance involves the exercise of powers which it had decided in the exercise of a lawful discretion not to exercise and which, in the absence of a request, it could not have been compelled to exercise . . . I think Northavon should have considered the matter afresh and not regarded the finding of intentional homelessness as conclusive, as it seems to have done. I very much doubt if, on such reconsideration, Northavon could properly have considered it as other than compatible with its own duties and obligations to house the Smiths.[31]

The latter part of this quotation is obiter, of course. No judge will claim he can make the actual decision—judicial review, as the judges repeat so often, is not an appeal on facts or on the substantive merit of a decision, it is a procedural control. What the Court of Appeal was saying was that Northavon did not abide by the legislatively required procedures, and must look again. Bingham was only making a guess as to what they would then see as their duty. But if he was right, there could be no objection that Mr Smith was evading the Act. Rather the intermeshing of Acts the Law Lords have relied on to soften their housing decisions would be operating. In other words rather than trying to do what was forbidden in *Garlick*, the *Smith* case represents an attempt to do what the Lords said should be done.

The Lords, in this case Lords Templeman, Jauncey, Mustill, Slynn, and Nolan, did not agree, and their reasoning throws us straight back to the attitudes in the earlier cases. Lord Templeman gave the only full speech. It starts with the characteristic scene setting to show how difficult the authority's problem is, and how basically unfair it is for Mr Smith to seek housing given that he voluntarily left adequate accommodation—there were already 2,632 applicants on the housing list, and ordinary families with children already had to put up with a wait of two and a half to three years. Mr Smith could not be given priority 'without destroying the fairness of the allocation of accommodation by the Housing Authority and without causing bitter resentment'.[32] This view is entirely Templeman's

---

[31] *Ex parte Smith* at 259.
[32] *Ex parte Smith* at 406.

own. His almost sociological interpretation of the facts may be true, but it involves a very special sense of 'unfair' in which obeying statutory requirements apparently plays no part, and such views ought not to figure in the decision as to the scope of section 27 of the Children Act at all.

In other cases their Lordships have hinted at their doubts about the probity of applicants, when lending judicial support to the idea of applicants seeking to evade the Housing Acts, or when expressing the sense of others having more legitimate expectations. Templeman's view of the probity of Avon County Council (which, as it happens, was not represented before the Lords) is a far more extreme, and quite unproven, accusation of bad faith:

The Social Service authority, no doubt short of money, declined to exercise their own powers to protect the children of Mr Smith by paying for accommodation and for that reason attempted to transfer responsibility to the Housing Authority . . . The Social Service authority would have been aware that the Housing Authority could not provide permanent accommodation for Mr Smith and his family without breach of the rules which had been devised to allocate accommodation fairly to people on the waiting list. The Social Service authority would also have been aware that their suggestion with regard to temporary accommodation would involve the Housing Authority paying for that accommodation instead of the Social Services authority.

This is an extraordinary legal argument, which amounts to asserting that local government departments are, if anything, more dishonest than indigent applicants. Such a view of local government officers sits curiously with the great trust we are told to have in them in the previous cases. It is not as though the possibility of buck passing had not occurred to the Court of Appeal. Bingham is quite clear about this, but equally clear that it is irrelevant:

The deputy judge felt, I think, that Avon was seeking to escape their statutory duty by unloading it on Northavon . . . I do not think that can affect the outcome. Reading these two statutory codes side by side, I find a clear parliamentary intention that children in need should not fall between them. That means that a clear duty to provide or secure the provision or give assistance must rest somewhere. I conclude that Northavon did not respond lawfully to Avon's request under s. 27(1) . . . If on reconsideration it concludes on valid grounds that it is not bound to comply with any of Avon's substantial requests, then a clear and enforceable duty remains binding on Avon under sections 17(1) and 20(1) of the Act of 1989.

None of the Lords had any sympathy with the real legal point—that Northavon had never carried out the requested consideration. It is largely brushed aside. Noting that Bingham had criticized the housing authority for not considering the Smiths' position afresh in the light of the request,

Templeman observed: 'but that request told the Housing Authority nothing they did not know when they made their decision under s. 65(3). The Social Services Authority had no power to make decisions under s. 65(3).' But it did not, of course, claim to have any powers under that Act. More to the point, they were not challenging the section 65(3) decision, but asking for a new consideration under section 65(2), and it is no more up to the Lords than Northavon itself to say that one inquiry, made under one section, automatically implied the result of a new inquiry under another section. Nor was Avon's letter meant to tell the housing authority anything they either knew or did not know. It was, purely, a legitimate request to do something new. For the Lords, in this case Northavon could do no wrong, however. Much had been made in the Court of Appeal, and in counsel's argument before the Lords, of the way in which Northavon's reply to Avon's letter could not possibly constitute an adequate giving of reasons for refusing the section 27 request. It was particularly argued that no adequate reasons were given for refusing permanent accommodation, and no reasons at all for refusing temporary accommodation. Refusing to take these points, Templeman goes on to say: 'That letter has been much criticised but it was no doubt drafted by a busy official at short notice.' Such sympathy is misplaced and irrelevant. There is probably no more important aspect of proper procedure than the clear and adequate giving of reasons, a doctrine at the heart of the English legal conception of natural justice. Unfortunately such a cavalier attitude to lack of proper reasons by the side a Law Lord supports is not uncommon. (A good example was the attitude of the majority to the Home Secretary's letter in the last of the immigration cases.) In the end the Lords interpreted the section 27 right to ask for co-operation as nothing more than an appeal for discretionary help rather than a right. Ignoring the fact that social service departments have neither housing stocks nor expertise in housing, the Lords accepted counsel for Northavon's view of the Act. This was only that Parliament intended co-operation. 'Parliament did not, however, intend that the nature or scope of those respective functions of the requesting local authority and the requested authority should change as a result of the imposition of a duty to co-operate.' This becomes, in a way, a vital secondary theme. It was taken up also by Nolan in the one supporting speech: it was quite wrong for one authority to use legal means to compel another to help. This position is adopted not only because the courts do not want to referee interdepartmental fights, but, once again, for a fear that if allowed this avenue, claimants might actually make frequent use of judicial review. Templeman again:

My Lords, these arguments demonstrate the need to prevent the functions of a Housing Authority and the functions of a Social Services Authority becoming blurred. If any of these arguments were accepted, every Social Services Authority will understandably seek to exercise their powers under s. 27 in order to transfer the burden of the children of a person intentionally homeless from the Social Services Authority to the Housing Authority. Every refusal by a Housing Authority to comply with a request under s. 27 will be scrutinised and construed with the object of discovering grounds for Judicial Review. The welfare of the children involved, the welfare of children generally and the interests of the public cannot be advanced by such litigation.[33]

What exactly is wrong with decisions being scrutinized to see if they are illegal is unclear, but Templeman is probably thinking of the same argument that occurs frequently where the Lords exempt local authorities or police services for potential liability in tort—they should not have to waste time and money on defending legal claims, they must just be trusted to get on with their difficult jobs. But even then, why should not the courts decide on the boundaries of responsibility between local authorities? If not the courts, whom? Yet Lord Templeman sees no role for the courts in such an area:

The Social Service Authority are responsible for children and the Housing Authority are responsible for housing. The two authorities must co-operate. Judicial Review is not the way to obtain co-operation. The court cannot decide what form co-operation should take. Both forms of authority have difficult tasks which are of great importance and for which they may feel their resources are not wholly adequate. The authorities must together do the best they can.

And the same view is expressed by Nolan:

It is to be hoped that as a matter of normal practice a Social Services Authority, faced with the problem of children who are threatened with homelessness, will explore the possibility of obtaining council accommodation informally and in a spirit of mutual co-operation rather than by an immediate and formal request, unsupported by any offer of contribution, under the provisions of s. 27.[34]

Quite simply, if the courts do not rule on matters like this, any resulting system will be a patchwork of regionally variable compromises which, if nothing else, will damage that supposedly great legal value of certainty. More broadly, it is again an expression of an unwillingness ever to think of rights, and always to see such problems as best left to informal mechanisms and the best, but not to be overseen, efforts of local officials who are to be deemed always to be well intentioned. Unless, of course, they themselves dare to invoke the courts. There was considerable interest in this case, because the effort by social service departments to get housing authorities to help them had become a common practice, and this was a test case much observed by those in the housing and child care

[33] *Ex parte Smith* at 409.
[34] *Ex parte Smith* at 413.

communities. In truth the Lords did decide, under the guise of telling social service departments to behave—they decided, yet again, that housing authorities were their own judges of their duties. This may be fair and proper. It does not appear to be the parliamentary intention, but parliamentary intent always breaks down when it has to be carried over two or more pieces of legislation. Certainly it is not fair, and it is actually improper, that the very use of judicial review should be so discouraged by those at its apex.

2. Local Authorities as Education Authorities

Housing is not the only good provided by local authorities. There is neither space nor need here to go at length into other areas, but it is useful to take one non-housing example to demonstrate that this overall 'trust the authorities' approach is endemic and not something peculiar to the Housing Acts. To some extent this has already been shown, in the cases previously discussed about local authorities' liability for negligence in matters of educational provision and social service care, but the precise points that judicial review focuses on are different. Though the thrust of judicial argument tends to be the same, it is rather clearer where judicial review is denied than where tortious liability, everywhere so much a matter of policy, is treated as inapplicable. One relatively recent case should suffice, R v. *Devon County Council, ex parte George*[35] from 1989. As often with these cases it is an example of the House of Lords, represented by Lords Keith, Brandon, Oliver, Goff, and Lowry, overturning a Court of Appeal presided over by a Master of the Rolls, in this case Donaldson, with Parker and Taylor LJJ. The Court of Appeal had found for the applicant against a local authority. (There is probably no structural tendency for the Court of Appeal to be more liberal than the Lords, though it has been a striking pattern throughout the last few chapters. More probably we are seeing only the consequence of a contingent assembly of different judicial styles.)

Although we spend some time on the Court of Appeal's reasoning in this case, it should not be thought that we are making a judgement that it is preferable to that of the Law Lords. The case is chosen in part to demonstrate how evenly balanced public law decisions can be, because of the way in which they are forced to avoid the substantive matters and focus instead on procedure. The case clearly could go either way, as it did. We offer it as more cumulative evidence of their Lordships' preference for supporting the local authorities. This they have done almost as regularly

---

[35] R v. *Devon CC, ex parte George* [1989] 1 AC 573.

with education as with housing cases. It might also be noted, however, that the local authority was probably always onto a winner here, because the case had a slightly odd history. The judge at first instance, though finding for the council, had granted a certificate allowing a 'leapfrog' procedure by which appeal could go straight to the Lords, as it involved 'a point of law of general public importance relating to the construction of an enactment'. The Lords nonetheless declined to hear the appeal, so the case went to the Court of Appeal instead. The applicant, Christopher George was a nine-year-old boy for whom the Local Education Authority had refused to provide a free place on the school bus, on the grounds that he lived within walking distance of the school. It was common ground that the distance of 2.8 miles on an unlit and dangerous road was such that he could only safely walk there and back accompanied by an adult. (Though it made no legal difference, it helps put the story in context to know that the bus already stopped at his house to take his older brother who, because he was certified as asthmatic, the LEA was obliged to transport.) The LEA believed that because his stepfather was unemployed, there was no problem about this restriction. It was part of his father's case that being thus required to walk sixty miles per week back and forth made it difficult for him to present himself to the local employment office as 'available for work'. The question of whether an LEA could require adult accompaniment had been decided in a slightly earlier case, *Essex County Council* v. *Rogers*[36] in 1987 by a Lords' panel with Ackner's as the sole speech. Probably as a result of this case the Education (No. 2) Act 1986 that applied to *George* had been amended slightly while passing through Parliament, immediately after the case, with the apparent intention of making LEAs look fairly closely at the appropriateness of their policy on walking to school. As the law stood an LEA was required to provide free transport if the walking distance to school exceeded two miles each way for a child under eight, and three miles each way for a child over eight. However, according to Donaldson MR, 'the Local Education Authority has still to consider, pursuant to s. 55(1) whether it is necessary to provide transport "for the purpose of facilitating the attendance" of the child at the school and, in so doing, pursuant to s. 55(3) it has to "have regard (amongst other things) to the age of the pupil and the nature of the route, or alternative routes which he could reasonably be expected to take"'.[37] Yet again it is vital to see the quite refined and limited question open to the courts, because nothing is gained, at this point in the analysis anyway, by lambasting the Lords for doing something their overall doctrine of judicial review forbids. To this effect it is worth quoting the Master of Rolls. First

---

[36] *Essex CC* v. *Rogers* [1987] 1 AC 66.
[37] *R* v. *Devon CC, ex parte G* [1988] 3 WLR 43 at 54 (the CA case).

he makes a useful point about terminology (with a pleasant little sting at the end), and then he goes on to give one of the clearest descriptions of the limits of judicial review in the judicial literature:

Application was made for judicial review of this refusal to provide free transport, on the basis that the decision was both illegal and 'Wednesbury unreasonable'. I eschew the synonym of 'irrational', because although it is attractive as being shorter than 'Wednesbury unreasonable' . . . it is widely misunderstood by politicians both local and national, and even more by their constituents, as casting doubt on the mental capacity of the decision maker, a matter which in practice is seldom, if ever, in issue . . . Let me stress the role of the courts in this controversy. The school which the applicant attends, the parish council, Devon ratepayers and the media are all fully entitled to say that if they were members of the education committee, the applicant would, of course, have been provided with free transport. And they have done so. Judges do not enjoy such a freedom. In judicial review proceedings such as these their role is much more limited. They can only consider whether (a) the council misapplied the relevant law or (b) it reached a decision which no council applying the law could reasonably have reached.

Part of the reason for quoting Donaldson MR at this stage is to absolve him from any suggestion that he, unlike the House of Lords, was committing the judicial sin of 'replacing the authorities' view with his own'. If the lower court had stepped outside the proper judicial role, we would not be able to rely on their finding as a way of underlining exactly what the Law Lords did. But the Court of Appeal was every bit as aware of the need for judicial self-restraint. Donaldson's argument is that the LEA denied Mr George's son a right to have something *considered* as the statute required, *not* that they made the wrong decision and denied him something he was entitled to. Refined though the distinction is, public law works on that point. The trouble with the distinction is not that it is refined, but that it is easy to ignore when one basically wants to support administrative authorities. A summary of Donaldson's view may most usefully be stated first, before his detailed argument, further to press this point. He characterizes the council's decision letter as stating, first, that Christopher is of the right age to be required to walk up to three miles each way to school and then as stating 'this is not a case where in the council's discretion transport should be provided free of charge'. But, according to Donaldson:

This betrays a fundamental error. This is that free transport is to be provided 'in the council's discretion' . . . Under s. 55(1) the council has no discretion. It has to exercise *judgment* on whether the statutory criteria exist, but that is quite a different exercise . . . I would add that, although the minute of decision was obviously drawn with very great care in the light of these proceedings which were already afoot, it does not in terms record that the education committee concluded not only that the applicant *could* walk to school with reasonable safety if accompanied, but that he could do so sufficiently easily that it was not necessary to provide him with transport in order to *facilitate* his attendance. [Stress in original.][38]

This reference to the decision letter not stating those things which would have to be true for the authority's decision to be a legitimate one was brushed aside in the Lords, as a similar problem had been in *Smith*. Yet the only control courts can exercise over administrative decisions has to be based on such a duty to give reasons, and if the relevant reasons are not stated, it is necessary to assume that they did not exist. The actual details of Donaldson's argument are not particularly important to us. They may well be no better than the reasons the Lords might have given for deciding the other way, and we consider them here only briefly as a further example of how one can, if determined, read a statutory code in the interests of applicants rather than of authorities. Donaldson's argument does need to be looked at briefly, to elucidate the distinction he drew in the quotation above, sadly rather too elliptically. This is the distinction between exercising *discretion*, which he says the council may not do under the relevant part of the Act, and exercising *judgment*, which he says they are required to do. This point, and a further related point he makes about the role of policies and norms in administering public provisions, are where the core difference between his approach and that of the Lords resides. They could also stand as a textbook thesis about the proper nature of administrative behaviour.

What one might call Donaldson's substantive argument is that the council has misread the legislation. Where the legislation intends to set maximum limits of two miles each way for under eights and three miles each way for older children, further distances automatically entitling them to free transport, the council has decided it means that all children of these ages can be expected to walk such distances, and thus no transport needs to be offered (except for special medically certified reasons) for shorter distances. The judgement Donaldson believes the council is required to make, however, arises from reading the Act closely, or, one might rather say, actually thinking about the Act rather than reading minimum duties from it. There is no substitute for Donaldson's own words here:

The basic question which the authority has to ask itself is whether any, and if so what 'arrangements' are *necessary* for the purpose of *facilitating* attendance of pupils at school. The two emphasised words have to be read in conjunction with each other. The question is not whether particular arrangements would facilitate attendance, door to door transport would undoubtedly do that. Nor is it whether arrangements are necessary to secure attendance. Section 39(2)(c) indicates clearly the legislative view that such arrangements are not necessary *to secure attendance,*

[38] *R v. Devon CC, ex parte G* [1988] 3 WLR at 59.

where the child lives within walking distance, unless there is some special factor . . . The question under section 55(1) is whether arrangements are *necessary* in order to *facilitate* attendance. This at once raises the question of why education authorities should be expected to facilitate attendance when this is primarily a parental responsibility. The answer I think is that a child who is subject to undue stress, strain or difficulty in getting to and returning from school will not benefit from the education offered to it at the school. And in speaking of stress and strain on the child, I include stress and strain unavoidably induced in the child by stress and strain on the part of the parent, either as an accompanying person on journeys to and from the school or otherwise, for example, anxiety that the child may not be safe. [Stress in original.]

Yet the authority, as far as Donaldson can see, shows no evidence of ever having considered this question. They did not form a judgement on whether or not young Mr George would have his education facilitated to a worthwhile degree by not having to make his particular journey on foot at his age. Thus, in the classic formula of *Wednesbury*, they failed to take into account something they should have considered. What he means by saying that they had no discretion under section 55(1) is that they did not have a discretion as to whether to bother considering this point or not. He does not mean that the answer they had to come to was determined by the statute. This goes to the core of administrative decision making, as enunciated in a doctrine that Donaldson, again too briefly, expounds on the role of policy in such matters. The Act provides, according to Donaldson, that a council must 'have regard (amongst other things) to the age of the pupil and the nature of the route, or alternative routes which he could reasonably be expected to take' pursuant to section 55(3). Against this expectation he raises two questions about such 'discretionary' policy making. One refers to the use of standardized norms, the second to the application of general policies:

While it is of course, permissible, and probably administratively essential to have certain norms in mind, each application has to be considered on its individual merits and the age of the child and the nature of the route are not the only factors to be taken into account. The words 'amongst other things' are a not a throw away expression. Full effect must be given to them.

Donaldson gives some examples of the sort of 'other things' in this case— the easy assumption that the father is available because he is unemployed, the sheer fact that it involves sixty miles a week on foot for him, the asthmatic brother, and the effect on the younger having to leave so much earlier and return so much later than an older brother. But he insists these are matters for the council to consider when they decide 'whether the criteria set out in 55(1) read in the light of 55(3) are met'. He fully accepts that the court may only intervene if the council has acted in a way that is *Wednesbury unreasonable*, which he paraphrases in a way that shows just how little objective content there really is to the idea: 'To put it in the more homely language of May LJ in . . . "my goodness, that is certainly wrong". Or, the other part of the *Wednesbury* test, the council "erred in law by misunderstanding their powers and duties and, as a result, failed to take account of relevant matters or took account of irrelevant matters".' As it happens it is never stated outright in Donaldson's opinion which branch of *Wednesbury* Devon CC did fail, but it would be appear to be the second branch. He refers, though, also to the very idea of a generalized rule or policy:

The council had a policy. There is nothing wrong with having a policy, provided always that it is appreciated that each application must be considered on its own merits . . . It is, I think a fair reading of that policy in its 1986 version that the general rule was that no free transport would be provided for 'within distance' children, save in the following . . . [What follows are considerations not germane to this presentation of Donaldson's argument, though they are important for a completely separate argument he addresses on which we choose not to focus.]

In other words the very policy that the council used was one that essentially forced it to fail its duty, except for the exceptions he goes on to mention, which themselves were made somewhat automatic. These reasons for holding that Devon CC had failed in its duties to Mr George are a classic statement of English public law on administrative action—general rules and administrative norms can only be used where they themselves incorporate a proper consideration of everything the statute requires to be considered. Unless the court is satisfied from whatever evidence or record it has before it that all such matters were considered, the administrative entity will be held to have acted either unreasonably or illegally.

The House of Lords overturned this result. They could only do so if either they thought the interpretation of the Education Act (No. 2) 1986 did not require the council to form the judgement Donaldson reads into it, or that the council did exercise this judgement. Lord Keith, who provides the only speech in the Lords, choses mainly the latter strategy, and what one gets in the end are two conflicting readings of evidence, the evidence in question being the real meaning of the council's communications, and the role in their decision that seems to have been played by their standing policy document.

Keith does not disagree exactly with Donaldson's reading of the duty imposed by the Act to interpret the provision of transport where 'necessary . . . for the purpose of facilitating' attendance in section 55(1) with the requirement in section 55(3) to 'have regard (amongst other things) to the age of the pupil and the nature of the route . . .'. But he gives very much a dictionary treatment—'facilitate' is literally defined, by reference to the

Concise Oxford Dictionary, as 'to promote', and 'necessary' is defined from case law as meaning 'really needed'. The effect is to give a sense of the duty that while correct and not incompatible with Donaldson's, does not begin to have the richness Donaldson gives to it. Donaldson's rich interpretation of the duty came from reflecting on why a council should 'facilitate' in order to give full and purposive meaning to the duty. Keith applies the same literalist approach to the core question—did the council consider these matters fully when making their decision about Christopher George? Where Donaldson is suspicious of the council's use of a standing policy, Keith uses the policy statement itself as evidence that they did everything they needed to do. The council's decision letter had, according to Donaldson, betrayed 'a fundamental error'. After saying that 'this is not a case where in the council's discretion transport should be provided free of charge', the council had justified this by a reference to the policy document:

None of the circumstances set out in paragraphs 3(d)(i)–(iv) of the council's policy exist. There is no suggestion that Christopher is not a normal healthy boy for his age. We would expect a child of Christopher's age walking this route to be accompanied but are not satisfied that it would not be reasonably practical for one of Christopher's parents to accompany him or otherwise secure his regular attendance at school.[39]

The paragraph in question is concise. Sub-paragraph (i) simply quotes the duty in the words of the Act's section 55(1); sub-paragraphs (ii) and (iii) provide for transport where certified by a school medical officer or the director of social services, and sub-paragraph (iv) covers cases where 'the education committee decides, on the merits of a particular case, that special arrangement should be made'. As far as Keith is concerned the record shows clearly that the council has followed the policy of the Act, and has documented so doing, because all matters that might be germane are covered by that policy statement, and the council says they applied the policy. The route had been inspected, and the council had, as it said, taken into account his age and the nature of the route, and had considered that it would require accompaniment but that this was available. Thus 'There is nothing to suggest that the panel was not exercising a judgment as to whether free transport was necessary for the purpose of facilitating the applicant's attendance at school.' Donaldson had concluded that the panel had decided only that Christopher George 'could walk to school with reasonable safety . . .' but not 'that he could do so sufficiently easily that it was not necessary to provide him with transport in order to *"facilitate"* his *attendance'* (stress in original). Keith attacks this. As the council has said that none of the circumstances set out in the policy document apply:

[39] Taken from Keith's speech in *R* v. *Devon CC, ex parte George* at 602.

... this means that the panel did not consider free transport to be necessary for the purpose of facilitating the applicant's attendance at school. The words desiderated by the Master of the Rolls would not have conveyed any additional meaning.

What we have here is a fine example of minimalist versus maximalist application of pure *Wednesbury* doctrine, not a rejection by either side of that doctrine. Because *Wednesbury* can be as generous or as restrictive as its user wishes it to be. It is in its very essence a legal compromise, which is probably why it has never been replaced. For the Court of Appeal, all the council has done is slap on a policy that is clearly cut to a narrow interpretation of its duty. With this reading the slightly unusual language of 'necessary to facilitate' is otiose, because it really means 'physically necessary', and that as applied to a norm which effectively means that anyone between eight and sixteen is equally capable of walking six miles a day without detriment to their education. No one can really doubt that the council was taking such a rule of thumb, and treating the legislation as permitting it to make a child walk up to a certain distance, rather than setting maximum distances it could allow children to walk. But, as Keith says, there is nothing in the policy document that says this outright. The Court of Appeal is reading the duty itself more broadly, one might say more 'richly' and thus finds the council in breach of the requirement to consider matters fully. The House of Lords is leaving the council free, not only as it must, to decide for itself whether its policy does cover all that it must consider, but by giving a much narrower reading to the primary duty, making it much easier for the council to pass that test.

There is not, perhaps, a 'right answer' to the question of whether or not Dorset was acting within the restraint of public law. This is because public law doctrines, here with education, above with housing, and in fact with all service provision, are cast in a way that allows a court, quite legitimately, either to leave state agencies massive freedom to interpret their duties themselves, or to exercise a good deal of covert substantive control in a procedural guise. Only judicial preference, subject to the haphazardness of who hears the appeal, really determines what a council can do in any particular case. Taken along with the previous chapter on immigration rights, it seems that the inevitable, massive, and largely unconstrained nature of judicial discretion in a common law country makes any talk of rights, as opposed to executive convenience, very ill supported. In the final chapter we try to bring together these discussions, along with the comments on public law generally from Chapter 7, the analysis of policy arguments in Chapter 6, and the treatment of judicial methodology in Part One of the book. What we seek, in the last chapter, is some account of the nature of law as it is practised that makes sense of these patterns, and often of the precise absence of pattern, in both public and private law.

10

Conclusion—Legal Argument and Politics

> Law, says the judge as he looks down his nose,
> Speaking clearly and most severely,
> Law is as I've told you before,
> Law is as you know I suppose,
> Law is but let me explain it once more,
> Law is the Law.

W. H. Auden, *Law like Love*

But the common law of England has not always developed upon strictly logical lines, and where logic leads down a path that is beset with practical difficulties the courts have not been frightened to turn aside and seek the pragmatic solution that will best serve the needs of society.

Griffiths LJ in *R* v. *Deputy Governor of Camphill Prison,*
ex parte King [1985] QB 735

Yet, despite Auden's tautology, and continuing his poem, '... law-abiding scholars write: law is neither wrong nor right ... Law is the clothes men wear, Anytime, anywhere', his stanza captures very well the frustration of anyone trying, from outside the profession, to grasp what legal argument is actually about. The frustration comes in equal part because lawyers often seem to accept something like that tautology, but simultaneously to accept Griffiths' view of English legal development, and not to mind. The debate about the nature of law is, of course, a standard concern of legal philosophy. In the last couple of decades the professional legal philosophers' debate has largely centred round the Hart v. Dworkin contrast between law as a system of rules, and law as a collection of principles, with excursions into the idea of law as an autopoietic system. Outside the mainstream of the pluralist tradition, legal thinking has its characterizations, inevitably, amongst post-Marxist thinkers influenced by Habermas, or postmodernists of various French hues. Little of this is of any use to us, because even the most unconventional of such writers start from within the experience of legal discourse, and all seek to find some overall characterization which makes legal thinking and praxis coherent, self-contained, and valid. Our starting point must indeed be that lawyers (unless otherwise indicated, that noun covers, indiscriminately, practitioners, academics, and judges) all do think there is something separate and coherent about law.

Ordinary language usages amongst lawyers all indicate that, in some sense, they see law as a system of thought with its own validating tests, and as a system which produces truths the rest of the world has to accept and respect. Lawyers talk about cases being 'wrongly decided'; they assert, confidently, that one interpretation of the law 'is better than' another. They do this from the bench, and they do it, for example, in academic argument:

1. 'Are you saying, then, that X v. Y was "wrongly decided"?'
   (Question to a candidate during interviews for a Law Fellowship)

2. 'Regrettably we must conclude that X v. Y was wrongly decided'. Or

3. 'It must follow therefore that X v. Y was wrongly decided and is overruled'.
   (Commonly found in the Law Reports.)

4. 'But the better view is . . .'.
   (Commonly found, quite as bluntly, in law textbooks)

The sense of law as a self-contained and 'learnt' art is self-conscious and non-inclusive: 'It may be impossible for you as a non-lawyer to come to understand what counts as a good argument.' This comes from an interview with one of the Law Lords. It is a consciousness of a particular talent—'She has real promise, she thinks like a lawyer'—a law tutor's comment on a student to another law tutor. Sometimes the sense of law as separate is held with an ironic respect for other modes of thought, as when a judge congratulates a legal solution as corresponding with common sense, or castigates a colleague's opinion because the man in the street will view it as ludicrous: but even then the separateness of law is not doubted. Perhaps especially then.

Lawyers do indeed talk about principles, 'I am unable to reconcile this with any principle . . .', and also of rules, ' the rule has always been that'. And, of course, they talk about 'not cheating'. All the Law Lords insisted that there are times when one simply cannot stretch an argument to get to the result one wants. They talk of justice and just results, though not as all-powerful trump tokens. Indeed they may attack colleagues for being so concerned to do instant justice in a case that they will use any argument they can find. Lawyers talk about fairness, in a way which makes it clear they accept no Rawlsian identity of 'justice as fairness'. They talk about policy, though with an ambivalence. Sometimes a policy argument is offered as the legal solution, sometimes as a necessary conclusion when law cannot provide an answer. They talk about 'bright lines', that is, very clear demarcation rules adopted for pragmatic convenience. They do not often think of themselves as deducing results, though they do talk sometimes of analogical argument. More commonly they think of legal decision as some form of induction. (This is well documented in some of the cases from Chapter 6.)

Viewed from outside, legal argument is a hodgepodge of methodological rules, core constitutional understandings of the judicial function, 'common sense', economic motivation assumptions, assumptions about organizational prerequisites which amount at times to complex sociologies, human nature assumptions, core justice touchstones. Yet although law is, to lawyers, a special systematic method of thought, something that can be learnt, taught, something for which natural talent may vary, it is still possible, apparently, for Griffith LJ, as he then was, to speak as in the other head quote to this chapter. To say 'where logic leads down a path that is beset with practical difficulties the courts have not been frightened to turn aside and seek the pragmatic solution' *seems* to be a confession that courts sometimes deliberately give the wrong answer, yet it is doubtful any lawyer would agree to this description. For them, *both* the logical conclusion, *and* the intentional departure from logic, constitute well-formed legal solutions.

One way we might hope to grasp this special nature of law is to look at legal argument *in extremis*. By this we mean a situation where judges have to come up with something they can defend as genuinely being a *legal* solution to a problem that just cannot be avoided, when there seems to be no orthodox legal justification for even hearing the case. One might have taken something like a War Crimes Tribunal attempting to justify a retrospective application of positive criminal law in an international perspective where only sustained fiction can pretend any right to prosecute. But at Nuremberg and later the problems of justification were largely dealt with by deliberate silence. We have to hand a case almost as morally dramatic from the very recent history of the Law Lords, *Airedale NHS Trust v. Bland*.[1] If the Law Lords can succeed in finding a legal answer to the question posed in *Airedale*, we may be able to see why law is entitled to think of itself as a real and separate system of thought and analysis.

This was the case where the victim of a terrible disaster at a football match had been in a persistent vegetative state for over two years, kept alive by artificial feeding and by constant medication, but with no hope of ever returning to consciousness. Unlike the more familiar situation of someone on artificial respiration, it was not a question of simply switching off a machine which was keeping the body alive. Anthony Bland's body was working perfectly well except that he was completely helpless. He needed to be fed and cared for. If he was not fed he would indeed die, but

---

[1] *Airedale NHS Trust v. Bland* [1993] 1 All ER 821.

of starvation and dehydration, and it would take some time, unless one of the infections he regularly got came mercifully. Bland presented a legal problem for an unusual reason. His doctors agreed with his parents that he should be allowed to die. But they were frightened that if they did stop caring for him, they would in fact be committing a crime, possibly as serious as murder or manslaughter, and they asked the courts for a ruling on this. Technically their Lordships, and the courts below through which the case travelled, had no right to grant this request. English courts always refuse to answer hypothetical questions. The normal justification for the courts as an institution neither entitles nor requires them to act as a general moral tribunal. Even now, the Lords having given the answer that the doctors would not be committing a crime, it is unclear what the legal status of that pronouncement is. But when challenged on this matter, a senior Law Lord produced a classic defence of necessity—'Who else could, what else could we do?' In this sense it was a legal argument *in extremis*. Not only was there no existing law on the matter, but the tribunal in question had no legal or constitutional right to entertain it. Yet the answer they decided they must give absolutely had to be a legal answer, not simply the best intuitive moral answer five wise and decent men could come up with. The answer may have been wrong, and maybe they should not have given one, but it is no part of our intention here to suggest they were anything but deeply and sincerely seeking to do well something they felt they could not avoid.[2]

So, how does one find a legal answer, and what does its 'legality' tell us about the supposed special nature of legal argument? For most of the judges concerned, at all levels, the *legal* as opposed to ethical problems of Bland's case were not really as difficult as they themselves suggested in their prefatory remarks. They even managed to find something like a precedent, on which we comment shortly. In all honesty one cannot really believe that most of the judges saw an ethical problem either. The moral responsibility was obviously awesome, but none of them seem to have had any personal doubt that Anthony Bland's parents should get their wish. They found no difficulty constructing an ethical category for him, or putting him into it. The ethical arguments vary a little in terminology but in little else. They have the following steps: Bland had no consciousness and no sensation at all; expert medical evidence was unanimous that he never again would; resources were being tied up keeping him insensately

---

[2] This is one of the rare situations where an author cannot refuse to say what he thinks should have happened. The Lords should have refused to entertain the case. The doctors should have gone ahead. The Crown Prosecution Service should have declined to prosecute under the public interest justification. Two valuable points would have justified the fears and sufferings of the doctors and parents and given meaning to Anthony Bland's death, and therefore his life. It would have been established that there is not, necessarily, a correct legal answer to every question. It would have forced Parliament to cease to dodge its responsibilities, and it might, even, have furthered the cause of a Bill of Rights.

alive; watching him continue in this state was dreadful for his family. Very little importance was attached to public moral views, even by those like Lord Browne-Wilkinson who recognized that there was no moral unanimity in society on the issue. He admitted that Roman Catholics and Orthodox Jews are opposed to what he guessed was a majority support for withdrawal of life support in Bland's case. Given the stress on unanimity in medical advice, it is interesting that he even notes:

Within the medical profession itself there are those, including one of the very distinguished doctors who gave evidence in this case, who draw a distinction between withholding treatment on the one hand and withholding food and care on the other, the latter not being acceptable.

Indeed Browne-Wilkinson notes that the very reason the case is before them, following the coroner's warning that failing to feed Anthony Bland might be murder, is because of the lack of unanimity in the health care profession.

In the past doctors exercised their own discretion, in accordance with medical ethics, in cases such as these. To the great advantage of society they took the responsibility of deciding whether the perpetuation of life was pointless. But there are now present amongst the medical and nursing staff of hospitals those who genuinely believe in the sanctity of human life, no matter what the quality of that life, and report doctors who take such decisions to the authorities with a view to prosecution for a criminal offence.[3]

Yet what this recognition of moral conflict does is not to make Browne-Wilkinson, or almost any other judge apparently, struggle to know what is right, but to make it quite crucial that they be seen merely to be giving a *legal* answer. The only Law Lord to speak at all directly on the ethical— more properly metaphysical—questions involved is Lord Mustill. He produces a perfect rationalist answer, but that is better than a refusal to do anything but note, *en passant*, that some would not agree. Mustill does, at least, tell us what he believes ethically:

... I still believe that the proposed conduct is ethically justified, since the continued treatment of Anthony Bland can no longer serve to maintain that combination of manifold characteristics which we call a personality ... I do not assert that the human condition necessarily consists of nothing except a personality, or deny that it may also comprise a spiritual essence distinct from both body and personality. But of this we can know nothing, and in particular we cannot know whether it perishes with death or transcends it. Absent such knowledge we must measure

---

[3] Lord Browne-Wilkinson must be wrong if he thinks that the presence of those 'who genuinely believe in the sanctity of human life, no matter what the quality of that life' in the medical profession is new. What is new is such people doing anything. Oddly this does not seem to have caused him any anxiety about his argument.

up what we do know. So doing, I have no doubt that the best interests of Anthony Bland no longer demand the continuance of his present care and treatment.[4]

Lord Browne-Wilkinson acknowledged the partiality of the ethical arguments canvassed by the courts, and the inevitability that:

... if the judges seek to develop new law to regulate the new circumstances, the law so laid down will of necessity reflect judges' views on the underlying ethical questions, questions on which there is a legitimate division of opinion. By way of example, although the Court of Appeal in this case, in reaching the conclusion that the withdrawal of food and Anthony Bland's subsequent death would be for his benefit, attaches importance to impalpable factors such as personal dignity and the way Anthony Bland would wish to be remembered it does not take into account spiritual values which, for example, a member of the Roman Catholic church would regard as relevant in assessing such a benefit.[5]

But this is, for him, a strong reason why what the Law Lords do should be presented as 'to determine this particular case in accordance with the existing law, and not to seek to develop new law laying down a new regimen'. Comforted then, by the knowledge that they are doing no more than saying what the law already is, all of the Law Lords except Lord Mustill take a very simple tack. The argument runs thus:

1. Discontinuing Bland's feeding and antibiotics is an omission, not an act.
2. Omissions can only be criminal if there is a duty to act.
3. There was initially a duty to act because there might have been some chance of saving Bland.
4A. Bland was unable to consent to invasive medical treatment and giving this treatment would have constituted, in the absence of consent, a crime.
4B. The absence of consent was nullified by the legal doctrine that where consent cannot be given, doctors are entitled to act in a patient's best interests.
5. Expert medical opinion is that, as he cannot revive, it is no longer in his best interests to continue this invasive treatment.
6. Therefore the implied consent must be missing, and invasive treatment, far from being a duty, now has no legal justification.
7. As there is now no duty to act, the omissions cannot be a crime.

It is worth noting that the precedent they rely on for intervention 'in the best interests' in the absence of the possibility of consent comes from a case, *F v. West Berkshire Health Authority*,[6] where the Lords permitted

---

[4] *Airedale* at 896.
[5] *Airedale* at 879.
[6] *F v. West Berkshire Health Authority* [1989] 2 All ER 545.

doctors to sterilize a mentally deficient women who lacked the capacities either to manage birth control or bring up a baby, but who could not be prevented from sexual intercourse. It is vital that their Lordships find a precedent, because in this case far more than in most, they are insistent that no new law is being created. Yet the analogy between the best interests of someone who is going to live but cannot handle one aspect of living and yet is incapable of understanding that, and the interests of someone who is going to die as a result of a legal decision is vastly overstretched. The real problem with their Lordships' entire analysis is their need to cling to this 'best interests test'. It requires some very complex argumentation to work at all. For example, a distinction Lord Goff draws:

In circumstances such as [Anthony Bland's] it may be difficult to say that it is in his best interests that the treatment should be ended. But, if the question is asked, as in my opinion it should be, whether it is in his best interests that the treatment that has the effect of artificially prolonging his life should be continued, that question can sensibly be answered to the effect that it is not in his best interests to do so.[7]

A very similar interpretation of what is the right question to ask is given by Lord Browne-Wilkinson:

. . . [the question is] whether it is in the best interests of Anthony Bland to continue the invasive medical care involved in artificial feeding. That question is not the same as 'Is it in Anthony Bland's best interest that he should die'. The latter question assumes that it is lawful to perpetuate the patient's life; but such perpetuation of life can only be achieved if it is lawful to continue to invade the bodily integrity of the patient by invasive medical care. Unless the doctor has reached the affirmative conclusion that it is in the patient's best interest to continue the invasive care, such care must cease.[8]

The beauty of such precision of questioning is that the decision is no longer about whether Anthony Bland should die at all—the case turns out to be about his legal right not to suffer an assault! And no new law is created at all? Their Lordships were very keen, however, to establish one thing—their decision relates absolutely only to omissions, to discontinuance of life support, and may not in any way be taken to authorize any positive step to bring about death, for fear that this might legitimize euthanasia. To those who fail to grasp any real difference between stopping feeding Anthony Bland and giving him an injection that would speedily end his life, there is simply a reiteration that there is a real difference, because of the omission/action distinction, and because of the argument that shows the doctors have no right to feed Bland without his consent.

This speaks to our earlier point that judges do sometimes note a conflict

---

[7] *Airedale* at 869.
[8] *Airedale* at 883.

between legal and ordinary arguments. Lord Lowry, for example, finishes his speech with a very persuasive account of how the non-lawyer would insist it was still a justification for euthanasia, but fails to say how he would persuade his imaginary friend he was wrong. Even Browne-Wilkinson regards the problem as one of justifying an apparently irrational distinction, but entertains no consequent doubt about the legal validity of the distinction:

Finally the conclusion I have reached will appear to some to be almost irrational. How can it be lawful to allow a patient to die slowly, though painlessly, over a period of weeks from lack of food but unlawful to produce his immediate death by a lethal injection, thereby saving his family from yet another ordeal to add to the tragedy that has already struck them? I find it difficult to find a moral answer to that question. But it is undoubtedly the law and nothing I have said casts doubt on the proposition that the doing of a positive act with the intention of ending life is and remains murder.[9]

This surely establishes beyond doubt that lawyers do see law as a separate and self-contained thought system. But Lord Browne-Wilkinson's statement here must also be one of the clearest presentations of law as a pragmatic, amoral, and unprincipled construction of *ad hoc* problem-solutions anywhere in legal literature. What the Lords did was to make a policy decision. They do this very frequently—it is no more than a routine application of Griffiths' statement in the opening quotation—'where logic leads down a path that is beset with practical difficulties the courts have not been frightened to turn aside and seek the pragmatic solution that will best serve the needs of society'. Here, apparently, the needs of society are to allow those in a permanent vegetative state to lapse into real death once it becomes clear they will never revive. At the same time society does not perceive a need to allow the termination of life in less utterly clear-cut situations. If the Lords had to take the case, would anything have been lost by using the usual language of policy making in the Lords, given the patent absurdity of the claim here to be applying pre-existent law? Because here, the answer to the question, what constitutes a *legal* answer, is both intellectually and, arguably, *legally*, meretricious.

One feels easier saying these perhaps harsh things, because the decision in *Airedale* was, in truth, much less united than appeared at first glance, or than it has generally been presented. Lord Mustill wrote a speech which concurs in the result, and contains the occasional consensus implying sentence such as, 'The reasoning I propose is, I believe, broadly in line with that of your Lordships', or, on the ethical question, 'With the general tenor, if not with the details, of what was said in the courts below I respectfully agree.' Actually his arguments are not compatible with the

[9] *Airedale* at 884.

position of his colleagues on the legal matter, and on the ethical dimension it is, naturally, the detail that matters. Quite probably Lord Mustill was tempted to dissent completely in this case, and refrained from a sense that such a dissent would cause more harm than good. In truth what he does say largely destroys the majority argument, though he, too, and very clearly, is twisting in a legal wind in an attempt to find a legal answer to a non-legal issue.

The careful question formation of Goff and Browne-Wilkinson can hardly stand up to Lord Mustill's opening demand for the legal issue not to be 'brushed aside as an empty technicality'. This must be resisted, Mustill argues, more honestly and bluntly than anyone else, because 'the authority of the state, through the medium of the court, is being invoked to permit one group of citizens to terminate the life of another'. Nor is he prepared at all wholeheartedly to adopt the stance that the court is not legalizing euthanasia. Interestingly he shows one consequence of sticking to a 'legal' answer:

> I will also abstain from debate about whether the proposed conduct will amount to euthanasia. The word is not a term of art, and what matters is not whether the declarations authorise euthanasia, but whether they authorise what would otherwise be murder.[10]

Lord Mustill accepts, with deep misgiving, that the only way through what he describes as 'a legal and ethical maze' involves the acts/omissions distinction, admitting that 'the ethical status of the two courses of action is for all relevant purposes indistinguishable'. He does though give a very good reason for not taking the case in the first place:

> By dismissing this appeal I fear that your Lordships' House may only emphasise the distortions of a legal structure which is already morally and intellectually misshapen. Still, the law is there and we must take it as it stands.

(Technically the case arrived before the Lords as an appeal on Bland's behalf by the Official Solicitor against the Court of Appeal's decision to grant the hospital declarations that their proposed course of action would not constitute a criminal offence.) The first part of Lord Mustill's speech is a powerful analysis of whether the Lords have any legal basis for pronouncement at all, which, interesting as it is, need not delay us. Except, that is, to point out that, presumably deliberately, he never actually answers the question. What appears to be his position is that all the Lords' decision amounts to is reassuring the doctors that 'what they proposed to do was lawful when proposed and will be lawful when carried out'. To his own question—'Just how is it that the civil courts can do in a criminal

---

[10] *Airedale* at 885.

matter what the criminal courts themselves cannot do?'—he does not even try to sketch an answer.

Lord Mustill's speech is merciless to anyone seeking comfort in easy legal answers and in analogies to what happens elsewhere in the common-law world. He alone, for example, makes the point that of the thirty-nine American states which have legislated for 'living wills', the legislation in twenty specifically excludes termination of life by the proposed mechanism in Bland's case—withdrawal of nourishment and hydration. Our reasons for saying that Lord Mustill's speech amounts, *de facto*, to a ringing dissent can only be presented by quoting the relevant passage at some length—nothing could be gained by paraphrasing such powerful prose. He refuses to accept the key point in the speeches of his colleagues, the extension of the crucial precedent in *F* v. *West Berkshire Health Authority*. He describes the logic of that case as being that where a patient cannot make a decision herself, not to take a decision is to choose one course of action by default, and therefore someone else must make it in her best interests. Therefore so that the decision on Bland's future not be taken by default (which would leave him medically alive), someone else must decide 'whether in his own best interests his life should now be brought to an end'. What Mustill says thereafter removes most of his brethren's case, including the 'no euthanasia' insistence:

I cannot accept this argument which, if sound, would serve to legitimate a termination by much more direct means than are now contemplated. I can accept that a doctor in charge of a patient suffering from the mental torture of Guillain-Barré syndrome, rational but trapped and mute in an unresponsive body, could well feel it imperative that a decision on whether to terminate life could wait no longer and that the only possible decision in the interests of the patient, even leaving out all the other interests involved, would be to end it here and now by a speedy and painless injection. Such a conclusion would attract much sympathy, but no doctrine of best interests could bring it within the law. Quite apart from this the case of Anthony Bland seems to me quite different. He feels no pain and suffers no mental anguish. Stress was laid in argument on the damage to his personal dignity by the continuation of the present medical regime, and on the progressive erosion of his family's happy recollections by month after month of distressing and hopeless care. Considerations of this kind will no doubt carry great weight when Parliament comes to consider the whole question in the round. But it seems to me to be stretching the concept of personal rights beyond breaking point to say that Anthony Bland has an interest in ending these sources of others' distress. Unlike the conscious patient he does not know what is happening to his body, and cannot be affronted by it; he does not know of his family's continuing sorrow. By ending his life the doctors will not relieve him of a burden become intolerable, for others carry the burden and he has none. What other considerations could make it better for him to die now rather than later? None that we can measure, for of death we know nothing. The distressing truth which must not be shirked is that the proposed conduct is not in the best interests of Anthony Bland, for he has no interests of any kind.

After that it is perhaps inevitably disappointing that Lord Mustill cannot actually do better than his colleagues in a positive way, though he admits this himself. His claims are entirely modest, for all he says is: 'I turn to an argument which, in my judgment is logically defensible and consistent with existing law.' His version is simply that Bland has no interests at all, and therefore there can be no duty to keep him alive 'in his best interests'. It is, at the very least, both more honest, and preferable because it makes no pretence of precedential justification. It is not in Bland's best interests to be allowed to die, but also not in his best interests to be kept alive. In fact the whole of this 'positive' part of Mustill's speech occupies only two paragraphs before he returns to attacking two other assumptions of his colleagues. He denies their comforting beliefs that the nurses in question will not have a harrowing time, and that doctors are somehow or other more fitted to make such decisions than anyone else. This last attack is important, because much of the emphasis of the others, especially Lord Browne-Wilkinson, is to find a way of turning the decision back over to the doctors. The doctors are to judge whether Bland's best interests now require a cessation of treatment, and the test proposed, a standard civil law test, is that the doctor's judgement will be acceptable if it is in accord with 'a respectable body of medical opinion'.[11] Browne-Wilkinson, in fact, is unconcerned by the possible moral relativism implied:

The doctor's answer may well be influenced by his own attitude to the sanctity of human life. In cases where there is no strictly medical point in continuing care, if a doctor holds the view that the patient is entitled to stay alive, whatever the quality of such life, he can quite reasonably reach the view that the continuation of intrusive care, being the only way of preserving such life, is in the patient's best interests. But, in the same circumstances another doctor who sees no merit in perpetuating a life of which the patient is unaware can equally reasonably reach the view that the continuation of invasive treatment is not for the patient's benefit. Accordingly . . . the court's only concern will be to be satisfied that the doctor's decision to discontinue is in accordance with a respectable body of medical opinion and is reasonable.[12]

This part of the argument disturbs Mustill, on the grounds that the essence of these decisions is not technical diagnosis or prognosis, and medical expertise seems no special qualification for an inherently ethical decision. This must surely be correct, but the faith in medical expertise argument is necessary, because it is part of the general strategy of demon-

---

[11] The test is derived from the standing case on medical negligence, *Bolam v. Friern Hospital Management Committee* [1957] 2 All ER 118.
[12] *Airedale* at 883.

strating that a purely 'legal' answer, put together by referring to well-established precedents, can be furnished. So we can see that this application of legal argument *in extremis* involves 'routinizing' the whole problem, and producing the most limited possible judgment, so that, if at all possible, absolutely nothing follows from the decision for future or analogous cases. The use of a medical expertise test based on 'a body of respectable opinion' pushes the issue even further out of law, as it is meant to. The courts do not even have to be the judge of the 'best interests', or even of what would constitute evidence about best interests. It may seem slightly contradictory, but the 'purely legal' *in extremis* answer consists largely of refusing to see a legal issue at all, while for policy reasons ensuring the instant reliance on doctors' private ethics stands no chance of being used as a justification for anything else they may feel like doing in such situations. In a way the Law Lords' solution to this case is entirely consistent with the main thrust of public law, as we have descried it. It is nothing more than an extreme version of the 'trust the professionals' establishment-oriented preference found in housing cases or educational negligence cases. Apart from showing the complete artificiality of 'legal argument', the way in which it can only be likened to opening a tool box and screwing together whatever pieces can be made to produce a workable answer, with no concern for the context in which the pieces were originally crafted, this example helps us further. Fundamentally *Bland* does not, as we suggested it might, show us what it is that a legal answer consists in. It shows us how to *construct* a legal answer. But we saw that in Chapters 3 and 4, and had here hoped for something more than a further demonstration of judicial methodology. The most one could derive from *Bland*, as an answer to the question 'What constitutes a "legal" answer to a problem?', is that a legal answer is 'an answer that is derived, somehow, from another legal answer'. Yet there must be some basic sense to the idea of legal work, because thousands of lawyers routinely carry out their tasks every day. Most cases coming before courts, even appeal courts, are disposed of fairly quickly and apparently easily. How can law be both so routine a process, and yet so invisible a thing *in extremis*? There is a clue in our analysis of how, methodologically, the Law Lords disposed of the *Bland* case. By raising the idea of 'routinizing' a legal question, our analysis does help solve the puzzle of how law can be treated as a real and self-contained system of knowledge despite the manifest creativity, discretion, and unprincipled policy making in much of what the Law Lords do.

In his seminal work *The Structure of Scientific Revolutions*[13] Thomas Kuhn introduced a vital concept of 'normal science'. Kuhn's main thesis was

---

[13] Thomas S. Kuhn, *The Structure of Scientific Revolutions*, Chicago UP, 1970.

that most scientific activity is not the critical attempt to test a theory, with complete preparedness to reject it, that some philosophers of science have suggested. Most science is the routine application of well-tried and understood techniques and theories, faithfully learned in graduate school. Where observation and theory clash the first reaction is to doubt the observation. The next reaction is not to reject the well-established theory, but to modify it to account for the new observations. Normal science is governed by what Kuhn calls 'paradigms', successful model solutions or research projects, which come to be the standard to be emulated, and which define the boundaries of a scientific endeavour, as well as identifying what are to constitute suitable problems for consideration and the nature of acceptable answers. Kuhn himself draws the analogy to law. A scientific paradigm is '. . . like an accepted judicial decision in the common law, it is an object for further articulation and specification under new or more stringent conditions'.[14] Initially paradigms offer promise of useful extension and elaboration, and require refinement, and it is this sort of scientific work that constitutes 'normal science', which Kuhn also describes as 'mop up work'. (This is very close to the way Oliver Wendell Holmes once regarded his own work in law.) In words that could very well be applied to 'normal law', or routine law as we call it here, Kuhn describes the activity:

Closely examined, whether historically or in the contemporary laboratory, that enterprise seems an attempt to force nature into the preformed and relatively inflexible box that the paradigm supplies. No part of the aim of normal science is to call forth new sorts of phenomena; indeed those that will not fit the box are often not seen at all. Nor do scientists normally aim to invent new theories, and they are often intolerant of those invented by others. Instead, normal-scientific research is directed to the articulation of those phenomena and theories that the paradigm already supplies.[15]

The defects of such an approach, according to Kuhn, include the facts that 'the areas investigated by normal science are, of course, minuscule', and 'the enterprise now under discussion has drastically restricted vision'. For science these restrictions have enormous positive consequences. Do they for law? The paradigms of accepted explanation can become increasingly unwieldy, cumbersome with tacked on riders to cover special cases, long before they are rejected and replaced. In science the most famous example is perhaps the endless additions to the pre-Copernican model of the universe needed to make calculations fit with observations. Kuhn argues that science does not, therefore, progress smoothly and incrementally. Instead it moves by sudden scientific revolutions, 'paradigm shifts' when the whole of the old explanatory order is junked and replaced with

---

[14] Kuhn, op. cit., p. 23.
[15] Kuhn, op. cit., p. 24.

an alternative model, created by one or more revolutionary scientific thinkers who discredit the work of the leaders of the field, which is still aimed at polishing and patching the old paradigm. Something very much like this seems to be true of law.

Most law activity is 'normal law', applying uncritically the existing paradigms. One judge described the difference between our reading of cases and a professional lawyers' by saying that lawyers were taught to read cases 'canonically'. Certainly barristers often talk about reading cases just to find a way to solve their clients' problems. One eminent practising lawyer interviewed who held this view of the craft, although the co-author of an indispensable practice textbook, emphatically denies that he would be competent to do academic legal research. Very seldom will a critical alternative paradigm be the way to win a case. Rather the barrister, and the judges up to and including the Court of Appeal, will accept that the problem must fit inside the paradigm, and, like any good but junior research scientist, will make it fit, by interpretation, fact selection, rephrasing of the question. The Law Lords are in an ambiguous position. They are, like the scientific leaders of a generation, essentially in charge of the paradigm. If it really will not answer a problem, if the equivalent of an unexpected observation comes up, a new pre-Copernican epicycle will be added if absolutely necessary, but preferably the observation itself will be interpreted to be compatible. The acceptance of liability for negligent advice discussed in Chapter 6 may be an example of a new epicycle, because no tweaking of the liability paradigm could fit in the need to allow damages to be collected where financial references were carelessly given. But usually problems will be handled by the 'normalizing' of an observation. This is what happened with Bland. No one outside the profession of law believes that what the doctors were doing to keep Anthony Bland alive was a form of assault. Invasive medical care is not in any sense an excusable assault—it simply bears irrelevant external physical similarities. But by stressing this misplaced analogy the judges were able to bring the entirely new problem of ending the nutrition of someone in a permanent vegetative state into the existing legal paradigm. Hence the claim that a non-available consent was required to justify continued treatment, and thus the arguments about best (or non-) interests. Much the same process was at play in the criminal law case studied in Chapter 4 on homosexual consensual sadomasochism. What was undeniably at stake was whether the courts were going to permit a form of homosexual sex play. The debate between the majority and the dissenters on how far along the dimension of physical harm consent could yield a defence to an assault charge was the process of 'normalizing' or 'routinizing' something the law had taken good care not to notice in the past. Most of the cases we have analysed can be considered in this light.

But there is a serious restriction to how far one can take this analogy between normal science and routine law. The Law Lords have vastly more power than scientific leaders, because ultimately both senior and junior scientists have to bow to the force of prediction, however long the old scientists may try to fend it off. At some stage a ruling paradigm will fail to predict correctly just too often where a rival paradigm predicts properly. Predictive capacity is extremely important to the lawyer—much of routine legal work consists of predicting how judges will react to the various arguments counsel can choose to present. Talking of judicial motives, in the quotation at the beginning of Chapter 1, Oliver Wendell Holmes says:

whether these other motives are, or are not, equally compulsory, is immaterial, if they are sufficiently likely to prevail to afford a ground for prediction. The only question for the lawyer is, how will the judges act?

Oliver Wendell Holmes, as we have said, was a precursor to the judicial realists. He was also one of the most distinguished judges in American legal history. The need to predict applies even to courts looking upward to those who will hear an appeal from them. But it is important only to the inferiors in the hierarchy—the Law Lords do not face a predictability test. For the Law Lords a paradigm only fails when they want it to. How would a leading case, or related batch of interpreted cases, 'fail'? Such a legal paradigm fails, essentially, if it produces manifest injustice, or if the answers it regularly produces to a category of problems are deemed inefficient by an important sector of opinion. Of course public opinion itself demands predictability—especially public opinion in the shape of lawyers with rich clients for their commercial or tax practices, so there will also be an inbuilt tendency not to offer the Lords arguments which would lead to a prediction-breakdown. A legal paradigm cannot fail by not generating an answer at all, because it will not be brought under a paradigm which cannot resolve it. A human conflict which cannot be brought under any paradigm does not represent a failure of any paradigm, or of law as a body of knowledge. At most the inability to produce an answer may perhaps be said to constitute a failure of the legal system—such a problem is simply non-justiciable. Technically there is always an answer anyway, because if the courts do not act, some pre-legal status quo survives. Thus when a court strikes a plaintiff out on the grounds that he has not made a case for the defendant to answer, it is not leaving an 'unexplained observation' hanging in theoretical space, as happens if a scientific finding cannot be explained by a paradigm.

Injustice matters only if the Law Lords themselves feel it is being done, and then only if it is not seen as an unfortunate but inevitable cost of 'certainty' or one of the other excusing concepts like parliamentary sovereignty. Thus in the case of *Woolwich* v. *Inland Revenue Commissioners*[16] a manifest injustice arose under the existing paradigm of when a taxing authority had to repay moneys it had levied improperly. The minority in the case, led by Lord Keith, were completely unaffected by the question of injustice, because they felt not only that the existing common law paradigm worked well most of the time, but that changing it involved an act of judicial legislation in an area it would be improper to proceed in. What made the case interesting from the viewpoint of the analogy to the structure of scientific revolutions is not that the leader of the majority in *Woolwich*, Lord Goff, not only thought the decision of the lower court unjust. What makes it interesting is that he is an advocate of an alternative overall paradigm, the doctrine of restitution, which is slowly challenging (especially amongst academic lawyers) the whole way certain problems involving unjust enrichment are conceptualized and solved. But Goff was quite aware of, and had to defend himself against, the charge of judicial legislation. Referring to overstepping 'the boundary which *we traditionally set for ourselves* [our emphasis], separating the legitimate development of the law by the judges from legislation' he makes the point:

... although I am well aware of the existence of the boundary, I am never quite sure where to find it. Its position seems to vary from case to case. Indeed, if it were to be as firmly and as clearly drawn as some of our mentors would wish, I cannot help feeling that a number of leading cases in your Lordships' House would never have been decided as they were. For example, the minority view would have prevailed in *Donoghue* v. *Stevenson* ... ; our modern law of judicial review would have never developed from its old, ineffectual, origins; and *Mareva* injunctions would never have seen the light of day.[17]

Goff was citing paradigm shift cases, and probably hoped that *Woolwich* would become one. A point Kuhn stresses in all his writing is that old paradigms do not collapse because they are inadequate—they collapse only when there is a replacement in the wings, and had Lord Goff not been an advocate of restitution (he co-authored the first major textbook on the field long before he was a judge), it is doubtful that any degree of discomfort with the injustice of the case would have forced him to cross the boundary he talks of. In fact the law is protected against injustice-prompted change by the dictum known even to laymen, that 'hard cases make bad law'.

Paradigms do change in law, or they have in the past, when they are economically inefficient from the viewpoint of important socio-economic actors, as with the development of contract law in the eighteenth century, but this requires a shared understanding of the desirability of certain

---

[16] *Woolwich Equitable Building Society* v. *IRC* [1993] AC 70 at 176.
[17] *Woolwich* at 173.

economic changes between judges and entrepreneurs, land owners, or some other important economic group. Such a model is probably only applicable in circumstances where a much more fully blown quasi-Marxist theory of law makes sense. There are, of course, important areas of the law which do exist not so much to regulate as to facilitate major economic relationships. By this we mean that the law does not aim to rule what intentions of the actors are legitimate, but to help them achieve whatever their intentions are. Contract law and the law of trusts are obvious examples of such facilitation. And such areas can be robustly defended when their consequences occasionally produce manifest injustice—no progress has been made in reshaping contract law to deal with the problem of third party rights, even though so august a legal reformer as Lord Denning tried hard to do so. In fact it takes statute to change such matters as legal treatment of unfair terms in contracts, because the common law clings to a sociologically inaccurate model of equal contracting parties. These areas may well be candidates for a form of normal law where there really is more sense to the idea of 'a legal answer', and where law may be a self-contained and self-sustaining system. If so it will be because entities like the legal contract are genuinely creations of law, and where an expertise in working out the ramifications of changes in a purely legal doctrine can constitute such a private discipline. Contract bears only a residual relationship to the external world's idea of a promise, and as long as we are thinking of technical contracts between corporations or similar economic actors, efficiency in meeting the needs of business to organize its relationships becomes the sole touchstone. Such a paradigm can be seen to fail when it does not serve the needs of clients, and external conceptions of justice and rights have little bearing. Much legal activity, and many high-profile cases, are indeed concerned with such matters, and they may properly be seen as constituting the sort of law where legal answers and legal knowledge can be insulated from other disciplines and other forms of knowledge. For example, arguably the biggest and most important case to occupy the Law Lords during the period this book centres round, the mid-nineties, is hardly discussed in these pages. It was a negligence case dealing with the liability of agents of members of Lloyd's whose alleged incompetence cost insurance syndicates millions of pounds. It is quite clear that the relevant paradigm could, perhaps did, fail here in a way that judges would have to recognize as failure. They could be forced to recognize failure because the entire machinery of insurance and reinsurance is so much a matter of technical legal provision of mechanisms to serve special clients. Fixing the paradigm was not something the Lords could dodge. But little of our concern, which is inevitably with law as it touches the generality of the population, is insulated in such a way as to produce genuinely autonomous 'legal' problems and 'legal' solutions.

Because major areas of day-to-day law are for these special reasons capable of generating specifically legal answers, being 'routine', law as a whole seems a perfectly suitable mechanism for handling social conflicts where there is no legislation, and for sorting out what to do where there is legislation. But this is a quite false reliance, arising from a special and untypical aspect of law. It was noted in Chapter 6, for example, that some legal thinkers actually see contract as an area 'taken out of' the main current of legal obligations as represented by tort law. The ways in which law is a hermetically sealed system capable of generating its own technical answers to its own technical problems do not begin to justify using law as a solution mechanism for the general problems of society.

So we are forced back to the idea of paradigms, and the problem of how, if at all, they can change and develop. Changes in public opinion, are said to bring about changes in the law. Perhaps they do, when judges choose to notice public opinion. Perhaps such changes can bring about paradigm shift, as with the decision on a man's capacity to rape his wife discussed in Chapter 4, but it is very much a matter of judicial choice. Leading scientists also have some degree of choice in whether or not to notice awkward facts about physical reality, but the degrees of freedom are far fewer. One is left with the idea that, on the whole, legal paradigms shift almost as a matter of taste amongst the paradigm wielders. Was there, for example, any very widespread and impatient public demand for a change in the law of rape? There was no tabloid campaign for such a change. Yet a year or so later there was such a tabloid campaign in criminal law, when a British soldier was found guilty of murder when on duty in Northern Ireland and fell foul of the extremely complex law of homicide. The Law Lords saw the point of the campaign and expressed sympathy—but they upheld the conviction. The most important difference between law and science in terms of paradigm shift, however, is not that legal paradigms seldom change, but that they are capable of uncontrolled change. Although science may progress through revolutions, there is no recorded example of a counter-revolution. Yet legal paradigms can fight back and retake the field, as we tried to show in Chapter 6 with the restoration of an almost pre-*Donoghue* 'pockets of law' approach in negligence.

The standard theory of judging held by practitioners and legal academics sometimes comes close to ideas like that of paradigm rule, though in different language. Much is made of argument by analogy, because the argument by analogy has always been seen as essential to precedent. A form of argument by analogy also applies in statutory construction, where a difficult phrase can be given a meaning because the same form of words has been judicially considered in another statute. Furthermore the value of incrementalism is held very highly indeed, even if it may be as true in law as in science that incrementalism is not a method of progress. Over and again Lord Keith won acceptance from his colleagues for the doctrine that incrementalism was the way forward in the law of negligence, during his battle to overturn the implications of *Donoghue* v. *Stevenson*. Analogy of course has virtually no role to play in science—probably only meteorology makes any serious use of it, because meteorology's problems, the problems of fluid dynamics and chaos, are inherently uncomputable. Analogies work in law because of a refined sense, almost like that of good taste, for what constitutes an elegant legal argument. There may be very deep historical roots for this approach to law as paradigm-manipulation. English common law, as opposed to the rival equity jurisdiction, grew from an approach in which there existed a set of specific remedies, the old common law writs, rather than a set of common law rules. The rules of justice were more in the background, so that particular common infringements of justice might come to be provided for by the construction of a new writ or cause of action. The whole of legal talent came, for a period, to be the skill of bringing a factual situation under a writ, and getting the complex formulas of the writs precisely correct.[18] These writs are not so very different from modern legal paradigms: the modern barrister or judge looking for legal bits and pieces to construct an elegant case is doing much what his ancestor did in drawing his formulas with care and precision.

The law thus provides a set of paradigms which are accepted, which can be taught and learned, the capacity for manipulation of which constitutes legal talent. The paradigms can grow very clumsy by accretion, but they can nearly always be made to work in some way or other, and therefore can be taught and replicated. The *Wednesbury* test is such a paradigm, and the early discussion in Chapter 7 goes to show how clumsy and incoherent accretion has made it. But its power is demonstrated in our whole section on public law, because it is only when counsel can somehow or other get their case out of reach of *Wednesbury* doctrines that plaintiffs win against the State. Yet attempts to refine or recast the paradigms, like Diplock's attempt to restate *Wednesbury*, are often ignored, or simply incorporated as further refinements. There is, though, a crucial difference between normal law and normal science. Kuhn makes a vital point when he insists that a dominant scientific paradigm will never collapse under its own weight—it will not be given up until the revolutionary rival is ready in the wings. Einstein had to create special relativity before the increasing inadequacy of the Newtonian framework could lead to it being dropped. It can hardly be otherwise, because science has to go on. Law has to go on even more pressingly, but the legal revolutionary with his new and rival paradigm has a much harder task than Einstein.

---

[18] Joshua Getzler, 'Patterns of Fusion' in Peter Birks, *Expanding Obligations*, OUP, 1997.

This is because there cannot exist in law the crucial experiment, the case which must be answered and can be seen objectively as capable of solution only in terms of the new paradigm. The Law Lords will never face a case that can, with complete objectivity, be shown not to be answerable with *Wednesbury*, or with the modern doctrine, whatever it may actually be, of negligent liability. They will never face such cases, because only they are entitled to admit their own failure to make the paradigm work. The Lords will certainly not give up a paradigm until a replacement is available, but they need never give one up regardless of the alternative. It may, for example, be the case that a doctrine based on the European administrative law concept of proportionality would do better than *Wednesbury* in dealing with cases against the State. Proportionality exists, and even has its English admirers. But the difference is that proportionality can provide answers some people think are better than *Wednesbury*, not that it alone can provide answers at all. And when we talk of a legal answer being 'better' we mean that it is morally or politically or socially preferable, not that it is superior in terms of an objective standard of explanatory power. In fact the situation is worse, because the courts can refuse to regard questions as justiciable at all—what arguably they ought to have done in Bland's case—whilst a scientist cannot easily refuse even to consider some observation on the grounds that physics just does not deal with the matter in question. Lord Mustill took exception to a piece of paradigm tweaking in *White* v. *Jones*,[19] where negligence was fitted with a new part to allow a firm of solicitors to be held liable to disappointed intended inheritors under a will they had negligently handled. He only had to say that this was a case where the law could not do instant justice without damage to the paradigm. He did not have to find an alternative paradigm, or even to suggest an alternative new piece for the old paradigm. This point we made above—there is always the status quo as an answer, so the response to a case that it cannot be handled without unacceptable damage to the paradigm is a feasible move. (Though not one likely to be described in that way.) In other words, a legal revolution can only happen when the legal ruling class itself feels like having one. This is not absurd. Political sociology has long recognized the idea of a 'revolution from on top', but such revolutions are necessarily limited both in frequency and scope. Furthermore a legal paradigm shift can be reversed. As we noted above, it is entirely fair to claim that the work of judges like Wilberforce did convert Lord Atkin's achievement in negligence into an alternative paradigm, culminating in cases like *Junior Books* and *Anns* v. *Merton*. Elsewhere, in New Zealand certainly and perhaps Canada, this became the new ruling paradigm. But in the UK the new paradigm has

---

[19] *White and another* v. *Jones and others* [1995] 1 All ER 691.

been overthrown and a much older set of normal law rules for negligence have returned to dominance, precisely under the argument that incrementalism not revolution is the way forward.

Normal law, then, is the application of paradigms by most practitioners, and the modification of them by the Lords. This helps account for the curious dual nature of law as a set of learnable rules moderated by policy flexibility. But there remains still the problem of paradigm strain. In the absence of an unforgiving physical reality that scientists face, we need to alter Kuhn's approach slightly. As far as law goes there seems a need to conceive of a higher-order paradigm, a more general construct which helps judges to decide when injustice, economic inefficiency or clash with public attitudes has gone so far as to constitute a paradigm failure in some area. What does this super-paradigm consist in? We want to suggest an analogy of our own which we think catches the nebulous common character of most House of Lords decisions in difficult cases. In the 1960s the Civil Service Selection Board used a set of tests on those applying for the then Administrative Class of the Civil Service. One was an exercise in which candidates were given a file on a policy problem—where to site a new university was one problem used. The file contained various facts and statistics which might have some bearing, and the candidates were expected to write a briefing paper to a minister suggesting the correct answer and its justification. Those who did well in this and similar tests progressed to a final interview. The other tests included serving both as a member, and in turn as chairman, of a committee where one was expected to steer one's preferred solution to similar policy problems through, or make contributions to the committee's overall deliberation.[20]

What was notably lacking from the problem file was any set of rules about what values or goals were to be optimized in the solution, or what costs, financial or otherwise, were to be minimized. One was told nothing about which bits of data were to be regarded as relevant. Somehow or other the intuitive selection of a university site maximizing unspecified values and minimizing unspecified and unordered costs could be gauged by one's assessors in a way likely to measure one's potential for high administrative and policy-making office. Presumably also the nature of one's contributions to one's committee, and the speed and way in which one chaired it, also told the assessors the same thing. What the tests seem to be picking up was a generalized talent for thinking the way the administrative class already thought, some intuitive sense of what constituted a

---

[20] The final test, sometimes called 'Buddy Ranking' was to nominate from amongst the small group of fellow candidates with whom one worked the person (a) whom one thought would make the best civil servant and (b) the person one would most like to go on holiday with. What little is known about the process of selection for the bench suggests the spirit of the process is not much different.

good policy answer, or proper chairmanship of a committee, an understanding which had to be intuitive because one was not told what to achieve. Throughout the British administrative echelons, and in similar positions in other institutions like universities, there does seem to be a common, unspoken, probably indescribable conception of 'soundness'. This connotes a sensible, moderate, and consensual approach to policy. Without ever being able to spell out what it consists in, good administrators recognize a solution arrived at by similar sound judgement. All the relevant factors are considered, and no irrelevant matters are allowed to influence judgement, decisions are as limited in scope as possible, as consistent as possible with previous decisions, compatible with parallel decisions, as bereft as possible of implications for future decisions. Recommendations are justified by comparisons and analogies from the immediate experience of the decision makers, the whole matter is treated with virtually no reference to overarching norms or guiding principles. It is administration on a case by case basis, heavily dependent on deference to experience on similar committees, rather than expertise in the technical matters discussed. In short it is the British generalist civil service culture, redolent with the need to express 'The Whitehall View', to carry all ministries along, with due deference to entrenched interests and tremendous respect for each other, and for all fellow administrators. The deference is coupled with a hierarchical doubt about the ability of others, lower in the chain, to cope with difficult decisions, but always with a group loyalty and an 'us and them' attitude to the general populace. Of all the paradigms in English law, the *Wednesbury* test speaks most clearly of this. The test is to consider all that should be considered, and not to consider anything that should not be considered. It has the familiar ring of the Book of Common Prayer, especially of the General Confession: 'We have done that which we should not have done, and left undone those things that we should have done . . .'. We have said much about that test. The worst thing about it is that it amounts, in many cases, to advice on how to describe one's making of a decision, rather than a rule for making it. What is meant by 'giving due consideration' to some matter? According to cases like *Brind*, it is enough to say that one has considered X. If one had to consider both X and Y, to balance, perhaps, two values enshrined in a statute, there is no obligation to explain how the balance turned out to tilt in a particular direction. Such is a matter of 'judgement', beyond argument.

This is equally a good characterization of judicial decision making at the top, at least in this country. The following are some salient characteristics of the Law Lords decisions as revealed in the published cases:

They are very consequentialist in that they are deeply concerned about potential future consequences of their decisions. This makes a form of argument to the effect 'you can't do X, even if it is right here, because it might be taken to imply Y in another case'. (Where the Y is chosen to be a deliberately absurd consequence.)

They rely on Parliament as a longstop. Issues they do not wish to face are deemed unsuitable for the courts, but other issues equally complex or equally dependent on empirical assumptions and sociological analyses are happily accepted.

Their decisions are commercially pragmatic. It is always a powerful argument that commerce will find some decision difficult to accept—even when the implications suggest that commerce as we know it will cease rather than face, for example, product liability claims. But these views are never backed by anything remotely like empirical evidence or expert witnesses from the business world.

They are patronizing to other rule appliers. Legal tests which might produce a more just result in an instant case are rejected because they will be too complex for others, say medical examiners in a social security case. Sometimes even the lower courts are thought not able to handle complex assessments. Such, for example, was part of the argument for the majority in the sex equality cases discussed in Chapter 3. Or lower level actors are thought too prone to worry about the legal consequences of their actions if they can be held liable at all—thus the police are immune from negligence cases, writers of references cannot be sued.

They have great respect, often, for the decisions of other common law jurisdictions because the idea of an internationalization of the common law furthers the sense of an internal logic to law which can transcend political and economic differences.

The Law Lords are, as noted, consciously incrementalist. In all sorts of cases issues are left undecided because it is thought better to decide as little as possible and to leave the implications to be considered only when a new fact set absolutely requires it.

They are consciously problem solvers, with a particular concern to 'make the Act work', to ensure the smooth running of the machinery of public administration.

They trust other administrators—we say 'other administrators' because this is the point. The Law Lords are, in many ways, just another branch of the British administrative class. Consequently they are concerned not to disturb the working of administrative machines by forcing their fellow administrators to worry about the courts. Although the Civil Service itself may be equipped with a booklet titled 'The Judge over your Shoulder', they really do not need it, because the judges, for the most part, are desperate not to intrude.

In the end these assumptions within which the paradigms are developed are dependent on common, shared, professional expectations which are largely inchoate, and which are quite unsuited as the basis of creative law making which shapes our lives. Many have sought a description of judicial ideology, but the truth about their attitudes, in some sense, is that they are not ideological enough! Or at least, they are not ideological in the sense of a developed theory and set of overt assumptions. In the sense of ideology which precisely refers to the largely unconscious expectations of what constitutes normal, rational, decent, responsible behaviour, there is a judicial ideology. It is a class ideology of old middle-class men, as the more radical suggestions have it. But they are untypical even of that social category—they have soaked up the ethos of a tough minded liberalism of those who run an administrative State. The ideology is one of pragmatism, indeed the sort of pragmatism that is unable to conceive that it is an ideology. Such a set of attitudes and expectations is in part the consequence of the barrister career they have all led, with its stress on today's quick argument for a client and the need tomorrow to cobble together another argument that would contradict it were the two to be held simultaneously. The ethic of the advocate whose duty is to advocate whatever works, the ethic enshrined in the very ideas of the 'argument in the alternative', and the 'cab rank rule' is altogether too present in the working assumptions and techniques of the higher judiciary.[21]

The problem, for those who, like us, see these characteristics of judicial decision as a problem rather than as a supreme achievement, is the absence of a constitutional code. Because Britain has so little in the way of a substantive code, the Lords may have little choice but to shadow the administrators. Of course in a sense Law Lords use a constitutional code all the time, with the reference to parliamentary intent, or the use of the argument from parliamentary supremacy. But this is based on a quite consciously aware use of the myth of Parliament. The judges know as well, or better than most, the huge democratic deficit implied by the British system of party discipline and Cabinet control of the backbenchers. They acknowledged that in *Pepper* v. *Hart*, and there are plenty of references to the Treasury as the real power behind Parliament, such as Lord Goff's explanation for why the Lords would have to legislate in the Woolwich case, which we have quoted before:

I fear that, however compelling the principle of justice may be, it would never be sufficient to persuade a government to propose its legislative recognition by Parliament; caution, otherwise known as the Treasury, would never allow this to happen.[22]

---

[21] The 'cab rank rule' is the rule that prevents a barrister from refusing to take a case he is competent to handle. It is said to ensure that unpopular cases still get good counsel. It equally serves to absolve anyone from exercising conscience about taking a morally dubious case.

[22] *Woolwich* at 176.

Yet parliamentary supremacy is normally a code-language deferring to the administration. About the only time when the real working of competitive democracy comes into judicial argument is when it is dismissed—the scorn, for example, poured on the idea of an electoral mandate in that most famous of post-war reactionary judgements, *Bromley* v. *GLC*, or, from the very first case analysed, the horror at the notion that the general ideology of the government that passed a statute might be used to interpret it.

In truth the Law Lords do nothing wrong. As long as the British Constitution is Hobbesian rather than Lockeian, there cannot be a real separation of powers, and the courts cannot but be a part of the administrative State. Nor, without a constitutional statement of values, can law be developed as anything but pragmatic paradigms disciplined only by a keenly honed professional sense of the fitness of one argument over another, something to be learned like any other craft and not capable of resolution into abstract principles. Were there to be a Bill of Rights, a written constitution with a preface establishing core values, even a systematic codification of law, the paradigms would operate differently. Because there would then be a set of principles against which the collapse of an old paradigm with social change, and the greater suitability of a new one, could become evident. With a written constitution judicial argument could indeed become principled and idealist rather than pragmatic and deferential to the judges' best guess at what commercial and administrative actors required. Above all law could be driven by a conception of citizen rights, not state generosity. Legal Realists will never be convinced that anything could take away the radical discretion of the judge, and those with a feeling for the Law of Equity over the Common Law might not even wish that discretion to vanish. But discretion is too rife in the English system. And the proposed incorporation of the European Convention on Human Rights will not change much. The problem of discretion lies not in the moral values of the judiciary, but in their own sense that they are not imposing them, and their conviction that their decisions are indeed technical and pragmatic solutions that right-minded people must agree with, reached by a specialist professional technique that outsiders cannot understand. To the extent that law does exist as such a craft, it is not a fitting material to generate answers to human problems. Keynes' famous quotation could well be adapted, and expanded out of the merely economic to describe our senior judiciary:

Practical men, who believe themselves to be quite exempt from any intellectual influences, are usually the slaves of some defunct economist.

Statistical Appendix

1. The Data Set

The data set consists of the detailed voting record of each of the 28 Law Lords who heard any of a total of 407 cases between 1986 and 1995. Each Law Lord is coded as voting either in a unanimous court, in a majority or in a minority or absent from each case. Each case is coded on a variety of variables to indicate whether it was won by, for example: appellant, respondent; original plaintiff/prosecutor or defendant; whether the winning or losing party can be coded as being 'stronger' than the other in terms set out in the chapter; from where the case came to the Lords; whether it had been decided by a unanimous or split lower court; what legal category the case exemplifies. It is available free of charge from the author as an SPSS Saved File. Anyone wishing a copy should send him a formatted $3\frac{1}{2}$ inch disk to St Hugh's College, Oxford. Further details of any of the analyses will also be provided on request. All statistical analysis presented in this book was carried out using the package SSPS for Windows Version 7.1.

2. Logistic Regression

To demonstrate the power of the technique, the following fully reported model is additional to the two discussed in the chapter—it is only one of many that can be derived. This model takes three Law Lords whose appearance was not found significant as single actors in the other models because we preferred to demonstrate the role of interaction. These are Lords Goff, Ackner, and Lowry. They are analysed over a smaller range of cases, only those covering public law issues, further to demonstrate that the models are not restricted in their applicability to one subset of the data. The results for the equation are:

		Chi Square	df	Significance
−2 Log Likelihood	58.333			
Goodness of Fit	48.757			
Model Chi Square		10.771	3	0.0130
Improvement		10.771	3	0.0130

Table A.1 Classification Table

Observed Result	Predicted		% Correct
	Weak Wins	Strong Wins	
Weak Wins	14	7	66.67%
Strong Wins	9	21	70.08%
		Overall	68.63

Variables in the Equation

Variable	B	SE	Wald	df	Sig	R	Exp(B)
Ackner	1.3549	0.70705	3.667	1	0.0555	0.153	3.877
Goff	1.4071	0.7019	4.018	1	0.0450	0.170	4.084
Lowry	−1.1620	0.6453	3.2427	1	0.072	−0.134	0.313
Constant	−0.4018	0.688	0.341	1	0.5593		

This model might be regarded as marginally significant inasmuch as Lord Lowry's result is significant only at the 7 per cent level rather than the 5 per cent level, but such a level seems entirely adequate for our purposes. The overall equation package is itself significant at better than the 5 per cent level.

The probability of a positive result for an equation is given by: Probability $= e^z/(1 - e^z)$, where z equals the sum of the B * variable terms. Thus for the probability of getting a pro-State result where all three Law Lords are present $z = (-0.4018 *$ for the constant, $+1.3549 * 1$ for Ackner, $+1.4071 * 1$ for Goff, $-1.162 * 1$ for Lowry. Thus in this case we have: $e^{(1.1982)}/1 + e^{(1.1982)}$, which gives a probability of 0.768 for the State winning a case where Lords Ackner, Goff, and Lowry sit with two others unrepresented in the equation. Similarly for a panel including only Ackner and Goff plus three others the equation would be prob. $= e^{(2.3602)}/1 + e^{(2.3602)}$, which equals a probability of a State win of 0.914. A panel of Lord Lowry and four others would give a probability of only 0.173.

Multiple Discriminant Analysis

The Discriminant Function scores for each Domain analysis for each Law Lord from the 'Core Court' are given in Table A.2 below.

Table A.2 Unstandardized Multiple Discriminant Scores

Law Lord	Constitutional Cases	Public Law Cases	Tax Cases	Criminal Law Cases	Civil Law Cases
Ackner	1.014	0.523	−0.313	1.526	0.824
Brandon	−0.045	−0.391	−0.642	1.382	0.554
Bridge	0.789	0.798	0.994	2.199	−0.516
Browne-Wilkinson	−0.095	0.136	0.196	1.434	−0.435
Goff	0.548	0.127	0.872	1.291	−0.046
Griffiths	−1.004	0.179	1.606	1.725	0.368
Jauncey	0.162	−0.181	−0.650	0.956	−0.263
Keith	0.336	0.945	−0.472	2.209	−0.868
Lloyd	0.651	−0.560	0.367	0.509	0.509
Lowry	0.615	−0.513	0.108	0.280	−0.218
Mustill	−0.533	0.075	−0.360	1.241	0.587
Oliver	0.245	0.055	0.329	1.304	0.136
Templeman	0.981	−0.494	1.789	1.874	−0.282
Slynn	−0.427	0.076	0.741	1.080	−0.138
Woolf	0.424	—	—	0.562	—

Index